Conflict at Work

Warwick Studies in Industrial Relations

General Editors: G. S. Bain, R. Hyman and K. Sisson

Also available in this series

Conflict at Work

A Materialist Analysis of Workplace Relations

P. K. EDWARDS

Basil Blackwell

First published 1986

Basil Blackwell Ltd
108 Cowley Road, Oxford OX4 1JF, UK

Basil Blackwell Inc.
432 Park Avenue South, Suite 1503,
New York, NY 10016, USA

British Library Cataloguing in Publication Data

Edwards, P. K.
  Conflict at Work: a materialist analysis
  of workplace relations.—(Warwick studies
  in industrial relations)
  1. Industrial relations   2. Labor disputes
  I. Title   II. Series
  331.89   HD6971

  ISBN 0-631-15272-5

Library of Congress Cataloging in Publication Data
Edwards, P. K. (Paul K.)
  Conflict at work.
(Warwick studies in industrial relations)
  Bibliography: p.
  Includes index.
  1. Labor disputes.   2. Industrial relations.
  3. Strikes and lockouts.   I. Title.   II. Series.
  HD5306.E42   1986   331.89   86-13677
  ISBN 0-631-15272-5

Typeset in 10 on 11½pt Times
by DMB (Typesetting), Oxford
Printed in Great Britain by
Billing and Sons Ltd, Worcester

Contents

Editors' Foreword

This is the first volume in this series to appear since Hugh Clegg retired from the editorial board. His contribution to it has been immeasurable. He was the University of Warwick's first Professor of Industrial Relations, and he played a key role in establishing the teaching of the subject in 1966. He was also the first Director of the Industrial Relations Research Unit, which the Social Science Research Council (now the Economic and Social Research Council) established at the University in 1970. Since 1984 the Unit has been a Designated Research Centre of the ESRC within the University's School of Industrial and Business Studies. Hugh was instrumental in the launch of this series, which is designed to disseminate the results of the Unit's research projects and also to include the work of staff teaching industrial relations in the University, in 1972.[1] He has managed the series with skill; he has contributed his own work to it; and he has maintained very high standards of scholarship, yet has done so in his characteristic modest and unassuming manner. We hope that we can maintain the tradition that he has established.

The latest title in the series undertakes a wide-ranging investigation of a central aspect of industrial relations, namely conflict. After identifying some difficulties in existing theoretical approaches, it develops a new and rigorous framework for the analysis of industrial conflict. This gives particular attention to the ways in which co-operation and consent are connected with conflict, thus aiming to develop an integrated approach to features of industrial relations that have often been seen in isolation from, and indeed in opposition to, each other.

---

1 The first six titles were published by Heinemann Educational Books of London; subsequent volumes have been published by Basil Blackwell of Oxford.

Editors' Foreword

The book argues that conflict and co-operation are produced jointly and are not separate: a piece of behaviour can contain both. The book's particular concern is the level of the workplace. A set of empirical illustrations of the theory of conflict is presented, in which the author draws on his own previous research as well as on the work of others to provide a detailed and comprehensive account of patterns of workplace relations. The book tackles many contemporary debates in industrial relations and industrial sociology. Its theoretical perspective and extended empirical discussions will also be of interest to students of labour history.

George Bain
Richard Hyman
Keith Sisson

Acknowledgements

This book has taken shape over several years, and the identification of particular sets of issues as being pertinent to its overall project, together with ways of approaching these issues, has been influenced by many people. Some points have been taken up from apparently unrelated discussions, so that some people have had an influence without necessarily being aware of it. It is thus best to limit, with one exception, personal acknowledgements to those who have been involved with the manuscript in something like its final shape. Braham Dabscheck, Anthony Ferner, Paul Marginson, and the editors of this Series have all made some very helpful comments. I am also grateful to John Goldthorpe who read drafts of what are now the first two chapters and who, although sceptical of the approach, generously made comments and suggested alternative lines of inquiry. Connie Bussman typed numerous drafts of the manuscript, as well as of various papers whose arguments have been absorbed into it. I am very grateful to her for the patience and dedication which she has shown throughout.

Since this is the first of the Warwick Studies in Industrial Relations to appear after the retirement of Hugh Clegg from the editorial board, it is appropriate to add to the appreciation by the present editors the thanks of the authors of previous volumes. His enormous knowledge and reputation might have overawed contributors, worried that their efforts would be dismissed from on high. But his understanding manner and his concern for scholarship enabled him to give his comments in a positive and unfailingly helpful way. Hugh has read the present manuscript with his customary care and eye for detail. Like its predecessors, it owes an enormous amount to him.

Acknowledgements

I hope that institutional acknowledgements will indicate other debts. Some of the basic features of the theory of conflict were outlined in a paper to the first conference on the Organization and Control of the Labour Process, held in Manchester in 1983; and the comparison between Britain and America was made in a paper given to the annual conference of the British Association for American Studies in the same year. The reactions to these papers have been of great help in clarifying and developing the relevant arguments. The Industrial Relations Research Unit provided a stimulating environment; it would be difficult to think of a better place in which to undertake a study of this kind. I am very grateful to my colleagues for their support and encouragement.

My remaining personal debt is to Hugh Scullion. Between 1978 and 1982 we worked very closely on a study of workplace relations which is reported in our joint book, *The Social Organization of Industrial Conflict*, and elsewhere. The present study is the direct descendent of this work; it enlarges on a theoretical approach to conflict which was sketched in the earlier work, it uses that work to illustrate various arguments, and, perhaps most importantly, its conceptualization of the nature of workplace relations has been intimately affected by the earlier research. Although the present study is of a theoretical and general nature, it depends on an understanding of the social relations of work derived from empirical inquiry. The earlier study relied on Hugh Scullion's ability to deal with the demands and difficulties of fieldwork with energy and good sense. The present debt is thus considerable, although neither he nor the other people mentioned should bear the responsibility for the final product.

Introduction

This book is about work relations, and in particular the origins and nature of conflict within them. Work relations are the relations between employers and employees at the point of production which govern how work is carried out. They are a specific aspect of workplace behaviour: this study is not concerned with such features of this behaviour as friendship groupings or the internal organizations of managements or workers except in so far as they impinge on work relations. Neither is it about every aspect of industrial conflict. It does not deal with, for example, the many theories of strike causation that exist. It is about the patterns of conflict which exist at the shopfloor level. Although having this precise focus, it is in some ways broader than supposedly general treatments of conflict, for these tend to concentrate on strikes and other collective matters to the neglect of the many other ways in which conflict can be expressed. It also aims to go deeper than an analysis of patterns of behaviour: instead of asking why strike rates vary between industries, it asks how work relations are organized so as to produce some forms of behaviour and not others, and what significance these forms have for the structure from which they emerge.

In adopting a focus on the point of production the study deals with a major area of scholarly debate. Work relations are concerned with the control of the labour process, that is the process wherein workers' capacity to labour is translated into actual work; and the labour process has been a topic of intense discussion. There are two features of this debate which are unsatisfactory, and which provide one reason for writing this book. The first is the tendency for writers to point out the limitations of existing conceptual schemes without providing any new framework of their own. The result is a bewildering array of detailed arguments and a lack of a sense of direction. No attempt will be made here to provide a new synthesis of work on every aspect of the labour process. But the study aims to provide a detailed and coherent statement about one key aspect, namely the place of conflict, and to illustrate the applicability of that statement through extended empirical discussion.

Second, the overall drift in the labour process debate is worrying. In reacting against the drift, the study swims against the tide of opinion; if it has any effect, it may be able to stem that tide. The general tendency is to play down the importance of the labour process. There has always been some scepticism about the labour process debate, and there has been some justification in the view that it has been pretentious. Yet doubts have also arisen within the debate itself. Central to these have been three points. Typologies of managerial control have been unsatisfactory, for example in their tendency to reduce a firm's approach to the management of labour to one simple formula. The control of labour can take place at levels of the firm other than the point of production; investment and marketing decisions will have a profound effect on the workplace, and there need be no strategy of control on the shopfloor itself. Related to this is the view that the control of labour is not the firm's main aim: capitalist firms exist to make profits, and workplace control may be a secondary objective. Finally, analysis of the labour process leads to too great an emphasis on relations inside the workplace, with external influences on workers' and managers' attitudes being neglected; among the main influences identified is gender, for it is argued that men and women enter the workplace with significantly different experiences and resources and that differing behaviour inside the factory has to be related to gender relations in society at large.

These are substantial arguments, and they will be considered in detail at the appropriate points: specifically, all three are analysed in chapters 1 and 2, while the third point about the relative autonomy of the labour process from external influences is taken up in relation to empirical material in chapter 6. The basic argument is that, correct as each point may be, work relations have an importance in their own right, so that the criticisms should not be seen as reasons for abandoning an interest in them. On the question of types of managerial strategy, it will be argued that the criticisms are correct. Indeed, an effort will be made to go further than pointing to the difficulties of existing schemes to suggest that there are fundamental problems with any typological approach. These stem from three connected points. Any employing organization will use a range of ways of persuading workers to work, some of which, moreover, may stem from a series of 'ad hoc' adjustments and not from any deliberate policy; the extent to which any one firm has an articulated strategy of labour control is thus questionable, and the idea that all firms of a similar type are characterized by the same strategy is even more questionable. Second, the actions of workers can powerfully affect the forms of control that are practised. Third, external influences, notably the behaviour of the state, can prevent some types of managerial control and encourage others. The dynamics and dialectics of the organization of work tend to become lost in models of control strategies. This is not to deny that patterns of control exist in workplaces. It will be argued, on the contrary, that the shape of such a pattern is the key factor in the form taken by concrete manifestations of conflict. But a structure of control should be seen as the result, and a potentially unstable one, of past interactions between employers and workers, in the context of specific external influences.

To make a radical break with typologies of control is, however, to invite the question of what should replace them. Is the only option to explore workplace relations in microscopic detail, and is there no overall logic of development governing the ways in which firms seek compliance? The present study can, to an extent, evade these questions. Its concern is the nature of conflict in work relations, and to demonstrate that a typology of control strategies does not assist the analysis is quite proper. But it also proposes some methodological arguments that bear on the question of strategy. The aim is not to replace typologies with micro-sociological exploration of specific cases, but to begin to develop concepts that can grasp the complexities of behaviour without losing sight of the forces affecting this behaviour. What is required is a set of analytical tools that can be used to understand work relations at several different levels. This point is developed below. All that needs emphasis here is that this approach is quite consistent with the analysis of 'macro' questions concerning the overall development of a pattern of control; the discussion in chapter 3, of changing forms of conflict as capitalism developed, and in chapter 5, of differing trajectories in Britain and the United States in the post-war period, should help to resolve any doubts on this score.

The arguments that the labour process is affected by decisions elsewhere in an organization and by relations in the wider society are both correct at the empirical level. Labour processes are not isolated, but neither are they the mere reflection of forces emanating elsewhere. Such forces have to be interpreted within work relations. This is true of structural conditions such as product market circumstances and of the attitudes that individual workers and managers bring with them. The structural conditions establish only broad constraints or opportunities for action; how they work depends on how the labour process is organized. Imported attitudes can be significant, but they do not determine behaviour once people are inside the workplace. To take an admittedly extreme example, a worker entering a newspaper print room is (or, until very recent developments, was) subject to very clear rules about behaviour, including how hard he works and with whom he socializes, that override his personal predilections. Work relations develop their own traditions that are important in shaping a wide range of behaviour. They can also influence 'external' factors, as the newspaper case again shows: recruitment to the industry has traditionally relied on kin networks, so that controls on recruitment that emerge within work relations affect who gets what jobs. The personal characteristics of the workforce are not an 'independent influence' but are shaped by relations within the labour process.

Most importantly for a theory of work relations, there is the question of whether the labour process has characteristics which are peculiar to it. If not, then the theory would have only limited value because it would be addressing a part of social life, albeit an important one, that had no clear differences from any other part. If it has distinct features, it makes more sense to develop a theory about it, for that theory will apply distinctively to it. The nature of conflict is one distinctive element of the labour process, and it will be useful briefly to indicate how conflict is generated by looking at a study of workplace relations.

This focus also serves to underline one other feature of the present approach, namely that it tries to deal with issues which have been as central to traditional industrial relations and industrial sociology as they have become to the labour process debate. These issues include the reasons why effort bargaining differs between different groups of workers and the reasons why there is conflict at the point of production. A well-known study that assessed such questions is Lupton's (1963) analysis of piecework bargaining in two factories. Lupton found that in one of them workers engaged in a set of practices, known as the fiddle, by which they altered the timing and amount of their own efforts; examples included working on one job when booked on another, and not booking work when it was completed but saving the booking slip for use subsequently (the aim being to smooth out fluctuations in earnings). Some fiddles shifted the relationship between effort and reward in the workers' favour, and might therefore be seen as 'conflict', but others had no direct impact, while yet others, notably doing jobs in ways that were quicker than those formally prescribed in work study standards, actually assisted in production. As Lupton stresses, moreover, even those fiddles that shifted the effort bargain might suit management to the extent that they gave workers satisfaction and reduced the likelihood of potentially more damaging conflicts. Work relations thus involve co-operation, adaptation, and accommodation as well as conflict. And these things are not separate but are produced together.

But if conflict and co-operation are jointly produced, why give the former special status? A major aim of the study is to show that conflict is the more basic principle, and thus to provide a theory of conflict at work which has hitherto been lacking or has been stated only partially. Although it is often said that conflict is a central feature of work relations, detailed analyses of why this is so, and in particular of why conflict is more important than co-operation, are rare. The term conflict covers a wide variety of meanings, from a basic principle of work organization ('capital and labour are necessarily in conflict with each other'), through tensions in a set of work relations ('there was a running conflict over manning levels'), to a particular dispute ('conflict broke out when the workers went on strike'). All these meanings will be addressed here. But because of the ambiguity of terminology, and because, as will be seen in chapter 1, elaborations such as 'conflict of interest' are unsatisfactory, the term structured antagonism will be used to refer to the most basic level of conflict. There is a structured antagonism in all work organizations in which workers' ability to work is deployed in the creation of a surplus that goes to another group.

This clumsy formulation is required to stress several points. It relates to workers and another group, and not to workers and capitalists, because the theory is designed to apply not just to capitalism but to any system of production that is exploitive; such a system is one in which the production and appropriation of the surplus is organized in ways which are not under the effective control of the producers. Serfs in feudalism and wage labourers in capitalism are exploited, whereas an independent worker who organizes his or her work and who secures the proceeds is not. A further key point is that exploitation is not just about the distribution of the surplus, although that is certainly important. It is also about the organization of production. Suppose that all the profits of a capitalist firm were distributed among the workers. Anyone seeing conflict in purely distributional terms would have to accept that conflict had been eliminated. But a structured antagonism would still remain because of the way in which production was organized: the subjection of workers to the authority of management and the need to plan production in accord with the needs of a capitalist market would still be present. It should not be inferred that the subjection of workers to management is total; the example from Lupton's work plainly demonstrates the reverse. But there is a need for employers to develop means of extracting work from workers, and a structured antagonism is necessarily part of the process: workers have a capacity to labour, but this capacity is turned into actual effort in a system of production in which employers aim to channel the capacity in ways that suit themselves.

An important analytical distinction here is that between what will be termed detailed and general control. As noted above, it has been argued that capitalist firms are interested in accumulation and not necessarily in the control of the labour process. This is true when the former type of control is considered, but not as a general proposition. Detailed control refers to the details of work tasks: whether managers decide such things as line speeds, manning levels, the allocation of overtime, and the application of discipline, whether workers decide them, or whether there is joint regulation. General control covers the accommodation of workers to the overall aims of the enterprise. Managers can secure a high level of general control without maximizing detailed control, and substantial amounts of detailed control need not imply that workers acquiesce in the arrangements to which they are subject. This distinction will be elaborated in subsequent chapters. Its present purpose is to highlight the fact that, even if detailed control is not on the bargaining agenda between workers and managers, the general problem of securing compliance remains.

The labour process is thus governed by distinct principles, and these principles derive from the character of conflict within it. There is a basic antagonism in the production process. This is different from conflicts that occur between the buyers and sellers of goods and services. There certainly can be disputes in such market transactions, but the outcome is that one party gains what the other loses. In the production process, there is no such simple result. There undoubtedly are disputes about the distribution of the surplus, but there is also the question of how it is generated. The problem of how workers' creative capacities are deployed can be solved in various ways, and each way tends to carry particular implications for the forms and significance of overt conflict. It is not a matter of employers gaining what workers lose, or vice versa, but of the coming together of the two sides in a relationship which is inherently contradictory: employers need workers' creative capacities, but cannot give them free rein because of the need to secure a surplus and to maintain a degree of general control; and workers, although subordinate, do not simply resist the application of managerial control.

A model of 'control versus resistance' cannot grasp the complex interplay of conflict and accommodation within the labour process. The concept of struggle is more adequate although, largely because of the concentration on issues of control, it has received little theoretical attention. Labour process theory has been observed to lack 'any well-specified theory to explain variations in the sources and consequences' of struggles at the point of production (Jackson, 1984: 11). By 'struggle' is meant here the behaviour that employers and workers use within work relations to influence the terms on which those relations are carried out. It need not be consciously seen by the participants as to do with control of the labour process. Thus, workers who use fiddles to improve the effort bargain may not see themselves as being engaged in struggles with the employer, but the consequences of their behaviour can be assessed in terms of struggle. Neither is workplace struggle to be equated with class struggle. Indeed, a basic argument running through this study is that conflicts in work relations carry no necessary connotations for wider class conflict. Whether or not workers see their relations with their employers in class terms (that is, whether they perceive in their relations of conflict and co-operation a relationship of exploitation, and whether they see struggle at the point of production as a means of overcoming exploitation), and whether or not they see these relations as putting them in the same class as other subordinate people, are empirical questions.

The concept of struggle is used to make three points. Empirically, workers and employers are engaged in continuing relationships which tend to develop their own specific features and logics. Analytically, it is necessary to try to understand the interactions involved in a set of work relations instead of reducing them to control and resistance. Methodologically, it is important to recognize that the activities of social agents are crucial in the interpretation of structural pressures. This may render accounts of particular developments more complex and less immediately appealing than explanations based solely on the working out of a structural logic of development. But it is essential. Indeed, it necessarily follows from the generally accepted point that the labour process contains within it an area of uncertainty which reflects the fact that no contract can specify workers' duties in exact detail. This indeterminacy means that there must be room for social actors to affect the situation. How they do so is, of course, influenced by many structural constraints. But part of the 'relative autonomy' of the labour process is the autonomy of struggles. The theory developed below is therefore one of the dialectics of work relations.

The theory does not pretend to be totally novel; many of its elements are already in existence.[1] But it tries to bring together

1 The points made above about struggle, for example, parallel many of Przeworski's (1977) about class struggle, in particular the argument that 'objective' and 'subjective' elements are not distinct. He argues against the traditional view that class-in-itself develops as a result of objective features of society, with class-for-itself being a

arguments that have tended to be made independently, in order to provide an overall framework for the analysis of conflict in work relations. And it attempts to deal explicitly with issues that have often been considered on the basis of assumption or assertion.

A theory needs to stand or fall on its intrinsic merits. But in industrial relations, as in other social sciences, matters are not so simple. Existing theoretical frameworks are identified by labels such as pluralist, radical, sociological, and Marxist. These labels are far from arbitrary or unimportant, for they categorize a theory according to the assumptions that it makes, the modes of analysis that it employs, and the issues that it addresses. The present theory will be called materialist, because it tries to identify the material bases of industrial conflict and to demonstrate how concrete features of work relations are necessarily connected, albeit in a mediated and indirect way, with these bases. It is critical of both Marxist and non-Marxist approaches. In particular, an attempt will be made to differentiate a materialist from a Marxist analysis.

Why does this matter? It is widely argued that attempting to distinguish between Marxist and other approaches is increasingly difficult and decreasingly important. Abercrombie and Urry (1983: 89–92), for example, point to such a degree of overlap between 'Marxist' and 'Weberian' theories of class that trying to separate them becomes meaningless. Many modern treatments of Marxism have been seen as consistent with conventional social science. The present view has two components. First, there has been a fruitful dialogue between writers claiming to adopt a Marxist standpoint and non-Marxists, and new theoretical approaches are beginning to emerge (see, for example, Lash and Urry, 1984). The present materialist approach can be seen as part of this movement. Second, however, there remains a good deal of suspicion of Marxist analysis among non-Marxists. At the same time, there is debate as to whether the amendments to traditional views which recent schools of analytical Marxism

---

subsequent and separate 'subjective' element. Classes develop only through struggle and as they struggle they affect the conditions under which they come into being. Structure and action are thus reciprocally related. The present argument is in line with this view, although being critical about a certain vagueness in Przeworski's definition of struggle. In addition, it is focused on struggles at the point of production, and is sceptical about how far these turn into class struggles. Similarly the points made by Stark (1980), notably that workers have considerable discretion at work and that their powers of resistance depend on the particular struggles in which they are embedded, are echoed below. But Stark concentrates on broad 'macro' questions of work re-organization and, like Przeworski, is interested in the formation of new middle classes. The present concern is much more with the specifics of work relations and the complex nature of struggles at the point of production.

have made mean that these schools have in effect, if not in name, broken from classical Marxism. So the question of what Marxism is remains an issue, and one whose discussion has not been helped by the looseness with which terms such as Marxist and neo-Marxist have been employed.[2] In short, the materialist theory stands in the tradition which draws on some Marxist ideas while not itself being Marxist, but there is also a case for trying to specify in what a Marxist approach consists. The theory can be read independently of the discussion of the connection with Marxism; moreover, even if the account of the distinctiveness of materialism is not found convincing, the theory itself is unaffected.

Since one aim of a materialist approach is to provide what non-Marxist accounts have hitherto lacked, namely a theory of the bases of conflict in work relations, it is pertinent to assure adherents of such approaches that they are not being offered Marxism by the back door. More importantly, such an approach can be shown to be based on arguments that stand in their own right: it is possible to go beyond the merging of arguments from different discourses, which has been a persistent theme of recent literature, to the statement of a theory which is more than an eclectic assembly of elements from different traditions. (One aspect of the book follows from this point. Various of its arguments can be traced back to Marx and other writers, but no explicit discussion of their work is included. This is partly because numerous accounts already exist, but also because it is desirable to expound the materialist approach without returning to its origins. There is no need constantly to rely on the 'founding fathers' of social sciences for inspiration.) Many Marxists are, it will be argued in chapter 2, in fact materialists, since they have abandoned a distinctively Marxist approach. This is, ironically, to treat Marxism more seriously than those who use it as a talisman or who are attracted to it because of dissatisfaction with other theoretical approaches, for Marxism is given the credit of having a distinct theory of social relations. Materialism stands in contrast to any Marxism worthy of the name, and it therefore claims to appeal to non-Marxists and to those who have found Marxism attractive without necessarily endorsing all of its tenets. In short, there is now the possibility of moving beyond

2 An illustration of the need for precision comes from reactions to an earlier study (P. Edwards and Scullion, 1982a), from which the present one is derived. Labels such as neo-Marxist have been applied to it. And Batstone (1984: 304), in replying to the study's criticisms of his own earlier work, says that these fail because the extent to which its 'detailed analysis in fact derives from a specifically Marxian starting point is open to doubt'. Since the study never claimed to be Marxist, this misses the point. But it suggests that clarity may be helped by trying to specify what a Marxist approach entails.

the debate between 'Weberians', 'Marxists', 'neo-Weberians', 'neo-Marxists', and other groups, to establish a genuinely distinctive theory of social relations. The present contribution is part of a move in this direction.

Several recent studies can be seen as part of this move. A detailed analysis of their materialist leanings would be out of place here. But the sort of approach involved may be briefly indicated. The work of writers such as Przeworski (1977) and Stark (1980) has been mentioned above. A major concern is to develop a theory which allows for both 'structure' and 'action' and which does not reduce one to the other. A rather different example is the comparative analysis of French and Italian unions by Lange *et al.* (1982). This includes (at pp. 219–27) a theoretical approach to unions that treats them as actors who are shaped by their contexts without being wholly constrained by their contexts and with their being able to influence them. Such an approach, which neither treats action voluntaristically nor reduces it to structure, and which sees struggle as developing a logic of its own, is consistent with the views developed below. In short, the present argument is part of a wider re-orientation of social theory. Its claim to distinctiveness lies in its explicit theoretical framework and in its concentration on an area which is sometimes assumed or taken for granted, namely the point of production.

To be anything like comprehensive, a theory of conflict must be able to deal with the many meanings of the term 'conflict'. Different levels of analysis have to be employed to refer to these various meanings. Three main ones will be used. The first is the basic level of structured antagonisms. Then there is the organization of work relations. Co-operation comes in here, for employers need to persuade workers to work, and cannot rely on coercion alone; workers are similarly not wholly opposed to their employers. Work relations can be organized in many ways. It is less a matter of some reflecting conflict, and some co-operation, than of different ways in which conflict and co-operation are produced together. The analytical task is to try to tease out the interconnections within, and dynamics of, a set of work relations so as to understand how conflict and co-operation are organized within it. Finally, there is the level of concrete behaviour. What forms of behaviour are feasible, how far they reflect conflict, and how far they represent forms of adaptation to the situation will reflect the character of work relations in which they occur. If just workers' behaviour is, for simplicity, considered, an action such as going absent can reflect at the same time resistance against a system of control, a partial adaptation of the loopholes of that system to meet workers' own needs, and a form of accommodation to the system. Again, it is necessary to draw out the implications, and in particular to relate the behaviour to the pattern of work relations that exists.

The levels of analysis parallel another way of identifying levels of abstraction, although this second way relates more to the treatment of the real world than to purely conceptual considerations. At the broadest level there is the whole of a mode of production, together with the distinct forms of exploitation associated with each mode. Then there is the social formation, that is the individual country within a mode of production. Even within one mode, work relations vary according to the specific strategies adopted by employers and workers, and according to the context in which they operate. Third, within each country, there is considerable variation between industries and individual establishments. Each of these levels of empirical analysis will be used to illustrate the theory of conflict.

This identification of three levels of analysis closely parallels that proposed by Wright (1985: 8–12) for the consideration of class. Wright speaks of the mode of production, the social formation, and the specific conjuncture as distinct levels of abstraction. Such an arrival at similar means of conceptualization is interesting but perhaps not surprising. What requires more comment is a difference between the present argument and that of Wright concerning the nature of exploitation. This study's view of exploitation, as a characteristic of production relations but not exchange relations, is a fairly orthodox one. For Wright, following Roemer (1982), exploitation can occur outside the labour process: it exists whenever the fruits of the labour of one group are transferred to another group. In a society of independent producers, for example, there is no labour market and there is no exploitation in the orthodox sense, but in Roemer's terms exploitation will exist if the sale of goods results in the transfer of the fruits of labour. This difference is no mere quibble. The point of the orthodox definition is to provide a means of establishing that the labour contract is different from other forms of contract because it involves exploitation. Roemer's approach denies this. Its attraction is that it seems to be more general, for it can take account of such cases as an artisan who is formally independent but who is poor and oppressed because he has to sell his goods to a powerful merchant.

No detailed consideration of Roemer's views will be attempted here; some brief comments on one key aspect of them are given in the appendix to chapter 2. But it is necessary to explain how the following analysis of exploitation should be seen by someone adopting Roemer's perspective. As Wright (1985: 72) notes, his own initial reaction was to reject it because it does not treat relations within the sphere of production as crucial in the definition of exploitation and class relations. He now accepts that, although relations within production are of great practical importance, the basis of the capital-labour relation lies deeper, in the effective control of productive assets. Yet at least two sorts of problem remain. First, broadening the definition of exploitation can lead to some odd results, such as that the working class of advanced capitalist countries exploits workers elsewhere because the power of the advanced countries enables them to secure the products of less developed economies at a price less than their value. Second, if relations inside the productive system are so important, how are these relations to be conceptualized? Wright would presumably accept that there is something special about production, namely the use of labour-power to create a surplus which is not controlled by the direct producers; this has no parallel in the sphere of exchange. It may be that such points can be dealt with. If this is so, then for those adopting Wright's viewpoint the present account of exploitation should be seen as an attempt to develop a rigorous approach to the special but important case of that exploitation which takes place within the production process. In particular, it tries to explain what is distinct about the process and why conflict is inherent in it. That is, even if Roemer's 'general theory' is accepted, there remains a place for a more specific theory of the nature of relations at the point of production. Production relations are of special importance; the general theory does not itself provide the means of explaining why, and it carries with it the danger of treating production and exchange relations as though the same principles governed them. It may be that a general theory could be developed to take account of these points, but, until it is, the orthodox view of exploitation, as a characteristic of production but not exchange relations, may be retained.

The foregoing arguments about the specific character of the social relations of production and the place of conflict within them are developed in chapter 1 by indicating limitations in existing treatments, whether these adopt a 'conventional' or a labour process perspective. These limitations do not invalidate everything about the treatments, and some crucial insights from a range of writings are identified. These are used to build up, in chapter 2, a theory of conflict. This theory is then contrasted with a Marxist approach.

The remainder of the study illustrates and extends the theory, using examples at different levels of abstraction. In chapter 3 the focus is the broad development of capitalism as a mode of production and the changing ways in which conflict was generated (although to make the discussion manageable most of the illustrations are taken from Britain). A major argument is that, because capitalism is a mode of production with distinct characteristics, forms of conflict have displayed a greater degree of uniformity than is often thought. There have obviously been enormous changes, but these have occurred in a context in which some of the basic parameters have been constant.

In the next two chapters the level of analysis moves to the social formation, the specific focus being contrasts in the development of work relations in Britain and the United States. One element in the contrast was the role of the state. Chapter 4 therefore outlines an approach to the state before applying it to cases of state intervention in labour relations in the two countries (with some other illustrations being drawn from Australia). In line with the basic premises of a materialist approach, it is argued that state intervention is neither the result of the needs of the mode of production nor the activity of a state which is a self-contained entity. Instead, intervention can be traced to the base of economic development, but this base created only broad constraints and pressures which had to be interpreted in practice, which gave considerable leeway to actors in the precise decisions that they made, and which depended for their outcome on the specific character of the state in terms of its organization and powers. Once states had begun to intervene, moreover, their activities exerted an effect on subsequent developments that was unpredictable, and was independent of other parts of society. Thus chapter 5 charts trends in labour relations in the two countries since the 1930s and relates these to the interaction of state and employers' policies. It also examines some of the consequences of the two patterns for productivity. It again follows from the basic approach of the study that these consequences should not be seen in terms of the supposedly greater amount of resistance or shopfloor power in one country than the other. Patterns of work relations have several elements, some of which may enhance production while others may interfere with it. And both types of these elements may be as much the creation of management as of workers. The outcomes of work relations cannot be reduced to variations in the resistance of workers.

This perspective is continued in chapter 6, where the focus is the most detailed one of the individual workplace. Five types of detailed control are identified, and the related ways in which concrete activities, of a collective and an individual kind, arise under each type are considered. It becomes possible to treat an activity such as sabotage not as a self-explanatory 'form' of behaviour but as a reflection of a type of control, with the activity taking on very different characteristics in different workplaces and with, indeed, the very label of sabotage being problematic and requiring explanation in terms of why and how it is applied to certain outcomes of struggles in work relations.

As mentioned above, the materialist theory claims to apply to any exploitive mode of production. In chapter 7, therefore, work relations under three non-capitalist modes of production, feudalism, slavery, and state socialism are considered. The basic argument has two aspects: under any mode of production, the transformation of labour-power into labour is an uncertain process, with workers necessarily having the opportunity to alter the terms of their subordination; but the nature of this uncertainty differs between modes because of differences in their fundamental ways of organizing exploitation. It is correct to argue that workplace conflict is not unique to capitalism, but incorrect to infer that there are no distinctive features of this mode of production.

The overall aim, therefore, is to understand the basis of conflict in work relations, how conflict and co-operation are intertwined, and the ways in which the expression of conflict can vary. Although analytical and theoretical in purpose, the study has some implications for 'practical men'. These implications are briefly indicated in the epilogue.

Although wide-ranging, the study has some obvious gaps. One which requires some comment is the lack of attention to employees other than manual workers employed in factories. This is a necessary limitation, given that most studies concentrate on such workers. It is not as damaging as might appear, for the general principles are applicable to other workers. A study such as Blau's (1963) investigation of clerical workers in an American federal employment agency, although not using the language of control and struggle over the effort bargain, reveals a range of covert means that such workers can deploy to subvert formal rules and create some space for themselves. The precise concepts relevant to such workers may differ from those that are familiar for studies of blue-collar workers, but the basic principles of analysis are the same. Perhaps more difficult are cases where the division between exploiting and exploited groups is not clear-cut. Managers and supervisors of all kinds control subordinates while themselves being controlled from above: are they covered by the theory, and in what respect? No attempt will be made to consider their position in detail, but two points may be made. First, those who fall unambiguously into the 'exploited' category, that is those who do not own any means of production and who exercise no authority over the labour of others, are a substantial part of the work force: 55 per cent in America, according to Wright's (1985: 195) figures. Second, the presence of 'intermediate' groups is not really a problem when different levels of analysis are taken into account. There is a structured antagonism between capital and labour, but there is no reason why this antagonism should create two internally homogeneous classes of capitalists and workers. Workers meet the power of capital through supervisors who are themselves subject to authority from above. This has important consequences for the self-identity of supervisors and for patterns of concrete behaviour. But it does not bear on the fact that capital, although internally differentiated, is in an antagonistic relationship with labour. Matters involving the internal differentiation of capital and labour pertain to a different level of analysis from that concerned with the basic features of the mode of production. The failure to make this kind of distinction has been the source of much confusion.

A further limitation is the empirical focus, within the discussion of capitalism, on Anglo-Saxon countries. Is this not a severe limitation in view of the fact that the point of production is much less of a focus of conflict in, say, Sweden or France? And is not the role of neo-corporatist accommodation between unions, employers, and the state so significant in countries such as Sweden or Germany that a focus on the workplace is partial to the point of being misleading? It is true that, in their different ways, writers such as Korpi and Shalev (1979), Streek (1984) and Cameron (1984) have advanced the understanding of patterns of strike activity and of the degree of integration of the working class within the social structure. By exercising bargaining restraint at the workplace level, it is argued, unions can reap gains at other levels. A theory of conflict would then focus on the conditions under which this is possible. The present approach does not deny the importance of such analysis or treat the workplace as the only important level of analysis, although having some reservations about some of the arguments of the writers in question. But their approach is to assess what happens once workers have been mobilized, that is once particular interests have been identified and forms of organization to express them have emerged. The present concern is to examine the bases of conflict, that is how and why workers and employers are in a state of antagonistic relations; it is out of these relations that particular organizations to express conflict emerge. A materialist theory could certainly be applied to, say, the ways in which unions and works councils in Germany are engaged in relations of conflict and co-operation with employers. And its analysis of the role of the state could certainly be extended to a case such as Sweden. This would not, however, assist the development of the theory which is, in short, not directly about the conditions of neo-corporatist exchange in capitalist economies but about the relations between capital and labour which necessarily underlie such exchange. To criticize the theory for neglecting cases in which the workplace is not the focus of most day-to-day conflicts is to confuse form and substance: it is an empirical question why potential conflicts do not occur, but the need for employers to extract effort within an antagonistic relationship still exists.[3]

There are thus various respects in which materialist analysis can be extended or modified. The first task, however, is to develop it and to apply it to those cases which are most important to it. This is the aim of the present study.

3 There is, moreover, the danger of assuming that conflict can be shifted permanently away from the level of the workplace, even though in several countries, including Sweden, high levels of absenteeism, for example, have been persistent worries for management. It thus becomes pertinent to ask how social relations are organized at this level and what forms of action are open to workers. Some of the key aspects of the effort bargain may be determined away from the point of production, but this should not be allowed to lead to a neglect of this level of analysis. Some treatments come close to assuming that day-to-day workplace relations in corporatist structures have an entirely routine and unproblematic character.

1

Problems in the Analysis of Conflict

Two of the most frequent statements about industrial conflict are that it is inevitable and that it can take a wide variety of forms. To move beyond such truisms an adequate theory must be able to operate at three distinct levels of analysis. First, there is the identification of the bases of conflict, that is why conflict is inevitable and what are the chief groups in industry which are said to be in a state of conflict with each other. 'Conflict' here refers to what are sometimes called conflicts of interest, that is basic contradictions or divisions that may not be reflected in overt disputes; as explained later, the concept of a conflict of interests is not in fact the most useful for the purpose, and it will be replaced by that of structured antagonism. Second, there is the development of analytical tools to move from this fundamental level to the consideration of specific forms of work organization. It is obvious that a degree of co-operation is necessary if any social work process is to continue, and a means must exist to incorporate co-operation systematically into the analysis. It is also obvious that work organizations differ in their characteristics: some workers are individualized, others are members of powerful work groups, and so on. Tools are required to analyse these differences; examples are the concepts of the wage-effort bargain and the frontier of control. Finally, it must be possible to analyse concrete instances of conflict: how do these instances stem from specific organizations of work; what explains the occurrence of one 'form' of conflict and not another; how far does observed behaviour such as sabotage or output restriction reflect an underlying conflict; and so on.

In this chapter, various approaches to worker-management relations are assessed against these criteria. The question of the bases of conflict is in many ways the most important, for if an approach cannot explain why conflict exists a statement that conflict is inevitable or endemic lacks any real meaning or foundation. A major purpose of the chapter is to demonstrate the absence, in many approaches, of a way of analysing the bases of conflict, and thus to lay the ground for chapter 2, one of whose main purposes is to provide this vital missing ingredient. But the second and third levels of analysis are important, particularly in the assessment of theories of the labour process. In these theories the twin concepts of managerial strategy for the control of labour and worker resistance to this control are widely used. The connections between these concepts and the bases of conflict are not always clear, and the theories would benefit, it will be suggested, from some explicit theorizing such as that attempted in chapter 2. In addition, the 'control versus resistance' model has difficulties in dealing with co-operative aspects of workplace relations and in exploring how far observed behaviour, for example a manager and a shop steward agreeing a manning level for a job, reflects control and resistance.

The chapter has four main sections. In the first, some traditional industrial relations approaches are briefly reviewed. This is followed by a consideration of what has become known as the 'radical' approach. This is a rather specialized label, for the term 'radical' is widely used to denote approaches that are critical of the prevailing orthodoxy; in economics, for example, radical theories of the labour market are contrasted with neo-classical ones, and the radical theories can be differentiated into several distinct strands. In the present context, the radical approach consists of the sociological tradition of analysing work relations; it has Weberian roots and is non-Marxist and often anti-Marxist. The third and fourth sections examine approaches that focus on the labour process, the former concentrating on writers who have stressed conflict over the control of this process and the latter considering those who have stressed the generation of co-operation and consent within it. The concluding section draws out some of the elements of an adequate theory of conflict which can be identified in the disparate writings examined in the body of the chapter.

Conflict in Industrial Relations Theory

A detailed critical exegesis on what industrial relations specialists have had to say about industrial conflict would be impossible. It is also unnecessary, for the key issues can be considered in terms of the perspectives identified by Fox (1966, 1973): the unitary and the pluralist approaches. The following account is brief and selective, but it also tries to be more sympathetic and adequate than some critiques of the approaches, which tend to present them as straw men.

Unitary Perspectives

According to Fox, the unitary approach is characterized by a belief that work organizations are unified bodies in which everyone shares the same goals. As Crouch (1982: 18) puts it, conflict is then seen 'as rather unnecessary, the result of misunderstanding or mischief; in other words, as pathological'. It is not surprising that, presented thus, the perspective is simply rejected as wholly inadequate. There is a mass of evidence that organizations are not unitary structures but are coalitions containing competing interests; conflict is too common and too obviously based on genuinely different interests to be written off as the outcome of misunderstanding; and so on. But Fox and Crouch then have a problem, for they both recognize that a unitary view is probably adopted by a large number of what Crouch (1982: 18) calls 'non-academic practitioners of industrial relations, especially on the managerial side'. That is, many people think that firms have common goals and that, given sufficiently good communications and sufficient good will, conflict can be eliminated. In addition to managers, one might want to include among holders of this view those workers who subscribe to the 'football team' idea of industrial relations: that is, those who, when asked whether the firm is a football team in which managers and workers have the same aims, or is an organization in which interests are fundamentally in conflict, agree with the former option. In addition, several academic perspectives, particularly those associated with the human relations tradition, have been seen as having unitary views. How is it that so many people adopt a view which not only conflicts with the academic wisdom of pluralists and radicals but which must also clash with much of their own daily experience of conflicts in industry?

The answer lies in two distinctions: between descriptive and normative statements; and between coherent world views and vague and inarticulate understandings of everyday practice. If the normative view that conflict is pathological were treated as a description of reality, unitarists would not need to try to account for the existence of trade unions, for they would have to believe that unions, as reflections of differing interest within firms, could not exist. In fact, of course, various explanations are offered (Fox, 1973: 190). These explanations involve, in effect, attempts to explain why labour relations cannot be described by purely normative statements. Similarly, if normative statements were treated as descriptive, there would be no need for 'practitioners of industrial relations', for the very existence of industrial relations implies differing interests.

On the difference between general world views and concrete understandings, research into managerial attitudes towards industrial relations is instructive. This points to the widespread adoption of a unitarist perspective. Winkler (1974) has argued that members of boards of directors tend to see industrial relations in very simple terms, with conflict arising from misunderstanding or the behaviour of troublemakers; the reason was their lack of direct knowledge of labour issues and their insulation from shopfloor workers. Fidler (1981: 148–67) found in a survey of chief executives of large firms that the most frequent explanation for the presence of two sides in industry was that it was an aberration and that conflict was the result of poor communications; there was no enduring view of the firm as a set of coalitions. A more broadly based survey of managers at all levels came to a similar conclusion. Its authors argued that such findings contradict the common argument in industrial relations literature that managements have sponsored the growth of shop-steward organizations, have often found the closed shop to be useful in the stabilization of industrial relations, and have generally acted in a manner which accepts the legitimacy of shopfloor organizations (Poole *et al.*, 1981: 82–3). If managers are unitarists, why should they do these things?

Such a way of posing the issue represents a fundamental confusion. It is not clear why a general and normatively based view of what firms ought to be like is contradicted by concrete practices based on acceptance of shopfloor organizations. It is perfectly possible to believe that firms are 'really' based on shared interests while also accepting that, in fact, trade unions exist and can make demands for such things as the closed shop. A unitarist manager may be prepared to accept that in the real world in which he operates there are concrete benefits to be gained from formalizing arrangements by, for example, agreeing to a closed shop. World views are not, in any event, clearly articulated statements. It has become a commonplace in recent studies of workers' attitudes that workers do not have coherent and consistent views, and that there may be a contrast between general statements of belief and actual practice (e.g. Nichols and Armstrong, 1976). A generalized view that strikes are the result of agitators, for example, may co-exist with respect for one's own shop stewards and a willingness to strike if this action seems necessary. There is no reason to suppose that managers are fundamentally different: they can readily hold views that might appear to be contradictory.

The unitary view is certainly inadequate as an analysis of the causes of industrial conflict. But it is not simply to be dismissed. It is important to try to understand why 'practitioners' hold the views that they do instead of treating them as wrong. More importantly for present purposes, a unitary perspective contains a vital element of truth which tends to be neglected when the perspective is treated as a self-contained system and rejected as a whole. There are substantial areas of co-operation in work relations. Workers are not always going on strike. Managers can devise means to generate a sense of loyalty to the firm, for example, through schemes for participation and profit-sharing. Firms may well have an idea of removing a 'them and us' approach on the shopfloor. And such things are not to be seen as simply the result of manipulation of workers. There is a very real sense in which workers stand to gain from arrangements that promote co-operation. There are the immediate financial advantages of better wages and fringe benefits, together with the advantages of job security to be derived from working for firms that are not driven by conflict and that are thus able to produce at low cost.

This argument should not be misunderstood. It is not being suggested that harmony is a natural condition in industry or that the pursuit of co-operation can be divorced from struggles for control. But a theoretical approach is needed which can incorporate the issues identified by the unitarists. It is not a matter of a conflict model of society *versus* a co-operation model but of a model which can embrace conflict and co-operation and thus transcend the simple division between approaches which has tended to exist in the past.

Pluralism

If the unitary view has been disregarded, the pluralist perspective has suffered from over-attention from its opponents. It is common to find it argued, for example, that pluralism assumes 'a roughly equal balance of power between employers and workers organized in trade unions' and sees industrial relations problems as 'pathological' (Clarke and Clements, 1977: 132, 134). The accusation that pluralism necessarily assumes a balance of power has been denied by Clegg (1975), one of the leading pluralists. And Ross Martin (1983) has shown that another common accusation, namely that pluralists assume that the state is simply neutral as between the interests of employers and workers, is also false: the view was held only by a particular school of American pluralists, and it has been disavowed by many self-professed pluralists.

A more subtle explication and critique of pluralism is advanced by Fox and Crouch: institutional pluralists, who are held to occupy the dominant position in academic studies of industrial relations, concentrate on formal institutions and believe that the inevitable conflicts which arise in industrial relations can be tamed through appropriate institutional means. There is certainly no view that conflict is pathological. The Donovan Commission (1968: 79–80), a widely quoted source in the construction of the pluralist view, for example, argued that restrictive practices were the product of particular industrial relations contexts and might be perfectly rational from the point of view of those engaging in them. It also held, however, that such practices reflected merely a sectional interest and that the reform of bargaining arrangements would solve the problem. Similarly, there is no view of an equality of power between employers and workers. Clegg has poured scorn on the very idea of what equality might look like. All that needs to be held is that groups exist and come into conflict with each other, and that appropriate institutions can channel this conflict into peaceful means.

As Hyman (1978) has argued, most versions of pluralism start from a statement that conflict is inevitable and natural, but they rapidly qualify this by focusing on the means through which conflict is institutionalized and by treating conflict as a contained and limited phenomenon. The whole logic of the analysis is to move away from a focus on what Hyman (p. 32) calls the 'material basis' of conflict to an assessment of how conflict is organized and channeled. But what is wrong with a 'minimalist' as against a 'strong' pluralist position? The former would hold only that there are bound to be conflicts of interest in industry, and that groups emerge around particular interests and use their resources to seek their overall aims.

Clegg (1979) has outlined such a position. He says that pluralism and Marxism are similar in so far as both are concerned with conflict and with stability: 'both regard conflict as inevitable in industrial relations as in other aspects of social life' and both face the problem of explaining how conflict can exist without its destroying society (p. 452). But why is conflict inevitable? For Clegg (p. 1) industrial relations is the study of 'the rules governing employment'. These rules cannot be understood without understanding the organizations which take part in their creation. 'Each of these organizations has its own sources of authority, and whenever there are separate sources of authority there is the risk of conflict. When organizations are in conflict, they may apply pressure to persuade each other to make concession'. The logic of this argument should be carefully noted. Overt conflict is equated with the application of sanctions by organizations; and a broader conflict of interest exists because organizations have different sources of authority.

Such a view is not limited to self-proclaimed industrial relations pluralists. In its essential elements it is, ironically, shared by some critics of pluralism. Such influential writers as Shorter and Tilly (1974) and Korpi and Shalev (1979) have attacked the assumption, made within what they see as the pluralist tradition, that conflict occurs solely within collective bargaining; they suggest that the use of organizations' power resources within the political arena is also important. Yet, as shown elsewhere (P. Edwards, 1983), this is not a decisive criticism, for the focus on collective bargaining is merely a reflection of the pluralists' concentration in and on the Anglo-Saxon countries, where collective bargaining is the main means of determining wages and conditions of employment. Analysis of the use of power resources outside collective bargaining is perfectly consistent with a pluralist programme. The critics' own mode of analysis, moreover, is in fact no more than an extension of a pluralist position, based as it is on the deployment of power resources by already constituted organizations. The following critical comments apply, then, not only to traditional pluralists but also to several other influential approaches to labour relations.

In the traditional and in these newer forms of pluralism the focus is overwhelmingly on conflict which arises out of clashes between organizations. The size of this defect depends on what is included under the heading of an organization. If the focus is on formally constituted bodies such as trade unions, the problem is substantial. It is reduced if less formally organized collectivities such as shop steward committees or even individual work groups are included. Historical studies (e.g. Tilly, 1982) for example have examined changing 'repertoires' of public protest, looking at any collective gathering regardless of how amorphous and unorganized it may be. Yet the problem remains of assuming that articulated interests exist, which groups then express. In practice, attention has been paid almost exclusively to what happens once groups exist. As Hill (1974) points out, traditional industrial relations pluralism assumes that work groups exist instead of considering the conditions which permit such collectivities to develop.

A phenomenon such as piecework bargaining, for example, would have to be seen as the product of clashes between work groups and managements. The idea that workers can engage in such bargaining as individuals is neglected, as is the important fact that groups are likely to emerge through the process of bargaining itself: the existence of groups depends on the presence of opposing interests, and not the reverse. Even more importantly, potential expressions of conflict such as absenteeism and quitting are not even considered because they are not part of the deployment of sanctions by organizations.

It might be possible to extend the approach to consider the behaviour of individuals. But this would be difficult, given pluralism's view of society as being composed of competing groups. And it would not avoid the difficulty of treating groups as the means of expression of already articulated demands and wants. The generation of these demands and wants would remain a problem.

There is in pluralism, moreover, little view of the nature of the society in which groups are engaged in their struggles. Some groups are certainly allowed to be more powerful than others, but the groups are seen as autonomous in the sense that power resources can be deployed in any direction and that the outcome will rest simply on the relative powers of different sides. There is no sense of the ways in which there may be systematic pressures which prevent various groups from using their full 'resources' or indeed of the complex processes which define these resources in the first place. The problem is particularly acute for those who espouse a 'political' approach, for they speak of deployment of resources in the political arena without having an articulated view of the nature of the arena or of the role of the state in shaping its boundaries. A pluralist approach does not tackle the problem of the nature or the basis of conflict, and merely concentrates on what happens when organizational expressions of conflict have already been articulated.

Concluding Remarks
Further detail could be added to the foregoing descriptions, but the main characteristics of the view to conflict taken by unitary and pluralist approaches should be clear. Despite their limitations as adequate theories of conflict, in particular regarding the identification of the bases of conflict in work relations, they have some strengths which should not be dismissed. The unitary view recognizes the importance of co-operation and consent. Numerous studies have shown, moreover, that workers may not aspire to an influence over many aspects of firms' behaviour; although the assumption of shared interests is very wide of the mark, unitarists are correct in assuming that workers are not in a state of permanent conflict with their employers and that they may adopt or at least take for granted the aims of the firm. The pluralist perspective, although lacking a view of the bases of conflict and tending to focus only on concrete forms of conflict that are collectively organized, can be effective in the analysis of clashes between organized groups.

Radical Perspectives

As noted above, the radical perspective denotes in the present context writers who have tried, often on the basis of critiques of pluralism, to develop a sociological account of workplace relations. Crouch (1982: 27) notes in his statement of a radical theoretical position on trade unionism that the approach emerges 'from the heartland of modern British sociology', citing as representative names Fox and Goldthorpe, and locating their work in the tradition exemplified by writers such as Rex, Lockwood, and Parkin. He expounds a view of conflict only briefly, but in essence it does not assume that institutions will be able to channel conflict, that there is a common interest in the resolution of what look from above to be 'problems', or that there is an overarching normative order. Neither does it 'take for granted the character of industrial conflict' but instead stresses the 'endemic nature of conflict and the fact that its sources lie beyond the reach of institutional tinkering' (p. 26).

The approach is difficult to summarize more cogently than this, for it has grown up in the course of criticisms of pluralism and of Marxism and is hence characterized more by its rejection of particular tenets of each than by a specific list of attributes of its own. It certainly has a strong tradition, but this is a tradition of methodological approach rather than broad theoretical statements. There is, for example, the tradition of investigation of the attitudes of occupational groups and the demonstration that consciousness is more complex than at least some Marxist views imply. Similarly, there is a willingness to discuss matters such as the structured inequalities of power and advantage which are seen to characterize capitalist societies, and indeed to use terms such as capitalism, which receive little attention from the pluralists.

The argument here is that these radical approaches have one central weakness: they lack a means of explaining why conflict is 'endemic' and why inequalities are more than contingent results of differences in groups' access to rewards. This is not, however, to follow the normal Marxist-influenced lines of criticism such as that offered by Wood and Elliott (1977). These writers take as their focus the work of Fox (1973, 1974) and argue that its attempted radicalization of industrial relations theory is not successful. They identify an ambivalence in this work. There is an element involving the modification of pluralism, to suggest for example that conflict is rather more deep-seated and that inequalities of power are rather greater than the institutional pluralists imply. But there is also a hint at 'some kind of Marxist analysis' which would 'involve a questioning and rejection of the *sine qua non* of pluralism, namely the notion that all groups in industry have a common interest in the survival of the whole of which they are part' (p. 110). This argument is misconceived. First, as Fox (1979) pointed out in a celebrated reply, it confuses analysis and prescription. There is a difference between holding values which can be described as liberal-pluralist and accepting that these values are adequately realized in existing societies. A 'radical' method of analysis need not involve commitment to a Marxist programme of social change. Second, what can it mean to insist that a radical approach rejects the idea that groups have interests in the survival of society as a whole? It is certainly necessary to criticize the pluralist notion that there is an automatic sharing of interests and that no interest group will pursue its aims beyond some limit set by what is socially acceptable. But all groups plainly have some interest in the continued operation of society so that the means of subsistence continue to be available. Wood and Elliott provide a good example of the tendency to suggest that a radical analysis, by moving away from assumptions of a natural tendency towards order, should assert that conflict is ubiquitous and total and that trust and co-operation are either impossible or the outcome of manipulation by powerful groups in society. What is needed is not a rejection of the possibility of trust or of the idea that there are some shared interests in society but an analysis which can incorporate trust and shared interests while also seeing the employment relationship as being based on conflict.

The real problem with the radical approach is that, like that of the pluralists, it lacks a view of the basis of conflict. There is a very simple choice to be made. Either conflict is equated with observable manifestations of discontent, or an attempt is made to specify the bases of conflict independently of any particular observable indicators. The former option would go beyond pluralism in so far as it was able to take account of behaviour other than that undertaken by groups. Grumbling to a supervisor, going absent, or engaging in covert 'fiddles' such as booking more output than had actually been produced, could all be included. But it remains incomplete. To show its inadequacy, a number of formulations will be considered, beginning with the most sophisticated attempt to escape the dilemma, that of Lukes.

Power and Interests
Although Lukes's (1974) 'radical' view focuses on power and not conflict, it is obviously closely related to present concerns. What Lukes aims to do is to replace existing views of power, which he feels are too limited because of their focus on behavioural manifestations of power, with a broader view which recognizes that power can be exercised even in the absence of observable manifestations. As he puts it, he wishes to take account of power which 'can occur in the absence of actual, observable conflict' and to allow for the presence of *'latent conflict'* which consists in a contradiction between the interests of

those exercising power and the *real interests* of those they exclude' (pp. 24–5, emphasis in original). He adds, in a significant footnote, that his account is different from that of writers such as Dahrendorf (1959), who tries to identify the objective basis of latent interests, because Dahrendorf 'assumes as sociologically given what I claim to be empirically ascertainable'. Thus, for Lukes the exercise of power means that a superordinate affects a subordinate in a manner contrary to the interests of the latter. Two conditions are specified as necessary if such a view is to be sustained: it must be possible to justify the 'relevant counterfactual', that is the expectation that the subordinate would have acted differently but for the exercise of power; and the mechanism whereby power is exerted must be identifiable.

This argument has generated considerable critical interest, which may be summarized under two heads. First came a series of questions about the empirical applicability of Lukes's ideas. A Lukesian analyst is plainly claiming to know better than people themselves where their real interests lie, which raises a vast range of methodological as well as moral problems (Roderick Martin, 1977: 165–9). On the latter, Lukes (1974: 34) admits, and indeed stresses, that any view of power is 'irreducibly evaluative', and it is not clear why his evaluations of what is desirable or what people would do in the absence of an alleged exercise of power should be given privileged status. On the methodological problems, consider for example the use which Lukes makes of the study by Crenson (1971) of air pollution in American cities. Lukes argues that this can be interpreted in terms of real interests by arguing that people have a real interest in clean air and that this interest was not being attained because of the exercise of power by corporations whose factories were producing the pollutants. Yet, even in so obvious a case 'there is a gap between the power subject's desire to avoid or mitigate some of the effects' of power and the guarantee that these effects can be removed without damage to other interests (Wrong, 1979: 186). That is, once the possibility is allowed for that people have numerous interests, it is not clear whether a failure to maximize one objective means that power is being exercised or merely that there are trade-offs between different objectives.

As Bradshaw (1976: 125–6) notes, Lukes takes over from existing approaches an individualistic methodology. The aim of these was to be able to say that in a specific case a specific actor had power over a specific matter. When the concern is with real interests in general a view of power as relating to individual cases becomes unworkable. It is not a matter of adding up a series of independent actions but of understanding the nature of a relationship between two parties. This leads into the second line of criticism, which has concentrated on the theoretical problems underlying Lukes's approach. As Benton (1981: 173) argues, Lukes lacks any 'conception of an inner dynamic of capitalist social relations' and thus faces the problem of finding an 'anchor which will secure a radical critique of the prevailing distribution of power . . . in the absence of any detectable social force whose standpoint is represented in the critique'. Lukes cannot limit his view of interests to wants and preferences, for these can plainly be 'distorted' by the exercise of power, but he has no means of establishing what the objective interests of a particular group are. This is why he has to insist that any notion of interests is evaluative: he has no way out of his dilemma of wanting to say that something is against the interests of a group without having a view of the objective conditions in which the group is placed.

It will be convenient to consider here some other points which have emerged from the debate about power, for they are of some significance for the argument to be developed below. First, Benton is correct to reject reliance on the concept of interests. There is a tendency to assume that there are (apart from Lukes's unsuccessful attempt to find a middle way) only two ways of looking at interests: either they are equated with wants and preferences, with all attempts to identify more fundamental interests being rejected as a metaphysical; or a Marxist approach is adopted in which all interests are supposedly reducible to, or at least based on, class position and in which the interest of the working class is held to be the overthrow of capitalism. The limitations of both will by now be apparent. The way out is to abandon reference to interests and to rely instead on analysis of the structure of the situation and how it affects the development of particular patterns of wants and preferences. That is, the need is not to presume that there are certain basic real interests but to consider how the location of people in objective conditions encourages the growth of some preferences and not others.

Second, Benton refers to the activities of the power-holder instead of simply examining power in terms of the position of the power-subject. This is plainly important for an analysis of industrial conflict, in that a proper understanding of conflict requires attention to the activities of employers and workers; indeed, which 'side' is the more powerful may be a point which requires specific attention. Benton's approach is to speak of the objectives, and not the interests, of power-holders and power-subjects, and he distinguishes between the power of the former to do something and power over the latter: the powerful may be able to attain ends without necessarily having to exert power over their subordinates. This is, again, important since there has developed a view that the sole matter of interest to employers is control over the activities of their employees. The distinction between 'power to' and 'power over' acts as a reminder that employers may have numerous aims, which may or may not directly involve relations with workers. Where 'power over' is involved, Benton defines power in terms of the capabilities and resources of the two sides, with one being powerful if it is able to achieve its objective even where the other is also deploying its resources in pursuit of an incompatible objective.

There are, however, some difficulties. Hindess (1982) identifies one set of problems in his critique of approaches to power based on capacities to secure ends: if outcomes depend simply on capacities, then any conception of results as depending on action disappears, for the result is determined in advance. Moreover, Hindess argues, there is a tendency to see interests as characteristics which attach to agents independently of the particular struggles in which they are engaged (p. 506). As suggested above, there is a tendency among some writers on industrial conflict to treat the resources of employers and unions as though they exist unproblematically outside particular sets of relations and as though they simply have to be put into action as the need arises. The logical outcome of this sort of approach is the view of strikes put forward by some economists: if the resources of both sides are known in advance, the only explanation of a strike is that one or both parties makes mistakes about its own or the other side's resources. Yet there are plenty of examples in which apparently hopeless strikes have led to victory. Not only can resources be miscalculated, but the nature of the resources can change during a dispute if, for example, workers generate solidarity and determination which was intially lacking or if employers decide not to use all the 'resources' which might appear to be at their disposal. To take another example, consider what has been called elsewhere (P. Edwards and Scullion, 1982a: 162) the 'tool-box' theory of sanctions: the theory that workers (and managers) have at their disposal a set of sanctions which can be applied according to the needs of the situation. There are two problems with such a theory. First, in circumstances in which workers have not developed a collective organization which has been tried in practice, certain sanctions such as the restriction of effort or a work-to-rule will be literally unthinkable because, although it is always possible in principle for workers to question some aspect of the way in which they do their work, unless some organization has emerged there is no way in which this possibility can be translated into action. 'In short, sanctions are constituted by organization and by the process of their use' (Edwards and Scullion, p. 163). Second, even where a tradition of organization exists, the process of applying sanctions can never be certain: outcomes depend on agents' conduct of a campaign, and the definition of resources is possible only through actions.

A second problem with Benton's approach is the absence of explicit consideration of the structure of the situation in which 'objectives' are defined. Despite reference to Lukes's lack of a view of the dynamics of capitalist social relations, Benton does not propound an account of these relations which could be used to explain why, for example, workers come to have certain objectives which then come up against the objectives of other groups. He has certainly undermined Lukes's approach and, followed by Hindess, has identified some of the elements to be incorporated in a more satisfactory approach such as the rejection of a notion of interests and the importance of treating conflict as involving action as well as the deployment of impersonal capacities. But he has not solved the problem which Lukes raised, namely the identification of latent conflict, by reference to objective considerations. This is one of the tasks of the following analysis.

Exploitation and the Production Process

Some further features of the radical or sociological approach are evident in the recent work by Hill (1981: vii–viii) which aims to 'reconstruct industrial sociology' by drawing on 'Weber's economic sociology' and 'the insights of the revived Marxist perspective'. This marks an advance in several ways, notably its attempt to produce a theory of work relations which can deal with latent conflict by providing an account of the objective basis of observable behaviour. Hill endorses a concept of exploitation, which he defines in terms of the monopoly of the means of production enjoyed by the capitalist. This monopoly 'is used to compel a workforce to do more work than its own wants prescribe, thereby producing a net gain for the capitalist which reflects the amount of this extra work' (p. 6). He later enlarges on this view by arguing that conflict is not simply a matter of the distribution of the surplus which is generated in the process of production but is also an aspect of that process itself (pp. 13–14).

This is a crucial point. Any adequate account of conflict in industry needs to be able to explain conflicts within the production process. The reason for competition over the allocation of the surplus is clear enough: the rewards going to the capitalist will increase if the share of profits increases, while workers will similarly gain by increasing the share of wages. There is more to it than the distributional struggle which is the sole focus of some schools of economics.[1] But why are

1 On this, incidentally, Hill displays some confusion, for he commends what he calls the neo-Ricardian perspective even though, as is now well established (e.g. Rowthorn, 1980: 24–47), a limitation of this perspective is precisely its focus on the distributional

there conflicts within production? A full answer will be attempted in chapter 2. All that needs to be noted here is that phenomena exist which cannot be explained by reference to distributional struggles alone. How can the systematic restriction of effort or other well-attested workplace activities be explained without reference to the process of production?

Hill's treatment of production and distribution through a theory of exploitation is on the right lines. But it is not entirely successful. This can be seen at two levels. First, there is the way in which the discussion of empirical material is carried out. The clearest example is the statement following the quotation of a frequently cited passage from Kerr (1954: 232) in which examples of the diverse range of individual as well as collective forms of conflict are given. Hill (1981: 128) comments that 'industrial sociology, however, is concerned primarily with collective rather than individual expression, and with organised rather than unorganised methods of conducting conflict'. Given the stated aims of the book, this is a remarkable limitation: instead of considering the ways in which the exploitative relationship between capitalists and workers creates a complex pattern of control and resistance, in which conflict is a major principle, industrial sociology is to consider only collective methods of conducting conflict. Second, Hill's theory of exploitation is developed in only the tersest way, the main aim of the discussion being to free the concept from any necessary connection with the labour theory of value. Hill does not explain whether workers who were found, through appropriate interviewing, to want to do as much work as they were in fact doing, or even more, should be considered to be exploited. If the term 'wants' is replaced by 'interests', the Lukesian problems re-appear: why, for example, is it in workers' interests to do less work rather than more, given that if they do not work hard they may endanger their other interest of having a job? As it is stated, moreover, the theory of exploitation contains more than a hint of being grounded in a distributional approach: there is exploitation because capitalists take part of the product, not because the process of creating that product is itself exploitative. Hill's proper insights into the production process are not integrated into such a theory. In short, therefore, the theory remains undeveloped, and is not used to inform analysis of empirical issues, such as the forms

---

struggle with no concern being shown for conflicts within the production process. The approach is called neo-Richardian after the tradition of economics established by David Ricardo, in which three classes are identified (rentiers, capitalists and workers), each deriving its income from a different factor of production (land, capital and labour). There is a struggle over the distribution of the surplus from production going to each class, but the production process itself is not examined.

taken by conflict, which should be addressed by a reconstructed industrial sociology.

The Effort Bargain

A final issue in connection with the radical perspective arises from the study of the effort bargain, in particular Baldamus's (1961) contribution. This is important for several reasons: as argued below, the effort bargain is a useful concept for bridging between analysis of the bases of conflict and consideration of concrete behaviour; one of Baldamus's key arguments, namely that the labour contract can never be totally specified in advance, is a further insight that several more recent writers have re-discovered; and Baldamus's work has influenced many 'radical' analysts, although it has never formed the basis of a 'school' (one reason for which may be that Baldamus subsequently concentrated on some idiosyncratic and unpublished studies of industrial accidents).[2]

Baldamus argues that the labour contract, that is how much work of what sort shall be expended at what times and in what ways for a given wage, cannot be specified in advance of the work's actually being carried out. However detailed a set of rules and instructions may be, an employer cannot foresee every eventuality and cannot describe exactly what must be done. Even the most unskilled task involves the application of the worker's abilities and practical knowledge of how the job should be done. There is thus an area of indeterminacy in the labour contract. The importance of this is that it points to a potential area of conflict within the process of production.

It is easy enough to show why there should be disputes over the distribution of rewards between workers and employers. But Baldamus began to ask about relations within the production process, suggesting that work is not merely a technical activity in which inputs are transformed into outputs; moreover it is not a process in which the interests of workers and employers can be assumed to be the same. Instead, he argued that there is a necessary uncertainty over how workers' capacity for work is turned into effective labour or 'effort' as he called it. The production process for Baldamus is one in which

2 On Baldamus's following, it is interesting to note the fame of work published in the same year, namely Rex's (1961) *Key Problems of Sociological Theory* which was widely seen during the 1960s and 1970s as a leading text in the 'conflict school' of sociology. As noted above, Crouch names Rex but not Baldamus among the key figures in the sociological tradition in which he places himself. The initial reception of the two studies was rather different: in reviews in the *Sociological Review* V. L. Allen hailed Baldamus's work as a contribution while T. S. Simey condemned Rex's book in powerful terms. For the studies of accidents, see Nichols (1975) and Baldamus (1969).

the relationship between rewards, or 'wages', and effort is variable, with the outcome having to be determined on the shopfloor itself.

Baldamus explicitly related his analysis to industrial conflict, arguing that the concept of a disparity between wages and effort located 'the very centre of industrial conflict' and that it was 'applicable to all manifestations of conflict, even if the participants themselves are not aware of their conflicting interests in terms of changing effort values' (1961: 105, 108). This is an important statement, for it recognizes that conflict may exist even in cases in which the participants are not aware of their conflicting interests. It plainly goes well beyond the pluralist concern with the conscious deployment of collective sanctions. It is also an attempt to deal with a central problem posed in the radical perspective, namely how the analyst is able to identify industrial conflict when there are no overt manifestations of it. Finally, it is a recognition of the problematic nature of the connections between behaviour and the concept of conflict. There is plainly no immediate correspondence between an activity such as going absent or committing 'sabotage' and the underlying notion of conflict. The behaviour can reflect many things other than conflict. And its significance has to be investigated through consideration of the social context in which it occurs and the social meanings that it has for participants. That is, the relevance of behaviour for the notion of conflict has to be assessed through empirical consideration of social meanings and social structures.

As noted above, however, Baldamus was not able to put the programme of work implied in this approach into action. There are also some difficulties with his arguments, although these represent an important recognition of what an adequate theory for conflict would look like. Some detailed criticisms are given elsewhere (P. Edwards and Scullion, 1982a: 6). In brief, Baldamus does not really deal with the third set of issues identified at the start of this chapter, namely the connection between a concrete form of behaviour and concepts such as the effort bargain. It may be possible to re-describe going absent, for example, in terms of a wage-effort disparity, but it is not clear what such a re-labelling will explain about the behaviour. What are the social circumstances which produce it, why do workers use it and not some other form of adjustment in their pursuit of parity, and what are its consequences for social relations within the factory? A second detailed point of some importance concerns Baldamus's concept of effort. He is highly critical of industrial engineers and others who claim to be able to measure effort objectively: his critique of industrial engineering and work study techniques is forceful and persuasive. But his own conception of effort seems to have two incompatible elements. The critique of scientistic pretensions in the measurement of effort stresses that how much effort a worker is making is necessarily a subjective judgement: if the job is going well, a worker may feel that less effort has been made than when things are going badly, even though more output is created in the former situation than in the latter. But against this there is the conception of effort as constituting some sort of shared understandings. Wage-effort bargaining, for Baldamus, is not solely a matter of subjective feelings, for a given bargain is likely to affect the whole of a workshop. Is effort therefore a subjective or objective phenomenon? The best answer, and one that is consistent with Baldamus's overall approach, is that it is not entirely subjective. It is common for groups of workers to develop standards of reasonable performance and to criticize those going above or below these standards. And foremen often share a view of what is normal and acceptable behaviour. These inter-subjective standards are not, however, totally objective, for they involve a range of imprecise and accepted notions and not exact measures. But they represent approximate and understood indications of performance. The 'effort' side of the wage-effort bargain should, therefore, be seen in this inter-subjective manner and not in purely subjectivist terms.

A more general question concerns Baldamus's view of the bases of conflict. Why is it that the uncertainty inherent in the employment contract leads to conflict? It is perfectly possible to argue, for example, that workers and managers will reach some sort of shared understandings about effort levels. Uncertainties will merely complicate the process but need not point to a fundamental antagonism between the two sides. It is useful to consider in this context relationships other than those within employment. Terence Johnson (1972: 41), for example, has discussed differing ways in which occupational groups can attempt to exert control over their social environments. The division of labour leads to specialization, and the social distance between groups

> creates a structure of uncertainty, or what has been referred to as indeterminacy, in the relationship between producer and consumer, so creating a tension in the relationship which must be resolved. There is an *irreducible but variable* minimum of uncertainty in any consumer-producer relationship (emphasis in original).

Now this statement almost exactly parallels Baldamus's argument, but it is not clear that one would want to treat all producer-consumer relations, for example those between doctors and patients or between shopkeepers and customers, in the same terms as relations between employers and employees. It may be possible, in formal terms, to speak about competing or conflicting interests but, as noted above in discussing Hill's work, this is not entirely satisfactory. Is the labour contract to be treated like any other contract? Plainly, Baldamus does not want to do so, and he is correct in this. But some means of identifying the unique character of the labour contract is required. This issue will be discussed in detail in chapter 2. For present purposes, it is sufficient to note that the essence of the labour contract is the sale of a capacity to work, labour-power, with the actual amount of work performed having to be established through the process of production. In a normal commercial contract, goods or services are provided in return for payment; this is equivalent to the sale of labour power. The goods or services are the desired object of exchange, and that is the end of the matter, whereas in the labour contract what the employer wants is not a capacity but its exercise. Indeterminacy is not the defining characteristic of this contract, since any exchange relationship involves a degree of indeterminacy. What is crucial is the use of labour power under the direction of the employer. It is in the use of labour-power within the production process that conflict is rooted.[3]

Baldamus's work does not represent a 'false resolution' of the problem of consent as Burawoy (1979: 11–12) has argued. Instead, it is an important but partial source of insights. In the terms used at the start of this chapter it is not very useful at the most fundamental or the most concrete levels of analysis. But it provides some crucial insights in the middle ground. Once the origins of conflict have been specified some tools are needed for intermediate levels of analysis, and the concept of the wage-effort bargain is of great value in two respects. First, it sensitizes the observer to the variability of the terms of the labour process. And, second, it is useful when analysing particular situations to investigate how controls over effort are established, what attempts are being made by managers and workers to shift the terms of the bargain in their own favour, and what conditions are conducive to particular types of bargaining.

Conclusions

The radical perspective has considered several important issues such as the nature of power, the effort bargain, and the indeterminacy of the labour contract. It has not, however, brought them together into an

---

3 It is this aspect of Baldamus's work which has been re-discovered by economists working within the 'transaction costs' approach (e.g. Williamson, 1981): all contracts have an area of indeterminacy concerning exactly what services are required. See p. 100.

adequate framework. The bases of conflict cannot be identified in struggles over effort bargaining or in the operation of power. In the case of the latter, even the post-Lukes literature does not deal with the problem of objectives: either objectives are aims and wants held by social actors, in which case they are in principle observable, or they are inferred by the observer, in which case a means of identifying them is needed. The theory outlined in chapter 2 therefore drops notions of interests and replaces them with the concept of a structured antagonism between workers and employers; this antagonism is identified through analysis of the exploitive nature of the employment relationship. The radical perspective also has some difficulties in linking conceptual analysis to patterns of concrete behaviour, in particular 'individual' actions, a problem which it shares with much writing in the labour process tradition.

Control and Conflict in the Labour Process

Labour process approaches take as their starting point the organization of work and struggles that take place within the production process. They have not, however, provided an analytical framework which can deal with all the issues that arise. In explaining why this is so, the following discussion aims to assist in the assessment of the labour process perspective more generally. Although the main terrain of the labour process debate is well known, an overall perspective has been lacking: numerous criticisms of the main texts exist, but it is not clear whether the criticisms are intended by their authors to amend some parts of the texts' arguments or to refute the logic of their approach. Some broader conclusions are attempted here. Some of them are surprising. In particular, there has been, and remains, a tendency to treat workers' 'resistance' as an entity, separate from managerial behaviour, whose internal characteristics are not examined: the ways in which concrete behaviour can reflect accommodation and acceptance as well as resistance are not examined, and 'resistance' remains an unsatisfactory residual category.

Typologies of Control
Interest in the labour process was stimulated by Braverman's (1974) study. But it gave no attention to workers' behaviour, preferring to look at what it termed the objective aspects of the situation and not the subjective ones of how workers interpreted it. This is plainly a large omission. It is not just that issues of resistance and accommodation were left out in order to highlight other things. If, as Braverman

himself says (at p. 56), workers are purposive and creative, the question arises of how this creativity is used in the labour process: workers' behaviour is not just a matter of subjective interpretation but is central to the 'objective' issues of how work is organized and controlled. Subsequent analyses have tried to put right Braverman's failings.

Friedman (1977) analyses developments in Britain, concentrating on Coventry and Leicestershire. He identifies two reasons why labour power is variable: 'because individual human beings are intelligent and guided by subjective states, and because workers are alienated from the labour process and actively build organisations to resist managerial authority' (p. 82). Friedman therefore posits 'two major types of strategies which top managers use to exercise authority over labour power' (p. 78). Responsible Autonomy aims to use the creativity of labour power by permitting workers freedom and the discretion to respond to changing conditions. Direct Control tries to limit variability by close supervision and minimizing the area of workers' responsibility. Friedman (pp. 106–7) is careful to stress that these two strategies are not self-contained entities between which firms may choose at will. Switching rapidly from one to the other would require considerable changes in work organization; for example, to move from a Direct Control to a Responsible Autonomy approach would require new ways of managing geared to flexibility and the removal of rules and procedures predicated on the assumption of fixed duties and lines of authority. Firms can, however, move closer to one approach or the other according to external circumstances such as the state of product market demand and to internal factors, notably the extent of organized worker resistance. In the Coventry car industry during the 1960s, for example, firms began to move away from the Responsible Autonomy strategy that they had formerly pursued as they aimed to regain control of manning levels and piecework prices. Each strategy has inherent problems, which Friedman calls contradictions: 'contradiction does not mean impossibility, rather it means the persistence of a fundamental tension generated from within' (p. 106). With Direct Control, the problem is that people cannot be reduced to the status of machines: discontent and the threat of disruption increase, and the positive aspects of workers' creativity are suppressed. Responsible Autonomy has the problem of trying to persuade people to behave as though the work process reflected their own desires and objectives instead of being directed at accumulation and profit.

The approach has a good deal to commend it. It stresses the difficulties of the managerial task, it gives full weight to the role of workers' resistance, and it recognizes that workers are not simply out to interfere with what managers want to do, but have aims of their own. The last point is particularly important. A simple response to Braverman's approach, which, as will be seen below, has informed some of the American writing on the labour process, is to add 'resistance' as a constraint on managerial strategy: managers create strategies and workers find ways to interfere with them. Friedman offers a more sophisticated approach which sees managers and workers as meeting with contradictory aims and as working out a pattern of accommodation based on these differing objectives. Workers do not simply resist but are active agents.

Yet the account of control strategies requires amendment. As Wood and Kelly (1982: 82) point out, Friedman's categories are not very clearly identified. Responsible Autonomy, for example, covers a whole range of techniques, which may appear together but which need not do so. There are at least two distinct ways in which firms may grant workers autonomy: they may be forced to do so, as when organized groups of workers struggle to challenge managerial control of work speeds, the allocation of work, the application of discipline, and so forth; or they may grant a degree of control over the immediate work situation largely on their own initiative, for example through plans for job enlargement and job enrichment. A sophisticated policy based on job redesign and autonomous work group is very different from a struggle for control between shop stewards and managers in the engineering industry. Although both cases contain elements of workers' autonomy their causes and consequences are likely to be very different, a point pursued in detail in chapter 6. Direct Control similarly conflates several rather different practices. It may involve close supervision and the imposition of strict discipline. But it can also reflect a paternalistic approach in which managers try to inspire a personal form of loyalty, in which workers accept the need to work to managerial directives, and in which harsh discipline is not necessary. Many other variations and combinations within each strategy of control are conceivable.

The circumstances in which firms adopt one or other strategy are not very clearly identified. Much of the emphasis in Friedman's analysis is on the role of organized worker opposition in forcing firms to grant a degree of responsible autonomy. But, even in situations where such opposition exists, there are many other influences on management. And, in general, there is very little evidence that forms of autonomy based on job re-design and the like have been introduced to quell worker resistance; many of the best-known experiments have occurred in sectors in which union organization has been weak (Kelly, 1982: 74–5). The key role of 'struggle' in producing autonomy for workers is thus not established. In some organized sectors of the economy struggle has not led to a great deal of shopfloor autonomy: the gang system in the car industry to which Friedman gives so much attention is a very special case, and in many other parts of industry struggles at the point of production, while certainly creating a set of customs that constrain management, do not produce substantial amounts of autonomy or discretion. And such autonomy can occur in the absence of organized resistance.

Perhaps most importantly, there is some ambiguity about the relationship between Direct Control and Responsible Autonomy. In his empirical discussion, Friedman tends to see them as opposite ends of a continuum. Yet it is possible that they can co-exist, for example in a firm which grants autonomy in the performance of work tasks while imposing strict rules on attendance. Such a view extends the logic of Friedman's view of the labour process as a social relation in which workers' creativity has to be harnessed: firms are likely to devise a range of methods of doing so. If the two types of control are seen less as self-contained strategies and more as aspects of managerial behaviour which can be blended together, it is possible to build on Friedman's work to investigate how different ways of eliciting effort are put together.

An approach which has obvious similarities with Friedman's is Richard Edwards's (1979) analysis of managerial strategy in the United States. Three types of control are identified. Simple control existed in much of industry during the nineteenth century and survives today in small firms; its main characteristics are the exercise of power personally by the entrepreneur, the enforcement of strict discipline, and the absence of formal rules. Problems of co-ordination in larger organizations, together with worker resistance against arbitrary discipline and strict control, led to the development of technical control in which machinery sets the pace of work. The third system, bureaucratic control, emerged in an attempt to deal with non-production jobs but has spread to production work as firms have tried to forestall unionization. Its defining feature is 'the institutionalization of hierarchical power', with direct orders from supervisors being replaced by a set of impersonal rules, which cover not only the performance of individual work tasks but also job gradings and promotion; the company uses the promise of promotion as a means of gaining workers' compliance (p. 21).

This classification cuts across that proposed by Friedman. Edwards pays virtually no attention to attempts by employers to give, or concede, autonomy to workers at the point of production. The classification is based on different techniques of control and not on different ways in which employers can seek the compliance of their workers.

That is, while Friedman stresses the creativity of workers and the role of Responsible Autonomy strategies in harnessing it, Edwards concentrates on changing mechanisms of managerial authority. This has some benefits. Thus, personal control in small firms is not the same as that deployed in large mechanized operations, and to treat both under the rubric of Direct Control may not be very illuminating. The disadvantages are, however, considerable. Friedman made a bold attempt to understand the complexities of workers' behaviour although it is necessary to go rather further in this direction than he suggested. Edwards displays little interest in this question, preferring to see 'resistance' as emerging under any form of control and treating its characteristics as unproblematic. Struggle certainly exists, but it is not seen as a process whose characteristics require detailed investigation. It is as though managers act and workers react through resistance. The role of workers' behaviour in generating accommodation to a system of domination is not addressed.

This tendency has been continued in more recent work. Together with David Gordon and Michael Reich, Edwards has considered the long-term development of the American economy, arguing that various systems of labour control have emerged, that these have contained internal contradictions, and that they have been replaced by new forms (Gordon *et al.*, 1982). These authors admit (p. 246, n. 12) that their earlier work 'exaggerated the power of capitalists to achieve whatever they wanted and also neglected workers' response to capitalists' initiatives', and they claim to rectify this deficiency. Yet they fail to do so. As argued elsewhere (Nolan and P. Edwards, 1984), there are many empirical problems with their attempts to show that worker resistance was the main reason for changes in systems of labour control. The approach itself, moreover, does not transcend Braverman's framework. Instead of Braverman's stress on de-skilling and a unilinear development of monopoly capitalism, Gordon *et al.* present a model in which capitalists faced resistance and followed one of a number of discrete strategies in dealing with it. Resistance is, in effect, added on to a model of capitalists' control. The character of resistance is not addressed. And each type of control is treated as a discrete entity.

On the latter point, it is important to move away from simple typologies of control. Typologies that start out as attempts to characterize differing empirical tendencies can easily come to be seen in what Gospel (1983: 12) calls an over-deterministic manner: as self-contained entities that, far from highlighting particular parts of reality, are put into effect in their entirety by managements. Critics of Edwards have noted that a category such as technical control was not like that. Geller (1979) points out that, in a case such as Ford's during the 1920s, which supposedly exemplified technical control at its most extreme, all three of Edwards's modes of control could be discerned: in addition to the technical control of the assembly line, there was the close supervision and exercise of arbitrary authority supposedly associated with simple control, together with welfare plans and other attempts to gain workers' commitment which reflect 'bureaucratic' methods. Lazonick (1983) argues that, in the mass production in-dustries as a whole, firms sought means to persuade workers to accept their work rather than leave or engage in protest. And he points to the very shaky basis on which pure technical control would have rested: there is no evidence that assembly-line workers have been under the illusion that the speed of the line is the outcome of an asocial technology. There is a range of other evidence that 'bureaucratic' methods were in operation well before Gordon *et al.* suggest and that a given form of control can occur in different social contexts and have different consequences (Nolan and Edwards, 1984: 206).

These problems with the typology are not just matters of historical detail. It is not simply a question of making a broad picture more detailed or of correcting historical inaccuracies. The problems reflect a deeper methodological failing. Firms will develop their practices of labour control with whatever materials they have available. They are unlikely to have explicit strategies and more likely to react to par-ticular circumstances as best they can. Even when they have fairly clear goals they are unlikely to follow a policy which conforms to an ideal-type: they will proceed according to their own needs. In par-ticular, they are likely to use a variety of means of controlling the labour process and tying workers to the firm. Reliance solely on arbitrary power or technology or rules would be a very limited and dangerous approach. Even 'simple' control is far from simple. Case studies of the types of firm indicated by Edwards, discussed in more detail in chapters 3 and 6, point to the complexity of social relations. Control is not simply imposed by management but emerges from an amalgam of different elements. In addition to close supervision, there are several ways in which workforces are fragmented; for example, workers with valuable skills may be given favourable treatment. Although the majority of the workforce tends to come and go readily, with high rates of turnover, a stable core group can be treated very dif-ferently from the rest. This has important consequences for the ability of management to legitimize its own control. There are also a range of practices which go under the heading of paternalism: firms try to look after at least some of their workers as individuals, they attempt to develop personal bases of loyalty, and so on. Such paternalism may give material benefits to workers while also acting at an ideological level to create acceptance of the system of control. In short, any system of control represents a complex array of managerial practices and of worker activity. It is not just that the ideal types are not a very accurate description of reality: they also distort that reality by implying that discrete strategies of control are formulated by management and actually implemented, whereas control is multi-faceted and is the product of past struggles within social relations of work.

Resistance and Accommodation

In view of such problems, where do broad attempts to understand the nature of the labour process stand? It is plain that an approach based on a simple 'capitalist control *versus* worker resistance' model is inadequate. Control and resistance are not separate things, and each contains contradictory elements, with capitalists needing to use workers' creativity and with workers often behaving in ways which do not simply interfere with managerial plans. Cressey and MacInnes (1980) have made an important step in stressing this point. They argue that the relationship between capital and labour has an inherent duality. Capitalists must harness workers' creative powers, and therefore rely on eliciting a degree of co-operation as well as using coercive methods. Workers, as well as trying to resist subordination, have an interest in the viability of the units of capital that employ them. The framework used by Braverman and others, of a shift from a merely 'formal' subordination of labour under early capitalism to the 'real' subordination implied by monopoly capitalism and de-skilling, is thus inadequate.

It is possible to take this argument rather further. As suggested above, analysis in terms of interests is unsatisfactory, and the use of the language of interests by Cressey and MacInnes can readily be avoided by speaking of objectively contradictory aspects of the relationship between capital and labour. More importantly, the contradictions from the workers' point of view go rather deeper than that between avoiding subordination and being dependent on a firm to earn a living. This contradiction cannot be made the basis of workers' dual relationship with capital, for not all workers are directly dependent on particular firms. In sectors where labour turnover is very high there is no such direct reliance on a particular enterprise. More important is the contradictory nature of workers' activities within the production process itself. Workers do not simply enter work and then seek means of resistance. Instead, they find means of living with the system as they find it. It is, for example, a commonplace in industrial sociology that workers find ways of doing work which are easier than the ways laid down by management. In using such 'angles' and 'fiddles' they help themselves but also help the firm to attain its production targets. Their activities reflect their use of their creative abilities. Behaviour which may be labelled as resistance emerges out of this situation, but there is no overarching interest, namely resisting subordination, which is neatly balanced by the opposing interest of keeping one's job. Workers have many interests, and these stem from the social organization of work; that is, it is incorrect to assume that all workers have discrete sets of interests which exist independently of work experience. Instead, workers discover their interests through the process of work.

One other elaboration of Cressey and MacInnes's argument is needed. It is evident that, in itself, it provides no answer to the question of why conflict is inherent in capitalist work organizations. In correcting an argument based on the real subordination of labour, it points to the mutual dependence of capital labour and thus treats conflict and co-operation as equivalent principles. This is not to minimize its contribution, but only to suggest that the treatment of relations of compliance and co-operation needs locating in a more explicit account of the structured antagonisms of the labour process than that provided by Cressey and MacInnes.[4]

The contributions reviewed above contain several useful leads, but much of the overall drift of the post-Braverman debate has involved the demolition of grand interpretive schemes. There are two separate elements in this drift. The first, evident in the above discussion, is the impossibility of applying simple conceptualizations of control, strategy, and resistance to concrete situations. The second is the need to locate the labour process in other aspects of capitalist development. It is increasingly being argued that to concentrate on the details of labour processes is to miss much of significance. The result has been some considerable theoretical confusion, for it has not been clear what status the labour process has once these two lines of criticism have been followed to their fullest extent.

The survey article by Littler and Salaman (1982) is a good example of the problem. These authors catalogue several problems with the Braverman debate. Drawing on the work of Cressey and MacInnes, they argue that the control relation is not just about conflict: 'control must be seen in relation to conflict and sources of conflict *and* in relation to the potential terrain of compromise and consensus' (p. 253, emphases in original). Control of the labour process, moreover, is not always the predominant concern of the capitalist: 'surplus value has to

---

4 The authors have, in private discussions and conference presentations, themselves stressed this point.

be produced but also *realized* in the market' (p. 257, emphasis in original). In particular circumstances problems of the realization of surplus value through exchange on the market may be more pressing than those of control. The writers point out, for example, that in industries where profits stem largely from sales efforts or the vagaries of product markets, matters of labour control are likely to be of secondary importance. They go on to suggest that attempts to improve on Braverman's scheme such as those of Friedman and Edwards remain flawed. These concentrate on the formal aspects of control, thus giving insufficient weight to the informal ways in which consent can be achieved and to the indeterminacy of any system of control. No system can prescribe in detail everything that is done within it, and characterizations of types of control give too little attention to the limitations and uncertainties inherent in any system. In addition, Littler and Salaman argue, there is an excessive concentration on the worker at the point of production, with a corresponding lack of consideration of the ways in which 'control of work' can be achieved 'away from the point of production, indeed away from the organization itself' (p. 264). Decisions on marketing strategies, accounting procedures and many other things will have control implications. 'The first priority of capitalism is accumulation, not control' (p. 265). Hence 'the subordination of labour . . . cannot be understood at the level of the labour process' (p. 266).

Presumably the authors mean by their last comment that subordination cannot be understood only at the level of the labour process. Even with this important qualification, however, their argument is unsatisfactory. It certainly helps to highlight some misconceptions and correct some misplaced emphases, but it is not clear what conclusions should be drawn. Neither is it clear exactly who, apart from Braverman and some followers, is being corrected. The need to take account of informal practices within formal organizations is a commonplace of much of the sociological and industrial relations literature. It may be that some broadly based treatments have neglected these practices, but they can readily be incorporated into a consideration of the labour process; indeed, they help to show in detail how struggles at the point of production are structured. Similarly, the point about consent and compliance has been made not only by Friedman and by Cressey and MacInnes but also by Burawoy, to whom Littler and Salaman devote only the most fleeting remarks even though, as will be seen below, Burawoy has proposed an approach to the labour process which is designed to replace that of Braverman while retaining a Marxist basis. The main feature of Littler and Salaman's approach is thus the argument that control is secondary to accumulation. The authors do not present a discussion of the system of production and exchange under capitalism, and it is thus not very clear what they mean by accumulation or why accumulation is central to capitalists. The more general view within mainstream economics is that profit is the main goal of capitalists. To insist on accumulation is to make a different point which has, of course, a well-established Marxist pedigree. The argument here is that the dynamic of capitalism stems from the need for capitalists to accumulate capital. Unlike feudalism or mercantilism, in which profits may simply be consumed and in which there is no inherent growth dynamic, capitalism is based on a circuit of capital in which capitalists are forced to accumulate fixed capital. This point will be pursued in chapter 3. Littler and Salaman do not, however, consider it or its several important ramifications.

Although they destroy any idea that capitalists are always and everywhere obsessed with control of the labour process, the authors do not establish an alternative view. At the level of concrete activity, firms may, as Friedman suggested, grant a degree of control over work operations to workers, or they may have no particular view about their 'strategy'. But this is not to suggest that the problem of control is unimportant. There appear to be at least two senses in which Littler and Salaman use the term control: to refer to the details of work operations and, as in the argument that 'control of work' can occur away from the point of production, to indicate that capitalists are in some broader sense attaining their desired ends. Even when firms are not actively pursuing a strategy of control, they still require a set of arrangements within the production process that will ensure that surplus value (another term, incidentally, that Littler and Salaman deploy without explication) continues to be produced. It is thus necessary to make two distinctions: between different meanings of 'control'; and between the level of concrete activities and that of theoretical analysis. On the latter, discussion of the complexities of particular cases should not be confused with conceptual analysis of the nature of the labour process. As Littler and Salaman say, surplus value has to be realized, but it also has to be produced. There are good reasons for treating the production process as an uncertain and conflict-laden activity in which 'control' of the terms under which labour power is transformed into labour is a central element.

With Littler and Salaman's review, we are left with a celebration of empirical complexity. The labour process is seen as one among a set of sites of social relations, but no attempt is made to develop analytical tools that comprehend the principles underlying these relations. It is for this reason that the Braverman debate can be said to have come to an end. Once worker resistance is brought into the picture, and once this resistance is seen not as a residual category or as something which simply interferes with capitalists' goals, many of the issues raised in the debate have to be addressed in a new way. As Burawoy (1981: 93) argues in discussing Edwards's work, a distinction has to be drawn between a contested terrain and a terrain of contest. Edwards sees the workplace as a contested terrain, that is as a site in which resistance is perpetual. Instead, it should be seen as a terrain of contest: this 'is to suggest that the workplace is an arena in which struggles are organized, but that these struggles by no means necessarily threaten the organization of work'. The implications of relations at the point of production have to be assessed and not assumed.

The Production of Consent

In stressing that workers' behaviour involves adaptation as well as resistance, Burawoy develops a view of the labour process which is very different from that of the 'control *versus* resistance' model. In his critique of Braverman, Burawoy (1978: 274n) argues that the term adaptation is preferable to resistance because workers' actions incorporate 'ideological mechanisms through which workers are sucked into accepting what is as natural and inevitable'. Such adaptation, moreover, reflects workers' purposive behaviour. As against Braverman's view that management can monopolize knowledge, Burawoy argues that workers are creative and that management relies on them to deploy their skills and experience. The labour process involves a clash between workers' conceptions and managers' conceptions of how work is to be done. The central problem for the capitalist is not to wrest knowledge of the production process from the worker but to persuade workers to co-operate in their own exploitation. In the labour contract, the wage is specified in advance, and the capitalist has to organize production 'so as to ensure the extraction of unpaid labor' (Burawoy, 1979: 26); that is, for the capitalist to make profits and for the system to continue, surplus has to be generated within the production process. But under capitalism, and unlike feudalism, for example, in which the 'surplus' labour that peasants perform for their lords is plainly visible, the capitalist's surplus is not directly observable. Goods are produced, and the 'necessary' and 'surplus' elements are not empirically distinct. Hence, for Burawoy the distinctive feature of the capitalist labour process is the simultaneous securing and obscuring of surplus value.

How is this achieved? Burawoy distinguishes between competitive and monopoly forms of capitalism. In the former there is intense competition in product markets, workers are poorly organized, and there is a permanent pool of unemployment. Inside the factory, workers are subjected to a harsh, coercive form of discipline. Under monopoly capitalism such methods are no longer possible, and workers have to be persuaded to co-operate with management through 'hegemonic' control. In his study of an American engineering factory Burawoy (1979) identifies three aspects of this control. First, there is the labour process itself. Workers were paid on piecework, and gaining a standard level of bonus, known as making out, gave workers considerable satisfaction, but at the cost of accepting the rules under which this 'game' was played. Playing the game generated consent to the principles of capitalist production. Second, the plant's highly structured internal labour market rewarded seniority by making access to the most desirable jobs dependent on length of service and by protecting the longest-serving employees from being laid off. Commitment to the enterprise was fostered, as workers relied on individual advancement and not collective struggle with the employer over the effort bargain. Third, an 'internal state', comprising the collective bargaining system and the grievance procedure, complemented the internal labour market. It gave workers rights as individuals and constrained managerial discretion, but in doing so it protected management's more basic power to plan and direct the labour process.

An important aspect of Burawoy's analysis is the argument that the labour process is 'relatively autonomous' from other aspects of society: consent is created inside the workplace and is not imported from outside. As against Littler and Salaman, for example, Burawoy suggests that matters away from the point of production are not as important as relations within the production process. His main evidence is the variability of output between workers: extra-work factors such as a worker's race or marital status were less important than seniority within the factory or experience of doing a particular job. Burawoy (1979: 156) admits that his data are 'flimsy', and says that 'it would be wrong to conclude that what happens to workers outside the factory is of little importance to what they do inside it'. But he provides little analysis of how 'external' forces impinge on behaviour at work, and it is thus difficult to judge how relative the relative autonomy of the labour process is.

This aspect of Burawoy's work has received considerable criticism. Thus, Paul Thompson (1983: 172–6) argues that consent is produced not just in the workplace but within the social formation as a whole, using two examples to illustrate the point. First, traditions of class, culture, and trade unionism affect how people behave at work; the work practices of white-collar workers, for example, reflect the wider conceptions of society held by these workers. Similarly, inter-industry and international differences in the extent of 'consent' will reflect differing traditions of trade unionism. Second, women workers' behaviour may reflect intra-work factors but it will also be shaped by socially constructed notions of femininity. Burawoy's argument, that external experience is irrelevant, 'is clearly wrong, for we are not all socialised in the same way' (p. 175).

Thompson is undoubtedly correct that Burawoy does not establish his argument and that forces external to the workplace cannot be neglected. But some refinement of the notion of relative autonomy suggests that it can still be used. On such influences as unionsim, Thompson (p. 174) implies that they are separate from the labour process: 'the prevalence of centralised, non-ideological and highly integrated "business unionism" cannot have failed to influence the tendency towards cynicism and acquiescence among the workers' studied by Burawoy. Yet the business union approach of American unions cannot be divorced from events inside factory regimes, as chapter 5 will indicate in detail. The character of trade unionism is not simply external to these regimes but is affected by them. There may be other factors which are more truly external. Thompson suggests the example of Vauxhall workers on Merseyside, who have traditionally been more militant than their counterparts in Luton, a difference which reflects different working-class traditions. Yet such militancy still has to be interpreted in the factory, and factory regimes will shape it: the Merseyside worker entering the Vauxhall plant is likely to have been exposed to different forms of managerial control from his neighbour working for Ford. Still greater contrasts could be observed between Merseyside workers working, say, on the docks and in the post office. The labour process, or more exactly the patterns of social relations that regulate the labour process, has a certain autonomy.

Burawoy is wrong to reject external forces, but the labour process is relatively autonomous in two senses. Conceptually, the problem of utilizing labour power in the production process is distinct from other aspects of social life. Empirically, patterns of regulation develop logics of their own, so that workers in identical situations outside the workplace can be exposed to very different conditions within it. It should also be noted that people do not enter jobs randomly: firms' recruitment and selection procedures are geared to look for some sorts of worker and not others. Factory regimes thus strengthen their own autonomy by influencing what 'external' forces are permitted within them. The idea of relative autonomy should be made more subtle and not abandoned.

In subsequent studies, several of which are brought together in a recent book (Burawoy, 1985), the analysis is extended to consider the relationships between forms of control at the level of the factory and 'global politics', that is the politics which take place at the level of the state as distinct from power struggles in the workplace itself. In addition to the 'market despotism' of competitive capitalism and the hegemony characteristic of monopoly capitalism, Burawoy (1980) identified a system of bureaucratic despotism characteristic of many state socialist countries. Drawing on Haraszti's (1977) description of a Hungarian piecework factory, Burawoy notes that the labour process itself shares many features with market despotism: arbitrary managerial power, and permanent pressure on workers to speed up their work. The difference lies in global politics: 'distinctive to the politics of bureaucratic despotism is a harnessing of party and trade union structures to the managerial function' (1980: 278). Whereas under market despotism the logic of the market is used to justify a coercive regime inside the factory, under bureaucratic despotism global politics and production politics are inextricably linked. Burawoy (1985) has also advanced an account of the varying links between global and production politics in capitalist countries.

Burawoy's contribution is of great importance. It recognizes that workers' behaviour simultaneously involves resistance to, modification of, and accommodation with capitalists' practices. It develops analysis of the problems facing capitalists. Thus, Burawoy argues, as against Richard Edwards in particular, that mere conformity to the rules may not be enough: 'management may secure *compliance* to rules through carrot and stick, but how does it secure the *consent* presupposed in the pursuit and production of profit?' (1981: 92, emphasis in original). He also addresses two other points raised by critics of a labour process perspective: the need to look beyond the labour process itself, and the question of the organization of work in non-capitalist societies. On the former, he analyses the internal labour market and the internal state, and relates developments in them in his case-study to changes in the character of product market competition as well as to forces within the factory. His analysis of global politics relates to both points, for it helps to consider how global and production politics have interacted to create different patterns of work relations in different capitalist countries while also throwing light on the contrast between capitalism and state socialism.

The details of Burawoy's consideration of the state and its connections with workplace relations will be taken up in chapters 4 and 5, and non-capitalist societies are considered in chapter 7. The present concern is the broad applicability of Burawoy's approach to the problem of conflict.

The contrast between despotism and hegemony is overdrawn. It has been noted (e.g. by Littler and Salaman, 1982: 266, n 3) that the equation of despotism within the factory with competition in the market is incorrect, for highly competitive conditions can go along with craft forms of organization and limited employer power, as was the case historically in the building industry for example (Price, 1980). More generally, the internal operation of a despotic system is likely to be less simply coercive than Burawoy suggests; the limitations of Friedman's and Edwards's model of simple or direct control apply equally here. Naked coercion is insufficient for the stable operation of a productive system, and ties between workers and employers are more complex than Burawoy's account allows. Thus, case studies of factories in competitive industries show that, although managerial power is certainly very great, management had to develop and sustain ideologies supportive of its own position and tried to create 'consent' to its domination (Armstrong *et al.*, 1981).

The exaggeration of the role of coercion under despotism is balanced by an excessive concern with consent under hegemonic arrangements. Burawoy himself cites the well-known article by Mann (1970), in which it is argued that workers are neither quiescent nor revolutionary but adopt a pragmatic perspective such that they tolerate their position but do not necessarily internalize broader sets of social values. Other research (Nichols and Armstrong, 1976) points to the contradictory and fragmentary ways in which workers make sense of the world. A high level of internalization of capitalist values may, indeed, be dangerous to capitalists in so far as it raises expectations and makes workers aware of the contradictions of the system. The notion of consent is too strong to capture the ways in which workers adapt themselves to the productive system. Now it may be that 'compliance' is too weak a term if it means mere conformity to the rules in a purely unthinking and mechanical manner. Not for nothing is one of workers' more potent sanctions against management termed a work to rule, for it is just such a rigid and literal interpretation of rules that impedes the performance of work tasks. As writers such as Baldamus and Friedman, as well as Burawoy, argue, capitalists have to secure the practical deployment of workers' skills together with a willingness to interpret rules by using their everyday skills and knowledge. If this is all that is meant by 'consent', there is no problem, but to draw too sharp a line between consent and compliance does not help.

A related issue concerns the extent to which hegemony is in fact established in the factory. Two recent contributions (Gartman, 1983;

Clawson and Fantasia, 1983) have argued that Burawoy lacks a dialectical approach to struggle at the point of production: in concentrating on the ways in which workers generate their own exploitation by 'playing games' he neglects resistance; and he denies that struggle has any independent role in threatening capitalist accumulation. The point is somewhat overstated, and there is the danger in the critics' approach of replacing one allegedly non-dialectical view with another. Gartman in particular speaks as though class struggle is a self-evident category; and in suggesting that employers' attempts to alter the production process were a response to workers' resistance he commits the error, criticized above, of reducing capitalists' behaviour to activities within the production process. But it is true that Burawoy tends to the opposite extreme of denying workers' activity at the point of production any significant role in the development of the capitalist mode of production, with everything being determined by forces outside the productive sphere.

One significant gap in Burawoy's categorization of types of factory regimes is thus the case of a continuing day-to-day battle over the terms of the effort bargain. This is particularly evident in his most recent contribution, which aims to be a general statement about *The Politics of Production* (Burawoy, 1985). This might be expected to contain an analysis of the factory politics surrounding the effort bargain and the battles between shop stewards and managers such as those described by Beynon (1973) and those which occurred in the United States between 1935 and 1945. Yet such things receive little attention. What is of concern here is a collective, organized struggle which is directed not just at the immediate effort bargain, in the sense of how much effort on a particular task is put in for what reward, but also at the conditions which govern such individual bargains. These conditions include the allocation of workers between tasks, the authority of supervisors, and the freedom of management to alter working conditions. Burawoy gives little attention to struggles to shape what he calls the factory regime, that is the ability of workers and their organization to affect the structures of power within which individual effort bargaining takes place.

This is not to suggest, as Gartman for example does, that organized struggle is ever-present. It is to make two points. First, Burawoy's analysis of hegemony under monopoly capitalism is incomplete to the extent that it ignores the more organized forms of factory struggles. It is, of course, a familiar argument that such struggles are limited to the terrain of the factory and do not constitute class struggle. But this is not Burawoy's point, which is that, within the factory itself, hegemony reigns. In some factories it does, but this is not a universal condition of monopoly capitalism. Second, and more generally, the category of hegemony seems to be too broad to embrace all the ways in which 'consent' is achieved. In his earlier work Burawoy implied that the forms of control that he observed in his factory were characteristic of America, and possibly even of advanced monopoly capitalism in general. His subsequent analysis of different countries modifies this view by pointing to differing connections between global politics and production politics. But within one country the implication remains that there is one dominant mode of gaining consent, whereas in fact there are likely to be several forms. In addition to the survival of direct forms of control in competitive industries, firms in more advanced sectors differ widely in the ways in which they treat their workers. In Britain, IBM, Ford and BL cars have practised very different policies, and these have, in line with the above argument, been variously affected by workers' workplace activities.

There is, then, considerable room for the extension and modification of Burawoy's approach. In many respects, it is a matter of alteration, for the approach is far more sensitive to the complexities of workplace behaviour than is the control *versus* resistance model. There are also some more general points about the issues which Burawoy has explored. In the terms used at the start of this chapter, one question concerns the analysis of concrete behaviour such as committing sabotage or going absent, in particular the connection between such behaviour and the bases of conflict. In his factory case study Burawoy concentrated on making out under piecework, giving little attention to other forms of behaviour; in his later work he has been more concerned with the differing shapes of factory regimes than with the detailed assessment of how forms of work behaviour are influenced by these regimes. The task remains of showing how behaviour which comes under a given rubric, for example 'sabotage', differs in different regimes and how far and in what ways it expresses conflict.

The above comments have dealt with issues at the second level of analysis namely the development of tools to consider forms of work organization and the interaction between conflict and co-operation. This leaves the first level, the identification of the bases of conflict. Burawoy, like other writers in the labour process tradition, locates conflict in the extraction of effort from the workers: conflict is not just about distribution of the spoils but is present within the process of production itself. He is also more explicit than some in explaining why this is so. As noted above, he develops an account of exploitation: capitalists secure unpaid labour from workers, by ensuring that the value of the labour expended is greater than the value of the labour power bought. Exploitation occurs in other economic systems too.

Thus Burawoy contrasts feudalism, with its clear distinction between the time which peasants spend working for themselves and the time which they work for their feudal lords, with capitalism (1979: 20–3).

A theory of exploitation is the necessary basis for a theory of conflict. There is a need for a rather more developed statement of such a theory than that provided by Burawoy. How, for example, is the concept of exploitation treated: does it refer to a purely technical analysis of the relationship between abstract categories of 'capital' and 'labour', or does it refer also to a sense of grievance that workers may hold about their lot? Is it argued that, because workers are exploited, they have an ultimate interest in overcoming their exploitation through struggle against their exploiters, or is exploitation no more than an analytical term with no implications for how workers will behave? The answer suggested in the following chapter is that the analytical aspects of the concept can and must be separated from those relating to the alleged interest of the working class in over throwing capitalism. Burawoy's position is not very clear. His empirical analysis suggests that hegemony is powerful, except in some vaguely defined periods of crisis, and that there are many important divisions between workers which make class unity problematic. But he is also clear that his analysis is a Marxist one. To anticipate the results of the discussion in the following chapter of what such a claim means, for the claim to be anything other than rhetorical there must be an argument that the fact that a mode of production is exploitive has necessary consequences for the experience of work and class action. There need be no presumption that exploitation will lead directly to class consciousness; numerous factors may legitimately be introduced to explain why workers tolerate exploitation. But there must be a claim that the organization of the mode of production creates a basic tendency for workers to become aware of their own exploitation, to identify with other workers, and to struggle against it. It is just this line of argument which will be rejected in the following chapter.

A theory of exploitation can, then, be stated in terms different from those proposed by Burawoy. In addition, there is a need to spell out some of the implications of the theory. How, for example, does it apply to cases other than feudalism and capitalism? How is 'surplus value' in capitalism to be conceptualized, and how is the labour process connected with other aspects of capitalism such as the drive to accumulate? Burawoy and other Marxists plainly have answers to such questions. All that is claimed here is that an explicit and rigorous consideration of them is necessary for the development of a systematic theory of conflict in the workplace.

Burawoy's analysis thus requires development in several respects, particularly in connection with the analysis of concrete behaviour and the ways in which workers' activities at the point of production can shape the organization of work. Managers and workers together create a means of organizing work in which conflict and co-operation are mingled. This process is continuous, and it has consequences for what either side can do. Burawoy argues that it is one of the forces, inter-capitalist competition being the other, shaping the development of capitalist work relations, but he tends to minimize the role played by struggle. Patterns of work relations develop, however, logics of their own and it is important to try to assess their causes and consequences. In addition, the analysis of the bases of conflict needs development; the line of development to be suggested here raises some large questions about a Marxists approach such as that presented by Burawoy.

Conclusions

This chapter has attempted, through a critical appraisal of different approaches to conflict, to document the claim that an adequate theoretical perspective had been lacking. Some very important points have certainly been recognized by many writers. These include the observation that co-operation as well as conflict must be a feature of any labour process, the argument that the terms of the labour contract cannot be specified in advance, and the location of conflict within the production process itself. A theoretical means of bringing together such points has, however, been lacking. At the same time, the attention which has been paid to broad characterizations of managerial control strategies and to the problem of class consciousness has not been matched by detailed consideration of the ways in which concrete behaviour reflects deeper antagonisms in the labour process between workers and managers.

Much of the analysis of the following chapters represents an attempt to build a theoretical approach that avoids some of the problems identified in current writings. The need to treat the production process as a social relationship in which co-operation and conflict are jointly created has, for example, been stressed. But two points warrant particular emphasis if the insistence on certain features of the approach is to be understood. First, analysis based on the concept of interests has been rejected. The concept does not provide a bridge between consideration of basic conflicts between 'capital' and 'labour' and analysis of concrete events. It is either equivalent to concepts such as wants and desires, that is the preferences of people in real-life situations, or it requires some grounding in analysis of social structures. Given the widespread use of terms such as 'interests', the need to make a sharp break from it will be indicated by using the term 'structured antagonism' to refer to the basic split between capital and labour. The break with the notion of interests is also important in the articulation between the three levels of analysis identified at the start of the chapter. Use of the notion, by Marxists and non-Marxist writers alike, can involve the claim or the implication that antagonism at the most basic level feeds directly into conflicts at more concrete levels. As argued elsewhere (P. Edwards, 1979), this view should be avoided. A basic antagonism between capital and labour need not imply that capitalists and workers will meet as opposing classes with clearly opposed interests. But neither should analysis go to the other extreme of denying that structurally based antagonisms exist. That is, those who oppose a Marxist view of class and class struggle can tend to the view that there are no materially grounded antagonisms between capital and labour. The following chapters try to state and apply a theory which avoids these extremes.

Second, it has been argued above that typologies of managerial strategy are flawed. The main reason is that they posit one mode of gaining workers' compliance within each distinct strategy. Firms' employment policies are in fact likely to be more complex than such characterizations suggest, embracing several different ways of gaining compliance. This is not just a point of empirical detail. It reflects a basic problem with a typological approach, namely a tendency to reduce the many ways in which patterns of workplace relations are generated by managers and workers to ideal-types in which managers are the only really active agents and in which only one mode of control is employed. Not only is the richness of actual cases lost, but there is also a tendency to characterize the development of capitalism as a series of jumps from one mode of control to another. Continuity is played down, as is the variety which exists within one apparently homogeneous form of control. It is certainly reasonable to try to characterize different systems of control and to identify emerging trends, but a typological approach does not necessarily help, and it may hinder, such exercises. The granting of 'responsible autonomy', the development of 'hegemony' via an internal state, and the creation of bureaucratic modes of control can all be important in specific circumstances. But they are tendencies which can co-exist with others, and the important analytical task is to assess how these various tendencies cohere and not to reduce them to self-contained systems of control. This is again a theme which will run through much of the following discussion.

In moving away from a typological approach, it is necessary to develop rather more complex accounts of social relations in the workplace. Once it is accepted that the generation of 'compliance' involves more elements that typologies allow, and once the role of workers in shaping the effort bargain is taken into account, it becomes clear that neat descriptions of control and resistance become impossible. The presentation in terms of contrasting models has to be replaced with a careful assessment of how particular features of an overall pattern of control cohere and how behaviour relates to this context. Ease of exposition has to be sacrificed to the exploration of complex and interlocking social structures.

Existing terminology is difficult to employ. As noted above, terms such as compliance and consent have a range of meanings. It follows from the above analysis that precise definitions will not help. It might, for example, be suggested that direct control can be equated with a pursuit of minimal compliance, while relative autonomy involves more active consent. But consent can also be produced under direct control, most obviously where the employer's authority is contained within paternalistic structures. And it is not clear how much 'consent' an employer using relative autonomy or hegemony wants or needs. The solution is to see employees' commitment, consent, or compliance as the product of the social relations of production and not as a distinct 'thing'. That is, how workers become tied to their firms, and how far and in what ways they willingly give up their capacity to labour will depend on a wide range of circumstances which cannot be reduced to categories such as compliance. Just as conflict is not to be seen as a clear and measurable phenomenon, but instead as a principle of work organization, so forms of co-operation and accommodation have to be understood in context.

These needs to make the analysis of the labour process more complex can be balanced by one important narrowing of scope. Writers such as Littler and Salaman have suggested that control at the level of the labour process may not be critical to all firms in all cirucmstances. This could imply that any number of influences outside the workplace would have to be included in any adequate theoretical treatment of conflict in work relations. Such a view would fit into the standard sociological criticism of workplace studies, namely that they neglect the sources of social attitudes that arise elsewhere in society: the factory is not an island. In an investigation of a particular factory, it will be necessary to consider influences from elsewhere in the organization and outside it. But, as Burawoy suggests, relations at the point of production have a 'relative autonomy'. Theoretically, the issue of the generation of effort in the production process can be distinguished from other aspects of a mode of production. Empirically, although workers enter the factory with expectations and attitudes shaped outside it, what they do inside it is influenced by its own customs and traditions. A worker going on the assembly line in Luton in the 1960s, where collective challenges to management over the control of the effort bargain were little-developed, would have had some very different experiences from someone with the same social background who entered the technologically similar plant at Halewood, where a running battle for control was going on (compare Goldthorpe *et al.*, 1968 with Beynon, 1973).

In developing an account which can amplify these points about the bases of conflict at work and the forms that conflict takes, a clear analytical approach is needed. The approach of this study is non-Marxist, and is best seen as an attempt to provide for non-Marxist social science a perspective on conflict which has hitherto been absent. Crouch (1982: 39) presents his work as an effort to remedy 'one of the defects of the radical or sociological school, its lack of a theoretical statement on trade unionism'. A similar claim may be made for the present study of industrial conflict.

2

The Theory of Conflict

In this chapter the materialist theory of conflict is outlined in its simplest form. Some elaborations and qualifications are then added. Two appendices deal with issues connected with the theory but not centrally part of it. The first explains why the theory is not Marxist, and is indeed opposed to any proper Marxism. The second briefly considers two other issues, the connections between paid work and domestic labour and the characteristics of non-materialist theories of exploitation.

The focus of the theory, conflict, has several meanings, as noted on p. 5. The aim is to deploy different levels of analysis to deal with these various meanings. Each level has a degree of autonomy. The basis of the theory is an analysis of exploitation and the identification of a 'structured antagonism' between dominant and subordinate groups within any exploitive mode of production. But this antagonism does not determine everything that occurs at the level of actual behaviour. It sets some basic parameters on this behaviour while permitting considerable variation in the ways in which conflict and co-operation are intertwined in practice. In particular, the idea of a structured antagonism is designed to break with the concept of a conflict of interest which is often assumed to underlie concrete behaviour. There is a basic antagonism in exploitive modes of production, but there is no need to assume that this feeds into the identification of particular sets of interests among workers or employers.

The theory developed below draws on many existing ideas. Any novelty lies in its combination of these into one statement. One tradition concentrates on the indeterminacy of the labour contract and the effort bargain. Another considers the general identifying features of a mode of production, without looking in detail at actual workplace relations. It is a matter of bringing together the appropriate elements of a theory, paying particular attention to the development of a hierarchy of concepts that provides a connected statement about the nature and forms of conflict, and not of starting from scratch.

The Theory Outlined

Scope and Method
The theory is about industrial conflict, by which is meant the relations of antagonism that exist within exploitive employment relationships. It is not about social conflict in general. This is not to deny that the productive system will influence, and will be influenced by, other parts of society. But for the purpose of theoretical consideration it can be analysed in its own right.

This will be seen as a contentious statement by those who argue that the labour process cannot be understood apart from influences from outside the workplace. Yet, conceptually, the problem of transforming labour power into effective labour is distinct from other social processes. And, empirically, the workplace is generally distinct from other spheres of life and it has its own customs, norms, and understandings. Relations within it can thus be treated as distinct from other sorts of social relationships, although it is, of course, true that in any particular case the expectations and social statuses that workers and managers bring to the workplace will affect their behaviour. Such influences are important, but they are external to and different from relations which develop around the work task itself.

This argument will not be defended at length here; it is more important to state the positive features of the theory. A brief consideration is given in the appendix to this chapter in relation to one candidate for inclusion as a necessary part of a theory of the labour process, namely the gender of workers. This candidate is also discussed, in relation to some empirical issues, in chapter 6. One partial exception to the argument concerns the role of the state. The state does not directly enter the production process and the exception is thus only partial. But in some cases a mode of production cannot be defined independently of the state, the clearest example being state socialism. In others, notably capitalism as it has developed from its early stages, the state has been heavily involved in shaping the development of the economy and the context within which workplace activities take place. An extension to the theory is thus an account of the nature of the links between the state and the labour process. Since this raises issues distinct from the main part of the theory, the account is reserved for chapter 4.

As indicated above, the main methodological feature of the theory is the identification of different levels of analysis. This is essential if various common confusions are to be avoided. Within the labour process debate, for example, the points are often made that workers have some autonomy at the point of production and that control at this level may not be the capitalist's sole or major aim. The points are correct, but the inference that control of the labour process is unimportant or that workers are not 'really' subordinate to capitalists is incorrect. Distinguishing between levels of analysis avoids such problems by providing a means of taking full account of empirical complexities without sinking into an empiricist form of analysis. More generally, the metaphor of levels helps to deal with the long-standing analytical problem of relating structure and action: if the structural context of behaviour is stressed through analysis of a mode of production, the role of action and struggle may be neglected, and yet, if the focus is on concrete activity, structural conditions and constraints may disappear into the background. An approach in terms of levels of analysis is not a solution to this central dilemma of the social sciences, but it is a way of recognizing and handling it. The more basic or fundamental levels establish some of the conditions of operation of the more concrete levels. But such constraints do not determine everything that happens at the more concrete levels, and it is possible for influences to run in the opposite direction.

Three levels of analysis may initially be identified. These are the mode of production in general, the broad principles of the organization of the labour process, and the concrete operation of the labour process in the real world. Further distinctions and elaborations may be introduced to make the analysis applicable to different situations.

The Mode of Production and the Basis of Exploitation
A mode of production is a way in which people are brought together in social relationships in order to produce goods and services. Within any mode there is an analytical distinction between production which is necessary to replace the means of production which are used up and the surplus which remains. Raw materials have to be provided. Machinery wears out and has to be replaced. Workers require sustenance in order to live, and they, like machinery, have to be reproduced if production is to continue in the long run. Over and above this necessary production there is the surplus. Modes of production differ according to the ways in which they bring together human and non-human resources and in the ways in which they allocate the

surplus. Exploitive modes are those in which producers are subordinate to others within the process of production. The basis of a structured antagonism between superordinates and subordinates is thus the existence of relations of domination.

These statements apply to any exploitive mode of production. Reference was made above to capital and labour, but such terms apply usefully only to capitalism and they need to be replaced by others for the analysis of other exploitive modes. Writers such as Dobb (1963) and G. Cohen (1978) distinguish between slavery, feudalism, and capitalism. The characteristics of a fourth mode of production, state socialism, are more rarely formally adumbrated. It will be discussed briefly here, and more fully in chapter 7. For Dobb (pp. 13–16), the first three types of society are based on class antagonism, and it is the form in which surplus labour is appropriated that is critical. Under feudalism, the direct producers are in possession of the means of production such as ploughs, and they are not divorced from the means of subsistence. Surplus labour is extracted from them by extra-economic means: they are compelled to perform labour services on the land of the lord. Under capitalism there are no such extra-economic obligations. Dobb later (p. 36) clarifies the argument. Under capitalism there is a divorce between the producers and the means of production, which now lie in the hands of the capitalist, and the sale of labour-power is the mode of production's defining characteristic. Under slavery there is some similarity to capitalism in that the slave is also divorced from the means of production, but the difference is that capitalism is based on a free market for labour-power whereas the slave is not free to choose his or her master. To summarize:

	Capitalism	Feudalism	Slavery
Divorce of workers from means of production	Yes	No	Yes
Presence of extra-contractual relations	No	Yes	Yes

There are three problems with this approach. First, it is not really the mode of appropriation of the surplus which is crucial. The concept of a mode of production refers to the social organization of the production process and not just to the means used to extract a surplus. Second, as G. Cohen (1978: 83–4) points out, the distinction between feudal producers who can set the means of production in motion and lords who obtain their surplus through extra-economic coercion is not satisfactory. The reason why lords are entitled to labour services or feudal rents is that peasants hold their land from the lords, and can be dispossessed if they do not carry out their obligations. 'The serf does not have burdens forcibly laid upon him *because* he controls his own little territory: they come with the territory' (p. 84, emphasis in original). It is thus not clear that peasants can in fact set the means of production in motion independently of the lord, as Dobb, together with more recent writers such as Burawoy (1979: 20–30), claims. Third, the distinction between modes of production according to the worker's ability to put the means of production in motion is less sharp than appears at first sight. The contrast between the feudal peasant, who can till the land and consume the crops, and the factory worker under capitalism, who performs a fragmented task and cannot consume what is produced, may seem to be clear. But replace the factory worker with a labourer on a capitalist farm and the distinction becomes murky, for such a worker can plant and tend a crop, and what is produced is, in principle, consumable.

Cohen's solution (pp. 65–9) is to distinguish between modes of production according to the ownership rights in productive forces. The productive forces are labour power and the physical means of production such as machinery and raw materials. A member of the subordinate group can own all, some, or none of each productive force, as shown in Table 2.1. Thus, independent producers own all of their

TABLE 2.1
Classification of Ownership of Productive Forces

| | | Subordinate's Ownership of Labour Power | | |
		All	Some	None
Subordinate's Ownership of Means of Production	All	Independent Producer	X	X
	Some	Property-owning worker	Serf	M
	None	Classical proletarian	Worker in State socialism	Slave

Source: G. Cohen (1978: 65). The classificatory scheme is Cohen's, but location of a worker under state socialism in one cell is not. The cells labelled 'X' are deemed by Cohen to represent impossible combinations. The cell 'M' is of only minor importance. See text for explanation.

labour power and the means of production that they use. They are not exploited in the sense used here, although they can, of course, be subjected to the power of other producers in the market place. An independent artisan may suffer as the result of the power of large firms over him, as expressed, for example, through the prices they pay for his goods. He may well be materially worse off than a worker for a large firm, but he is not exploited. (Some related cases such as workers' co-ops are mentioned below).

The three main cases of concern to Cohen are the proletarian, serf, and slave. Proletarians, or more precisely, 'classical proletarians' as distinct from those in the cell marked 'property-owning worker' discussed below, own all their labour power because they can choose to which capitalist they sell it. ('Ownership', Cohen stresses, is conventionally discussed using legal terms, but this is merely a convenience: what is important is not legal ownership but the effective power over a productive force). But they do not own the means of production with which they work. Serfs own part of their labour power because they have effective control of that part of it which they employ on their own land. They also have some ownership of the means of production that they use, that is they have some effective control of their ploughs, oxen, and so on. But they also depend on the lord for their right to use the land, and the lord can require them to work on his land, so that they own neither all their labour power nor all their means of production. The slave lacks effective control on both dimensions.

This leaves five cells. Of particular interest here is that combining some ownership of labour power and no ownership of any means of production. For Cohen, this is a possible transitional form between the serf and the proletarian, wherein serfs have lost control of the means of production but are still tied to their feudal lords and lack the full control of their labour power. Another important candidate for this cell is the emerging proletariat in colonies run by capitalist states. As described briefly in chapter 3, workers here have often been subject to systems of annual contracts and other forms of forced labour. They have lost the means to support themselves on their peasant holdings but are far from free in their control of their labour power. A third case, it may be suggested, is the worker under state socialism. Such a worker owns none of the means of production, for these are owned, both legally and in practice, by the state, which determines how they shall be used. Workers 'own' their factories only in a rhetorical sense. They do not own all their labour power because there are restrictions on the freedom to move between one enterprise and another and because the state imposes a duty to work. At times there have been very strict controls on the voluntary movement of labour, combined with forcible direction of workers to key sectors. Such controls have been relaxed, and, as described in chapter 7, there is often a considerable degree of toleration of labour turnover. Workers are not the property of their employing organizatic.n in the way in which a slave-owner owns his slaves. But neither are they free wage-labourers. They cannot sell their labour to the employer they choose, not least because there is no class of capitalists each seeking workers but only a group of state enterprises that are subordinated, to a greater or lesser degree, to the central planning organization.

Of the remaining four cells, Cohen argues that two, marked 'X' in Table 2.1, represent impossible combinations. It is not possible for someone to have complete control of the means of production that he or she uses while his or her labour power is even partially controlled by another: to do as one wishes with one's means of production implies that one can deploy one's own labour power in their use, which is what is denied in both cases. The situation of owning some of the means of production but no labour power is possible but, as Cohen argues, of limited interest. This leaves the case of owning all one's labour power and some of the means of production. Cohen's discussion (pp. 70–3) is a very important analysis of the basis of proletarian status. He considers a case in which a worker works in a clothing factory and is required to take his own sewing machine with him; he owns some of the means of production, and is worse off than if the capitalist supplied and maintained the machine. In principle, moreover, he could set up as an independent producer on his own. But he could produce on such a limited scale that he would be unable to compete with large capitalist firms. He cannot support himself as an independent producer. 'Lack of means of production is not as essential to proletarian status as is traditionally maintained. It is better to say that *a proletarian must sell his labour power in order to obtain his means of life*' (G. Cohen, 1978: 72, emphasis in original). The property-owning worker is as much of a proletarian as is the classical proletarian.

Three features of this scheme warrant emphasis. First, it allows for a variety of cases intermediate between those of the classical ideal types of slave, serf, and proletarian. These ideal types are no more than reference points for more complex analyses. Second, it sees capitalism as a distinct historical product. The property-owning worker is a proletarian because he has to sell his labour power to live, and the reason that he must do so is the emergence of large firms against which he cannot compete as an independent producer. The ways in which independent producers lose their independence, and the emergence of capitalist forms of work organization from earlier forms, can be accommodated: capitalism is not seen as a 'mode of production' existing outside time or space. Third, workers in new forms of work organization can be compared with the model of the classical proletarian to assess the basis and nature of their exploitation. Workers employed in a workers' co-operative in a capitalist country, for example, own their firm but, to the extent that they have to sell their labour power in order to live and that they have to organize the labour process on lines similar to those of capitalist firms, they continue to hold a proletarian position. They may differ from employees of capitalist firms in such respects as their autonomy in the workplace and their involvement in the running of the enterprise, but they continue to be proletarians and thus to be distinct from other groups such as feudal serfs.

Modes of production thus differ according to the way in which exploitation takes place. The capitalist can exploit the worker because the latter lacks the means of production and must sell his or her labour power in order to live; exploitation takes place by means of the labour contract. In slavery and serfdom non-economic pressure is required. But, as Cohen (1978: 83) stresses, the two modes of exploitation can accompany any form of surplus labour. The standard connections are between a contractual form of exploitation and surplus taking the form of surplus value that has to be realized in the market; and between extra-economic exploitation and surplus not taking the form of value. But other connections are possible. For example, it is possible to coerce someone into working for a wage and producing surplus value. (The distinction between a surplus in general and the particular form of surplus value is taken up further below.)

But what characterizes a subordinate producer? Cohen (1978: 69) identifies three features which are possessed by proletarians, serfs, and slaves alike. They all produce for others, but these other groups do not produce for them. They are subject to the authority of a superior within the production process, and can exercise no countervailing authority. And they tend to be poorer than their superiors. The first two are crucial, while the third should be seen more as a consequence than a characteristic of subordination.

Now, one obvious criticism of Cohen's approach is that workers can in fact exert some influences over their superiors. As noted in chapter 1, any labour process involves the application of human capacities to non-human means of production, and the duties of workers cannot be fully specified in advance. Superordinates therefore need workers' abilities, and this need can be used by the workers to establish some control of the conditions under which they perform labour. In moving to more concrete levels of analysis this point is of central importance; Cohen admits that his models of modes of production are idealizations, and a major aim of the discussion of subsequent chapters is to consider the actual working of different productive systems. But the elaboration and development of basic ideas as they are applied to concrete cases does not diminish the essential point. Subordinates produce for others under the broad authority of the latter. They may be able to alter some of the terms on which this authority is exercised but they cannot escape their subordination without leaving the mode of production entirely. Such escape may be possible for a few individuals, but for the great majority it is impossible.

Here, then, we have a statement of the nature of exploitation.[1] Exploitation does not rest on the contingent fact that one group happens to be more powerful than another. It is inherent in production relations. In exchange relations, it may be possible to say that one trader exploits another when bargaining power is used to secure exchange on advantageous terms. But such language is imprecise and unnecessary, for it is not apparent how fair and unfair exchange can be clearly separated, and it is preferable to use the more limited concept of bargaining power. As the balance of power shifts, so one party or the other will make the more advantageous deal, but no new value will be produced: what one gains, the other loses. In exploitive production relations, by contrast, there is no such balance: a surplus is produced within social relations of dominance and subordination, and there is no sense in which the production of the surplus can be seen as a process in which the dominant and subordinate groups are in equivalent positions.

As most writers agree (Cohen, 1978: 333; Burawoy, 1979: 20–30), a key difference between feudalism and capitalism is that exploitation is visible in the former and invisible in the latter. The feudal serf's obligation to labour for the lord is clearly stated and entirely public. The distinction between necessary and surplus labour is not apparent in capitalism, for there is no clear separation between work done to reproduce labour power and the means of production and that done to create a surplus. The necessary and surplus elements are fused together. There are some other characteristics of the capitalist mode which require explication, for these help to show how the antagonistic relation between capital and labour is structured.

1 The statement is intended to be basic and to represent a position that would command a broad degree of support from writers adopting a materialist position. There are, however, some new theories of exploitation which take a very different view. They represent a move away from attempts to locate exploitation within the sphere of production and are thus fatally flawed; they are discussed briefly in Appendix 2.1 to this chapter.

First, the processes of production and exchange, although conceptually distinct, are fused together in what is known as the circuit of capital. In any form of production that is geared to the market, goods are produced not for their inherent desirable qualities (their 'use-values') but for their ability to be sold at a profit (their exchange-values). Under feudalism, merchants became increasingly important as trading developed. But production and exchange remained relatively distinct: the merchants did not directly organize production, and, although they were calculative and acquisitive, their pursuit of profit was limited to the sphere of exchange. For capitalism to emerge, a class of men with large amounts of money is insufficient. 'Men of capital, however acquisitive, are not enough: their capital must be used to yoke labour to the creation of surplus-value in production' (Dobb, 1963: 8). Capital must enter the production process directly, and mercantilism gradually gives way to capitalism, one of whose distinguishing features is the circuit of capital. This circuit (described by, for example, Aaronovitch *et al.*, 1981: 24–8) involves money capital being used to purchase labour power and the means of production, which are then put to work to produce goods which are then sold; the resulting money is used to start a further circuit. The surplus created in production can be termed surplus value because it has yet to be realized in monetary terms and is of no use to the capitalist until it is.

This fusion of exchange and production may seem to be remote from the understanding of industrial conflict. But it is of great importance. Under feudalism the production of the surplus is not directly tied to the market; under state socialism it will reflect political decisions as to what goods should be produced and in what quantities. Under capitalism production is driven by a law of value, namely that the purpose of production is the creation of surplus value. The capitalist labour process is necessarily closely connected with the capitalist market, and the capitalist aims to exert a direct influence over the organization of work. One of the most obvious connections between the market and the labour process is the effect of crises of profitability on the number, location, and organization of jobs. The labour process is not an independent aspect of the economy although, as will be seen below, it has principles of organization which are specific to it.

A second important feature of the capitalist economy is its proneness to long-term growth combined with short-term crises. Its central dynamic is provided by the drive to accumulate. Unlike other modes of production, it contains within itself a necessary pressure to expand; firms create surplus value, and if they do not use this to increase their productive capital they will find their markets taken over by other firms. The pressure to accumulate capital is general, and 'the circuit of capital is thus a process of self-expanding value' (Nolan, 1983: 301). But expansion does not take place smoothly, for there is no guarantee that the surplus-value created in production can be realized in the market. It is self-evident that economic growth has been punctuated by recessions and crises; these are to be expected in a system in which production and exchange are not integrated and in which falling profits and over-production are ever-present possibilities. For capitalism as a whole there is a contradiction between the needs of the production and exchange systems, and this is exacerbated by the fact that capitalism does not operate as a total system but is characterized by competition between firms, the result being a continuing battle for markets and a struggle for survival.

The concept of a contradiction is of some importance for the theory of conflict. A contradiction is not a logical impossibility but is a state of tension between two or more features of the social structure. This tension is not, moreover, the result of a clash between independently existing factors but stems from the very operation of the system: the operation of the economy generates forces which tend to undermine the principles on which it is based. In capitalism, for example, competition between firms tends to drive down the rate of profit, and is thus in contradiction with the need for growing profits if the process of accumulation is to continue in the long term. Similarly, unregulated capitalism requires some central co-ordination, but the development of such co-ordination through the state means that an independent body has been created which can, by influencing how the market operates, undermine the principle that markets are free of external pressure. But perhaps capitalism's most widely discussed contradiction is its tendency to bring into being a class of free wage-labourers who are tied to the capitalist only by the wage and whose potential for resistance can challenge the whole of the capitalist social structure.

The idea of a contradiction provides a means for the analyst to assess the development of the mode of production which is neither determinist nor voluntarist. Features of the economy, such as the drive to accumulate and the proneness to crises, can be identified; these are structural characteristics, and an explanation of social change which turns on them is not voluntarist. But, because these characteristics are general tendencies, no determinist predictions are made about how contradictions will be resolved. The rise of the state in capitalist societies, for example, has greatly affected the operation of the economy but it has not destroyed it. And, crucially, the existence of a proletariat has not led to the overthrow of capitalism. A contradiction creates permanent tensions in the social structure, but how these tensions are dealt with depends on what people do. As will be seen below, there are also some important contradictions within the labour process which help to shape how employers and workers interact.

Capitalism is not unique in its possession of contradictions. Feudalism, for example, contains tensions between production on the manor, where serfs perform surplus labour for the lord and where market relations are undeveloped, and the emergence of trade and commerce, which threaten the stability of the manorial order by importing the principles of a market economy. But contradictions take on different forms in different modes of production.

These brief remarks on the principles of economic organization of different modes are meant to be no more than indicative of some broad issues. The central purpose of the present discussion is not to analyse economic relations in general but to deal with relations between dominant and superordinate groups within the labour process.

Organization of the Labour Process

The labour process also contains contradictions which are specific to it and not just the reflection of forces emanating elsewhere in the economy. In any exploitive mode of production the central problem for the dominant group is to extract effort from the subordinate group. The nature of the problem varies between different modes. For the feudal lord the task is to get the serf to work for him, when such work is plainly additional to the labour that the serf needs to perform for his own requirements. Extra-economic means are normally employed to do this. Thus, the lord has the legal power to insist that the serf carries out the required task, which is backed up by political power and ultimately by military might. In addition to these relations of power, there are elements in the relationship between lord and serf which moderate the nakedness of exploitation and add other strands to the relationship. The lord is supposed, for example, to establish the security of the manor by defending it from attack and acting as an arbiter in matters of internal dispute. Such activities do not alter the nature of exploitation, but they place it in a social context in which mutual rights and obligations are stressed. As Cohen (1978: 333) argues, in feudalism the fact that relations between the groups is utilitarian is concealed behind the pretence of a community of shared interests.

The slave-owner's problem is that, despite his formal legal title to dispose of his slaves as he wishes, if he wants to produce goods he has to deploy the slaves' labour-power. Unlike the feudal lord, he has to organize the labour process directly. Although he can use physical force to make the slaves work, there are costs in doing so: excessive force may destroy a valuable asset, and force is not necessarily the best way of having labour performed in an effective manner. Even apparently simple work tasks can be carried out grudgingly and with no concern for the quality of the product, and slaves can find ways of sabotaging the product. There is a contradiction between the right to use force and the need to achieve some level of willing compliance among the slaves such that productive tasks can be carried out effectively. Slaves' creative capacities have to be released and cannot be taken for granted.

The capitalist shares some of these difficulties: he has purchased workers' labour power but has to realize this in production. But he also has problems of his own in that capitalism is characterized by a system of free wage-labour. He cannot use force as readily as can the slave-owner. In addition, he has contracted to pay his workers a wage: the slave-owner has to keep the slaves fed and housed but how he does so is within his discretion and is to an extent variable, whereas the capitalist has agreed in advance to pay a given wage and then has to organize production so as to generate surplus value. How is the deployment of labour-power controlled in such a situation? One obvious means is the threat of dismissal if tasks are not carried out properly. But the threat has limited effect in times of full employment or in particular occupations that are in short supply. In addition, just as pure force may not be the best way to get slaves to work, so the threat of the sack will be of limited value in inducing compliance. So modes of control internal to the labour process are necessary as the capitalist seeks a balance of inducements and penalties. Among these modes are payment systems that link pay to effort, the development of hierarchies of responsibility, promotion ladders, rules on attendance, and penalties for breaking workplace rules. The balance between different methods will depend on circumstances.

State socialism also has its contradictions. The major one within the labour process is that between the idea that workers own the means of production (and can therefore determine how work is organized) and the fact that work is bureaucratically organized, with workers having to work under the command of others to meet targets over which they have little or no control. Again, workers have to be persuaded to work, but the context of this persuasion, and the means used to achieve it, are distinct from those prevailing under capitalism. The political institutions of the state and the institutions of the enterprise are closely integrated, whereas under capitalism they are formally separated. The threat of unemployment is removed, but instead there is a variety of pressures put upon workers to work hard, including those stemming from socialist ideology.

In any of these modes of production dominant groups have a variety of means of seeking the compliance of subordinates. Each mode involves a contradictory relationship between dominant and subordinate groups in which elements of antagonism and co-operation are necessarily intertwined. In such a situation, the problem for dominant groups is to live with and manage the consequences of the various contradictions that operate within the labour process and, as noted above, outside it. They will develop means of managing the labour process in the light of their specific circumstances. Some of the broad principles underlying these means will reflect the character of the mode of production as a whole. A capitalist, for example, is dependent on realizing profits in exchange and has to manage his labour relations accordingly. But there is a considerable degree of leeway in the precise ways in which work relations are organized. There is no one model of labour control which applies to all capitalist countries. There are two related points here, which need to be made separately.

First, there is a wide range of means of gaining compliance. These cover methods of attracting and retaining workers and of organizing the work task itself. On the former, workers can be forced into the workplace through the absence of alternatives, or positive inducements can be offered. They can be retained through the material benefits of wages and related rewards, or through relations of debt and dependence. In many parts of the world the development of capitalism was marked by the use of contract labour and a requirement that workers live in company-provided housing and buy goods from company shops; wages have often been paid in kind and not in money. Such practices make it difficult for workers to sever their connections with the firm. At the point of production itself there is an array of means of eliciting effort, including supervision of work, payment systems relating reward to effort, promotions to more desirable jobs, and disciplinary sanctions for non-compliance. Not all of these means of attracting workers and persuading them to work will be equally salient in all modes of production. The feudal lord, for example, can hardly institute piecework payment systems. But some of the issues are common: even though feudal lords and slave-owners do not have the problems of labour turnover associated with free wage-labour, they cannot totally rely on workers' legal ties to them and can face considerable difficulties with serfs and slaves who run away. Problems of retaining labour may loom large if alternative ways of making a living look more attractive. More generally, what is important about particular techniques is their location within a whole set of ties between employer and worker. Each aspect should not be seen in isolation. How, for example, did a feudal lord get workers to fulfil their obligations? Not by assembling distinct modes of control, such as the right to dispossess tenants and the existence of specific obligations to perform labour, into a deliberately created package but by operating within a social structure in which obligations and understandings came to be taken for granted. Serfs' various obligations became tied together in a system in which economic, political, legal, and ideological relationships operated in unison. To understand how work relations operate it is certainly necessary to investigate their constituent parts, but in doing so, their links with other parts should not be neglected.

Second, as against the tendency noted in chapter 1 to identify a few ideal-types of modes of control, it is very unlikely that concrete work organizations will reflect such types. Several features of modes of production suggest that a more complex picture will necessarily exist. The management of several sets of contradictions will not lead to neat solutions. Different members of the dominant group may come to different views of the best ways in which to operate. And, crucially, subordinate groups have an influence over the terms of their own exploitation and can affect the precise ways in which work relations are managed. There is no particular reason to expect that labour processes will be organized in similar ways either within a whole mode of production or even within a specific industry or one country.

The central feature of the organization of any labour process is the need to deploy workers' productive capacities within a relation of structured antagonism. At the level of analysis of the labour process, it is impossible to see 'conflict' or 'co-operation' as the key feature, for both are necessarily involved, albeit in a relationship in which there is a deeper antagonism. Conflict and co-operation are created simultaneously in the organization of production itself, and it becomes meaningless to try to separate them.

The Organization of Conflict

Within these broad principles, day-to-day relationships between dominant and subordinate groups have to be worked out. How are actual labour processes organized, and what is the place of conflict within them? This question has conventionally been addressed by starting with specific 'aspects' or 'manifestations' of conflict and then, as it were, working backwards. Thus Kerr's (1954: 170) well-known discussion lists a large number of 'forms' of industrial conflict and notes, rather despairingly, that the range of forms is limited only by 'the ingenuity of man'. The problems of such an approach have been considered in chapter 1: it begs the question of what conflict is, it does not relate forms of behaviour to a theory of conflict, and it treats these forms as alternatives to each other without considering why one form occurs in some situations and not in others. For present purposes the key difficulty is that connections are not made between forms of behaviour and the organization of the labour process. The result is that questions concerning the characteristics and significance of the behaviour are neglected: a given form of activity can involve co-operation and adaptation as well as conflict. As suggested in chapter 2, similar problems confront analyses of 'resistance' that do not place this resistance in the context of the social relations of work.

The present argument deals with these difficulties by seeing behaviour as the outcome of participants' attempts to work through the consequences of their relations of conflict and co-operation. A particular form of behaviour arises in response to particular circumstances and can contain within it elements of conflict and of co-operation. The analytical task is to identify these elements and to explore how the behaviour fits into, and develops, a given set of relationships. It is a commonplace that, even under slavery, workers have means of slowing down the pace of work, committing sabotage, and otherwise altering the amount and quality of labour-power deployed. Both amount and quality are important: the amount is dependent on workers' ability to do less work than employers want or expect, while the quality reflects the extent to which labour-power is deployed to achieve the goals of production or alternatively is used to sabotage these goals.

Now, neither amount nor quality is precisely measurable. How hard people are working, whether or not more effort can be given, and who is responsible for the quality of the final product are questions that are frequently debated between managers and workers. At a more theoretical level, the amount and quality of labour-power are not objective categories but rest on the social and contested nature of the production process: the whole point of seeing production as exploitative is to escape from the view that it is a purely technical process in which amounts of labour are measurable. Despite this, however, it is also true that, within particular work situations, there are some broad, if fuzzily defined, standards as to what amounts of labour power, and of what quality, will constitute the norm. Slaves on a cotton plantation will know through experience how much work is acceptable and what short-cuts in picking the cotton will be tolerated. They will also realize that there are some technical standards by which the quality of work can be assessed. Although the production process is not entirely a technical process involving the transformation of inputs into outputs, it plainly has some technical aspects. The quality of labour power may not be exactly specifiable but it is possible to say that there are rough standards which enable increases or decreases in quality to be assessed. A slave will know the difference between high-quality and low-quality labour power in terms of how much skill and application are devoted to the task at hand. It may well be the case that there are contradictions between different aspects of the labour process, for example between a demand for high quality of output and one for high quantity, and there may be disputes between slaves and owners over how these conflicting demands are to be balanced. But the concepts of the amount and quality of labour power are clear.

Workplace behaviour involves social relationships around the effort bargain, that is the continous negotiation that occurs in the workplace over how much effort, of what quality, shall be expended for a given reward. (Terms such as bargaining and negotiation should be taken as referring not just to explicit collective bargaining, over such a thing as a piecework price, but also to informal practices that affect the terms of the effort bargain). A particular practice, such as a standard over how much work constitutes a normal day's labour, or the use of 'sabotage', determines how this continuous negotiation works out in practice on a day-to-day basis. That is, the amount and quality of labour power are in principle variable, but every day a certain amount of work of a certain quality gets done. The resulting effort bargain contains a whole set of practices and understanding over what work is done and how it is performed. Some of these practices may appear in forms that can be labelled as sabotage, absenteeism, or whatever. But they are to be understood not as self-contained expressions or aspects of conflict but as forms of behaviour that emerge out of bargaining over the organization of work. There is little point in asking whether absenteeism is a form of conflict. The interesting questions include how the behaviour is related to the labour process, how far it serves to alter the effort bargain, and to what extent participants themselves see it in terms of conflict between workers and managers.

A good example is labour turnover. As will be seen in subsequent chapters, this can have a variety of meanings and consequences. Under slavery, running away can be a way for workers individually or collectively to express their desire for freedom; whether it is an individual and isolated action or a more organized one will depend on such things as conditions of labour in slave encampments and on the size and stability of communities of run-aways. Under early capitalism in some colonial countries, desertion was a widespread reaction to poor working conditions: it was not just a response of 'pre-industrial' workers to the demands of industrialism but was a rational reaction to conditions within the labour process. Under state socialism it can be an informally acknowledged way in which workers bargain with employing enterprises: enterprises may tolerate and indeed encourage turnover if it helps to bring them the skills that they need. It makes little sense to ask whether these various activities are really forms of conflict, and it is even less useful to treat them under the same rubric of 'Turnover'. What is relevant is to assess how the behaviour reflects particular forms of work organization and what significance it has. It is, for example, likely that quitting will be the action of workers with specific discontents, and it may suit management to have such employees leave instead of 'causing trouble' within the workplace. Similarly, the behaviour's significance from the point of view of employees can be investigated: is it the activity of a few relatively isolated individuals, or does it reflect a more broadly based sense of grievance; and so on?

Seen in this way, conflict is not something that only workers engage in. Most obviously, employers have ways of shifting the effort bargain in their own favour: the promulgation and enforcement of new rules on attendance are as much to do with 'conflict' as is sabotage. And, as just noted, employers can find benefits in behaviour that at first sight is against their interests; this, again, is a point that will be developed in much more detail in later chapters. More broadly, because the labour process involves the interplay of contradictory demands, which stem both from differences between workers and employers and from tensions within the employer's own position, employers have to make choices as to how they try to organize work relations. One choice may carry with it a particular set of consequences. Strict discipline and close supervision are likely to lead to absenteeism and turnover. A less strict approach may avoid these problems but lead to various 'restrictive practices' in the workplace. And so on. This is not to suggest that employers make clear and conscious choices regarding behaviour in the workplace. Some consequences of a given work organization may be unintended. Their freedom of choice may be constrained by competitive circumstances, the need to ensure an adequate supply of labour, the degree of collective organization among the workforce, and many other things. And in many cases they may not make choices about a pattern of behaviour (for example, between a high and low level of turnover) but may instead operate a given work organization and learn to live with the consequences. But their role is central in that they are involved in the organization and control of the labour process, and the approach that they adopt will powerfully affect the forms of concrete behaviour that emerge.

A given form of behaviour can, then, involve aspects of accommodation and adaptation to a system of work relations as well as being in conflict with or a form of resistance against it. In addition, work relations are not static. It is not as though employers establish systems of control to which workers accommodate or against which they protest. Workers' behaviour can help to share structural features of the situation. For example, workers may respond to managerial rules by developing their own informal practices, and these practices may, given a sufficient degree of shopfloor organization, achieve the status of rules that significantly modify the formal rules. The structure of workplace relations at a particular time will reflect the outcome of past activities on the part of workers and managers: structure and action are not separate but interact.

The term 'struggle' can be used to refer to the behaviour of managers and workers with respect to the effort bargain. In some usages (e.g. Burawoy, 1979: 162) it is limited to activities that alter the terms of the effort bargain: struggle alters the relative returns of capital and labour, whereas competition refers to activities, such as conflicts between workers, which accept the existing distribution of rewards. This approach unduly limits the concept of stuggle. Workers can, for example, seek what they see as a fair distribution of easy and difficult jobs, and success can be important in limiting managerial freedom to exercise favouritism. The terms of the effort bargain may not have altered although the context in which the bargain takes place will have changed. Plainly, not all forms of behaviour that take place in workplaces, or even all contacts that occur between individual workers and managers, involve struggle. The term should be taken as including activities which affect the terms of the effort bargain and which reflect the ways in which managers and workers relate to each other as buyers and sellers of labour-power. Whether or not their various activities affect the balance of effort and rewards is a separate question. The degree to which workplace struggles involve self-conscious attempts to assert control will also vary. 'Struggle' thus refers to that part of workplace behaviour concerned with the control of the labour process. Within individual workplaces, industries, or countries struggles will develop characteristics of their own. These will, in turn, help to determine what courses of action are subsequently open to managers and workers. In short, a pattern of workplace relations reflects previous developments, so that current struggles are shaped by the history of previous struggles.

Concluding Remarks

So what exactly is the conflict which the theory attempts to understand? 'Conflict' can mean so many things that different terms have been introduced to deal with its various aspects. The sense of a basic conflict of interest between capital and labour has been rendered in the notion of a structured antagonism. Conflict as efforts by managers and workers to control the labour process has been considered in terms of the dual relationship between the two sides, in which each depends on the other while also having divergent wants. Conflict in this sense is intertwined with co-operation: the two are produced jointly within particular ways of organizing labour processes. And how far a given concrete 'form' of conflict such as going on strike or organizing a work-to-rule is possible will be strongly influenced by the existing pattern of relations; similarly, how far behaviour such as absenteeism, which plainly contains many elements apart from 'conflict', has characteristics which can be related to the idea of conflict will depend on the organization of work. This organization is not the product of a deliberate managerial strategy counterbalanced by workers' resistance. It is created by the day-to-day activities of both sides as they try to deal with particular sets of circumstances, and adaptation and accommodation are as important as deliberate efforts to assert or resist 'control'. Behaviour around the issue of control can be termed struggle. Struggles vary in their character and intensity, and they have histories which shape subsequent developments. The outcome of action shapes the structure in which subsequent actions take place.

Discussion and Elaboration

Several points are likely to come to the reader's mind concerning the application of the above approach. Is not the division between dominant and subordinate groups, for example, too crude to deal with the range of different positions that will exist in any complex division of labour; and how does one deal with forms of work organization that do not correspond to one of the modes of production, for example, non-profit-making services in capitalist societies? No attempt will be made to deal with all such questions, and answers to a few of them will be no more than indicated in broad terms. More important, in any event, are various elaborations which may be presented with reference to a capitalist economy, for it is in relation to such an economy that most of the discussion of relations within the labour process has taken place.

Control and Management Strategy
Much of the labour process debate has been taken up with demonstrating that managements do not try to maximize their own

control of the details of work operations and that managerial strategies are complex and need not involve any clear foresight or well-thought-out plan for the regulation of the labour process. In addition, it is commonly pointed out that managements have financial and other aims that are remote from the labour process, the result being that it is incorrect to reduce managerial action to action in the sphere of labour relations. Such points can be handled within the approach outlined above by noting, for example, that firms have to operate in the sphere of production and also exchange, that the development of the economy reflects the outcome of sets of forces that are in contradiction with each other and not the working out of a logic of managerial strategy, and that relations within the labour process itself should not be seen in terms of the 'management control *versus* worker resistance' model. Control remains an important analytical tool, however.

Control of what, and to what ends? At a general level, the answer to these questions is implicit in what has been said above. The object of control is the way in which the labour process is organized. The end of control for the capitalist is the continued production of surplus value. For the worker the situation is somewhat more complicated, for workers do not have a precisely opposite end of resisting the creation of surplus value. But they have to face the power of capital and find ways of adapting to and also modifying this power. How in practice they do so will, of course, vary. It does not follow from analysis at a theoretical level of the uncertainties surrounding the labour process that workers will always and everywhere try to make use of these uncertainties. Neither does it follow that capitalists will be trying to minimize the uncertainties, for they rely on workers' creative capacities as well as on their ownership of workers' labour-power. So how can the struggle for control be viewed?

At the level of real work situations 'the' labour process becomes a multitude of different labour processes with their own histories and organizing principles. In particular, each will reflect the activities of employers and workers and their unions, and will be characterized by a 'frontier of control' which is the product of these activities and which is shifted as the parties respond to changing circumstances. The frontier will indicate where control of a particular aspect of the production process lies. Although the translation of labour-power into labour is a process which cannot be specified in advance, every day a certain amount of labour is expended under certain conditions. The frontier summarizes these conditions. It indicates whether a particular issue such as the movement of workers between jobs is decided by the arbitrary decisions of management, by the implication of rules which delimit managerial rights, by customary arrangements which are not written into rules, by the power of workers and their respresentatives to refuse to move between jobs, or by other mechanisms. The frontier is conceptually important in understanding the significance of observed behaviour, or the absence of behaviour. As pointed out on p. 29, there is a view of workplace relations, which can be called the tool-box theory of sanctions, which holds that workers have any number of forms of resistance to capitalist control which can be deployed, given the will. Such a view seems to stem naturally from the point that the labour process is conflict-laden and that the capitalist cannot automatically rely on workers to work. Its error lies in making a direct link between this general point and specific practices. In particular cases the history of struggles will have led to a frontier of control under which some sanctions are ruled out in advance.

The idea of a frontier of control depends on a zero-sum conception of control, for if control of the allocation of labour lies with management it cannot also lie with workers. It therefore differs from control in the sense of the deployment of labour-power to secure the continued production of surplus value. This contrast points to an important distinction between what may be called detailed control and general control. The former refers to who controls all the decisions about how immediate work tasks are to be carried out, and is conveniently analysed using the metaphor of a frontier. The latter covers the broader issues of securing workers' commitment to the aims of the enterprise. The distinction between the two helps to deal with some confusions in writings about the labour process. As noted in chapter 1, when Littler and Salaman point out that capitalists do not always try to maximize their own control, they mean that maximizing detailed control is not necessarily the employer's aim; general control, however, remains important. Consider, for example, the many schemes that have been introduced to increase workers' participation in the enterprise. These include job enrichment, industrial democracy experiments, and the currently fashionable quality circles and briefing groups. Underlying such schemes is the wish to persuade workers to use their creativity to overcome problems in the production process: workers are not to be de-skilled operatives doing fragmented tasks but competent people thinking about how to produce good effectively. The aim is to improve general control while reducing the employer's detailed control.

Note that general control is not simply increased or decreased, for it is not a zero-sum concept. A firm which improves its general control is not necessarily taking something from its workers. For example, many American firms have been responding to Japanese competition by trying to introduce more flexible ways of working. In so far as such efforts help to secure the existence of the firms they are 'in the interests' of workers. General control may have been enhanced. This example also illustrates three points about control. First, changing policies for general control need not stem from failures within the existing system of labour control. A pattern of detailed control may be operating acceptably on its own terms, with few 'problems' such as strikes. But competitive pressure from other capitalists may force a change: managerial policies of control depend as much on changes outside the workplace as on struggles within it. Second, there need be no calculated policy of incorporating workers by giving them concessions at the level of detailed control. Managers are likely to respond to external pressures through a series of attempts to deal with what they see as the immediate problem. There need be no careful strategy. An increase in workers' commitment may result, but this need not be a well-formulated aim. And it may not occur if, for example, managerial concessions encourage demands for further changes. Third, improving general control may not be consistent with the interests of all workers or all the interests of each worker. Most obviously, those who are made redundant as a result of introducing more flexible ways of working are excluded from the system. Those staying with the firm will have to balance their interests in keeping a job and in having a job which is presumably more enjoyable against the fact that 'commitment' involves effort and obligations as well as new rights and the fact that some sources of bargaining with management may have been lost (for example, workers who have agreed to work flexibly across job boundaries have lost the power to impose sanctions by sticking strictly to narrow job specifications). Improving general control may also be opposed by junior managers who fear a loss of authority or by other groups in the firm. In short, improving general control does not solve the problem of gaining compliance but shifts the terrain on which the problem is managed, with accompanying changes in the balance of interests. In particular, efforts in this direction may fail or may have only a temporary effect.

'Control' need not, then, be seen as a matter of deliberate managerial policy. A system or a structure of control can contain a variety of elements which have been assembled as the result of particular responses to particular problems. Yet such a system or structure has real consequences for the way in which work is perceived and for what actions are possible. It is not simply imposed from above, for it reflects previous struggles; yet it constrains behaviour, on the part of managers as well as of workers. This lead to the issue of workplace rules and norms.

Informal Rules and Norms

As already noted, workers necessarily have the capacity to affect the terms on which their labour-power is deployed. They do not simply react to initiatives from on high, but can themselves play a part in the elaboration of rules governing the labour process. This argument reflects a long-standing concern in industrial sociology and industrial relations with informal practices and the ways in which formal rules are modified or ignored. But there is perhaps a danger of assuming that these practices are universal in their occurrence and identical in form. Their development will depend on the form of workgroup organization that exists in a particular setting, on managerial behaviour, and on a range of contingencies reflecting the nature of work tasks and technological and product market forces. Work groups, in the sense of teams of workers who share common work situations and who act as distinct collectivities, cannot be assumed to exist. The strength of groups, and hence the strength of the norms that can be imposed on other workers, will vary. It is, for example, unlikely that all work groups have clear norms on attendance and absence in the sense of explicit understandings that can be backed up with sanctions against those who either exceed or do not come up to understood levels of absenteeism.

Neither should it be expected that informality is the preserve of workers alone. Managers can exploit informal understandings just as much as workers can. The basic organizational rules laid down by management do not constitute a maximum level of compliance from which workers can, to varying degree, escape. The rules cannot, by definition, establish precise levels of performance. All that they can do is try to lay down the broad principles to be applied. They consititute resources which either side can use in struggles over the effort bargain. It is not a matter of managerial formality and worker informality but of a continuing struggle in which elements of the formal and the informal are necessarily intertwined, for formal requirements cannot cover every eventuality. Rules are part of the structure of the situation in so far as they lay down basic guides to and contraints on action. But rules will plainly differ in the extent to which they can guide and constrain: some will be more firmly established than others. And they still have to be interpreted in action, and in this process of interpretation they become resources which have to be identified, defined, and applied.

One point of terminology needs clarification. As discussed in chapter 1, the concept of the effort bargain is widely used. The present analysis distinguishes between an effort bargain, that is a particular relationship between effort and reward, and the frontier of control within which it takes place. A frontier of control embraces all the influences on the detailed organization of work tasks. Its position can determine the contours of specific effort bargains. Where, for example, management has the right to determine piecework prices, workers' ability to bargain will be constrained. Where, by contrast, workers have established collective controls on manning levels, management's power to operate within individual effort bargains is limited. The importance of this distinction is that workplace struggle is not just about effort bargains but embraces the wider balance of power; as shown in detail in chapter 6, work relations in workplaces in which the frontier of control has been shifted in workers' favour differ markedly from those where struggle is limited to individual effort bargains.

Divisions in the Ranks of Capital and Labour

It is a commonplace in workplace studies that shopfloor managers are active in the creation of informal practices that are disliked by more senior managers. There are thus significant divisions within the ranks of management, which are matched by mutual hostility between groups of workers. How, therefore, is it possible to construct a theory based on only two fundamental categories, capital and labour?

There is a crucial difference between analytical categories based on functions performed in the production process and groups which exist in the real world. The functional division between those who produce a surplus and those who organize the creation of the surplus and whose income derives from a share in the surplus is clear enough. Direct producers create the surplus. Some of this is taken by those who own the means of production: the share-holders and so on. And some of it is used to pay those who do not themselves produce the surplus but who are instrumental in organizing production so that it is created. Senior managers would come into this category. But in the real world it is impossible to make such a sharp distinction. One of the manager's roles is co-ordinating different tasks, and this can reasonably be seen not as a straightforward appropriation of surplus value that would exist if co-ordination was not carried out but as an activity which, while not directly producing goods, is necessary for any production to take place. Investigation of the position of managers might well want to give attention to the different elements of their role; it has been suggested, for example, that they occupy an objectively contradictory class position because they are neither workers nor capitalists (Wright, 1978: 61–88). But such investigation need not obscure the basic point that the principles underlying the organization of the economy permit the analytical identification of different functions. How the performance of these functions operates in practice is a question for a different level of analysis.

In the particular case of foremen, Armstrong (1983) has usefully clarified some to the key issues. It is not helpful, he suggests, to see foremen in terms of the traditional stereotype of 'the man in the middle', that is as a group caught between the shopfloor and management and belonging to neither. Nor is it useful to concentrate on an alleged proletarianization of the supervisor, wherein levels of income become similar to, or even lower than, those of manual workers and jobs become fragmented and de-skilled. The supervisors in Armstrong's case study were proletarianized on these and other dimensions, but in terms of their relationships with managers and workers they were not proletarianized: they exercised authority over workers and did not share the same position in the division of labour; and managers assessed them in terms of their contribution to managerial aims. The foremen's 'interests conflicted with those they supervised' and were 'inextricably linked to the performance of capital functions' (p. 355). A similar perspective could be applied to other 'middle groups', assessing how they fit into the relationship between capital and labour. In short, analysis in terms of such basic categories does not inhibit consideration of the position and behaviour of different interest-groups within concrete social structures. On the contrary, it facilitates a proper analysis because, as Armstrong demonstrates, instead of relying on such characteristics as income to measure 'class location' it is possible to investigate actual behaviour and relate it to the principles underlying the organization of production.

The Problem of Groups outside the Capital–Labour Relation

There are various groups in society whose work is not addressed by the present theory. A small-holder, an independent shop-keeper, or a self-employed contractor does not come within the scope of the theory, although such people will be powerfully affected by the operation of the capitalist market. Much larger groups may also appear to be excluded. How far, for example, can relations between a senior official in a department of a local authority and his or her subordinates, or relations between a head teacher and teaching staff, be understood in terms of an effort bargain that is located in antagonistic interests in the production of surplus value? One answer is that they cannot, with the theory being limited to organizations that are directly involved in the production of surplus value. But it can also be suggested that some to the key features emerging from the theory have a wider application.

Relations in local authorities or schools plainly differ from those in capitalist factories. And there are also important differences between organizations that do not produce surplus value: banks, hospitals and government bureaucracies differ in the work tasks carried out and the control systems that develop. Influences stemming from the capitalist nature of the economy are not, moreover, felt directly. Thus, in their study of the Post Office and British Telecom, Batstone *et al.* (1984) argue that in state enterprises there is a 'political contingency' which mediates the effects of economic forces: whereas in private firms the need to make profits according to market signals is relatively clear, in state enterprise the state itself shapes the 'market' through decisions on the prices that may be charged. And the enterprises themselves are likely to have goals of public service as well as profitability.

Yet the political contingency should be seen not as an autonomous force but as a mechanism that shapes how the principles of capitalist organization work through the practice. It mediates but does not counteract forces stemming from the organization of the economy. Many capitalist countries have seen the growth of overt industrial protest among groups such as teachers and nurses. There is plainly some connection between this and pressures put on these groups in terms of pay levels and the organization of work. These pressures can in turn be related to attemps by governments to tackle problems of inflation and the cost of funding the public sector, problems which reflect difficulties in managing the capitalist economy as a whole. The details of work organization, such as systems of wage payment and the use of job evaluation techniques, reflect, moreover, the systems employed in capitalist organizations. The labour process of workers in the state sector is powerfully influenced by the principles governing the economy as a whole, albeit in an indirect manner.

A similar point applies to profit-making organizations which do not directly produce surplus value, such as banks. Although a strict argument that they contain within them a structured antagonism over the generation of surplus value cannot be sustained,/it would be quibbling to suggest that exploitation is thereby absent. Such organizations exist to make profits in a capitalist economy, and relations between workers and managers will reflect this fact. In short, the framework outlined above can be applied to work relations within any society which is dominated by a given mode of production, although there will plainly be variations in the precise ways in which work is organized.

Concluding Comments

These remarks do not resolve the problem of demarcating exploited and non-exploited workers. It has, indeed, been argued that attempting a sharp differentiation between them may be not only difficult but also of limited value. As long as the exploitive character of a mode of production can be identified, it is reasonable to argue that this character will affect all members of the relevant societies: a self-employed craftsman in capitalism is subjected to different influences on his life-chances from those affecting an identically skilled worker in feudalism. But it is also necessary to indicate what kinds of people should be considered to be exploited. The criteria suggested by Cohen (see p. 62) help here. The fact that an industrial manager does not own all the means of production with which he works does not make him a proletarian, for he exercises authority over others, and, according to some writers, performs the 'global functions of capital' by his involvement in the extraction of surplus value. The exercise of authority is not in itself sufficient to identify an exploiting group, for this can take place in voluntary organizations, for example. But when such an exercise takes place within an exploitive mode of production the link with exploitation is clear. For present purposes, the exploited group can be taken to be those who fall into one of the relevant cells in Table 2.1 and who exercise no significant control over the labour power of others. The decline of industrial blue-collar occupations notwithstanding, this group remains a large one in modern capitalist societies; as noted earlier (p. 14), Wright has estimated that a similarly defined group comprises 55 per cent of the American work force. Distinguishing between routinized and intellectual labour, and defining the former as those in occupations requiring less than three years' vocational training, Himmelstrand *et al.* (1981: 161) put their 'extended working class' at 77 per cent of Swedish wage-earners. These estimates are, however, less important than the basic points that exploitive characteristics of different modes of production can be identified, that these characteristics powerfully affect work relations between subordinates and superordinates, and that the bases of workplace conflict can thereby be established.

Concluding Remarks

This chapter has outlined an integrated conceptual approach for the understanding of relationships within the workplace. The approach draws on the work of a range of writers, and none of its various elements can be seen to be original. In particular, although criticisms of various writers have been made in the two previous chapters, this does not mean that their contributions are considered to be of no account. Some of the specific arguments of Friedman (1977) for example were criticized, but several of the points that he makes concerning the need to incorporate struggle into a theory of the capitalist labour process and the importance of taking account of the co-operative as well as the conflictual aspects of these process are plainly consistent with the argument developed above. This argument is intended to draw together the many useful insights that have developed, while avoiding a mere eclecticism.

An exercise of this type obviously carries with it the danger that it will be seen as so all-embracing that it merely states the obvious. The reader may be tempted to conclude that we knew all of this all the time. It has, however, been noted at several points in the discussion that existing theories fail to develop a coherent theory of conflict within the production process: if what has been said above is obvious, then this is so only in retrospect. It is hoped that a materialist framework can bring some order to debates about the labour process and provide a theoretical account which has hitherto been lacking. But the development of the framework is another matter. In the rest of this study a number of issues that arise from the framework are addressed.

APPENDIX 2.1
Materialism and Marxism

The theory outlined above has been called a materialist one. The label does not matter, and terms such as radical or sociological could equally well be applied. What is important is the attempt to link discussion of concrete forms of workplace behaviour to an analysis of the operation of the economy as a whole. The term materialism serves to stress the material, as opposed to the contingent, bases of workplace conflict, and also to indicate that these bases differ in different modes of production.

The differences between such an approach and a Marxist one require consideration for several reasons. First, one of the aims of the analysis is to develop the radical or sociological perspective on work; since the perspective has grown up in conscious opposition to Marxism, users of it will need to be persuaded that they are not being offered Marxism by the back door. Second, many recent debates in the area of workplace relations have overlapped with Marxism in their anxiety to address questions concerning the nature of the labour contract and the control of the labour process. Yet it has not always been clear whether contributors to the debates take a Marxist position, and if so in what sense. Some clarification of the issues is needed; and it is hoped that a position can be outlined that will form the basis of non-Marxist accounts that have hitherto had a somewhat uncertain status. Third, Marxist perspectives have become increasingly common in recent years: although the debate with Marx has a long history which does not need repetition here, some novel issues concerning the nature of Marxist social science have arisen, and the attempt to distinguish between Marxist and non-Marxist approaches has more relevance than it appeared to have a few years ago. Finally, the features of the theory relating to the possibility of non-exploitive modes of production and to the understanding of the sense of which conflict is said to be 'inevitable' stand out if it is contrasted with Marxist approaches.

Characteristics of Marxism

There is the familiar difficulty of deciding what constitutes Marxism, a difficulty which has greatly increased with the growth of Marxist and *marxisant* approaches. Not only are there differences between Marxists, but there are also questions concerning the basic criteria that permit an approach to be identified as Marxist. Several accounts in new areas of Marxist writing such as the role of the state have tried to deal with some of the standard criticisms of Marxism, the result being that they may have ceased to be Marxist in anything but name. As Marshall (1982: 201, emphasis in original) comments on attempts to develop a theory of ideology, it is not clear 'what it might be (other than a specific rhetoric and style of discourse) that makes such attempts distinctively Marxist in a *methodological* sense'. Similarly, in the area of work relations, there are 'Marxist' accounts which abandon the fundamental tenets of Marxism. The brief discussion in Appendix 2.2 points to theories of exploitation that do not treat the labour contract as distinctive. Another good example, since it comes from two well-known Marxists, is the paper by Bowles and Gintis (1981) in which the authors retract what they call the correspondence principle. This is the principle developed in their earlier work (Bowles and Gintis, 1976) that the requirements of the capitalist production system place definite demands on other parts of society, such as the educational system, in terms of such things as the inculcation of norms of obedience to authority. The principle, they suggest, gives insufficient attention to the 'contradictions' that develop between the productive and educational spheres.[2] Their solution is to argue that capitalism contains different 'sites' which exert pressure on each

---

2 The term contradiction may be too strong to characterize the tensions that Bowles and Gintis consider. As noted above, a contradiction is more than just a clash of opposing principles.

other. This abandons the view that the development of productive forces is the basis for the growth of social relations.

The solution adopted here is to indicate some criteria that any account claiming to be Marxist must meet; differences between materialism and Marxism may then be outlined. A fundamental requirement is that the labour process is treated as a special sphere of social activity because of the relations of exploitation that exist within it: there must be an analytical distinction between the processes of production and exchange, and the former process must be seen as having distinct characteristics. And there must be a view as to why exploitation exists. A Marxist must also hold that any mode of production has an internal dynamic provided by a growth of the productive forces such that modes tend to be superseded by more advanced modes.

Capitalism, for example, is seen to supersede feudalism and then to develop the productive forces. But as it does so crises of growing severity emerge and at some point capitalism becomes inappropriate for the further development of the productive forces and it is replaced by socialism. Now, Marxists can properly disagree between themselves on a range of issues such as whether there is a long-run tendency for the rate of profit to fall; whether capitalism will simply break down or will be destroyed by class struggle; and on the nature of socialism. But they must agree that modes of production have internal dynamics which lead to their demise and that socialism, meaning in particular a non-exploitative mode of production, is feasible and, in the long run, inevitable.

Materialism shares some of these characteristics: Marxists must be materialists, but not all materialists need be Marxists. There is the stress on exploitation within the labour process, the use of the concept of contradictions, the willingness to analyse modes of production in terms of abstractions such as capital and labour, and the insistence on making struggle within work relations a central aspect of the account of historical development. But Marxism needs to go further. Cohen (1978: 198), for example, is very clear that pre-capitalist class societies are characterized by a level of productive development which produces a low amount of surplus, that capitalism leads to a larger amount of surplus, and that socialism is associated with a 'massive' surplus. He goes on (p. 206) to discuss societies which have ceased to be capitalist without a high level of development of the productive forces, suggesting that it is questionable how far they have achieved socialism and pointing out that they have often adopted technologies from capitalism; and he concludes that the Marxist thesis about the development of socialism would be refuted if a fully socialist society emerged which remained largely agricultural.

Presumably, a major characteristic of socialism is felt to be not just a massive surplus but the generation of the surplus in non-exploitative ways. This is one point at which materialism and Marxism part company. The former makes no statement about the conditions which will lead to a development of 'true' socialism; it does not try to assess what level of productive forces is necessary for capitalism to cease to be progressive; and it does not speculate about how non-exploitative modes of production might appear. It certainly accepts, as stressed above, that there can be production without exploitation, the independent producer being a case in point. But it does not suppose that a whole mode of production, generating a massive surplus, can be brought into being in such a way that exploitation is ended.

Marxism must propose some logic of social development such that exploitation will be transcended, whereas materialism makes no such claim.[3] In view of the obvious difficulties with arguing about the nature of 'true' socialism, the point may also be made with reference to the transition from feudalism to capitalism. As argued below, the Marxist view is that the development of the productive forces in feudalism placed such strains on the social relations of production that the mode of production could no longer continue. An alternative view, which is consistent with a materialist account, is that, although there certainly were contradictions within feudalism, the reasons why the social formation broke down reflected changes in such things as the legal system and the growth of non-feudal systems of production, notably in the towns. The collapse of feudalism was not caused by a contradiction between the productive forces and the productive relations, which merely placed certain constraints on the social structure. The emergence of capitalism, moreover, was not the result of the collapse of all types of feudalism, for capitalism developed from feudalism only under the specific historical circumstances affecting Western Europe, as distinct from those in the East. The importance of productive forces is not to be neglected. The whole point of the foregoing approach through levels of analysis is to suggest that specific events can be related to basic forces within a mode of production. Thus, the breakdown of Western feudalism cannot be explained simply by legal and other developments but also has to be related to the contradictions of the productive system. But the contradictions

---

3 It may be suggested that, although Marxism of *praxis* may argue that socialism is inevitable, a methodological Marxism need make no such claim. Yet such a Marxism is indistinguishable from materialism if it merely derives concepts to apply to capitalism without suggesting that there is a law of motion of the mode of production. A materialist account as outlined here is designed to appeal to, among other groups, those who use Marxism as a methodological quarry.

were not sufficient to destroy the mode of production, and they were significant only alongside other changes in the social formation. Modes of production have identifiable structural characteristics but these do not determine historical change.

A further key characteristic of a materialist account is the distinction between basic characteristics of a productive system and the attribution of interests to particular groups. Although it is 'better' not to be exploited than to be exploited, this way of looking at the problem is not helpful since it conflates a particular interest (not being exploited) with the whole set of interests that groups are likely to have. To say that a mode of production is exploitative is not to condemn it, for other modes are also exploitative and the question of whether one form of exploitation is better than another has to be settled by individuals making their own judgements and not by analytical deduction. Indeed, when exploitation is seen in the purely technical sense of the extraction of surplus from direct producers, a high rate of exploitation may be 'better' than a low rate; for example, capitalists practising direct control may create small amounts of surplus using autocratic and coercive methods while those using more participative forms of management in high technology sectors may produce a higher rate of exploitation with less obvious suffering on the part of their workers. Finally, exploitation is a concept for understanding the principles of work organizations. It is not reflected in simple divisions between people, for some people control the work of others while themselves being controlled from above. Exploitation is a category at a fundamental, and not a concrete, level of analysis.

Base and Superstructure

These contrasts between Marxism and materialism may be made more specific by looking at the familiar problem of base and superstructure. Such a consideration also helps the explication of a materialist mode of analysis: it will be argued in later chapters that certain parts of the 'superstructure', notably the state, have played an important role in the development of labour relations in capitalism, and some preliminary consideration of how base and superstructure are related will help to clarify the status of the argument.

Cohen (1978: 134, emphasis deleted) deals with the issue with his usual incisiveness. He defends the 'primacy thesis', which is that 'the nature of a set of production relations is explained by the level of development of the productive forces embraced by it (to a far greater extent than vice versa)'. One consequence of the thesis is the view that a capitalist economic structure emerges when the productive forces can no longer develop within previous sets of production relations.

Capitalism thus necessarily arose from the demise of feudalism. Dealing with the argument that it was only in Western Europe that this happened he says (p. 248),

> The fact that capitalism did not arise spontaneously outside of Europe is a serious problem for historical materialism. It will be solved, if at all, by finer distinctions among production relations proper, together with attention to different strictly material conditions in different regions. If the problem cannot be solved in that way, then so much the worse for historical materialism, not for the claim that historical materialism distinguishes between base and superstructure.

This argument gives a stringent definition of what a Marxist account must involve. Thus, Cohen rightly criticizes Anderson (1974) who, having himself attacked explanations based on differences in the superstructures of European and non-European societies, tries to rescue a 'materialist' account by redefining parts of the superstructure such as the law into the base of productive forces. As Cohen argues, this is just as 'idealist' as the procedure that Anderson criticizes, and is not a Marxist approach.[4]

So why did capitalism emerge only in Western Europe? This question, hotly debated in the 1950s, has recently received renewed attention. The historical controversies cannot be assessed here; Holton (1985) provides a useful introduction to them. But four positions may be identified. At one extreme is the Marxist view outlined by Cohen in which capitalism is seen as the necessary result of the collapse of feudalism. At the opposite extreme is the 'idealist' view, in which no special explanatory significance is given to production relations, and such things as demographic trends are seen as adequate explanations of the problems of feudalism. Third, there are the Marxists, notably Sweezy, who take an 'exchange relations' perspective in which forces outside the feudal economy itself, such as the rise of commerce and of towns, are seen as the prime movers in the rise of capitalism. Finally, there is the production relations view, taken by Dobb and by Brenner, in which contradictions of the productive system are seen as fundamental.[5]

The last of these is consistent with a materialist position. It is usually stated as against the second and third, and some of the points of

4 Anderson (1980: 72–3) has acknowledged the force of this criticism. Yet he does not make clear whether he wishes to withdraw his argument or with what it should be replaced.

5 The major contributions, by Dobb, Sweezy and others, to the 1950s debate, together with later writings, have been brought together by Hilton (1978).

criticism are identical to those made above of non-materialist views of industrial conflict: a tendency to treat exchange and production relations as equivalent, a failure to locate conflict in the character of the productive system, and so on. But it also contains implicit criticism of a properly Marxist view. Brenner (1977: 78), for example, argues that the emergence of capitalism in England reflected a specific conjuncture of class forces. In Western Europe as a whole, the peasantry had been slowly escaping from feudal obligations and was no longer unfree; the lords could not, therefore, deal with the problem of extracting more surplus by increasing feudal rents, for this would have been met with resistance. But the English ruling class was in a good position to increase surplus in another way, namely through the introduction of improved agricultural technology. It also differed from its counterpart in France because it could secure control of the land in order to introduce the technology and claim the benefits. In France, by contrast, the peasants' escape from feudal obligations had developed to such an extent that the lords could not hold the land themselves, the result being that the peasants could retain a non-innovative form of agriculture, which meant in turn that the growth of capitalism was retarded. In short, feudalism as a whole was a mode of production which generated what is called here a structured antagonism between the exploiting and the exploited classes. This antagonism was the basis of specific struggles in specific countries. Each struggle took on a character of its own and affected the possible future trajectory of the productive forces. Capitalism emerged in Western Europe and not elsewhere because of the character of the social relations of production.

This is a materialist explanation because developments in social relations are linked to the base of the productive forces without being seen as determined by them. Cohen does, of course, allow the superstructure to have significant effects. Thus he says (1978: 165) that the relations of production can condition the forces by helping to determine the particular path that development takes and by influencing the rate of productivity growth. But the 'productive forces on the whole dominate the production relations'. Thus the timing and precise character of capitalist development in different countries will reflect their production relations and will not be reducible to the forces. Later (p. 231) he also makes the important argument that 'bases need superstructures': a superstructural element such as the law can strengthen the stability of the base by rendering forms of domination legitimate. Such arguments are major developments of a Marxist account, for they show that it does not have to be assumed that the base determines everything about the superstructure or that the superstructure can have no effect on the base. They do not, however, solve the problem of the development of modes of production. An explanation of the rise of capitalism can be provided which focuses on the character of social relations of production. The social relations determined whether or not capitalism emerged in a particular country, while the productive forces merely placed various constraints on these relations.

Materialism thus distinguishes between base and superstructure. It also accepts the primacy thesis in so far as this argues that constraints stemming from the structural characteristics of a mode of production are basic to social development. But this is not the same as saying that the development of the productive forces requires certain changes in the relations of production. The failure of capitalism to emerge spontaneously from feudalism is indeed a serious problem for Marxism.

Position of the Working Class

Once capitalism has emerged, it brings with it a proletariat which has to sell its labour power in order to live. How do Marxist and materialist accounts of the role of the proletariat differ? A distinction needs to be made between the logic of a Marxist account and what Marxists actually do. Consider, for example, Lockwood's (1981) critique of the Marxist programme. A key weakness is found to lie in the elucidation of the link between the theory of capitalist development and the behaviour of the working class. According to Lockwood, Marxists wrongly presume that there is an inherent tendency for workers to recognize their own class interests. There is the error of assuming that 'through their power of reason workers will be quick to learn from their experience of capitalist relations of production that their ends can only be realized by the abolition of these relations' (p. 452). In fact, says Lockwood, there is no evidence for this assumption, and there is no natural tendency for class interests to be recognized, articulated, and developed. Marxists might well argue that this is a caricature of their position, in that they have tried to explain the various forces that enmesh workers in capitalism and prevent the growth of class consciousness. They might also point to the error of one of Lockwood's charges (p. 460), namely the familiar stricture that they rely for evidence not on their own primary research but on 'bourgeois' studies that they are otherwise quick to condemn. A range of contemporary and historical studies, either by professed Marxists or by analysts who use Marxian categories and ideas, now exists, within which various explanations are made of the character of class consciousness and of the reasons why such consciousness appears to be limited and fragmentary. The present argument is that Lockwood, together with many critics, may be wrong about what Marxists do, unnecessarily slighting their contribution and making it easy for them to dismiss the criticism as being directed at a straw man. He is substantially right, however, about the logic of Marxist analysis. There must be some claim that there is an inherent tendency for the working class to identify and struggle for specific class interests, in particular the overthrow of capitalism. Lockwood identifies some of the flaws in such a claim.

Within a materialist approach such problems are avoided by seeing class relations and class struggle as matters that do not stem directly from the nature of the mode of production. That is, capital and labour are analytical abstractions that help to assess how the productive system operates. How far the structured antagonism between them is translated into a specifically class struggle will depend on a variety of influences. These influences can be classified into four areas: the degree to which capitalists see themselves as a class with distinct interests; the degree of class unity among workers; the extent to which a particular struggle between a capitalist and his workers is seen in class terms; and the extent to which such individual struggles are generalized into an overall class struggle. A materialist approach does not deny the possibility that class consciousness can become a significant force. But it does not assert that there is any inherent tendency for relations between capital and labour to produce this result. The category of 'capital', for example, relates to a particular position in the productive process. Individual capitalists are likely, through their competition with each other, to perceive many differences with each other; and there will also be differences between different types of capitalist such as the large corporation and the small independent firm. It is, strictly speaking, possible to refer to struggles in a particular workplace as class struggles in the sense that a connection can be adduced between them and the fundamental categories of capital and labour. But such usages conceal more than they reveal about the struggles in question. It is preferable to avoid the unfortunate implications of simply attaching the term 'class' to specific struggles.

There are, no doubt, Marxists who could agree with this view. It has, for example, become common for discussions of class consciousness to stress that class unity is variable and that working-class aims are often limited and sectional. A good deal of value has emerged from some of these discussions. But the question arises of how far they remain Marxists and of how far the adjustments that are made to the Marxist theory of social change permit them to be called Marxist.

Burawoy's Marxism

The foregoing comments have had to be rather general, for it has been necessary to consider some broad features of an approach that can be termed Marxist and not the work of individual authors. It will be useful, therefore, to turn to a more specific case, of which the most pertinent, given its place in the discussion of the previous chapter, is the definition of a Marxist approach offered by Burawoy (1979: xii–xiii). He says that his study 'is not an exercise in neo-Marxism, Marxist revisionism, or any other label social scientists may apply to the Marxism they may wish to take seriously'. Instead, 'it is a Marxist study', which means at least three things. First is a concern with 'change and continuity in capitalism conceived of as a particular way of appropriating unpaid labor from direct producers'. Second is the refusal to assume that capitalism is the last type of society in history. Third is the 'possibility and desirability of a fundamentally different form of society – call it communism, if you will – in which men and women, freed from the pressures of scarcity and from the insecurity of everyday existence under capitalism, shape their own lives'.

The first two points do not make a study Marxist. It is true that non-Marxists have tended to neglect analysis in terms of the productive relations of a society. But raising an area of attention is not sufficient to define the approach of a study, especially when the study claims the very special label of Marxism. And surely no one, except someone clinging to the more extreme of the now-discredited theories of the convergence of industrial societies, would argue that capitalism is the end point of the development of all societies. Burawoy's third point is more pertinent. His image of the future would be shared by many Marxists and, as he points out, dimissed as utopian by non-Marxists. The view here is that it is indeed utopian and, moreover, that it is strictly irrelevant to the analytical task which Burawoy has set himself. That is, to analyse the complexities of the capitalist labour process does not require an image of a non-exploitative arrangement. Indeed, Burawoy seems to recognize this, for in his discussion of the characteristics of capitalism he contrasts it not with communism but with feudalism. His analysis of capitalism appears, moreover, to hold out a bleak prospect for the achievement of communism. The focus is on the creation of consent and not on the tendencies of capitalism to destroy itself. Thus, Burawoy's empirical analysis lends support to the conclusion that capitalism is a robust mode of production and hence that any commitment to a Marxist theory of working-class action has tacitly been abandoned.

Burawoy (1979: 73–4) suggests that it is possible to conceive of an emancipated society in which there 'are no unintended consequences' and there is a 'coincidence of individual and collective rationality'. There would be conflicts, but these would be resolved through open and public discussions. A pejorative application of the term utopian is not out of place. How is it possible to operate without unintended consequences unless one assumes perfect knowledge and perfect foresight? How can individual and collective rationalities be brought into line without the need to enforce the collective will through majority vote or some other procedure? How can it be assumed that all individuals will share perceptions of the way in which society should work? In short, Burawoy's vision involves a utopia without a history and without progress.

Conclusions

To summarize the difference between materialism and Marxism, the discussion by Wright (1983) of Giddens's (1981) critique of Marxism is illuminating. Wright makes many pertinent criticisms of Giddens, which are unimportant here. He concludes by suggesting that the main defence for the Marxist theory of history and class relations is the argument that

> class relations have a specific primacy in that dynamics rooted in class relations provide an overall directionality to the trajectory of historical change. If this argument is . . . rejected, then there is no longer any justification for Marxist class analysis as such. Without the theory of history and without a general theory of class analysis, it is hard to see what remains as the distinctive theoretical core of Marxism (Wright, 1983: 35).

It is just this attempt to develop an evolutionary theory of history based on class relations that a materialist account rejects. The analytical distinction between capital and labour does not provide the grounds for explaining historical change.

Any account which claims the status of being Marxist in anything other than a merely rhetorical sense has some serious difficulties. The materialist approach tries to avoid these difficulties while retaining some elements of a Marxian perspective. It is, therefore, not an anodyne blending of Marxist and Weberian approaches but is an attempt to develop a consistent theoretical position.

APPENDIX 2.2
Paid Work and Domestic Labour;
and Non-materialist Theories of Exploitation

This appendix comments briefly on two issues which arise from the main discussion of the theory of conflict. These are the connections between work relations and non-work relations, and the difference between materialist and non-materialist theories of exploitation.

Paid Work and Domestic Labour

The links between the labour process and other parts of social life may be considered in relation to one of the most hotly debated issues of recent years, the question of gender. Paul Thompson (1983: 181) argues that 'it is impossible to understand the distribution of skills, methods of control and organization of work, different rates of exploitation, or any other factor connected to the labour process' without attention to the sexual division of labour. Yet this confuses the fact that the division of labour between men and women is an important feature of work organizations and the capital-labour relation as a distinct analytical issue.

The following statements are all true. Women tend to be segregated into the worst-paying jobs. The skills that women deploy are often undervalued as compared with those of men. Employers often feel that women work only for pin money and that they are less committed to work than are male employees, a feeling often shared by male workers. Women are subject to the 'double burden' of paid work and housework. The role of gender in the workplace has been neglected in traditional industrial sociology (R. Brown, 1976) and in Marxism, whose categories of analysis are 'sex-blind' (Hartmann, 1979: 1). It is also true that there are other significant lines of division. Thompson mentions racial ones. Religious differences can also be significant. In Northern Ireland, for example, not only is access to jobs heavily dependent on one's religion but, to the extent that employers can play on religious fears and rivalries, religion can also have a role in the control of the labour process. Yet it does not follow that all the lines of cleavage existing in a particular society have to be incorporated into a theory of the labour process. They have a bearing on the organization of work in particular situations but are analytically distinct from the capital-labour relation.

One reason for giving special attention to the role of gender is that there is a necessary connection between the use of labour power in the production process and the creation of labour power in the family. Various arguments have been offered, but the strongest statement is as follows. Any exploiting class needs to ensure the production of a supply of labour power. Labour power is produced in the family. The work that women do in bearing and raising children and in other domestic tasks is thus essential to the continued operation of the economy. Although they do not directly produce a surplus, they help to ensure that the conditions exist in which a surplus can be generated. Modes of production differ in the demands that they make on the domestic economy. Although it may be true that gender divisions within the workplace do not have to be made an integral part of a theory of conflict at work, there are, within any mode of production, necessary connections between the labour process in which the surplus is produced and domestic labour. A theory of the operation of the mode of production must thus attend to these connections. The work of Gardiner (1976), Beechey (1978) and West (1980) contains detailed discussion of the general analytical questions involved here, while Humphries (1981), for example, has studied particular historical developments using a perspective in which gender is explicitly included.

As Beechey, for example, notes, however, the development of a mode of production exerts a powerful influence on the activities performed by the family. Forces operating in the other direction seem to be rare, and there is thus justification for treating the productive system without giving detailed scrutiny to the family. In addition to this empirical point, there is the analytical one concerning what is to be explained. If the concern is to chart, for example, the development of the proletariat as a class it probably will be necessary to consider such hitherto neglected issues as the emulation in the factory of forms of male authority over women characteristic of the family. But where, as here, the concern is with patterns of conflict and accommodation in the workplace and the theoretical understanding of them, the role of domestic labour is not central. The different characteristics of different sorts of labour power are pertinent to the forms of control practised by management as well as to the expectation of groups of workers and the types of pressure that they can bring to bear on their employers. In some circumstances capitalists may even have to deal directly with problems of labour supply, for example through providing company housing; and capitalists may try to affect the behaviour of workers outside the factory, as in attempts to encourage habits of thrift and sobriety. But a theory of what happens inside the labour process need not concern itself directly with the conditions under which labour power is produced or the ways in which the productive system impinges on other parts of society.

Non-materialist Theories of Exploitation

The approach to exploitation outlined above is common to Marxist and non-Marxist but materialist theories. It defines exploitation in terms of relations within the process of production, distinguishes rigorously between exploitation in production and competition and conflict that may occur in the sphere of exchange, and insists that in capitalism labour-power is different from other commodities because it can produce new value. Such an approach, which was not really a source of dispute between Marxists, has recently been challenged. Giddens (1981: 60, emphasis in original) defines exploitation as 'domination *which is harnessed to sectional interests*'. He goes on (at p. 111) to discuss a key element in the analysis of exploitation, namely the identification of the surplus. He suggests that, if a surplus is defined as that which is produced over and above the traditionally accepted standards of living of a particular community, then it is not clear why appropriating this surplus should be seen as exploitation. He suggests that a surplus can be defined as such only in terms of the unequal distribution of power between classes, with a surplus being what one class extracts from another. Exploitation is here reduced to power relations, with the term not being restricted to production relations but embracing any form of relationship between one class and another. Any specific reference to production is lost. As argued in the text, this is a very serious loss since it removes the possibility of identifying the reasons why conflict is inherent in the labour process. Thus, while Giddens (e.g. p. 121) argues that in capitalism class struggle is inherent in the organization of work, he lacks a developed theory to explain this fact.

Since Giddens's comments are made in the course of a critique of historical materialism, they might be dimissed. But they are very similar to those made by Roemer (1982) who has produced a widely acclaimed 'Marxian' theory of exploitation. For Roemer, exploitation results from unequal exchange and does not necessarily involve relations at the point of production. How unequal exchange is defined and how Roemer develops his theory are unimportant here. They key point is his abandoning of the view that exploitation is something specific to the use of labour-power.

Broadening the term to cover any unequal exchange means that there is no way of addressing the specific nature of production relations, with exploitation being equivalent to the exercise of power. Analytically, one is back at the sort of approach criticized in chapter 1, in which conflict is a contingent consequence of the fact that some groups have more power than others. How these groups become constituted as 'classes' is not demonstrated: although Giddens, for example, uses the concept of a class he cannot ground it in relations within production but instead relies on ownership or non-ownership of property. In the present account, owning property is not in itself crucial; what is important is the set of relations which emerges around particular ways of organizing production. Power, moreover, is to be seen not as the basic analytical category but as something which is less basic than the structured antagonisms which exist in exploitative modes of production.

It is notable that 'Marxist' attempts to broaden the analysis of exploitation are paralleled by non-Marxist arguments which have a great deal in common with them, in particular in treating the labour contract as no different in principle from any other form of contract. The 'transactions costs' literature associated with the name of Oliver Williamson (e.g. 1981) represents a notable attempt to consider all forms of contract not in terms of the costless transactions with perfect information that characterize neo-classical economics but in relation to more realistic situations. The literature warrants a brief digression here for two reasons: it shows that, when certain fundamental tenets of a materialist position are abandoned, Marxist and orthodox approaches become indistinguishable; and its substantive analytical problems are identical to those faced by those, Marxists and others, who see exploitation as characteristic of exchange as well as production relations.

The transaction costs literature notes that there are costs in any transaction and, in particular, that there are costs and uncertainties involved in trying to ensure that the obligations implied in a contract are met. No contract can be precisely specified in advance. A merchant contracting with a farmer for the delivery of an order of corn, for example, can specify the amount, but the grade and quality of the corn, together with the precise timing and mode of its delivery, will be variable. Is this example not the same in form as that of labour services? Various forces of custom and tradition will help to ensure that there is a taken-for-granted set of understandings between merchants and farmers as to their mutual obligations, but these forces are external to the contract itself. There appears, then, to be nothing distinctive about the capacity of workers to resist managerial demands, for farmers can equally be said to be able to resist the demands of merchants for corn of a high quality.

It is true that, at the level of the contract itself, the labour contract is not unique. The uncertainties surrounding it are not qualitatively different from those surrounding other contracts. It would thus be incorrect to identify the sources of conflict within the labour process in terms of the capacity to resist alone. There is, however, a sharp distinction between the circumstances of the labour contract and those of other contracts. To the extent that uncertainties permit the farmer to amend the terms of his obligations to the merchant (or to engage in 'opportunism' as the transactions costs writers call it) money will end up in his pocket and not in that of the merchant. No new value has been created. The labour process, however, is a process designed to create new value. To the extent that the capitalist is successful in harnessing labour-power, the amount of surplus value is increased. It is not a matter of the worker simply behaving opportunistically in evading contractual obligations but of a structured antagonism concerning the way in which labour is extracted. Opportunism is external to the contract in the sphere of exchange, whereas the gap between workers' capacity to work and the performance of labour is integral to the labour process. Exploitation and opportunism are based on fundamentally different relationships.

Why should a Marxist want to recast the theory of exploitation? Roemer's answer is that Marxism has failed to account for the political and economic development of state socialist societies: there is no private ownership of property, so that theories of exploitation based on ownership or non-ownership cannot work, and yet inequality still exists. What is needed, in his view, is a theory of exploitation that can work even in the absence of private property. Roemer seems to have set himself a false problem. It is true that inequality exists in state socialism, and also that industrial conflict has not been abolished. But an account of these facts does not have to abandon the theory that exploitation is peculiar to the process of production. As argued above, a proper model of exploitation does not rely on ownership of the means of production as a criterion. Workers can own some of the means of production and still be exploited. The abolition of private property is not, therefore, as decisive in its effects as Roemer thinks. And a model of the form of exploitation in state socialism can be created within the analytical scheme employed above. In this model, the productive system remains the centre of attention, and exploitation is not identified with inequality.

State socialism has several important similarities with capitalism. For example, strikes, absenteeism, and sabotage, as well as bargaining about piecework prices, have been observed in both systems. This is not surprising since both are based on large-scale industry with complex divisions of labour. But there are also differences reflecting their varying forms of social organization, even if the technical organization of work is similar. The legitimacy of labour collectivities is very limited under state socialism, and the power of management is directly reinforced by that of the state. Instead of the pursuit of private profit and the accumulation of capital being the impetus of the system, it is the development of the economy through central planning that is the chief mechanism of economic change. Workers 'lose' to the extent that bargaining about the terms of the labour contract is illegitimate, but 'gain' in so far as labour-power is not treated as a commodity in the marketplace; problems of redundancy, restructuring and unemployment are largely absent. In short, the mode of production has a logic of its own which can be considered without assuming that it is a replica of capitalism and without having to invent a whole new theory of exploitation.

3

The Rise of Capitalism
and Changing Forms of Protest

This chapter begins to illustrate the arguments developed above. The concern is not to analyse in any detail changes in the mode of production: such issues as the spread of capitalist organization throughout the economy, the character of technical progress, the emergence of the giant firm, and the cyclical nature of capitalist development will not be addressed. This is not a work of economic history. Instead, the focus is the character of social relations in the workplace, in particular how patterns of work relations changed as capitalism emerged and how these patterns created distinctive forms of 'industrial conflict'. Most of the illustrations are taken from Britain in the period 1750–1850.

There is now a massive literature on the history of work, inspired by the 'new labour history' in which the actual experience of work, together with links between workplace and community, is a central feature. No pretence is made that a synthesis of this literature emerges below. What is offered is a way of looking at some of the perennial issues arising in the literature. Is it the case, for example, that capitalism's development produced a proletariat accustomed to new forms of work and that, as a result, struggle in the workplace once had a potentially revolutionary character which it has since lost? And is it possible to reconcile the persistence of frequent and bitter industrial disputes with an apparent growth in the political quiescence of the working class? A way of looking at such questions will be proposed which derives from the theory outlined in chapter 2 and which will, it is hoped, help in their consideration. Several labour historians have begun to turn to debates on the labour process for theoretical tools to understand concrete developments. The present account aims to assist in this effort.

Four issues are addressed. First, some introductory comments are made on the nature of capitalism and the reasons for its distinctiveness from other modes of production. Changing patterns of collective workplace action are then addressed. There are important continuities in patterns of protest under capitalism. As against the view that there has been a move from a 'formal' to a 'real' subordination of labour, it is argued, on the basis of the theoretical statement that the terms of the labour contract cannot be fixed, that there has been no straightforward and unilinear progression in patterns of labour relations or in the type of conflict to which they give rise. Third, the discussion is extended to the less commonly discussed but very important 'individual' forms of action: how did workers as individuals come to terms with capitalism and what significance did activities such as quitting have? Finally, the problem of the link between industrial action and class conflict is addressed.

The Rise of Capitalism

Two issues will be briefly discussed. First, there is the rather neglected question of the origins of one of the key characteristics of capitalism, namely the accumulation of capital. If this was new, where did it come from? Second, there is the creation of a class of free wage-labourers. How was this managed? An answer to this question has a direct bearing on the analysis of forms of protest, for patterns of workplace relations continued to be governed by traditions from an earlier age, and these customs and understandings were re-shaped under capitalism, with important results.

On the first question, it is important to be clear what is meant by accumulation. It does not mean simply a pursuit of profit or the growth of wealth through trade. Medieval city-states such as Venice built up large stores of wealth through their trading activities, but they were not engaged in the accumulation of capital. This occurs when the pursuit of profit through trade is transformed into the use of the profits as productive capital, with the merchant being turned into a capitalist who plays a direct role in the production process: instead of just making profits in the process of exchange, the merchant begins to organize production, using his profits not as a store of wealth but to purchase the means of production and labour power so as to generate a surplus within the production process itself. Numerous conditions were necessary for the birth of a distinctively capitalist production process. In his classic study of the rise of capitalism, Dobb (1963: 161) lists three: the breakdown of the monopolies over the supply of particular goods held by local guilds; the freeing of industrial capital from the restraints created by existing monopolies in the sphere of trade; and circumstances favouring a high level of investment in agriculture. On the second, for example, the state had granted monopolies to control the trade of various goods to individuals or groups, and it was necessary for such restraints to be removed so that independent manufacturers could begin to produce and market their goods freely. This is not to suggest that there was any functional necessity in the process: there was no requirement that capitalism be brought into existence and that therefore ensured a decline of traditional monopolies. There were, rather, certain conditions that had to exist before a distinctively capitalist system could emerge. And there was no guarantee that capitalism would be the end product of given historical change. Dobb (p. 195) cites the case of the Netherlands during the eighteenth century, where mercantile growth had been considerable and where some of the conditions for capitalism were developing. Even 'the launching of a country on the first stages of the road towards Capitalism is no guarantee that it will complete the journey'; in this case the attractions of financial speculation meant that money was not invested in nascent capitalistic enterprises.

In addition to change in the mercantile system, control of the production process had to alter. Control of the means of production had to be removed from the great mass of artisans and placed in the hands of a relatively small number of potential capitalists. Dobb (p. 150) provides an account of how this might have come about, and thus of how petty artisan production became transformed into a system based on the propertyless labourer, which in turn formed the basis of a fully capitalist arrangement. The domestic producer could retain his independence from the merchant if he owned land and used domestic manufacture merely to supplement his income. But if manufacture was his sole source of livelihood, as it was in the case of those who were being forced off the land, then the artisan was likely to become increasingly dependent on the merchant. Any downturn in the market or personal misfortune or other contingency would force the artisan into complete dependence on the merchant. In time, he would be transformed from an independent contractor to a homeworker carrying out operations on a piecework basis on materials supplied by the merchants.[1]

1 Kriedte *et al.* (1981) have recently discussed this process. They argue correctly that 'capital does not have a built-in tendency to penetrate into production, but merely an inherent interest in profit' (p. 94). The rise of a capitalist mode of production, in which capitalists organize the production process itself, cannot be taken for granted. The authors' own explanation is that commodity producers become increasingly dependent

There thus seems to have been a growing integration of production and exchange. Alongside the rise of the merchant-capitalist there was, in Britain at least, a rationalization of agricultural methods and the emergence of large firms, as described by Pollard (1965). In this environment of growth and change it is not suprising that a stress began to be placed on finding new ways of producing, harnessing water and then steam power to replace hand operations and developing the large factory. Such processes were intimately connected with the growth of new markets. Thus production and exchange came to be increasingly closely integrated, and accumulation became a major dynamic of the system. Once expansion and rationalization were adopted as policies by a few capitalists the remainder had to do likewise or risk going out of business.

The point of this schematic account is to stress that capitalism was a distinct historical product, with its growth depending on specific conditions. This had important consequences for the development of workplace relations, with pre-capitalist traditions often being significant and having to be reworked in the light of changing conditions. A class of free wage-labourers had actively to be brought into existence. It is notable that in many industries early capitalist organizations relied on contract labour, with workers being tied to work on an annual basis. Campbell (1979) charts the virtual serfdom that was used in parts of the Scottish coalfield, and similar arrangements existed elsewhere. In other industries, annual hiring was common. As will be seen below, such non-capitalist arrangements could be turned to the workers' benefit, but what is important for present purposes is the phase of semi-free labour, which was far from being a passing phenomenon and which reflected the difficulty with which capitalism was established. Two related features of a capitalist production system are a labour market with the free buying and selling of labour-power and a labour process in which the employer has the formal authority to deploy labour-power so as to produce surplus value. Both features are matters of degree. Labour markets can vary in the extent to which free contracting is constrained by legal and other restrictions on such things as the right to dismiss and the level of wages that may be paid. And the employer's authority in the workplace will be limited by workers' efforts to assert their own control. Much of the following discussion will be taken up with examining the consequences for workplace behaviour of developments in labour markets and within labour processes. In particular, and in relation to the latter aspect, it

---

on merchants during slumps, with power increasingly shifting to the latter. This is essentially Dobb's explanation, advanced over thirty years earlier, although Dobb is nowhere mentioned.

will be suggested that developments in the control of the labour process do not fit a model that has been widely deployed in the historical accounts, namely that of a progressive movement away from traditional modes of job regulation, with a high level of worker control of effort, to modes in which employers successfully established their own rules of the game. As argued in chapter 2, the distinctiveness of the capitalist labour process lies not in the growth of employers' control of the details of work operations but in the position of the labour process within the circuit of capital and in the direct role played by the employer in the production process.

Before moving to cases drawn from the industrialization of Europe, it will be useful to underline the generic nature of the problems of the labour market and the labour process facing an emergent capitalism. Thus, Robin Cohen (1980) has used a wide variety of research materials on the industrialization of Africa to draw out some of the main themes of the process, with particular reference to the covert forms of worker resistance that can emerge. He notes that the capitalist labour process involves the habituation to industrial production in five respects: workers are made into proletarians by being forced to abandon their own means of subsistence; the employer asserts authority within the workplace; labour creates a range of physical and psychological costs; there is an unequal distribution of rewards; and political and legal structures serve to reinforce capitalist social relations. Cohen relates workers' behaviour to each of these conditions. Enforced proletarianization is related to desertion and revolt by local communities; managerial control is met by effort bargaining and sabotage; the costs of work are reflected in accidents and absenteeism; and so on.

Now, it is questionable whether a direct correspondence can be made between aspects of capitalism and particular forms of behaviour. Effort bargaining, for example, obviously reflects attempts to deal with the inequality of reward as well as a response to managerial control. And absenteeism should be seen as a response to this control as well as being an individual reaction to the physical conditions of work; if it is not so regarded, it can be seen merely as a negative, individual, and spontaneous reaction and not as a rational act stemming from the social relations of work. Each form of behaviour needs to be related to changing work relations in general, instead of one form being seen as the product of one aspect of proletarianization, with another being seen as the consequence of a quite separate aspect. This problem notwithstanding, Cohen's account is valuable in drawing attention to forms of behaviour that have been little studied and in relating them to material factors in the development of the production process. As Cohen argues, desertion from capitalist organizations is too easily seen as 'pre-industrial' behaviour instead of as a rational response reflecting the type of labour control imposed on new industrial workers. The patterning of behaviour, moreover, reflects employers' activities as well as those of workers. Thus Cohen shows that tribal dances were altered in the light of workers' new circumstances. They were permitted by management as a form of what Cohen calls repressive tolerance, that is, as activities which allowed workers to express their discontents but which simultaneously meant that protest was channeled into such harmless forms and that workers acquiesced in the system of domination as a whole.

The ways in which behaviour contained elements of rejection of, as well as accommodation to, the capitalist system are thus illustrated. The importance of previous traditions in the development of social relations in the capitalist workplace is also clear. These points may now be pursued in more detail with reference to the European case.

Changing Forms of Collective Protest

Perspectives on worker protest have been transformed over the past twenty years. Few writers would now endorse the view that protests involved a series of 'negative reactions and responses to the impact of industrialization' and that conflict during early industrialization tends 'to consist of short-term incidents and to involve spontaneous fights, riots, demonstrations, violence, and mob action' (Kerr *et al.*, 1973: 200, 212). Riots and violence there certainly were. But these are no longer seen as spontaneous outbursts reflecting pent-up frustration with destruction of the old order. Instead, they are viewed as rational uses of the available resources which were governed by a web of rules. In an essay originally published in 1952, Hobsbawm (1964: 7) coined the celebrated term 'collective bargaining by riot' to describe the machine-breaking which took place in the Midlands and north of England between 1811 and 1813 and which goes under the label of Luddism. Much of the destruction involved no hostility to machinery as such but was among the normal means of putting pressure on employers in pursuit of collective demands. Hobsbawm noted the use of direct action against employers during the eighteenth century, and subsequent research (summarized by Stevenson, 1979: 113–35) has elaborated on the picture. The destruction of property was not random, as would be expected on the view that protest was spontaneous and unorganized; instead, targets were carefully selected. Similarly, violence was not the prerogative of the desperate and poorly organized members of the workforce but tended to be used by groups of skilled workers in order to exert pressure on their employers.

Considering eighteenth-century disturbances more generally, E. P. Thompson (1971) has argued against the view that there was a direct connection between economic distress and protest. The view that crowd behaviour was a direct and irrational response to hunger was for Thompson (p. 136) the product of the new political economy which reduced human activities to the cash nexus. There was, in fact, an identifiable 'moral economy' of the poor, based on a consistent view of the rights and obligations of the members of the community. Direct action occurred when customary expectations based on this moral economy were breached. It has been argued that the concept of a moral economy may become too rigid, since many changes in customary arrangements occurred either well before the outbreak of riots or without any popular protest at all (Stevenson, 1979: 311). This argument seems to be based on a misconception. Thompson is arguing that a moral economy was one of the crucial factors intervening between material distress and protest, and not that it was the only influence at work. To argue that protests involved the mobilization of a moral economy is not to imply that it was always mobilized or that it was rigid and unchanging.

The importance of the work of Hobsbawm, Thompson and many others lies in its demonstration of the rationality of protest. Riots were not negative or disorganized. It is true that they were backward-looking in the sense that customary obligations were upheld as the proper basis of conduct, but this was not a blind clinging to the past but a reference to established ways of doing things which had worked well and whose defence was directly in the interests of the rioters. Yet there is a danger, or more precisely a limitation, in at least some of the new social history of workers' protest. This is the explicit or implicit acceptance that patterns of conflict eventually become rationalized or modernized. The characterization of 'early' forms of protest as spontaneous and negative is decisively rejected, and the development of modern forms based on collective bargaining and the strike is seen not as a smooth and inevitable process but as a long and messy battle. But whatever the reasons, the outcome, namely routine wage bargaining which does not challenge the capitalist order as a whole, is seen in terms which are essentially similar to those employed by the older school of writers. The following discussion attempts a slightly different perspective.

The Benchmark of Modernity
It is first necessary to establish that there has been a tendency to take as a starting point a distinctly 'modern' form of industrial action

against which more traditional actions can be measured. Hobsbawm (1964: 344–70) implied as much in his well-known discussion of the ways in which workers learned the 'rules of the game': there was a partial learning of the rules during the middle of the nineteenth century, whereby workers learned to see labour as a commodity to be sold but still fixed the asking price according to non-economic criteria, which was followed by a complete learning towards the end of the century, with workers demanding what the traffic would bear. Rudé (1981: 5) distinguishes between pre-industrial and industrial forms of protest, dating the change at around 1840. Shorter and Tilly (1974: 15–18) identify three types of strike corresponding to the development of industry from an artisan base through mass-production to science-based technologies. Geary (1981: 38) argues that modern industrial protest 'was no longer directed against industrial society as such but against either conditions of work within it or against the structures of authority and ownership. In short, it ceased to be backward-looking'. And Stevenson (1979: 67) notes that rioting tended to give way to other forms of protest which were appropriate as large-scale and anonymous relations replaced the direct face-to-face social relations of an earlier age.

There are plainly several different propositions involved here. The major distinction is that between writers who identify a contrast between pre-industrial and industrial forms of protest and those who consider changing patterns of protest within the latter category. But the logic of the analysis is identical. An ideal-typical contrast is drawn up between two, or sometimes three, stages, and the modern stage is often treated as the unproblematic foil for the investigation of an earlier stage and of the processes by which modernity was created. Some things about the procedure are unobjectionable. It is true that food riots, for example, waned in popularity during the early nineteenth century. It is also important to try to reconstruct the past on its own terms and without the 'enormous condescension of posterity', to use another celebrated phrase (Thompson, 1968: 13). Yet there is the danger of treating the 'modern' period as self-evident and unproblematic. An uncertainty over the characteristics of this period is reflected in the widely varying dates which are put on its beginnings. What tends to happen is that an author studying a particular period draws the analysis to a close by saying, in effect: this is how matters worked out, and afterwards the people in question were in the modern period and their behaviour fitted into our understanding of modernity which is so familiar as to require no special attention.

The key difficulty is the failure to treat capitalist development as a continuous process in which certain features have remained constant.

The most important of these is the inherent uncertainty of the labour contract and the impossibility of the capitalist's gaining complete control over the expenditure of labour power. Consider, however, the view of Stedman Jones (1975: 50): 'the transition from "formal" to "real" capitalist control over production was a long and bitter process – and even in the leading sectors of the economy was only partially achieved by the end of the Chartist period'. The implication is plainly that the real subordination of labour was eventually achieved. As argued at length in earlier chapters, this implication needs to be strenuously avoided. The 'modern' period is not all institutionalized bargaining based on a fundamental acceptance of the capitalist order, and real subordination is, in the strict sense of the term, impossible.

It is, of course, true that labour is subordinated to capital and that changes have occurred in the nature of this subordination and in the character of workers' protests. Something has changed over the century and a half since a trade unionist wrote in 1833 that the unions 'will ultimately ABOLISH WAGES, become their own masters and work for each other: labour and capital will no longer be separate but will be indissolubly joined together' (quoted in Thompson, 1968: 912). The change is a decline in the degree of open questioning of the basic principles of capitalist political economy, together with a learning of the 'rules of the game'. But it is necessary to keep separate two things which have tended to be conflated in discussion of whether or not there was a distinct class consciousness among workers in early nineteenth-century England. The first is the analytical issue of whether relations between master and servant can be analysed in class terms, that is as exploitative relations around the production of surplus value. The second is whether the language of class was used explicitly at the time, and by what groups, how far a specifically working-class consciousness had developed, and what possibilities were open for struggles with employers to grow into overtly class-based actions.

As will be seen in more detail below, Thompson's work, together with that of writers such as Foster (1974), suggested that there was a growing awareness of class, that a working-class identity was emerging, and that, in some cases at least, class action was occurring on a considerable scale. Critical reaction to this thesis has stressed, by contrast, the sectional and occupationally based character of many struggles, the importance of large groups which did not become involved in class actions, and the weakness of explicitly class-based movements. As Rule (1984) has pointed out in a survey of recent historiography, this revisionist approach tends to deny that class consciousness had any role and to imply that a working class did not really exist. The present approach, which applies as much to the 'modern' period as to earlier times, avoids this difficulty by separating the theoretical analysis of work relations from consideration of the experience of class. There is no inconsistency between arguing that capitalist relations of production began to emerge, and thus that the terms capitalist and wage-labourer became increasingly applicable, and suggesting that, because of the historical context in which capitalism emerged, class consciousness was often limited. As Rule puts it, there was a labour consciousness, that is a consciousness of labour as against capital in which the distinctive interests of the two 'sides' were recognized, even though this need not imply that different labour consciousness arising from different contexts necessarily cohered to form a view of class unity.

Thompson's (1978: 149) statement of the position cannot be bettered:

> classes do not exist as separate entities, look around, find an enemy class, and then start to struggle. On the contrary, people find themselves in a society structured in determined ways (crucially, but not exclusively, in productive relations), they experience exploitation (or the need to maintain power over those whom they exploit), they identify points of antagonistic interest, they commence to struggle around these issues and in the process of struggling they discover themselves as classes.

In looking at patterns of conflict, then, the question is not whether or not classes existed but how relationships were interpreted and what means were used to pursue collective demands and how these means changed.

There are, moreover, important continuities in the ways in which conflict has been expressed. These tend to become lost in discussions of the modernization of protest. Price (1982) has pointed to some of the very close parallels between some of the 'problems' of the post-1945 industrial relations system and practices in earlier periods, notably the 1890s. He notes the ahistorical way in which developments since the Second World War, or perhaps more precisely since 1960, have been seen as unique. In fact, the 'problems' of restrictive practices, informal shopfloor organization, attempts to control overtime, and demands for job security all have long histories. For Price, there is a dynamic relationship between resistance and subordination; workplace struggles should not be dismissed for being 'spontaneous', 'economistic', or whatever. Price's argument can be generalized to the development of forms of conflict over the broader sweep of capitalist development. Although precise parallels, such as attempts by workers to control the amount or distribution of overtime, may not be in evidence, it can be suggested that there has been a basic similarity of content in workers' actions. This has been the attempt to influence the terms on which labour-power is utilized. Different forms of behaviour have obviously been used as the technical and social relations of production have developed. But changes in form should not be used to infer that workers' whole approach to work has been modernized and rationalized. Some weapons have become inappropriate while others have developed, but the difference between the twentieth-century factory worker and eighteenth-century artisan may not be as great as it is sometimes portrayed: each would understand what the other was trying to do, even though some of the problems encountered and means used to overcome them would seem strange.

Organization and Collective Action

The literature on changing patterns of protest may, then, be reviewed not in terms of a drift to modernity but with respect to two questions: how relations of production altered such that patterns of worker behaviour also changed, and how differing forms of protest reflected different means to similar ends. An initial difficulty, however, is that research has naturally concentrated on the protests themselves, the rules governing their conduct and so on, and not on the organization of work out of which they developed. Some studies, looking specifically at work relations during the eighteenth and early nineteenth centuries have, however, begun to appear (e.g. Rule, 1981; Fisher, 1981; Dobson, 1980; Sewell, 1980). And other studies looking at incidents of conflict have located these incidents in the context of work organization.

The first and most obvious point is that labour disputes formed a small proportion of the total number of popular disturbances at least until the early nineteenth century. In Rudé's (1981) classic work, for example, only two out of twelve chapters on specific episodes are devoted to labour disputes. In the countryside food riots were the main form of activity, while in the towns a wide range of political and religious issues were also likely to provoke riots. Stevenson (1979: 306) cites research showing that in England between 1790 and 1810 labour riots came a poor fourth in frequency behind food riots, disturbances against impressment and the militia, and political riots. It was only gradually that the focus of protest shifted from consumer-oriented actions such as food riots to producer-oriented ones such as strikes and machine-breaking. The decline of the food riot appears to have reflected several influences. The proximate ones included improved methods of food distribution. But underlying them was a change in the character of economic and social organization. Rudé (1981: 226), for example, stresses the notions of justice which informed many of the actions of the eighteenth-century crowd: custom had established a just price for basic commodities, and breaches of customary expectation led to attempts to impose a just price through direct action such as attacks on warehouses. As the new political economy based on the 'laws' of supply and demand emerged, the concepts of a just price and a just wage waned in their relevance. Consumer protest tended to disappear.

The rarity of labour protests is not, of course, to suggest that production relations were necessarily harmonious. But three sorts of influences help to explain the rarity. The first involved the small scale of production and the dispersal of workers between many different workshops. This must have militated against the development of collective organization. The second factor was the way in which work was controlled. Divisions between managers and employees were often unclear, and customary understanding affected work relations as well as prices, not just in terms of wage levels but also regarding the hours of work, accepted standards of workmanship, and the organization of work tasks (see Rule, 1981; Holbrook-Jones, 1982). Third, as Bezucha (1979) demonstrates in the case of silk workers in Lyons, many of the main lines of division lay not between masters and journeymen but between these two groups, as direct producers, and merchants. The potential for conflict between masters and workers was not absent, but it was constrained by several influences which meant that overt disputes about the terms of the effort bargain were rare.

Customary and informal arrangements do not mean that there was no control over work or that control lay in the hands of the masters. As Rule in particular demonstrates, in trades such as hatting, tailoring, shoe-making, and shipbuilding combinations of workers developed considerable influence over the conduct of work during the eighteenth century. By 1810 tailors' employers were complaining of 'arbitrary and oppressive laws' imposed on the trade by the unions (Rule, 1981: 152; Dobson, 1980: 17), and customary workgroup controls over discipline and similar matters were established in several trades. It would thus be a mistake to infer from the absence of continuity of workers' organizations that they were ephemeral and insignificant. The Webbs' famous definition of a trade union as a 'continuous association of wage-earners' (S. and B. Webb, 1920: 1) fails to fit the case because it assumes that continuity of formal organization is important if unions are to assert a permanent challenge to management. But during the eighteenth century formal organization arose as

it was needed to pursue a particular dispute. There was no need for continuous associations because customary rules operated for much of the
time and informal organization could sustain a substantial control
over the trade.[2]

The violence surrounding many labour disputes should not, then,
be seen as an expression of frustration or spontaneous protest.
Violence was used by the well-organized skilled trades, not as a statement of frustration but as a deliberate bargaining tactic (Stevenson,
1979: 130). Neither should it be inferred that its use was any less
'sophisticated' than the use of the strike weapon by more modern
unionists. Stearns (1974) has attempted to chart the evolution of late
nineteenth-century strike movements in terms of their growing
sophistication, as measured by their size, rate of success, stated issues,
and so on. In particular, unsophisticated actions are held to lack formal
organization and to look to the preservation of existing rights rather
than the creation of new ones. Yet formal organization is a means to
an end, and it is arguable that the need for such organization indicates
a decline in sophistication because workers were no longer able to rely
on customary arrangements but had to band together if they were to
have any chance of resisting the growing power of their employers.
Similarly, it is not clear why it is unsophisticated to try to retain
customary arrangements. In some ways eighteenth-century workers
had a degree of job control which was more developed than that of
their more 'modern' followers. They had understandings with masters
over the conduct of work, and only when these understandings were
breached was it necessary for them to engage in overt protest. Such
protest, moreover, was purposeful and deliberate and seems to have
been used when the workers' bargaining power was greatest (Rule,
1981: 178).

The last point is of some significance, for it is often assumed that
'early' workers' movements responded blindly to economic conditions, protesting when circumstances were worst and when the chances
of victory were slimmest; it was only later, and in particular with the
rise of permanent trade unions during the latter half of the nineteenth
century, that workers have been felt to have the organization to use
the strike tactically by waiting until periods of prosperity to try to
enforce their demands. Such a view is often implicit, and sometimes

2 The need for issue-specific organizations has not disappeared. It is still common in
large disputes for strike committees to be set up to handle picketing and so forth. (I am
grateful to Paul Marginson for this point.) Not only does this indicate a further line of
continuity between past and present. It also shows that, even under modern conditions,
workers' organizations cannot simply swing into action: strategies have to be formulated and workers have to be mobilized.

explicit, as for example in the work of Stearns and a good deal of earlier writing (e.g., for the United States, Commons *et al.*, 1918: 11, 361–3). Given the lack of reliable quantitative data on the incidence of strikes and also on the pattern of business activity, it is impossible to establish whether the correlation between strikes and prosperity was positive or negative. The relationship in more modern periods is, moreover, a matter of some dispute, with by no means all studies finding a positive correlation (see, for example, Durcan *et al.*, 1983: 229–39 for an inverse relationship between strikes and prosperity, that is a positive correlation with unemployment levels, in Britain in the period 1946–73). It seems unlikely, however, that workers in the well-organized trades of the eighteenth century would be unaware of the tactical advantages of using periods of prosperity to press their demands, and, as noted above, Rule has provided examples of such tactical behaviour.

Three distinctions seem relevant. The first is between the well- and the poorly organized trades, or more elaborately the identification of the degree and character of organization. Although organized workers, that is workers in trades with some collective control of work operations even though this control may well have operated informally, are likely to have had considerable skill in the timing and conduct of their protests, less organized workers are unlikely to have been as fortunate. Hence a clear-cut pattern linking strikes to prosperity should not be expected, for two effects will have been at work: the pro-cyclical activity of the organized and the counter-cyclical activity of the unorganized. When further complexities are added, notably the fact that a given trade may be well-organized in some parts of the country but not in others and the presence of many mediating influences which would prevent any one-to-one correspondence between economic conditions and levels of protest, it is apparent that any overall picture will be highly complex. Even in the case of food disturbances, which might be expected to chart the activities of the 'unorganized', it has been found that the relationship between price levels and the number of protests was far from straightforward: high prices did not necessarily lead to disturbances, for example when people were expecting a fall in prices and thus saw no purpose in protest (Stevenson, 1979: 106–8).

Second, different types of protest must be distinguished. Thus it has been argued for the 'modern' period that strikes during prosperity will be frequent but brief protests to enforce wage demands, while disputes during recessions will be more lengthy battles over more fundamental questions. To the extent that the latter type of protest is more likely to leave a mark on the historical record than is the former, the available data may give a distorted picture. Or, at least, it is easy to see how historians such as Commons and the Webbs, who were predisposed towards permanent unions seeking collective bargaining agreements, looked back over the past and concluded that most protests were of a backward-looking and spontaneous type.

Third, the picture may have changed as capitalism developed. The pre-industrial trades came under increasing pressure from the growth of large-scale industry, and the forms of control which the skilled workers had developed were gradually eroded. These workers may then have begun to emulate the less skilled in their pattern of protest, being forced into costly battles to defend their remaining privileges when their bargaining power was at a minimum. Thus, instead of a process in which the rules of the capitalist game were slowly learnt by the workers, there may have been a more complex development in which old forms of behaviour were rendered inappropriate and a period of 'spontaneous' protest supervened before a renewed learning of the rules took place. In addition, it would not have been a matter of intellectual appreciation of tactics which the notion of learning implies. The idea of using one's power when circumstances are propitious is too obvious to require much learning. It was, rather, a matter of the presence of conditions which permitted the lesson to be put into effect. When workers had the organization to sustain tactical behaviour they acted accordingly. When they were put on the defensive, being faced with the options of giving in silently or putting up a probably hopeless struggle, they sometimes chose one course, and sometimes the other. They had not forgotten tactical lessons, but found them hard to apply in the circumstances.

The Case of the Swing Riots

Before looking more closely at the ways in which workers' workplace behaviour altered, it will be useful to consider one specific incident to illustrate some of the more general points being made. This example is the series of riots and attacks on agricultural machinery which occurred in Southern England in 1830 and which go under the name of the Swing riots, on account of the anonymous threatening notes sent to farmers and signed by 'Captain Swing'. This case has been chosen because the best study of Swing (Hobsbawm and Rudé, 1969) demonstates clearly some themes of general relevance: the rationality of protest, the connections between broad trends in production relations and specific influences in the generation of the action, and the role of the activities of employers and the state.

Central to the account of Hobsbawm and Rudé is the demonstration that English agriculture in the period up to 1830 was going through a series of changes which altered the social relations of production. It was these changes which laid the basis for widespread protest. Thus the authors argue (especially pp. 15, 42–6) that agricultural workers were increasingly proletarianized from about 1750. The process was not one of the creation of a rural proletariat, for that already existed, but of the increasing proletarian character of the workforce as the long boom in agriculture strengthened the cash nexus and reduced the role of customary rights. Specific changes included the growing importance of cereal crops which did not require year-round attention and which helped to transform the worker into a casual labourer. In addition, the upward trend of prices encouraged farmers to sell as much of their produce as they could and to pay their workers in cash and not in kind. When the agricultural boom burst, the workers were trapped in poverty. The crisis of 1828–30 increased discontent, which was further heightened by revolutions in Europe and the domestic political upheavals around parliamentary reform.

Given this background, it took only a few minor incidents to spark off a series of riots. As Hobsbawm and Rudé demonstrate, rioting was concentrated in the areas where proletarianization and poverty were most acute, that is in the south-eastern counties of England, where cereal farming was combined with low wages. They also show how different forms of protest were related. For example, one image of the riots is of an upsurge of spontaneous violence, involving arson, machine-breaking, and other attacks on property. But the authors show (pp. 200–3) that arson and machine-breaking tended to occur at different places and times: arson rarely took place when a mass movement was at its peak and, although it was a clear expression of the workers' grievance, it was at the fringe and not the heart of the movement. As Dunbabin (1974: 30) comments on rural protest in general, a great deal of rick-burning reflected personal discontents and not political protest. Yet such personal discontent was obviously fuelled by the sort of social changes charted by Hobsbawm and Rudé. Although it should not be assumed that incidents of arson were always deliberate and self-conscious protests, such events can be seen as indirect indicators of the depth of rural despair and as reflections of changing social relations. The behaviour should be seen neither as a simple individual action nor as a manifestation of a collective will, but as the indirect product of tensions in the countryside. The point about the Swing riots was that they began to move away from individual acts towards more collective demands for better wages. After the collapse of the Swing movement, incendiarism continued and public protests became relatively insignificant (Hobsbawm and Rudé, 1969: 284).

Several general points emerge from this example. First, there is the use of different forms of protest at different times: 'protest' was not a random or spontaneous activity. Second, there is the marked contrast with some of the organized urban trades discussed above which, while lacking formal trade unions, had a good deal of collective organization. Agriculture represented the unorganized majority, for whom there were no established channels of bargaining and whose protests were therefore pushed into other modes of expression. The Swing riots are a particularly good example of the way in which the protests of the unorganized reflected poverty and distress and tended to occur at times of hardship and not prosperity. But the riots were not simply 'spontaneous': they reflected the build-up of tensions over a long period, and they represented one of the few outlets of expression left to the workers. This raises the question of the eventual development of agricultural trade unionism in the 1870s (described by Groves, 1981, for example). It is plain that unionism put the expression of discontent on a more organized footing. As Dunbabin (1974: 69–70) comments, periods of unrest during the latter part of the nineteenth century tended to occur when wages were rising, for example in 1872–4 and 1890–2, and not in recessions. But the process was slow: Dunbabin notes that arson continued until well into the 1880s, with isolated outbreaks occurring as late as 1914. More generally, unionism obviously helped workers to develop organized forms of action. But it did not imply that earlier agricultural protests had lacked rationality. It was simply that in the circumstances of increasing hardship workers could accept their lot or turn to the few weapons at their disposal.

Finally, the role of farmers should be noted. Hobsbawm and Rudé stress that, although the farmers were the main victims in the Swing riots, the rural community was sympathetic to the workers' plight, and farmers generally tried to make the clergy and landlords bear the costs of the labourers' demands. There was no rigid division of interests. As noted above, a similar point applied to many urban trades where the major cleavage was not necessarily between masters and journeymen. Class relations took time to develop and solidify, and traditional relationships retained a powerful role.

The Rules of the Game
The development of unionism in agriculture was a slow process, suffering many reverses. In other trades, however, there were by the late nineteenth century some well-established workers' organizations. As noted above, Hobsbawm, following the Webbs, has seen in this development a learning of the rules of the game wherein workers ceased to rely on custom to challenge employers and used the logic of the

capitalist market to advance their own interests. The discussion of the organized trades of the late eighteenth century has already suggested that, instead of a one-stage movement from ignorance (or denial) of rules to their acceptance, there may have been a two-stage process in which the rules of organization appropriate to pre-capitalist trades were replaced with the new rules of the capitalist market (notably that labour-power was a commodity whose price should be fixed by the market and not by customary arrangements), which only then were learned. The question of how far the new rules had, indeed, been established by the late nineteenth century now requires attention.

Price (1980: esp. 144–58) has addressed this question in detail in the course of his study of building workers and their relations with their employers. He accepts that there probably was a shift away from customary behaviour towards a more 'economistic' approach. In view of the many meanings of the term 'economism' it needs some definition. For present purposes it can be taken as a shorthand way of referring to all the ways in which the terms of the employment relationship can be reduced to monetary bargains. For example, a traditional standard setting the length of the working day according to some conception of what was right and proper might be rendered economistic through an employer's claim that there was no logic in the standard and workers' agreement to monetary compensation for working overtime: a customary control would have become something limited to the price of labour-power. Price accepts that economistic approaches grew in the building industry. He cites such things as controls on overtime and masons' rules over the use of stone which had already been worked on before delivery to a building site as cases in which, from the 1860s, economistic definitions grew, with struggles for power being translated into financial terms. But he argues that there was no natural drift whereby economic man replaced customary man. He accuses Hobsbawm and the Webbs of three errors: failing to explain the trends which occurred; not dealing with the links between customary and economistic behaviour; and assuming that the shifts which occurred reflected forces that were purely internal to the working class (p. 130).

The first and third points amount to the same thing: Hobsbawm and the Webbs did not advance specific explanations of the trend towards economism because they assumed that the reason lay in a tendency internal to workers' organizations, namely the learning of the new rules of the game. In place of this assumption, Price argues that economism reflected changing patterns of relations between workers and the building masters. In broad terms, there was a shift away from an unformalized system, in which the power of individual groups of workers was considerable, towards a formalized system of codified rules and procedures. For Price, formalization reflected employers' attempts to establish their own control of the terms on which work was carried out, as against the powerful controls traditionally exercised by the members of the skilled trades. Economism reflected, not learning, but the structural constraints of the emerging system of industrial relations.

On the second point, the links between customary and economistic actions, Price argues that there was no rigid division between the two. He suggests, for example, that there was nothing new in the 'economistic' idea of assessing what the market would bear when making wage demands; what was new were the terms on which an assessment could be made and the rationales that could be used to justify it. Restrictive practices continued to exist: 'old forms are not displaced but co-exist with the new. It is the context in which they are translated and mediated that is different' (Price, 1980: 157). Indeed, Price argues, such practices have continued to exist down to the present day, but they are now, as a result of the further formalization of the industrial relations system, illegitimate and outside the system.

As a general statement, Price's argument has a great deal to commend it. Changes in the form and significance of workers' workplace behaviour are related to developments in workplace relations and not to some untheorized notion of learning. As noted earlier, Price (1982, 1983) has written some more general essays which bring together the concerns of labour history and writings on industrial sociology and the labour process. In particular, he has pointed to the continuities between present-day and historical actions and to the dangers of assuming a development from the formal to the real subordination of labour.

Yet there are some qualifications to be entered. In organizing his analysis around the tensions between 'freedom' and 'control', Price implies that workers naturally preferred the former and that the development of the latter, through both employers' attempts to regain control and the operation of trade unions within formal collective bargaining arrangements, tended to infringe on this freedom. This perspective is inclined to minimize the dialectical aspects of any pattern of work organization. In a pattern based on 'freedom', for example, potential workers' interest in developing forms of solidarity which went beyond the confines of a particular craft were not realizable. Similarly, although economism can be analysed in terms of a reduction of a struggle for control to merely financial matters, it is also true that higher wages bring concrete benefits and that achieving a high level of detailed control of work operations is not necessarily or obviously always in workers' interests. This is not to suggest that Price engages in a simple critique of trade union bureaucracy or formal agreements as such. He has, in fact, been accused of adopting a position which 'may with only a little injustice be described as "workerism"', (Joyce, 1983: 240). A consideration of workerism in general will be given below, but in Price's case the accusation means an exaggeration of the workers' desire for freedom and an unduly negative view of formal procedures. The accusation as such does not stand up. Price's concern is to challenge a conventional wisdom that collective bargaining marked a stage in the long and successful march of the labour movement and that economism was a natural and right form of behaviour. He does not necessarily argue for an opposite position in which all aspects of custom are unambiguously defended. Yet one can see how the accusation arises. A tendency to treat freedom and control as opposites and a lack of critical analysis of what 'freedom' implied permit readers looking for workerism to find it.

A second qualification concerns the place of present-day 'restrictive practices'. It is questionable whether they are always completely illegitimate. It is true that various working practices have been either removed or altered from being established parts of an industry's arrangements to tenuous and formally illicit practices. Montgomery (1979: 116) makes the point with reference to American engineering firms during the 1920s: 'the customary craftsman's stint had been an overt and deliberate act of collective regulation by workers who directed their own productive operations. The group regulation which replaced it was a covert act of disruption of management's direction of production'. But such covert acts have varying degrees of legitimacy. The contemporary literature on custom and practice, on which Price draws, shows that formally illicit rules can develop a good deal of authority and that management may have to recognize their legitimacy (W. Brown, 1973).

Consider, for example, the case of one factory in which shop stewards had developed substantial controls of overtime and recruitment, among other things (P. Edwards and Scullion, 1982a: chs 7 and 8; the factory is described under the pseudonym of the Small Metals Factory). The controls could be described as having a craft or craft-like basis. Notions of craft tend to be applied rather haphazardly, but Price has himself attempted a more precise approach: craft control involves one or more of three elements. These are a clearly defined handicraft tradition; managerial acceptance of the legitimacy of craft controls, on account of the power to restrict entry or the possession of genuine skills; and a distinctive ability to do jobs not possessed by other workers and acquired through recognized channels of training

(Price, 1980: 10–11). There is some circularity in the second and third elements. Managerial acceptance of controls, in particular, may be a consequence of the existence of the controls and not one of their defining characteristics. There are also numerous problems with the identification of 'genuine' skill, for definitions of skill are often tied up with social definitions of what is really skilled work. But it is reasonably clear what is being discussed.

In the present case, union organization in the factory was based on skill above all other considerations: the dominant trade union had initially recruited only workers who had been through an apprenticeship. It slowly broadened its recruitment to include workers doing ancillary operations, but these workers were organized in a separate ancillary section. Although they had their own shop stewards, the senior stewards of each shop could come only from the skilled section. The line dividing skilled from unskilled work was based on the ability to use certain tools of the trade such as files and hammers. There was, in short, a defined craft tradition, with recognized channels of training, as provided via apprenticeship, and a range of controls which management recognized as legitimate. Perhaps most significant was the control of recruitment. The factory made a range of metal components which were sold to other plants, and it suffered from large fluctuations in demand. Recruitment controls were used to control these fluctuations. The stewards refused to permit management to recruit new labour unless they were convinced that the likely level of demand justified this. In addition, they exerted considerable influence over the selection of recruits: they provided lists of names of workers, and management could not bring in other workers. These controls, together with other controls of overtime and manning levels, were exercised openly and were firmly established within the practice of the plant. Whether management saw them as legitimate, in the sense of accepting their correctness, is questionable. But they were certainly accepted as something that had to be lived with. In short, craft controls are not always illegitimate or marginal in the modern era.

This is to support the tenor of Price's overall argument, while qualifying some aspects of its application. Once notions of the real subordination of labour are abandoned, and once patterns of workplace relations are seen in terms of a dialectical relationship between capital and labour, there is no need to invoke arguments about learning the rules of the game. 'Customary' forms of work organization have not disappeared. Indeed, informal means of determining the conditions on which labour-power is transformed into labour are essential. Such means may have changed in significance, and the rise of large bureaucratic corporations may have reduced the power of custom.

But it would be wrong to suppose that it had been destroyed or that 'modern' industrial relations are different in kind, and not just degree, from earlier forms.

Individual Action

Attention has so far concentrated on collective actions such as strikes and riots, and on the nature of collective organization to which they gave rise. Yet more individual forms of action also warrant attention, for they may have had a more consistent effect on workplace relations than the relatively rare outbursts of collective protest. It has, for example, become something of a truism that a pre-industrial work force lacks the habit of regular attendance at work and that high labour turnover and absenteeism are endemic. Studies of developing countries have pointed to some of the problems (e.g. Morris, 1965). Yet two problems make an assessment of the argument difficult. First, much more attention has been paid to collective actions, for the simple reason that they are more prominent and raise more appealing issues about workers' consciousness and class action. Second, to the extent that evidence on such things as labour turnover is available, the implications of the evidence are far from obvious. A high rate of turnover can point to several influences in addition to 'protest', and it would be dangerous to infer that workers quitting their jobs were rejecting the work norms of the nascent capitalist system. Some more general propositions as to how the behaviour should be viewed may, however, be put forward.

Most generally, firms lacked elaborate bureaucracies of hiring and firing procedures, personnel policies, and works rules. The notions of attendance and absence, staying and quitting, were thus less clearly defined than they are now. Employees leaving a firm now routinely hand in their notice; similarly, absenteeism is a recognized and much-discussed managerial problem. When employment relationships were less codified, absence and turnover were less meaningful categories. A worker might move between employers according to the availability of work without this movement being seen as 'labour turnover'. Similarly, to the extent that employers did not try to enforce attendance at specified times, the notion of absenteeism lacked precision.

Employers slowly began to enforce work rules. As the classic studies by Pollard (1965) and E. P. Thompson (1967) demonstrated, rhythms of work determined by the harvest and the hours of daylight were replaced by a new time discipline established by the clock. Employers tried to enforce regular attendance at specified hours, and developed means of record-keeping to do so. It should not, however, be assumed that this was a natural or smooth process. In their rise to the status of classics, some of the key messages of these studies have been lost. Hence, discussions of Thompson (e.g. by Giddens and Held, 1982: 281–2) focus on his analysis of how time ceased to be 'task-oriented' and became dominated by industrial rhythms. But Thompson (1967: 80) is clear that he is not presenting a technologically determinist model in which the needs of industry simply destroyed pre-industrial modes of work: countries such as Britain in the eighteenth century had developed sets of social relations which cannot simply be characterized as 'pre-industrial'; and there has never been a single type of transition to industrialism. In addition, it was not a matter of a rise of industrialism in general but of industrial capitalism in particular. The imposition of time-discipline reflected the demands of a developing capitalist economy in which employers needed to challenge workers' control of their own time: it was not a rational process but was one of lengthy struggle.

Traditional modes of work were, moreover, slow to disappear. Thompson argues that it took many generations for new work rhythms to be established. Reid (1976) has shown in his study of Birmingham how the tradition of 'Saint Monday' persisted into the late nineteenth century, and even until the early twentieth century in a few places. The tradition reflected the long-established habit of not working on Mondays. In Birmingham by the 1840s it had become a recognized institution, to the extent that day excursions on the railways and cheap admission to the Botanical Gardens were arranged on Mondays. By the 1860s the tradition was being condemned by employers. This reflected, says Reid, the introduction of steam power in many of the city's industries. It was no longer possible for employers to tolerate Saint Monday. But it survived in the unmechanized workshops, and also where workers opposed the employers: unanimous opposition was sometimes sufficient to defeat the employers. Not surprisingly it was the skilled workers who were most able to sustain such opposition. How, then, were these workers persuaded to acccept the new time-discipline of the factory? Reid (pp. 93–7) identifies four main factors. The schools were important in inculcating into children notions of 'time thrift'. There was a lack of political opposition to employers in Birmingham, so that their authority was strengthened. Steam power was often sub-let, so skilled workers were sometimes induced to impose time-discipline on themselves. And increased demands for consumption, as expressed, for example, through the building societies movement, encouraged workers to expand their horizons and to reduce their preferences for leisure. There was thus a rift between skilled artisans; or, more precisely, there was an ambiguity within artisan culture, with old desires for traditional ways of working coming into conflict with 'modern' conceptions inculcated by the schools and strengthened through consumerist demands.

The results of this study have considerable wider significance. The role of the schools is one illustration of the more general argument developed by Lazonick (1978) that capitalism exerted distinctive pressures on educational and religious traditions: the capitalist mode of production exerted a strong and empirically demonstrable effect on the rest of society. The divisions between artisans in Birmingham exemplify the point that the working class is not an objective and homogenous entity but is instead a product of concrete experiences; these experiences may encourage class solidarity but will not necessarily do so. More fundamentally, there was a division within one stratum of the class, the artisans: artisan consciousness reflected contradictory demands and was not shaped simply by 'resistance' to capital or by a preference for old forms of work. This theme has been pursued in great detail by writers such as Crossick (1978) and Gray (1981). The outcome of struggles over Saint Monday was not determined by a straightforward battle between rationalizing employers and workers defending old practices. Workers had complex and contradictory sets of interests, and 'resistance' and 'co-operation' were intertwined. For each individual worker, desires for old ways of working and new consumerist pressures created conflicting currents of thought, and action can be understood only as the result of these complex pressures and not as simple resistance to capitalist domination.

New work disciplines thus came slowly. It is becoming increasingly clear that large-scale bureaucratic modes of control were not imposed overnight. In several industries the practice of 'inside contracting' survived until at least the end of the nineteenth century (Littler, 1982). This arrangement involved the owner of the factory in sub-contracting a section of work to an employee, who in turn recruited, paid, and controlled his own workers. In such circumstances the direct monitoring of workers' attendance by the company as a whole would serve little purpose.

This is not to suggest that attendance was of no interest to management or that workers did as they liked. The prime pressure to attend work was, of course, financial: no work meant no money. In addition, the very strict supervision exercised by foremen ensured that workers attended on time. Williams's (1915) account of work in the Swindon railway shops, for example, makes clear how, as late as the early twentieth century, very intense pressure was put on workers to attend on time and to work as the foremen demanded. Yet such pressure was personal, not bureaucratic, and it is doubtful whether 'absenteeism' was recognized as a distinct managerial problem.

It is possible that labour supply and retention were more important to management than was absenteeism, until quite late in the development of industry. To firms using inside contracting the important thing was to have enough workers, with details of how workers performed being left to the sub-contractor. It is true that traditions such as Saint Monday were attacked, but these traditions reflected a collective and time-honoured way of allocating time between work and leisure. They were not at all the same as casual absenteeism, that is the decision by the individual worker to take a day off. Such traditions were, moreover, part of a system in which workers collectively claimed the right to decide when to work, and it was this collective and general claim which was most insidious from the point of view of managements wanting a supply of labour-power which they themselves could control. One piece of evidence bearing on this relates to the well-known case of Ford and the introduction of the five-dollar day in 1914. The most detailed study of the case (Meyer, 1981: 80–3) confirms the view of other writers that labour turnover was massive: 370 per cent in 1913, that is, the rate of quitting was equivalent to the whole workforce having to be replaced 3.7 times within the course of a year. But it also shows that recorded absenteeism was running at only 10 per cent, which is, by present-day standards, not particularly high. Evidence on the casual nature of much of the turnover is provided by Meyer's breakdown of quits in March 1913: of a total of 7302, 1276 were sacked, 870 left voluntarily, and 5156 left without notice. This last group comprised those who were absent for five days, and were then removed from the payroll. Their preponderance in the turnover figures suggests that workers readily left and shifted between jobs at will. This example is, of course, from a relatively late date in the development of large-scale industry, but it is indicative precisely because of this: obtaining a steady supply of workers did not come easily, and 'modern' forms of recruitment and discipline emerged slowly.

A further factor to take into account is the casual nature of much employment until at least 1914. As Stedman Jones (1984: chs 2–5) has shown in great detail, the labour market in London was dominated by casual labour. Work was often seasonal, and engagements were of very short duration. Workers would move between jobs as work became available, with little attachment to any particular employer or occupation. Although London was probably exceptional in its industrial structure, casual labour was also endemic in other cities as, for example, Roberts's (1973) description of Salford suggests: beneath the stratum of skilled workers in established trades there was a shifting population of labourers who took jobs on a casual basis. For a substantial section of the working class, therefore, turnover and absence remained inapplicable concepts.

The First World War appears to have marked a considerable watershed in the recruitment and control of labour, in Britain and America and probably in other industrialized countries too. An unprecedented shortage of labour forced firms out of their previous lack of concern with labour supply. Close attention began to be given to the problem of turnover and retention, and several pioneering studies of the phenomena were published (e.g. Slichter, 1919; Douglas, 1919). These developments came on top of longer-term trends away from inside contracting and towards a more systematic approach to labour control (Garside and Gospel, 1982: 101–2). The long-term trends and the immediate crisis of the war, with the need for high levels of production, forced employers into a recognition of the need to plan production. The development of personnel management as a specialist function also owed much to the stimulus of the war (Niven, 1967). As employment became stabilized, turnover and absenteeism began to emerge as distinct managerial problems.

When 'individual protest' is seen in this context, it is possible to understand why it is hard to summarize any definite pattern or trend and, indeed, why the term can be misleading. To discern a trend would require not just a measurement of rates of turnover (which does not exist, except in very partial data) but a view as to what those rates signified. For casual employments, the concept is largely meaningless, and even for more stable ones it is not clear how far an observed trend could be taken as evidence of the amount of 'protest' taking place. The substantial amount of evidence concerning employers' attempts to regularize work shows that there was a contradiction between the 'needs' of industry and the character of the workforce. But it should not be inferred from this general point that there was a specific clash such that workers' behaviour could be seen as a deliberate protest or, to use a phrase developed later, a 'withdrawal from the work situation'. More detailed work is needed on patterns of attendance and their significance. A useful starting point would be a re-examination of studies of motivation and morale carried out during and after the First World War, when the need to analyse the 'problem' first came into sharp relief. Prominent in the analysis of health and fatigue in Britain, for example, were the Health of Munition Workers Committee of 1915–17, and its successor body, the Industrial Fatigue Research Board, established in 1918.[3]

3 The work of these bodies is described by Vernon (1940). Their concern was to relate turnover, absenteeism and accidents to such things as fatigue, hours of work, and

Despite the difficulties, there are some specific studies dealing with turnover and absence, three of which are particularly useful for present purposes. The first two refer to Germany during the second half of the nineteenth century, but they contain more general implications for the consideration of 'individual' protests, even though their precise conclusions may not apply elsewhere. Schofer (1975) has investigated the formation of a modern labour force during the industrialization of Upper Silesia. He suggests, echoing arguments about workers learning the rules of the game, that during the 1870s and 1880s turnover may have reflected a reaction against factory discipline by workers unaccustomed to industry, whereas by the 1890s there was a core of industrial workers, for whom turnover was a response to better wages elsewhere (p. 122). That is, the amount of quitting may not have changed, but its significance as a form of protest altered from being a reaction against industry as such to being a means of improvement within the confines of the industrial economy. Schofer quotes typical rates of turnover in the two industries which dominated the region: in mining, between 25 and 50 per cent of new hires would quit within a year; and in iron smelting there were 11,000 quits in 1901, compared with a total workforce of 18,000. Schofer goes on, however, to qualify the account of turnover as a reaction to industry. There were some groups of workers with long periods of service, high turnover is characteristic of all growing industries and there is no one turnover rate characteristic of an industrial labour force (pp. 126–7). Moreover, as against the view that quitting during early industrialization reflected the inadequacies of workers who were unable or unwilling to accept the needs of industry for regular attendance, Schofer puts the behaviour in context (pp. 128–30). The influence of work conditions on workers' willingness to stay should not be neglected, and employers were prone to exaggerate the costs of the behaviour: the problem was not a lack of labour force commitment but a management which put the blame on workers and was unable to develop an adequate policy on labour relations. Managements similarly complained about absenteeism, although absence rates were not high. Absence and turnover, Schofer concludes, did not necessarily involve a rejection of industry; they could also reflect the behaviour of workers well versed in the methods of industrial life.

These points are echoed in the study by Crew (1979: 109) of the town of Bochum in the Ruhr. Crew notes that in the coal industry

---

lighting and ventilation; there appears to have been no consideration of the possible connections with other forms of worker behaviour. But the fact that 'individual' behaviour was even thought worth study is significant.

workers could afford to take time off work when wages were high. He cites managerial complaints in 1899 at missed shifts and at the fact that Monday was often a complete holiday. The example is of some general significance, for it links earlier traditions such as Saint Monday with later work habits of miners, of whom high absence rates, particularly on Mondays, have remained a characteristic. It casts some light on the alleged tendency for 'early' industrial workers to have a 'backward-sloping supply curve' for labour, that is the tendency for workers to attend work less often as wages rise. The reason for this phenomenon is usually found in the limited earnings aspirations of 'early' industrial workers, the result being that workers preferred leisure to earning more than their wages ceiling. Such a preference need not, however, be a purely 'early' phenomenon, for it can reflect a 'rational' trade-off of wages against leisure as well as an (irrational) withdrawal from work. We need to explain, moreover, why the trade-off exists, that is, why there is a preference for leisure, which the backward-sloping supply curve re-describes but does not explain. Instead of general references to the limited wage horizons of early industrial workers, it is desirable to consider specific aspects of work and the workforce. The particular dangers and exertions of work in the mines are one obvious factor why leisure should be particularly highly prized here. Another is collective organization of the workforce. In the case of Bochum, Crew argues that the miners, unlike other groups, had an occupational community which provided them with the solidarity to create a collective organization and to engage in strikes and other actions. This community may also have enabled them to make absenteeism into a collective and semi-organized activity. Instead of being the immediate response of individual workers to their conditions, it became a means of asserting the demands of workers as a group. And, among workers with a strong sense of community, it would have been far more than a mere negative withdrawal from work, becoming instead a collective means of enjoying leisure.

It is, of course, likely that mining was something of a special case, for a similar sense of occupational community is rare. Yet this is precisely the point. It would be misleading to generalize about the nature of absence and turnover in general, other than to establish the broad arguments that they can have elements of a 'rational' adjustment to industry as well as of an 'irrational' and backward-looking response, and that they can reflect a collective identity outside work as well as a mere negative withdrawal from work. The extent to which they had these various characteristics depended on the organization of the labour process in the trade in question, in particular on workers' occupational solidarity and on the character of employers' strategies for the control of labour. In some cases absence may have reflected a negative reaction and in others it may have represented more of a collective and organized response, and to impose a rigid model on its development would be unwise.

Crew (1979: 146–57) illustrates the role of employers' strategy in relation to labour turnover. Employers in Bochum wanted to gain the co-operation of skilled workers, and deliberately set about the development of welfare and housing schemes to tie workers to them. These schemes were later extended to the unskilled because, according to Crew, employers were concerned about the high costs of turnover. Thus, an attempt to stabilize their skilled workforces, so as to withstand competition for labour from other firms, grew into a more general desire to integrate workers into a community dominated by the firms. The companies had a virtual monopoly of decent low-cost housing, for example. The paternalistic personnel policies which developed, Crew argues, were not a historical throwback but were a rational policy to control labour costs. This argument is wholly consistent with that advanced earlier about labour strategies, namely that paternalism can have a lasting significance and that firms develop many strands tying their workers to them according to the particular circumstances in which they find themselves.

Prude (1983) has examined the New England textile industry, concentrating on the small local mills which, he says, were more typical than the large and more widely studied mills of the bigger cities. He finds that patterns of attendance and quitting reflected a learning of the rules of the game. On attendance, for example, there was at first resistance to working in the hours of darkness during the winter. And quitting ran at very high levels (voluntary turnover of at least 45 per cent per annum was recorded in one village, and it was often much higher). But some workers began to use quitting, not to escape from mill work but as a bargaining lever to improve their position within it (p. 22). By the 1820s some collective forms of activity were emerging, as, for example, in demands for overtime payments: this reflected an acceptance of the industrial order while trying to modify it to their own requirements (pp. 16–17). Although essentially following the argument of Hobsbawm and others, that absence and quitting changed their meanings as workers accepted the basic premises of the industrial system, Prude's work also suggests some modifications. First, 1820 is rather early for workers to have reached Hobsbawm's stage of not resisting industry in principle but of trying to turn it to one's own advantage, particularly when it is recalled that these were not large factories but small, isolated mills. The 'stages' can be highly truncated, and learning the rules of the game is not as lengthy a process as Hobsbawm implies. More generally, 'there developed intricate patterns of give and take . . . [Managers and workers] deciphered – or, more accurately, they created – the rules of the game for being industrial employers and employees' (Prude, 1983: 3). The rules reflected the joint activities of both parties, not the learning of a logic by workers alone. And the patterns of give and take reflected the specific circumstances in which managements and workers operated. For example, the employers failed to deal with the problem of labour supply by introducing yearly contracts, because workers still left and persuaded their new employers to help them recover any wages that they had left behind. More successful was the tacit acceptance that firms would not use the draconian disciplinary codes characteristic of the large factories; they obtained a degree of labour stability in return for giving workers some personal freedom in the workplace.

This very early development of a system of accommodation indicates again the limits of a 'stage' view. Even in early and undeveloped capitalist factories the dual nature of the capital-labour relation was very evident. The idea that employers used labour as a commodity and relied on 'simple' control does not fit cases such as this. The mills had a complex set of relations with their employers. As Prude argues, some of these relations can be described as paternalist, for the welfare of workers was emphasized and the mills had a very personalized administrative structure. But there were also bureaucratic rules regarding attendance, and in contrast to some other cases paternalism did not involve any attempt to exert control over workers' lives outside the factory. It was not a matter of simple control and the use of force or of an integrated paternalist system but of the development of a set of rules, by workers and managers alike, to control the employment relationship. These rules reflected several different strands.

These studies by Schofer, Crew and Prude provide some very powerful insights into 'individual' responses to the growth of capitalism. In addition, that of Crew in particular broadens the analysis to consider social and geographical mobility as aspects of class formation. As Thernstrom (1974: 282) stresses, a considerable degree of stability of membership of classes within a given locality 'would seem to be a minimal necessity if mere complaints are to be translated effectively into class grievances and to inspire collective protest'. Mobility may have significant consequences and, even if the causes of workers' movements may not be directly ascertainable, Thernstrom and others have argued convincingly that quantitative studies of social and geographical mobility can help to assess how far classes existed as stable entities. The matter is thus of importance here, in so far as this mobility can be seen as a means by which discontents were expressed and were thus channeled away from overt protests at the point of production.

Thernstrom's own work (1964, 1973) has certainly pointed to the importance of both forms of mobility in the United States. Its basic conclusion is that the openness and fluidity of American society on which contemporaries placed such store were not as illusory as later commentators have suggested. There were very considerable rates of both geographical and social mobility, and it also appears that there were few rigid barriers in the class structure. If the reasonable assumption is made that those leaving the working class were the most able, then potential leaders of collective class-based organizations were being lost. As Thernstrom admits, it is difficult to be precise about the extent of social mobility, because the method of historical reconstruction, which is based on examining the careers of people living in one locality, necessarily excludes those who left. It is certainly likely that those members of the working class who left did not experience the same rate of upward mobility as those who stayed, and thus that overall social mobility rates would be lower than estimates based on the stayers imply. But, as far as class formation is concerned, the point is less important. Social and geographical mobility together meant that in America the development of collective protest was restrained by the high level of individual mobility. In addition, it may be suggested that a self-reinforcing process developed, whereby mobility undermined collective solidarity, with this lack of solidarity making a strategy of 'exit' and not 'voice' the most rational, which further contributed to mobility.

Crew (1979: 80) concludes from his study of Bochum that social and occupational mobility were lower than they were in a number of American towns and cities. The work of Sewell (1974) on Marseilles has also been used to suggest that stability was rather higher in Europe than it was in America during the late nineteenth century. Comparative research on this question remains rare, however, and interpreters have rightly been cautious of inferring too much from a few, possibly atypical, cases. But it has been established that individual mobility can be a powerful brake on the growth of collective organization and that, in the case of America at least, this possibility was translated into reality, with rapid movement making it hard for a sense of shared grievance to emerge.

The point should not, however, be taken too far. There is no automatic link between a high overall rate of mobility and a lack of organization. It is, for example, possible for rapid turnover of a transient population to co-exist with considerable stability among a core group, whose sense of collective identity may even be increased by the sight of a constant stream of short-service workers. In so far as movement tended to be concentrated among the unskilled, it was possible for fairly stable groups of skilled workers to develop. Movement itself is not, moreover, synonymous with a lack of organization. The tradition of the tramping artisan (Hobsbawm, 1964: ch. 4), for example, was based on the movement of skilled workers around fairly regular routes, and it was a well-organized way of balancing the supply of labour and demand: movement in this case was an expression, and not a denial, of the organized character of a trade.

It would also be a mistake to see those engaged in rapid geographical and occupational mobility as an amorphous mass, lacking commitment to industry. It was certainly difficult for them to develop any sense of stability. But their movement must be seen, not as the product of the survival of pre-industrial habits, but as a reflection of the character of the labour market. When employers took on unskilled labour on a largely casual basis, workers had little choice but to move around. High rates of labour turnover and geographical mobility during the early phases of capitalist expansion are more usefully seen as reflections of the labour markets which emerged and of the conditions of labour within the factories and mines than of the habits and characteristics of the workers themselves. As industry developed, and as the problem of turnover began to worry employers, a range of solutions for the stabilization of the workforce emerged: paternalism was one, and Ford's five-dollar day was another. The available evidence suggests that high rates of turnover persisted until well into the twentieth century, and it may well be that the particular crises of war, with the need to plan war production under unprecedented conditions of labour shortage, was the key factor in the development of personnel policies designed to reduce 'wastage'. It certainly seems implausible to argue that there was a long-term and natural trend towards the 'modernization' of forms of individual behaviour. Early capitalism did not encourage a sense of 'commitment', and, indeed, the development of a market-dominated economy was antithetical to notions of long-term commitment to a particular employer or trade. Turnover and other problems of labour supply reflected the conditions of the labour market, and these conditions lasted far longer than any presumed period during which workers lost their pre-industrial habits and learned the new rules of the game.

Industrial Action and Class Conflict

As already implied, the connection between actions at the level of the workplace and class conflict has to be considered in the light of two points. First, relations at the point of production reflect the character of the mode of production in that struggles for control can be related to the structured antagonism between capital and labour. Such struggles can be called class struggles in the sense that they reflect antagonism between the two basic classes of capital and labour. But, second, it does not follow that there is an inherent tendency for individual groups of capitalists or workers to ally themselves with other groups in a struggle in which the interests of the class as a whole are articulated and mobilized. A third point is the obverse of the second. It is sometimes argued that to focus on relations at the point of production is to neglect other aspects of class formation and to assume that class consciousness will be promoted only by struggles within the workplace. This argument is incorrect, as will be argued below.

The importance of these points may be judged by considering the state of the literature on the history of the working class. One useful example is the study by Glen (1984) of Stockport workers between 1770 and 1830. This makes some very pertinent comments on the nature of collective protest, adding to the work summarized above. Thus Glen (p. 92) shows that the Webbs were wrong to assume that unions were ephemeral and that strikes were desperate struggles interspersed with periods of passivity. But it is, for Glen, equally wrong to see an alienated and united proletariat. Trade unions were well-established, but there were deep splits on grounds of skill, sex and location. No trade endorsed radical politics, any conflict orientation was limited to very specific questions, and the evidence adds up to the view that there was no class-conscious proletariat (p. 284).

This type of argument has been generalized by Joyce (1984) in his response to the attempt by Price (1983) to introduce a labour process perspective to the study of labour history. Joyce's central point is that Price's approach is 'lop-sided' in giving too much attention to class conflict, and not enough to co-operation, and in concentrating excessively on the workplace, to the neglect of wider political questions. This argument appears to be based on something of a misapprehension, and it would be unfortunate if some of the less helpful aspects of the labour process debate were to be re-run among historians. It is possible to see how the misapprehension has arisen for, as noted above, Price has not in general stressed the dual nature of the employment relationship, as involving conflict and compliance.

In addition, the import of concepts from sociology and elsewhere is inclined to cause difficulty.

Joyce and other writers (e.g. Zeitlin, 1983) are keen to root out what they see as workerism or rank-and-fileism. This error was defined by one of the first to raise the charge as 'the belief that the struggle for power at the point of production leads to advances in class consciousness in and of itself and without the intervention of political organization in the working class' (Monds, 1976: 84). It is easy to see how an over-emphasis on conflict and on the workplace can stem from a workerist perspective, if it is followed consistently. But the charge seems to mistake two things which are plainly separate. The first is the analytical statement that the labour process is based on a conflict over the use of labour-power. The second is the assumption or assertion that overt conflict is the sole organizing principle of concrete labour processes and that such conflict is more important than political action. The first argument does not imply the second, as has been argued at length in preceding chapters. It may be the case that certain writers have slipped towards a workerist view, although even that charge is suspect, given the vigorous replies that the accused have made to the accusation.[4] But there is no logical need for a labour process perspective to involve such a view. All that this perspective tries to do is to provide some theoretically grounded account of why the labour process should be seen in terms of conflict, and how co-operation and accommodation can be viewed within this basic framework. To say that the labour process is important is not to say that the labour process is all that is important. In the case of labour history, writers such as Price argue that work itself has been neglected, and set about rectifying this deficiency. This endeavour is not the same as suggesting that relations at the point of production are the sole interest of historical or contemporary investigations.

A further parallel between historiographical and sociological debates is the lack of any articulated position of those who attack workerism or an undue emphasis on the labour process. Joyce, for example, is quite correct to argue that there were pressures towards accommodation as well as conflict in nineteenth-century Britain. He is also right to stress the role of politics in the acceptance by the labour movement of the emerging capitalist system. Yet it is not clear how such points address the theory of workplace relations. The same problem as that facing some of the critics of a labour process perspective in general (see p. 45) arises here: pointing to empirical complexity

---

4 For a devastating reply to the original critique by Monds, see Hinton (1976).

does not advance a theoretical understanding of the connections between conflict and accommodation.

The need for a theoretically based view of the character of workplace relations may be illustrated by reference to some of Joyce's own work. This is particularly important for present purposes, for it helps to show how a view of workplace relations as class relations does not entail the argument that there is a natural tendency for the working class to organize as a class against capitalists. Joyce (1982) examines the links between work and politics in nineteenth-century Lancashire. He argues that a profound stability emerged in Lancashire in which workers, despite their numbers and their apparent interest in opposing bourgeois domination, accepted a political system based on the existing parties and lost any interest in socialism. For Joyce, this reflected an all-pervading 'culture of the factory', which in turn rested on the destruction of craft autonomy in the cotton industry and the establishment by the employers of control over the labour process (p. 80).

There are three problems with this argument. First, Joyce's view that there was a widespread acceptance of the political order, together with a marked deference towards the leaders of that order on the part of the workers, sits oddly with his view that craft control in the factory was destroyed. If their control had been destroyed, workers would surely have been unlikely to internalize the culture of the factory or to accept as legitimate the political authority of the factory owners. Second, the assumption that craft autonomy was destroyed conflicts with Lazonick's (1979, 1981) evidence that, on the contrary, it was flourishing and that Lancashire employers did not root out the spinners' unions or the numerous controls over piecework prices and effort levels that they had developed. Third, Joyce seems to work with the assumption that workplace relations involve conflict or accommodation, but not at the same time. Thus he seems to hold that political deference could emerge only out of an employer's victory in which their power in the factory was established and the possibility of workers' challenges was ruled out. The assumption comes close to the errors of workerism which Joyce wishes to oppose.

All three problems can be resolved if it is recognized that conflict and accommodation are parts of the dialectical nature of workplace relations. It is more likely that workers accepted political structures if their work relations were based on an accommodation over the frontier of control than if the employers were engaged in an offensive to heighten their own control. Thus Lazonick's view that work relations in the Lancashire cotton industry were based on a significant degree of power for the unions does not contradict Joyce's stress on hegemony outside the factory; indeed, it gives Joyce's view a basis which Joyce himself is unable to provide. And the reason for Joyce's problem is his lack of any view of the character of workplace relations. More generally, there is no contradiction between the growth of a political acquiescence among the working class and a continuation of controls over the labour process. Joyce appears to reproduce the response to a labour process perspective which has characterized some writings in industrial sociology: the perspective is assumed to hold that conflict is the general feature of work relations, and it is thus easily rebutted. Once the error of the assumption is removed, the force of the criticism largely disappears.

It would be possible to extend this argument by looking in detail at other areas of dispute between labour historians. But this would be tedious and would not add to the points of analysis already made. A brief indication of the sorts of disputes which might be usefully tackled may, however, be given before rather fuller treatment is given to a study which exemplifies many of the points being advocated here.

The debate between Price and Joyce is part of a much wider discussion of the place of the labour movement in late nineteenth-century Britain, with heated exchanges taking place on whether and how far the working class was 'incorporated' into capitalism; on whether a distinct aristocracy of labour can be identified and, if so, whether the aristocracy was deliberately created by capitalists so as to split the working class; and on the role of political change and an allegedly uniquely flexible political structure in Britain in responding to the challenge from below. Debate on these issues has tended to be conducted in stark terms, with the alternatives being to accept that radicalism was wiped out or to insist that pockets of resistance remained. As Tholfsen (1976: 11–13) argues in his survey of the debate, radicalism did not collapse but persisted in different forms, preserving independence and pride among craftsmen. Hence, he argues, it would be a mistake to ask why there was a rapid shift from a radical and class-conscious working class of the 1840s to an incorporated and compliant class by the 1850s: if radicalism persisted, explanations of the alleged shift are mis-specified because there was no sharp shift.

The present account aims to locate arguments such as Tholfsen's in a theoretical perspective on the capital-labour relation. It would be wrong to equate a decline of political radicalism, as described by Joyce and others, with an acceptance of capitalist authority within the workplace. Struggles for control continued, even if their character altered. By the same token, there is a danger in exaggerating the extent of class consciousness early in the nineteenth century. Workers are located within their own specific relations with their own employers, and they are necessarily divided on grounds of skill, occupation, gender, religion, and regional position. There will be circumstances in which they come together as a class to press class-based demands. But there is no inherent tendency for them to do so. And it is also questionable whether the articulation of demands in class terms means that workers had in mind an alternative form of social organization. It is one thing to use the rhetoric of class to mobilize a strike and another to have an end in view other than the settlement of the strike in terms of its overt demand such as a wage increase. That is, even a considerable awareness of class and a high degree of solidarity do not directly translate into a clear view of how existing social structures are to be altered. These points are familiar enough. But it is hoped that they can be accepted without also accepting the whole of the 'conservative' or revisionist account of class, namely the account which virtually denies that class is useful as an analytical category and which reduces to vanishing point the idea that employers have faced systemic crises of control.

Consider, for example, the critical reaction to a work such as that of Foster (1974) on Oldham. Foster argued that during the 1830s and 1840s there was a crisis of control in Oldham's main industries, and that, for reasons connected with the high degree of working-class solidarity in the town and the nature of radical leadership, this crisis developed into a class confrontation. He sees the main reason why employers were able to survive the struggle as a deliberate policy of the incorporation of working-class leaders and the creation of a labour aristocracy which divided the mass of the class from its leaders. Revisionist criticism (e.g., Musson, 1976) has concentrated on questioning the degree of class unity in the 1840s, on asking whether the ruling class acted as deliberately as Foster argues, and on challenging the Leninist model of leaders and led which Foster deploys. Some of these points are pertinent, but they should not be allowed to lead to the conclusion that there was no class consciousness in Oldham or that there was not a serious problem of control for employers. It is possible to analyse the factors which encouraged or hindered feelings of class, together with the developments of labour relations in specific industries on the lines indicated by Foster without necessarily accepting the inferences that Foster wishes to draw.

Finally in this section a study which exemplifies these arguments may be considered; whether or not its author would see it in the light suggested here is, of course, a moot point. The study is that by Sewell (1980) on the development of workers' consciousness in France up to 1848. He begins by noting that most researchers agree that the early labour movement was dominated by skilled artisans, not workers in the new factories; this 'makes the problem of continuity with pre-industrial forms and experiences impossible to escape' (p. 1). Pre-industrial organizations were not destroyed, but instead took on new forms. In particular the language and forms of thought characteristic of the pre-industrial guilds, or (as they were called in France) corporations, continued to play a large role. The study is thus:

> about the "language of labor" in the broadest sense – not only about workers' utterances or about theoretical discourse on labor, but about the whole range of institutional arrangements, ritual gestures, work practices, methods of struggle, customs and actions that gave the workers' world a comprehensible shape (Sewell, 1980: 12).

In short, in the terms used here, it is a study of the labour process of skilled artisans and of the forms of consciousness to which it gave rise.

Sewell explores the tensions between masters and journeymen under a corporate system (pp. 40–1). Although in legal theory the relationship was a familial one, in practice in many trades masters employed several journeymen and the time spent as a journeyman was often lengthy. The relationship thus has a class nature, as was evidenced in the frequency of disputes. At the same time, however, journeymen did not oppose the existence of the masters' corporations. Indeed, their own journeymen's associations were modelled on the corporations and were equally committed to the notion of the trade and to the need to protect the trade from outsiders. Thus, during the eighteenth century there was a class struggle, that is a struggle between different groups within the process of production, but the struggle was fragmented in that the journeymen of one trade had few immediately shared interests with those of other trades, and indeed had many things in common with their masters. The relationship of masters and men 'combined elements both of harmony and of discord' (p. 58), but journeymen's associations saw conflict within the terms of the trade and did not represent a groping towards the class-conscious world of the nineteenth century.

Sewell goes on to analyse the development of the corporate idiom. Crucial in this was the revolution of 1789, for this aimed to sweep away all privilege, and in particular its emphasis on the unitary and indivisible nature of the republic was incompatible with the traditional model of corporations controlling individual trades. The attack on the corporations was thus more to do with the philosophy of the Enlightenment than with problems internal to them (p. 63). Sewell admits, however, that it may be that trade corporations, with their highly restrictive local basis, were incompatible with the development of large-scale capitalist industry. The importance of this for present purposes relates to the question of base and superstructure. In the case of the corporations, it cannot be argued, Sewell would suggest, that pressures from the economic base were significant causes of the attack on the corporations. Here is a very good example of the inadequacy of reducing all crises to systems of labour control, for the crisis of the corporations came as a result of political change and not as a result of internal problems. It is possible, none the less, that, had the corporations been permitted to remain, pressure from the economic base would have mounted. The outcome, however, would not be direct but would depend on how these pressures were mediated.

Journeymen, not surprisingly, used corporate idioms alongside revolutionary ones. There was, for Sewell, no natural and inevitable emergence of class consciousness but instead a blending of corporate modes of thought with Enlightenment notions such as the dignity of labour. Fundamental to the operation of the workers' corporations was their relationship with the employer. Sewell (pp. 171–87) describes the work relations which emerged during the early nineteenth century. The economic and legal system established under the Revolution was based on a denial of previous modes of organization and thus tended to split a trade organized under masters' corporations into a series of competing workshops. 'Workers' corporations attempted to impose order on a potentially anarchic industry, to create trade communities by concerted action where they would otherwise have no existence, and to maintain them in spite of the hostility of the legal system and the state' (p. 183). They did so by trying to control entry to the trade and fixing piecework prices. They thus shared many features with the organizations of skilled workers in other countries. In particular their whole approach was based on a specific trade, be it shoe-making, hatting, or whatever. Any broader consciousness of class was built on this trade consciousness and could not be understood outside it.

Sewell concludes that, although workers' world views had altered a great deal between 1789 and 1848, consciousness of class was quite different from that which developed later in the nineteenth century (pp. 282–3). 'Class' could still be used to refer to any social category, and not necessarily to relations of domination and subordination. And class conflict was not a matter of confrontation between employers and workers, for employers shared some of the workers' corporate attitudes and were seen as potential members of ideal trade communities. It is, perhaps, possible to generalize from this argument to suggest that, even when a more developed consciousness of class emerged, it was shaped by the same sort of divisions and contradictions as those analysed by Sewell. Workers experience class relations not as self-evident things but as part of a world which they have to try to understand for themselves. It is natural that the understandings which emerge are shaped by the particular experiences of particular groups of workers. As capitalism has developed, a sense of class has certainly grown. But, as the numerous surveys of contemporary workers' attitudes have shown, a view of society as divided into classes which are antagonistic towards each other is far from universal. Although the growth of capitalism has meant the emergence of a class of free wage-labourers and the development of new forms of property rights, it does not follow that it has thereby created a unified working class.

Concluding Remarks

The conclusion of the last secion is, of course, consistent with that of many studies of class consciousness, for example, 'it seems rather unlikely that the proletariat carries *in itself* the power to be a class *for* itself' (Mann, 1973: 73, emphasis in original). There has, however, sometimes been a gap between consideration of class formation and class action at the 'macro' societal level and analysis of work relations at the 'micro' level of the individual factory or trade. There has also been a division between the idea of class as an analytical construct and consideration of how far a particular group of workers displayed class consciousness.

This chapter has used the framework outlined in chapter 2 to indicate how some of these problems might be viewed. The relationship between capital and labour can be described as a class relation, but it does not follow that class consciousness will result from the coming together of particular people within the production process. As capitalism developed, the nature of work relations changed: capitalists and workers became increasingly distanced from pre-capitalist ideas of the labour contract, the large firm began to supplant the small independent capitalist, and so on. But the speed of this process should not be exaggerated: old habits and assumptions remained alive, and significant parts of the economy were not affected by the mechanized factory. Neither should the dynamic of change be seen as one of a new system imposing new logics of behaviour. It is certainly true that the increasing scale of production placed new pressures on capitalists and workers. But capitalists' responses were shaped by their particular circumstances, so that different firms worked out different forms of labour control. And workers were also able to shape their worlds of work instead of simply having to embrace a new logic. There was continuity as well as change. A major analytical point to emerge is the inappropriateness of the model of a shift from a formal to a real subordination of labour. 'Real' subordination, in the sense of having to work to produce surplus value, was as present in early as in later capitalism. And modern workers, as much as their predecessors, have been able to exert 'informal' influences on the labour process.

This last point is of particular significance. The foregoing discussion has argued not just that the process of 'modernization' was slow and uneven or that 'informal' means of accommodation between workers and employers have been important throughout capitalist development. It has also been suggested that changing patterns of protest cannot be analysed with a model that counterposes managerial rationalization with workers' desire to retain traditional forms of work organization. Workers did not cling blindly to the past but responded to changing circumstances, and in doing so they helped to shape the ways in which the labour process was managed. If 'resistance' is too strong a word to describe their efforts, it can still be said that their behaviour rendered some managerial attempts at control unworkable and amended other forms of control. As studies of artisan consciousness have suggested, moreover, an individual worker's world view is likely to have reflected the contradictory demands and assumptions of 'traditional' and 'modern' modes of thought. The rise of modernism involved attempts by workers to balance these two modes, and not just the imposition of rationalism by employers. Forms of protest could be simultaneously backward-looking and forward-looking.

The chapter has also tried to consider 'individual' as well as collective responses on the part of workers. Lack of evidence makes such a consideration no more than tentative. It is necessary to turn to contemporary fieldwork investigations to develop a fuller picture; these are discussed in chapter 6. Before patterns of work relations in the modern factory are considered in detail, however, two more macro level issues need attention. Capitalist countries differ in the trajectories which their workplace industrial relations have taken; consideration as to why this is so is carried out in chapter 5. One argument of that chapter is that the role of the state has been a significant influence. Indeed, one gap in the discussion of the present chapter is an assessment of the state's role. The following chapter tries to fill this gap and thus to lay the groundwork for chapter 5.

4

The State and the Workplace

The neglect of the state is one of the more serious gaps in the labour process debate. As Burawoy (1985: 125) notes, the dominant tendency, as exemplified by the work of Richard Edwards (1979) and Littler (1982), is to collapse political apparatuses at the level of the state into the labour process: the state itself is given no specific attention. Yet it is necessary to do more than note the state's importance. Just as the bases of conflict in the capital-labour relation require careful explication, so the conditions of state intervention need consideration. Forms of conflict cannot be 'read off' from the clash between capital and labour, and neither can the state's activities be reduced to the 'needs' of the economy. But, in the same way in which conflict cannot be seen as the contingent outcome of disagreements between workers and employers, the state's interventions in the capital-labour relation cannot be seen as separate from the nature of this relation. A more subtle approach, in which the state is seen neither as totally constrained by civil society nor as totally independent, is required.

The first task of this chapter is to outline such an approach. The second is to apply it to state intervention in labour relations. The precise focus warrants emphasis. It is not intervention in the economy in general, the regulation of labour relations as a whole, or even the role of the state in the management of industrial conflict. A treatment of even the last of these would require attention to the conciliation and arbitration services of state agencies, legislation governing strikes in 'essential services' the *ad hoc* interventions of government in specific disputes, and so on. It would also be necessary to look at a wide range of countries to investigate the very different roles played by different states. The focus is the more specific one of the intervention of the state in job regulation at workplace level. And the aim is not to discuss this in relation to all capitalist countries but to use some specific examples to develop some analytical points. Crucial among these are the reasons leading to state intervention, the ways in which interventions were shaped by the existing character of capital-labour relations, and the ability of states to act independently of the demands of capitalists and workers. A further key point, concerning the impact of state interventions on the subsequent development of workplace relations, is taken up in chapter 5. In the context of the study as a whole, concentrating on fairly specific issues is the best way of analysing the role of the state, for this is an area in which the state's substantive importance has been profound, but in which treatments linking broad theoretical statements about the nature of the capitalist state to concrete cases of state activity have been rare. Three countries, the United States, Britain, and Australia are used as examples; each offers some specific illustrations of how state intervention operates in differing circumstances. As noted in the introduction, this is to select a narrow range of cases, but the aim is not to account for differing patterns of state intervention throughout capitalism but to use concrete cases to illustrate a general argument that could, appropriately developed, be applied more widely.

State and Economy

It is obvious that the state intervenes in many aspects of society. The concern here, however, is not with state intervention in general or even with the role of the state in managing the economy. It is with the state's involvement in the regulation of the labour process. The role of the state in this particular area is not, of course, separate from its broader role of economic management. It is thus necessary to do two things: to indicate why the state plays a part in regulating the labour process; and to explain why its behaviour stems from the nature of the mode of production, that is why the state is not separate from civil society. Speaking in terms of roles or tasks raises the largest methodological issue of recent debates about the state, the problem of functionalism. If the state is said to perform certain duties for the capitalist system, does this not entail a functionalist mode of explanation in which the cause of an action is found in its consequences? A position on this problem will be sketched after a framework for looking at the state has been outlined.

Importance of the State
In what ways does the state intervene to regulate the relationship between capital and labour? As Burawoy (1985: 125–6) argues, there are

two main aspects. The first is the determination of the conditions on which labour power may be sold: the state intervenes to affect the reproduction of labour power, for example through social security legislation that guarantees minimum living standards, the result being that the supply of labour power no longer depends solely on the market. Second, there is the regulation of how that labour power is used. Burawoy cites compulsory union recognition and collective bargaining as means of constraining management's freedom to discipline workers. Other examples are legislation restricting the hours of labour and establishing standards of health and safety: the employer's freedom to use the labour power that he has bought is restrained not only by workers' own actions but also by state regulation. This second aspect is the more important for present purposes. Regulations on the price of labour power may set limits to what can go on inside the labour process, but they do not directly shape the pattern of relations. Regulations on the use of labour power directly constrain employers' power over labour and affect how the labour process is organized.

Burawoy goes on to consider the links between the state and what he calls production politics, that is the institutions and struggles that control the labour process at the level of the workplace. He compares the American engineering factory that he had studied earlier (Burawoy, 1979) with the British factory studied by Lupton (1963). Although their technologies and product market circumstances were similar, the production politics of the two plants differed, with the American factory being dominated by a formal, detailed contract which specified workers' rights and encouraged a bureaucratic approach, while the British one was characterized by a more fluid situation and constant bargaining between workers and managers. Some of the reasons for the contrast can be found in differences in the politics of production, but the state also played a role: in America collective contracts are legally binding, and the union is responsible for the behaviour of its members, whereas in Britain no such legal regulation exists. Burawoy proceeds to develop this contrast by outlining four models of the state's intervention in production politics. The contrast between Britain and America can be drawn on two dimensions. That just mentioned is the dimension of the direct state regulation of factory regimes, with America scoring high and Britain low. The second is the degree of state support for the reproduction of labour power: in Britain, there is a fairly developed system of unemployment insurance and state medical provision and the country scores high on the dimension, whereas America scores low. The other two cells of the categorization are exemplified by Sweden (high on both dimensions) and Japan (low on both).

There may be room to quarrel about the details of the categorization. Is it really the case, for example, that the Swedish state intervenes directly in the regulation of factory regimes? Although collective contracts are legally binding, the state generally stays at arm's length from the content of those contracts. State activity may underpin the behaviour of managements and unions, but it would appear, at the very least, that the character of the Swedish state's regulation of factory regimes has been different from that characteristic of the United States. There is a need to develop Burawoy's brief discussion of the links between the state and the shape of labour relations to take account of the particular historical circumstances in which the various actors found themselves. This is attempted in the second section of this chapter and in chapter 5.

This point leads to a second area in which Burawoy's analysis needs extending. Burawoy (1985: 148) argues that 'the different forms of state intervention are conditioned by class interests and class capacities defined primarily at the level of production'. That is, the state is not autonomous but is shaped by the mode of production. But why is this so? How is it possible to conclude that the forces from the mode of production that influence the state are more powerful than those running in the opposite direction, and in what sense can they be said to be the more powerful? Burawoy has, after all, shown that differences in state behaviour affect production politics. Is it not possible to conclude that states vary in their inclinations and abilities to intervene in production politics according to such things as the size of the state bureaucracy, the preferences of legislators, and other factors not connected with the economy? In fact, states act in the ways that they do because they are constrained by the character of the economy. But an argument to this effect needs to be mounted.

The Capitalist State
The study of the state is a major academic growth industry. There have been numerous debates about particular perspectives, and discussion has often become very abstruse (for a useful survey, which is none the less extremely complex, see Jessop, 1982). No more than a few basic propositions will be sketched here.

As a starting-point, it is possible to take the criteria suggested by Jessop (1982: 221) for assessing the adequacy of analyses of the state in capitalist societies. There are five criteria. An account is adequate to the extent that it: is founded on the specific features of capitalism as a mode of production; attributes a central role in the process of capital accumulation to interactions between class forces; establishes the relationship between the economy and the polity without reducing the one to the other and without treating them as totally autonomous; allows for variations in the form and function of the state in different societies; and allows for the influences of class forces rooted in non-capitalist relations of production and of forces which are not of a class nature.

The relevance of these criteria should be evident, but some comment is needed on the second. Jessop rightly stresses the importance of interactions between class forces in an attempt to avoid one of the problems in the debate on the state, namely the treatment of the state as though class struggle is absent and as though the state can be the ideal collective capitalist. States are, in fact, implicated in relationships between labour and capital which are characterized by struggle and whose solution may involve complex and contradictory actions by the state. Hence Jessop's (1982: 221) view that 'state power is capitalist to the extent that it creates, maintains, or restores the conditions required for capital accumulation in a given situation' requires some modification. States may be capitalist but may fail to attain their own express ends. The Tsarist Russian state in 1917, for example, would presumably count as a capitalist state even though it was failing to maintain the conditions for capitalist development. As Jessop says later (p. 226), the complexity and contradictoriness of the conditions of existence of capital accumulation 'invalidate all attempts to suggest that the state in capitalist societies is unequivocally and universally beneficial to capital'. Yet, in addition to suggesting that the state will have to act in ways which are not beneficial to capital, they suggest that the state may be unsuccessful in its endeavours. It is essential to distinguish between the intentions and the effects of a given set of activities. A state should be considered to be capitalist to the extent that it tries, or more accurately to the extent that it is structurally constrained by the economy to try, to secure the conditions for capital accumulation.

As writers such as O'Connor (1973) and Offe (1975) have suggested, the state's activities can be considered under the heads of accumulation and legitimation: assisting in the process of capital accumulation and in securing the legitimacy of the system of domination which characterizes the capitalist mode of production. There are contradictions within each sort of activity. Within accumulation, for example, the involvement of the state in the activities of privately owned capitals may mean that the very conditions which the involvement was designed to promote, namely the continuation of private capitalism, are negated by the need for the state to play a direct role. There are also contradictions between the accumulation and legitimation functions of the state, for example when actions that are necessary to sustain the legitimacy of the system interfere with needs of accumulation. There is thus no suggestion that the state can intervene smoothly and successfully or that it is the instrument of the capitalist class in particular: 'what the state protects and sanctions is a set of *rules* and *social relationships* which are presupposed by the class rule of the capitalist class. The state does not defend the interests of one class, but the *common* interests of all members of a *capitalist class society*' (Offe and Ronge, 1982: 250; emphasis in original).

How are accumulation and legitimation defined and analysed? Offe examines accumulation under three heads: exclusion, maintenance, and dependency. Exclusion is the principle that the state has no authority to order production or control it. The state cannot initiate production in private enterprises unless such production is thought to be accumulative, and it cannot stop production that is considered accumulative by the producing unit. This argument is, however, apparently contradicted by such things as wartime controls over what shall be produced. Perhaps a better way of putting it is to say that direct state interventions in decisions as to what to produce are unusual and that, when they do take place, they are premised on the assumptions that private ownership will continue and that the aim of production is the creation of surplus value. The state can be said to be excluded in that it does not interfere with the ends of commodity production. This leads to its second accumulation function, that of maintaining the conditions for accumulation: the state has a 'mandate' to try to resolve potential threats to the accumulation process. Finally, the state is dependent on the continuity of the accumulation process, for without continued accumulation the state cannot finance its own activities.

Block (1980: 230–2) has developed this last point: although state power cannot be reduced to class power, there are important systemic constraints on the activities of capitalist states. Four 'contextual elements' help to show how 'the exercise of state power has generally served the needs of the capitalist accumulation process'. These are: the existence of capitalism as a world system, which leads managers in each state to try to emulate other capitalists; the degree of control over investment held by capitalists; the disproportionate control by capitalists of wealth and the means of influence; and the contradictions of the capitalist accumulation process. Perhaps the last of these is the most important for a theory of the distinct role of the state. As Block notes, the unregulated search for profit is likely to be self-defeating, as proper provision is not made for the reproduction of supplies of labour-power and as periodic crises threaten social stability. State managers thus 'act to save capitalism from itself'.

The legitimatory aspects of the state's role have received comparatively little attention. This is particularly unfortunate in view of some general problems with the concept of legitimacy: is legitimacy to be equated with the degree of support given to the regime by subordinate groups, or does it encompass wider sources of legitimate authority; and, to the extent that subordinates' acceptance is involved, does the concept refer to subordinates' attitudes alone or also to their concrete practices? On the former question it has been pointed out that to see legitimacy in terms of subordinates' acceptance of a command leads to the problem that the same command can vary in its legitimacy according to the subjective state of subordinates. An alternative is to see the extent of the legitimacy of a command being 'indicated by the answer to question"by what warrant"?', with acceptability to subordinates being only one possible answer: legitimacy may come from above, in the shape of the law for example, as well as from below (Goldthorpe, 1977: 218, n. 15). In the present context, it is important to see legitimacy as embracing more than the consent of the working class. If the state is to defend the common interests of all members of society it needs to gain the compliance of capitalists as well as workers, and also the compliance of other social groups such as the petit bourgeoisie which are not directly connected to the capitalist labour process.

An approach to the problem of legitimacy may, however, be sketched. In view of the difficulties which surround the terms legitimacy and legitimation it is desirable to seek an alternative, just as the concept of compliance has been preferred to that of consent. It seems sensible to speak of the integration of the system in the sense in which Lockwood (1964) uses the notion of system integration to refer to relationships between parts of the social system. The task of the state is to try to integrate the activities of capital and labour, of different fractions of capital and labour, and of other groupings in society in such a way that the capitalist economy can continue to operate. The problem of integration is inherent in a capitalist economy given the tensions in the accumulation process considered above and given also the conflictual nature of the capital-labour relation: the state has the task of trying to contain the conflicts which arise in civil society. There is no suggestion that the task can be permanently fulfilled, for tensions and contradictions are permanent features of capitalist societies, and the state has to try to steer a difficult course between competing objectives. Neither is it claimed that integration involves consent and harmony. As Lockwood (p. 250) says, system integration is analytically and factually separable from what he calls social integration, namely the extent to which relations between actors are orderly or conflictful: 'it is perfectly possible . . . to say that at any particular point in time a society has a high degree of social integration (e.g. relative absence of class conflict) and yet has a low degree of system integration (mounting excess productive capacity).' Integration refers to the extent to which the parts of the social system are brought into line with each other, regardless of the degree of dissatisfaction which may exist. The reverse of Lockwood's example therefore holds. That is, a high degree of system integration can go along with a low degree of social integration. An economistic struggle by trade unions, for example, can lead to a high level of industrial conflict without there necessarily being any threat to the capitalist productive system itself.

Integration can, of course, involve the making of concessions to powerful groups: it is not simply a matter of fobbing them off with minor or meaningless rewards. The point is, as Offe suggests, that the state exists to create and maintain certain rules and procedures and not directly to serve the interests of one class. The rule of law is relevant as a means of promoting integration or compliance only when the law is genuinely independent of the demands of the capitalist class. The law creates rules which apply to all, and it constrains capitalists as well as workers. In trying to integrate competing demands, albeit within the need to promote the accumulation process, the state can have a real effect on the shape of the social formation.

Although there are certain constraints on the state which arise from its location within a capitalist mode of production, the activities of the state do not flow directly from these constraints and, since its activities have a degree of autonomy from class interests, its role cannot be reduced to one of pursuing the interests of a particular class. In addition, particular states will act in different ways because the constraints coming from the mode of production affect only the general shape of state intervention and not its precise form, because states are equipped with differing power, and because their activities take place in different contexts shaped by the development of capitalism in specific social formations.

The role of the state can thus be seen not in terms of deliberate attempts to 'incorporate' the working class but in terms of the consequences which its actions have for the integration of the system. These actions may be motivated for any number of reasons, and there is no guarantee that they will unambiguously add to system integration. The consequences have to be discovered and not assumed. Yet hegemonic consequences of state action can be identified, for example when the passage of labour law encourages the view among the working class that the state is a neutral arbiter and that the laws represent a just balance between the interests of capital and labour.

The basic argument, then, is that the state is a capitalist state because it operates within certain constraints which are created by the capitalist mode of production, but that neither the reasons for nor the consequences of state intervention in the economy can be read off from the existence of these constraints. There are complex and contradictory pressures on the state, and attempts to deal with these pressures can alter the character of the social formation. Capitalism is a dynamic mode of production, and the state is an engine of change and not simply a means of defending an existing pattern of class relations. Its actions can contribute to system integration, but in what ways and with what results is a matter for further investigation.

The Problem of Functionalism

As Crouch (1979) in particular has argued, Marxist accounts of the state face the major problem of attributing functions to the state: how can state managers know that their duty is to buttress the capitalist system, why should what they do necessarily have the intended results, and how can the reasons for their behaviour be explained in terms of the results that the behaviour is supposed to have?

Because of the bad name that functionalism has acquired, the fact that an account uses functional language tends to be taken as a damning criticism. But Cohen has shown that functional, as distinct from functionalist, explanations are in principle perfectly proper (G. Cohen, 1978: 278–96). Consider Cohen's example of religion (pp. 281–2). This begins from the supposition that a society requires religion for stability, and that it has a religion filling that need. It may have acquired a religion for any number of reasons, but once the religion is in place stability is enhanced. A functional explanation here involves no more than a mode of analysis which is commonly employed in the social sciences, namely the examination of the connections between different parts of a social structure and a consideration of how they cohere. As Cohen stresses, however, the identification of a function is not the end of the matter, for this does not explain the existence of a particular phenomenon and further evidence is necessary before a causal explanation of its presence can be said to have been produced.

Now consider one of Cohen's 'Marxian illustrations' (pp. 294–5) of functional explanation. This is of some substantive interest in the present context, for it relates to the passage of the Factory Acts and hence to the question of why the state intervenes to limit the rights of the capitalist over the deployment of labour-power. Marx put forward two reasons for the passage of the Acts: pressure from the working class for a limitation on the length of the working day, and the need to curb the tendency of capital to deplete the stock of labour-power by making workers work excessively long hours. The latter reason raises particular difficulties, for it suggests that the state's intervention was explained by the function which it perfomed, namely defending capitalism from its own blindness. Cohen suggests a connection between Marx's two arguments: changes which are in the immediate interests of the subordinate class tend to occur when that class fights for them and when they increase or preserve the stability of the system. 'The elements are connected because ruling class perception of the need for change is quickened by the pressure of underclass demand, and the latter gets bigger in consequence' (p. 295).

Cohen ends his discussion at this point, but some further comments must be entered. His defence of a functional form of explanation is proper, but he neglects to note the conditions which would have to apply in a particular case for a functional account to be correct. It cannot be assumed that state managers knew that their actions would increase the stability of the system. There is always the danger of *ex post* rationalization and of circular explanations: the Factory Acts were passed because they increased integration, and we know that they increased integration because they were passed. The danger can certainly be avoided. Thus, relevant evidence would include speeches by 'advanced' capitalists detailing the benefits of restricting hours of work and cases where working-class demands were equally powerful but were not successful because the subjects of the demands lacked integrative potential. To the extent that such evidence can be produced, it is proper to employ a functional account. In the case of the Factory Acts, Marvel (1977) has produced some relevant evidence. He argues that the Acts were not the result of popular pressure, for such a view cannot explain why the 1833 Act was passed in a Parliament dominated by the Whig manufacturers, who were hostile to legislation, and not by the previous Tory-dominated House, which should have been more open to such pressure. He suggests instead that the Act was drafted at the behest of leading textile manufactures, who wanted to increase the costs of production of the smaller mills and who found the legislation a convenient way of doing so; the Act's provisions related only to women and children, who were concentrated in the small mills, while the large firms used steam-powered mills that employed few women and children.

It may never be absolutely clear that the integrative properties of legislation are important factors in its passage, but dispositional and counter-factual evidence may be available. In addition, as Cohen stresses (p. 290), there has been an over-reaction against conspiracy theories of history. There are cases, as shown below, in which state managers have had the explicit aim of saving capitalism from itself, and here the problem of functionalism does not arise.

To speak of the duties and tasks of the capitalist state is thus not to engage in functionalist modes of explanation. Constraints and pressures from the economy can be identified. These affect the sorts of decisions that are felt to be reasonable by state managers. These decisions have consequences, some of which may be to increase system integration, in which case it is proper to say that they have this particular function.

State Managers and Relative Autonomy

The state thus has a relative autonomy: its actions are constrained by the nature of the economy, and the forces stemming from the economy are more 'important' than those running in the opposite direction. But it is not totally constrained by these forces, state managers have to decide between different alternatives open to them, some alternatives may involve concessions to subordinate groups, and the state's actions can alter the shape of production politics. 'Important' in this context does not mean that pressures from the capital-labour relation can overcome the state's attempts to intervene, for this would imply that the state's relative autonomy was virtually constrained out of existence. It means that the state can certainly act against the wishes of capitalists, and can alter a pattern of production politics in ways which none of the actors involved wants, but that, at a more fundamental level of analysis, the state is a capitalist state: in particular cases it may be more powerful than other social actors, but the context in which it uses its power and the broad thrust of its interventions depend on the nature of the economic system.

In some cases state managers may react to events in a more or less *ad hoc* fashion without having any particular view of where they are trying to go. In others, they may have a range of more explicit strategies from which they can choose. But, in either case, their actions will have consequences which tend to shift production politics in a particular direction. Such developments may be unintended, but, once begun, they develop a logic of their own and make interventions in congruent directions more likely, and interventions in other directions less likely. The conditions under which states can act, and will be required to act, also vary: in situations of crisis the state's freedom to take new initiatives increases. The state can thus be an important actor in struggles within the production process. As argued in chapter 2, these struggles help to shape subsequent patterns of relations: history is important.

The foregoing arguments point to the need to investigate particular instances of state intervention in some detail in order to explain the logic of the situation as it faced state managers and to consider why they acted as they did..The general framework outlined here can be claimed to be consistent with Jessop's five criteria for an adequate account. In particular, an effort has been made to treat the economy and the polity as distinct, without seeing them as completely divorced. As Jessop (1982: 142) also notes, once the general question of the form and function of the capitalist state has been addressed and 'once we focus on state power at the level of the social formation rather than the form of the state apparatus at the level of the mode of production, it is essential to introduce a much more complex system of concepts'. In moving to a more concrete level of analysis, it is certainly necessary to use different concepts. But they are less complex, or at least more immediately related to day-to-day issues of politics, than are concepts at more abstract levels. What is required is an understanding of the context in which decisions were made, and such familiar concepts as pressure groups, party political opportunism, and personal ambition are involved. The following section attempts to consider various instances of state involvement, not to provide a detailed legislative history but to relate specific events to the particular form which the state's relative autonomy took.

The State in Industrial Relations: Three Cases

To illustrate how state interventions are shaped by specific historical circumstances and also by more basic pressures stemming from the economy, there is no particular reason to choose one example rather than another. The cases discussed below offer, however, some valuable evidence on the different processes involved. They also lend themselves to reasonably clear-cut discussion: the reasons for state involvement are often murky, but in these cases the situation is clearer than it is in many others, and in some of them the participants analysed their own motivations, thus easing the task of reconstruction.

The United States is a case in which the state has traditionally been weak. Consideration of the American state's intervention in industrial relations thus illustrates clearly the conditions under which a state which is not pre-disposed to intervene none the less does so. The need for the state to regulate capitalism emerges more clearly here than it would in the case of, say, Germany where there has been a long tradition of a strong state and where intervention as a result of the specific pressures arising from the capitalist economy would be difficult to disentangle from pre-capitalist traditions of state activity. The American case also provides an example of a situation in which the state's law of workplace behaviour dovetailed with the private law developed by employers. In Burawoy's terms, factory regimes and global politics meshed together. The consequences are analysed in chapter 5, and the discussion in the present chapter lays the ground for this analysis.

Britain offers a useful contrast with America. In both countries, relations between unions and management at the level of the workplace have formed a significant part of labour relations as a whole. But the course of development in the two countries has differed. The differing roles of state managers have been part of the explanation of this divergence, and consideration of why state managers have acted in particular ways is thus necessary. The comparison is made the more useful by the obvious similarities in the countries' legal traditions, forms of trade union organization and other things: some of the parameters of state intervention can be held constant.

Australia has many traditions in common with these two countries: its legal system is closely modelled on the British one, its trade unions had strong links with Britain and in some cases originated as branches of British unions, and so on. Yet the state has played a substantially larger role in industrial relations than has its British counterpart. The contrasts with America are also revealing, for both countries were 'new' and had large tracts of unsettled land. Yet in America there developed a strong tradition of individualism, with the state performing a strictly limited role, while in Australia collectivism and state interventions have been more in evidence. It is true that this contrast should not be over-drawn. The 'individualism' of American workers has to be set alongside the solidarity which has been a lasting characteristic of strikes, and, to the extent that it does exist, it may reflect not the internalization of broad social values but the power of employers to prevent collective traditions from taking root. Similarly, Australian workers seem to have come closer to a radical egalitarian position than one of revolutionary class consciousness. Important contrasts remain, however.

The following analysis thus considers why state intervention has taken different forms in the three countries. Once a particular form of intervention was established, the state could exercise its powers, and indeed was expected to do so; for example, once it has become established that governments will try to mediate between the parties to large-scale industrial disputes, not only do governments have the power to intervene but there will also be demands from the parties themselves or from public opinion to resolve subsequent disputes. In short, once a tradition of state intervention has been established, the state is a 'relatively autonomous' actor. But the reasons for, and nature of, the initial involvement can be traced to the pre-existing character of capital-labour relations.

One initial methodological point must be made. International comparisons are fraught with difficulties because there is any number of differences between countries, and it may be difficult to establish which is the key factor or factors in explaining a particular difference. An apparently attractive approach is to identify a factor which seems to differentiate between two countries and to test the argument by finding a third country which has the factor in common with one of the first two and seeing whether the claimed effects are present here. Yet this may prove to be impossible either because no suitable contrast exists or, more fundamentally, because countries' characteristics are tied together instead of varying independently. An argument that Country X has characteristic P because of structure A is not necessarily contradicted by pointing out that Country Y also has structure A but has characteristic Q: it may be that, in the context of all the other features of X, A has a certain effect, whereas in the different context of Y it operates differently. These and other problems cannot be pursued in detail here. The approach to them may be briefly stated. Developments in a particular country need to be considered in terms of the situation facing the key actors and the forces leading them to act in certain ways. The aim is to reconstruct how certain choices were encouraged and how, once they had been made, they themselves influenced subsequent events. It may be that a particular influence that is attributed explanatory significance in the discussion of one country may strike the reader as being equally applicable in another. But the aim is not to explain everything about international differences in industrial relations, but only to account for the shape of state intervention. The fact that Country X shares a characteristic with Country Y does not prevent that characteristic from being pertinent to the explanation of state intervention in X. It is its operation in the context of X which is important, and the discussion will be convincing to the extent that it can indicate how a range of forces came together to produce a particular outcome. The aim is not to look at international variations as such, but to consider individual countries and to chart, albeit in broad outline and not in historical detail, how particular decisions came to be made.

The United States

State intervention in America is often discussed largely in terms of the New Deal of the 1930s. Yet direct involvement in industrial relations goes back to the late nineteenth century, and the tradition that was established created assumptions that powerfully shaped the New Deal legislation. It is here that discussion must begin.

1870–1916. State intervention began in relation to the railways: legislation successively promoted conciliation, required collective bargaining, established the eight-hour day (against employer opposition), and created a permanent body to adjudicate in disputes. The railways were in the forefront of industrial conflict during the last quarter of the nineteenth century, with several violent and lengthy strikes. State activity took a variety of forms: the use of troops to quell disturbances; the issuing of injuctions against strikers by the courts; the direct involvement of the executive branch in organizing responses to strikes; and the passage of legislation which had the aim of resolving conflict. In addition, the period was marked by governmental intervention in the business activities of the railways, notably through the Interstate Commerce Act of 1887. As Eggert (1967: 2) remarks, the railways were the country's first big businesses, and it was thus to be expected that federal intervention would occur here. And they were not just big but were crucial to the operation of the economy: as late as 1916, they carried 77 per cent of freight, and 98 per cent of passenger, intercity traffic (Stover, 1961: 238). But this economic importance shows only that, if intervention were to occur, it was likely to do so here: it does not explain why it occurred or what shape it took.

Three approaches to state intervention can be identified. The first is the standard view that the railways resisted external control of their affairs. Here, the reasons for the state's activities are not directly addressed, and the story is one of over-powerful corporations eventually being brought to heel by legislation. The state is seen as the autonomous reflection of an unexplicated public interest. The second approach was developed by Kolko (1965) in deliberate rejection of the first: state intervention not only failed to damage the railways' interests but was also welcomed by the companies because it helped them to rationalize the industry and achieve price stability in the face of declining freight rates and the inability of voluntary price agreements to prevent the re-emergence of price competition. Kolko shows, for example, that average freight rates per ton mile fell continuously from 1.88 cents in 1870 to 0.73 cents in 1900 and that railways were active in seeking legislation to regularize competition. He argues that 'if for some reason the power of various key business groups was endangered, even for causes of their own making, the state was to intervene to preserve their dominant position' (p. 12). This approach reflects a more general line of argument that began to emerge during the 1960s: the capitalist state is not neutral and it acts to preserve the long-term interests of capital, in particular to prevent cut-throat competition and to assist in the rationalization and develop-ment of the process of accumulation (see Kolko, 1967; Weinstein, 1968). As noted above, this argument has subsequently been criticized for seeing the state as the instrument of capital with no role of its own. In the present case, Skowronek (1981: 225–6) has argued that Kolko has merely replaced the view that the state reflected the public interest with the claim that it represented one or other of the private interests in civil society: what is missing is a consideration of the state in its own right.

Skowronek provides an interesting attempt to develop a positive argument, as distinct from rebuttal of others' claims, by focusing on the process of state-building (see also, for a fuller account, Skowronek, 1982). The American state was weak, not in the sense of being completely underdeveloped, but because its structure was irrele-vant to the tasks that were faced. Power was localized, the govern-ment had few institutional controls that affected the operation of society as a whole, and authority within the national government was split between the executive, Congress, and the judiciary. America, alone among the major Western nations, pursued a policy on railway regulation that was plainly irrational: because it tried to control competition but in fact failed to do so, with even the com-panies' most basic demand, for pooling of income, not being attained until 1917 (Skowronek, 1981: 234). The state was unable to operate effectively and failed to pursue any interests consistently.

This argument contains the important recognition that the state is not simply an all-powerful tool. Policy grew as state managers responded to the contradictory pressures placed on them, using the limited powers that they had available. So why did regulation emerge? The railway companies had a general desire to reduce competition. In addition, they feared that constraints on them might emerge at the level of the individual states. From the 1870s states with important farming interests began to regulate prices, for there was powerful resentment among farmers at their dependence on the railways and the high tariffs that they had to pay; Illinois led the way in 1871, in legislation that the Supreme Court declared to be constitutional in 1876 (Stover, 1961: 126–31). A national regulatory system was more likely to favour the railways. There was also a more general public recognition that something had to be done about excessive competition on long-haul routes and the very high rates charged on the short-haul routes which represented monopolies for the individual companies. The state thus came under a general pressure to do something, and an attempt at action slowly emerged. As Kolko (1965: 21) notes, the first bill in the federal legislature to try to ban rate discrimination was presented in 1876, but the Interstate Commerce Act was not passed for another eleven years.

As for the state's intervention in labour disputes, Eggert (1967) argues that, of the various agencies of the state, only the courts developed a consistent policy, whereas the legislature and the executive made a number of *ad hoc* interventions which lacked direction and which often came too late to deal with the problem for which they were designed. The courts' policy involved a series of innovations in labour law as new devices were discovered for restraining strikes. In 1877 contempt of court proceedings were brought against strikers working for railways in court-appointed receiverships on the grounds that court orders could not be carried out; in the Burlington strike of 1888 injunctions were granted against attempts to apply a boycott to trucks owned by the struck railway: in 1893 injunctions appeared which banned strikes as such; and in 1894 all judges agreed that the Sherman Anti-Trust Act, which banned interference with interstate commerce, applied to railway strikes. Yet these important judicial rulings contrasted with legislative attempts to provide a framework for resolving labour disputes. The Arbitration Act of 1888 provided that voluntary arbitration commissions could be established; in 1898 the Erdman Act empowered the Commissioner of Labor to mediate at the request of one party to a dispute, and contracts requiring workers not be trade union members (yellow-dog contracts) were banned (the latter provision was ruled to be unconstitutional in 1908); and in 1913 the Newlands Act set up a permanent mediation board. Although hesitant and uncertain, the legislature slowly developed a policy based on the encouragement of collective bargaining and the provision of state agencies to handle differences between the parties.

The logic appears to have been as follows. In the highly charged atmosphere of a violent strike the prime concern of state agencies was to restore order. Although there may not have been a simple dislike of all strikes or a hostility to unions, the effect of trying to restore order was to undermine strikes and to assist employers. The courts provided employers with some very powerful weapons. Yet there was also a more general sense that labour relations in a major industry could not be fought out in a series of damaging battles. The commission appointed to investigate the 1894 strikes, which was chaired by the Commissioner of Labor, Carroll D. Wright, derided the activities of the courts: 'some of our courts . . . are still poring over the law reports of antiquity in order to construe conspiracy out of labor unions'. It went on to argue that railway companies are not free to operate as they please, for they are 'creatures of the state, whose rights are conferred upon them for public purposes'. And it recommended that employers should be encouraged to recognize unions and that there should be a permanent strike commission to investigate railway disputes, with the power to compel the companies to obey its decisions (U.S. Strike Commission, 1895: xlvii, li, lii–liv). The state was thus seen as having a legitimate interest in controlling labour disputes on the railways and in restraining the companies from disposing of their property as they saw fit. As will be seen below, this argument was, in the New Deal legislation, generalized to commerce as a whole, but at the end of the nineteenth century this was far too momentous a step, and arguments were restricted to the special case of the railways.

The method of regulation adopted was, however, far from burdensome to the companies. They refused to co-operate with the Erdman Act until 1906, although, between then and 1913, 61 requests for assistance were made under the Act, of which 40 were settled through mediation or arbitration and 21 involved private agreement after mediation failed (Eggert, 1967: 224–5). It can reasonably be suggested that the companies found the peaceful settlement of disputes beneficial, as compared to the costs of lengthy disputes. The unions with which they were coming to deal were the 'operating Brotherhoods', that is the unions of workers who operated the trains. These unions were renowned for their conservatism, and dealing with them posed little threat to the companies. In other industries, moreover, union recognition could bring the danger that, as well as bargaining about wages, employers would have their right to manage challenged, as unions and workers tried to influence the operation of discipline and working rules. As argued in chapter 5, this fear was particularly strong among American employers. On the railways, by contrast, many of the rules governing work itself had begun to emerge from the 1850s: the linking of pay to miles covered began in the 1850s, by the 1870s contracts began to cover manning standards and promotions procedures in ways similar to rules that still exist, and the practice of promotion based on seniority became widely established (Richardson, 1963: 144, 234; Licht, 1983: 148–53). Companies knew that many aspects of work were already outside their unilateral control, that they could live with the situation, and that formal recognition and the mediation of disputes would be unlikely to impose any new threats.

Developments on the side of the state and of the employers can thus be described without resort to any notion that activities were functionally designed to buttress the capitalist system. Legislatures responded to certain problems of public order and slowly evolved a policy to deal with them, while the companies learned to recognize the costs of strikes and the benefits of mediation, particularly when the state was also acting to restrain competition and thus making it relatively easy to set prices that would cover the costs of any wage increases arising from mediation. The (largely unintended) outcome was the restructuring of the capital-labour relation to permit state involvement. Outside the railways, however, the state was unwilling and unable to make any widespread changes until the First World War brought new pressures.

The First World War. The state's involvement in industrial relations reached unprecedented heights during the war. The reasons are not hard to find. The government required large quantities of war materials, together with the transport to move men and materials within the United States and to Europe. Shortages and dislocations became severe on the railways and in the shipbuilding industry, and the government took effective control of both. On the railways, the unions took advantage of the increased demand for railway services even before the country entered the war: in 1916 they demanded the eight-hour day, which the companies refused, but the threat of a strike led to the passage of the Adamson Act which met the unions' demands (Stover, 1961: 183–4). Under government operation, which began in December 1917, many of the gains made by the operating crafts were spread to other workers: shop crafts were granted premium overtime pay, the seniority principle, and the practice if not the principle of the eight-hour day (Wolf, 1927: 14–38). The companies were also protected, being guaranteed a rate of return equal to the average profit of the previous three years, plus allowances for depreciation; the total cost to the government exceeded one billion dollars, and a further 530 million dollars was paid over when the companies were returned to private control in 1920 (Kolko, 1965: 228–9). In the major wartime industries the government was thus willing to take direct and unprecedented steps to organize production. In some industries, such as shipbuilding, the military played a large role not only in production matters but also in dealing with workers' grievances and establishing collective bargaining machinery (Bing, 1921). Military personnel were less concerned about establishing precedents concerning the right to manage than about securing production, and were more 'liberal' than many employers.

State intervention was, however, seen purely as a response to the wartime emergency, and the government's controls were subsequently dismantled. During the 1920s most of the country's mass production industries operated on an 'open shop', that is non-union, basis, and even in industries such as coal, where unionism and collective bargaining had a long history, the membership and influences of the union declined. It took the crisis of the Great Depression to challenge the employers' domination of the workplace.

The New Deal. A convenient starting point in considering the labour legislation of the New Deal is Skocpol's (1980) use of it to test three neo-Marxist theories of the state. The instrumentalist view sees the state as the instrument of capitalists and asserts that crises of accumulation force capitalists to act as a class despite their divisions in normal times. This has to be able to show, however, that there was a disciplined vanguard of capitalists with a clear strategy and the power to implement it; and that these corporate leaders were prepared to make concessions to labour. In fact, capitalists were divided and uncertain, and a policy of concessions was forced on them by politicians. The political functionalist approach sees the role of the state as being to organize capitalists by reflecting the interests of capital as a whole: the New Deal would be seen not as the result of capitalists' direct demands but as the outcome of a process of interest-aggregation. Two major problems are identified here: the failure of the National Recovery Administration to establish economic recovery conflicts with the expectation of outcomes functional to the long-term interests of capital; and the assumption that there will be a powerful centralized administration capable of managing economic intervention contrasts with the weakness of the federal government and its need to invent means of economic intervention from scratch. The class struggle approach argues that there are some general constraints on state managers to act in capital's interests; notable among these is their reliance on a healthy economy. In addition, however, crises can weaken capitalist confidence while increasing pressures from below, with the result that state power is relatively autonomous from the demands of capitalists. The strength of this approach, for Skocpol, is its analysis of labour legislation as the result of the intersection of class forces. There are, however, some questions about the notion of class struggle. There was, she argues, little by way of concerted pressure from the working class: there was neither an organized programme of demands nor industrial disruption on a sufficiently wide scale to force concessions. Concessions to labour stemmed from the political process, which suggests the need for close attention to state structures. For example, the organization of Congress gave rural areas a disproportionate influence, and tended to restrain liberal reforms.

It is possible to build on Skocpol's arguments by considering how the New Deal legislation came about. A useful distinction is that between intentions and effects: state managers or other actors may have aimed to achieve a certain goal but the effects of their action may have begun to develop a logic of its own. The failure to attain the goal should not be seen as evidence that the goal was unimportant. It is, for example, well established that the Roosevelt Adminstration began with the explicit aim of saving capitalism from itself and of restoring confidence in the operation of the capitalist economy (see Schlesinger, 1960; Leuchtenburg, 1963). Its early measures through the National Recovery Administration largely failed. But this failure merely shows that the problem was too large for the very limited recipes that were being employed. State managers can have the aim of acting functionally in the interests of capital, and it can hardly be denied that the Administration had this aim. But they can find that conditions prevent their success, in which case they have to amend their approach and possibly become more radical than they had first intended.

Howell Harris (1982b) has taken up Skocpol's suggestion that state structures should be given close attention in an important discussion of the New Deal legislation and the place of labour in the 1930s. He argues that labour's gains were won not through autonomous working-class pressure on the state but through a political process. And it was not the Administration but a group of political liberals in Congress who made the running. Prominent among these was Senator Robert F. Wagner, whose biographer (Huthmacher, 1971: 132) stresses that the New Deal was the result of a hectic confusion and not an ordered plan. To consider how the central piece of New Deal labour legislation, the National Labor Relations Act of 1935, usually known as the Wagner Act, came about, it will be useful to begin with the experience under the earlier period from 1932. The famous section 7a of the National Industrial Recovery Act (NIRA) had contained provisions protecting workers' rights to organize and to engage in collective bargaining. The central aim of the codes promulgated under the Act, however, was to assist business recovery. The theory was that prices were too low and that, to restore stability and increase effective demand, industries should be permitted to control prices (J. Johnson, 1979: 189–93). To be given a code, an industry had to include section 7a, but in the important case of the automobile industry this requirement was successfully avoided (Fine, 1963), and in many other industries the section had little practical effect. The main administrators of the National Recovery Administration (NRA) were explicitly concerned to help industry to help itself. At this point, 7a was seen as a symbol with no practical importance. The section stated some general principles about the desirability of workers' self-organization but imposed no requirement on employers to bargain and contained no means of enforcement; the legal provisions were also unclear and hence easily avoided (Ross, 1965: 51; I. Bernstein, 1950: 39; Schlesinger, 1960: 131).

Wagner was appointed chairman of the National Labor Board under the NRA, and he had some successes where employers were prepared to be conciliatory, but the weakness of the Board became increasingly apparent. In 1934 Wagner told Roosevelt that the Board's central problem was employers' refusal to bargain and their interference with unions' organizational activities. This problem led to the Board's eventual disintegration. This process was assisted by the hostility of the main figures in the NRA to unions: they were unwilling to use even the limited sanctions available to them, such as removing the right of a firm to use the 'blue eagle', the NRA's symbol of co-operation with its activities, against recalcitrant employers (Huthmacher, 1971: 161–2; Leuchtenburg, 1963: 108).

There the matter might have rested were it not for the broader failure of the NIRA to stimulate industrial recovery. This gave the liberals in Congress the scope to press for a more radical programme on labour relations. In 1934 Wagner drafted a new bill, which was met with silence or hostility from the Administration: Roosevelt in particular took little interest in labour matters and did not see the purpose of giving workers the right to free self-organization (Leuchtenburg, 1963: 107–9). Wagner made another attempt in 1935, and Roosevelt finally came round when in the famous Schechter case the Supreme Court nullified that whole NRA structure and forced him to act rapidly to rescue the main platform of his Administration, namely economic recovery (Hutchmacher, 1971: 167, 190–98). In short, a very special conjuncture of forces was required to permit the Wagner Act to succeed.

The political circumstances of the period thus created a space in which the liberals in Congress could act: capital was weakened by the Depression and the failure of the NRA to restore confidence, and the Executive, although itself not interested in labour reform, was willing to tolerate labour legislation as part of the attempt to generate recovery. Two questions remain unanswered: what was the role of 'class struggle' in the process, and why did the legislation take the form that it did? The answers are connected for the liberals saw the strikes of the period as indications of a need to provide legislation which would put capital–labour relations on a harmonious basis, and in seeking specific solutions they turned to existing precedents.

As noted above, Skocpol plays down the importance of industrial disruption in the passage of the Wagner Act, arguing that lobbying was more important and pointing out that strike activity was on the wane when the Act was passed. Yet this is to take an unduly narrow view of the effects of the strikes. In 1934 there were more strikes than for many years, including four major upheavals: strikes in the car and cotton industries, plus disputes that became virtual general strikes in

San Francisco and Minneapolis (I. Bernstein, 1970: 217–315). These latest manifestations of the American tradition of massive, violent confrontations must have brought the 'labour problem' home to the liberals. Without them, it is doubtful whether legislation would have concentrated on dealing with collective relations between managements and unions, as against other broader matters of social policy such as unemployment insurance. As noted above, Roosevelt's interest was in general social reform and the plight of the individual worker, and not in trade union rights. Skocpol rightly rejects a simply 'class struggle' view in which workers and employers are seen as putting competing demands on the polity, with the stronger side winning. But the background of industrial disputes was important in putting labour relations legislation on the agenda.

The shape of the legislation, it may be suggested, stemmed from past practice and assumptions. It was not invented from scratch. Although it certainly aimed to limit the power of employers, it did so within existing norms of how the employment relationship should be governed. This may help to explain why the basis of labour legislation laid by the Wagner Act has remained in being: employers found that they could live within it and, as shown in Chapter 5, even turn some of its provisions to their own advantage.

The basic argument was that large firms had accrued enormous powers and were acting in an autocratic fashion towards their employees, such that basic human freedoms were denied within the workplace. These firms were known as 'economic royalists' (e.g. Auerbach, 1966: 3). At the philosophical level, the denial of liberties and the development of industrial autocracies was condemned by reformers. Writing in 1929, the labour economist Sumner Slichter, for example, attacked employers' resistance to unionism and suggested that employees needed 'mental independence' (Dunlop, 1961: 211–12). Similarly, in his testimony to the Commission on Industrial Relations of 1916 the liberal judge Louis D. Brandeis identified the fundamental cause of industrial conflict as the contrast between political liberty and industrial absolutism; improving the material conditions of workers would not resolve this conflict, which could be dealt with only by attacking management's absolute powers (reprinted in Bakke *et al.*, 1960: 232). The liberal programme was therefore not one of attacking capitalism as such but of limiting the excessive powers of large corporations. The policy could also be justified, as noted above, in terms of its contribution to promoting economic recovery. When viewed in this light, it is possible to see how it gained support outside the small group of committed liberals. For example, Mulder (1979: i) has identified a group of 'insurgent Progressives' who were mostly 'dissident Republicans' and who were 'opposed to concentrated economic and political power'. Notable among them was Robert M. LaFollette Jnr, who between 1930 and 1940 chaired the Senate committee that revealed the massive investment by large companies in labour spies, private police forces, and weapons of all kinds, all with the aim of fighting off unions (Auerbach, 1966). A policy of curtailing the exercise of power by these companies plainly appealed to a number of groups which would otherwise be hostile to state intervention.

On the practical level, the drafters of the New Deal legislation turned to existing models for guidance in an area in which they felt very uncertain. Most immediately, Wagner turned to the United Mine Workers, several of whose officials worked on his drafting committee; section 7a was based heavily on the legislative history of the coal industry (J. Johnson 1979: 144). Interestingly, however, the UMW's president, John L. Lewis, did not see 7a as a means to organize the mass production industries, viewing it instead as a solution to his own particular problems of stabilizing the coal industry and rebuilding the UMW's organization (Dubofsky and Van Tine, 1977: 184). Thus, even the lobbyists in favour of the section had only limited expectations, and subsequent developments depended on the creativity of labour activists and not on any pre-organized plan to transform American industrial relations.

More general practical effects on the drafters of the legislation can also be identified. Harris (1982b) points to the tradition of collective bargaining that had grown up in industries such as coal and clothing. This provided a model of industrial government on which the reformers could draw. Central to this was the negotiation of terms and conditions of employment directly between employers and unions, with the state playing no direct role. In the clothing industry, for example, a period of intense conflict had been ended with the making of collective agreements in many key sectors (Budish and Soule, 1920). These involved permanent boards of arbitration to settle differences. As the chairman of the New York Men's Clothing Industry Board, William M. Leiserson, argued, trade agreements were 'constitutions for the industries which they cover', and he drew detailed analogies with parliamentary systems of goverment (Leiserson, 1922: 61). Proponents of the trade agreement exaggerated the degree to which permanent peace could be created, for the history of the coal industry was one of agreements breaking down whenever competitive pressures and overcapacity emerged, while in the clothing industry there was no sudden switch from conflict to bargaining, but instead a lengthy period throughout the 1910s during which agreements broke down

(Levine, 1924). Collective bargaining could not itself guarantee industrial peace if the forces impinging on it were too strong. But it is easy to see how the model of peace through industrial self-government appealed to reformers seeking a solution to violent and unrestrained labour conflicts.

This drawing on past practice had important consequences for the nature of the New Deal legislation. There was no attempt to institute direct determination of terms and conditions by the state through legislation on such things as minimum wages, holidays, and unemployment insurance. Instead, the model of the trade agreement was developed, with the role of the state being to secure the conditions under which collective bargaining could take place. Thus, the Wagner Act and the case law that followed it laid great weight on the employers' duty to bargain and on unfair labour practices: if employers were not bargaining in good faith or if they were using unreasonable means to interfere with union organization, they should be restrained by the law, but what they bargained about and what substantive terms they established with the unions were of no concern to the state. This preference can be related to the traditional weak role of the state, for state agencies were not used to the idea of regulating industry directly, and, as accounts of the early history of the National Labor Relations Board show, the state's role had to be invented as people went along.

Developments can also be related to the previous character of union-management relations. Employers had traditionally asserted their right to manage. Some had reluctantly been brought within the scope of trade agreements, but such agreements could be torn up. There was nothing in them which permanently restrained managerial freedom, whereas legislation would establish such restraints. In living with the intense hostility of employers, unions had come to rely on a 'business unionism' approach that stressed the trade agreement and was suspicious of outside interference. It is, for example, well known that the American Federation of Labor was opposed to something as commonplace in other countries as state unemployment insurance until well into the 1930s. In short, not only did the state lack the administrative apparatus to institute direct controls over the employment relationship, but employers' resistance would have been intense and there was little systematic pressure for it from the unions. The post-New-Deal system of industrial relations thus had important continuities with the preceding period, most importantly with the continuation of bargaining at the point of production. State intervention changed the balance of power but not the bases of work relations.

Britain

The discussion of the United States has tried to show in some detail how an approach based on the idea of the relative autonomy of the state can be applied. There is no need to repeat the exercise for Britain, and all that is needed is a broad indication of the ways in which the state has become involved in labour relations.[1]

As widely noted, the state's role has traditionally been limited to conciliation in industrial disputes; unions and management have preferred to settle matters directly, without state intervention. This has been described as the tradition of voluntarism. As Flanders (1974: 353, 362) noted of the unions' view of the state, voluntarism 'has never excluded a positive attitude towards some kinds of labour legislation', and it goes much deeper to reflect a belief among unionists that they must be free 'to order their own affairs according to their own preferences with as little outside interference as possible'. Similar points would have to be made about the employers, regarding whom Flanders is silent, so that voluntarism can be taken as a tradition in which the parties, although willing to use the law if it seems to give them a specific benefit, have generally concentrated on settling their affairs themselves. State intervention has dramatically altered this tradition. Some writers have been led to counterpose the non-interventionist stance of voluntarism and corporatism, in which unions and employers are brought together under the auspices of state agencies to create tripartite agreements on economic management. Attempts at national planning and incomes policies might support a corporatist thesis. But the thesis, at least in its strong version that there was a clear drift towards a corporatist policy on the part of the state, is plainly contradicted by the policies of the Thatcher government, with its desire to roll back the influence of the state. The thesis is, in any event, weak to the extent that it treats developments of the 1960s and 1970s as part of a conscious state policy; assumes that capital and labour are homogeneous blocs and ignores divisions within them; and implies that state interventions incorporated the organizations of capital and labour, instead of merely aiming to control some of their activities.

It is preferable to consider the factors leading to state intervention in a more general way, without becoming enmeshed in debates about

1 Jessop (1980) provides a useful review of the state's role in the economy as a whole since 1945. He argues that attempts to manage the economy have led to stop-go cycles, with the state being unable to exercise effective control of developments. He also points to the weakness of the organizations of capital and labour, arguing that neither side had the unity or sense of direction necessary to press through a re-structuring of labour relations; this point is taken up further below.

the notion of corporatism. Corporatist arrangements can obviously be used, but they are likely to be among a wider range of approaches and need not form part of a conscious strategy. Consider, then, the picture facing British 'state managers'. Throughout much of the period since 1945 they have been faced with problems of slow economic growth and balance of payments difficulties. Whether or not labour issues have been a prime cause of these problems, it has rarely been possible to try to meet them without affecting the conduct of industrial relations. The incomes policies of the first post-war Labour government, for example, were part of an attempt to deal with a lack of competitiveness by controlling wage costs. As is generally the case, the context of state intervention has been provided by an economic crisis which has required immediate measures. There has been little room for careful planning. In view of the government's own close links with the union movement, and in the context of unions' co-operation with the state during the war, it is not surprising that the post-war Labour government sought the unions' co-operation with wage restraint instead of, for example, trying to impose it. Neither is it surprising that governments during the 1960s and the 1970s tried to persuade the unions to co-operate with incomes policies, turning to more forceful methods when this failed. Governments have had to balance the perceived national interest in periods of acute uncertainty with the demands of particular groups.

It was suggested above that the American state enjoyed a period of relative autonomy during the crisis of the early 1930s. The British case seems to be different because successive crises have not involved a collapse of public confidence in business such as that which the slump inspired among Americans, who had become accustomed during the 1920s to rising standards of living and to claims that this was due to the free enterprise system: when the rise ended, the system itself was held to blame. The British state has been less able to restructure industrial labour relations in ways that would be opposed by important fractions of capital. In addition, the problem has been perceived not as one of 'economic royalists' but of unions which resist improved working practices and which make irresponsible wage demands. The aim has thus been seen as one of harnessing or controlling unions and their members. Yet because of the tradition of voluntarism and the powerful position of the organized labour movement, this aim has proved impossible to achieve. Incomes policies have broken down, and some attempts to legislate have been defeated.

This is not to suggest that unions have been more powerful than governments. As several commentators have pointed out, there is an important sense in which British unions have been too weak and not too strong: leaderships have been unable to impose settlements on the membership, and it has proved impossible to develop a corporate body in which the TUC could 'deliver' on the interest of labour as a whole. It is thus sometimes argued that unions' power is greater in defensive actions and in disrupting government or employers' efforts at reform than it is in aggressive campaigns. This is true to an extent, but what must also be taken into account is another sense of power, namely 'the production of intended effects' (Russell, 1975: 25). The power to disrupt the actions of others is not to be equated with achieving one's own goals. In this case, unions can reasonably be taken to have goals such as raising their members' standards of living and securing opportunities for employment. The rise in unemployment that occurred throughout the 1970s, together with periods of falling real wages and numerous uncertainties occasioned by the collapse of companies, has not been consistent with such goals. The British case has not been one of a power struggle in which one party's long-term aims have been met. Instead, it has reflected a continuing series of attempts by governments, employers, and unions to come to terms with the consequences of a continuing economic crisis. As Panitch (1976: 251–3) argues, in a weak and under-capitalized economy such as that of Britain, unions' demands on wages (or on other things) do not need to be very high in order to provoke a severe crisis.

Just as unions have been divided among themselves, so 'capital' has not been a unified bloc. Strinati (1982), in particular, discerns a range of competing approaches in managerial treatments of industrial relations. He suggests that the large, UK-based, manufacturing firms that were dominant within the CBI took a 'corporatist' stance, meaning that they favoured state intervention and the control of the internal affairs of unions. Small firms, together with the banking sector adopted what Strinati (perhaps not very felicitously) calls a paternalist view, which involved a generally non-interventionist state together with the internal regulation of union affairs. Finally, large multi-nationals preferred a non-interventionist approach without attempts at internal regulation. Strinati (1982: 161–4) sees the 1971 Industrial Relations Act, for example, as the outcome of the state's attempt to grapple with these contrasting demands. The state had an active role in trying to accommodate differing demands so as to develop an overall strategy. Many other writers (e.g. Ingham, 1982) have discussed divisions within capital and the effects of these on the development of a coherent policy.

The main period of state intervention in Britain has thus been one in which the opportunities for clear-cut action have been limited. Managing the economy has been increasingly difficult, and the need to deal with immediate problems has made a more strategic approach difficult. The position of unions has been far more entrenched than it was in America in the 1930s, and the possibilities for a state-imposed model of labour relations have thus been remote. It was argued in the case of the New Deal that American labour legislation has not fundamentally altered the basis of capital-labour relations, for collective bargaining remains the dominant focus, and direct state regulation of employment conditions is limited. The New Deal did, however, greatly change the conduct of bargaining: in this respect it was revolutionary. In Britain, state intervention has been concerned with managing the consequences of a mature industrial relations system in the context of profound economic difficulties.

It is useful briefly to relate experience since the 1960s to earlier traditions. As Clegg (1979: 291) summarizes the position, the law has generally kept out of industrial relations, apart from such 'limited areas' as social security legislation, health and safety, and the protection of groups considered too weak to look after themselves. The internal operation of collective bargaining was allowed to progress relatively unhindered. Unions and employers preferred to manage their own affairs, and there was no campaign by unions for the legal guarantee of organizational rights, for they had learned to rely on their own industrial strength (Lewis and Simpson, 1981: 9). The state's limited role was also reflected in its approach to overt industrial conflict. Fox (1983: 27) has recently argued that the government was unwilling to back employers directly when they were engaged in lengthy struggles with their workers; it might instead offer conciliation and arbitration. The state certainly wielded considerable force, 'but this was not in pursuit of modernization, but simply to settle large-scale disputes'. There were thus three roles for government intervention: to deal with 'limited areas' outside collective bargaining; to permit bargaining to occur where it appeared that judicial activity was interfering with its proper functioning, as in the reversal of the *Taff Vale* decision in the 1906 Trade Disputes Act; and to try to settle significant disputes on the basis of compromise.

The British case is thus one of a state being able to hold itself aloof from the battles between capital and labour. From the 1960s, accelerating economic problems rendered this position increasingly difficult, and the state began to take a far more active approach. But, in doing so, it was constrained by the strong tradition of voluntarism that had emerged and that had, indeed, been encouraged by earlier governments. The 'labour problem', moreover, was merely one part of a set of problems connected with low economic growth and a lack of competitiveness in international markets.

Since 1979, a radical change in policy has taken place, and some brief comments are required on how it affects the foregoing characterization. First, it exemplifies the point made in connection with the New Deal that the state's relative autonomy increases in times of recession (although in the British case it also has to be said that many observers see the government's monetarist policy as itself a cause of the depth of the recession). In the field of labour relations the government's legislative programme can be seen as an attempt to do for capitalists something that they were too pusillanimous to do for themselves, namely to take on the unions. Second, as part of the general policy of 'rolling back' the influence of the state, direct involvement in labour relations has been reduced: incomes policies have been rejected, and the government has refused to intervene in even the largest industrial disputes, whereas under previous Conservative as well as Labour administrations it had been accepted that ministers would try to resolve large and potentially damaging strikes. Third, however, this does not mean that the state has simply withdrawn. On the contrary, financial controls and demands for increased efficiency have led managements in the public sector to take a new, tough approach on working practices (Ferner, 1985; Ferner and Terry, 1985). And the private sector has been affected by attempts to 'make labour markets work' by, for example, reducing the statutory protection of wages in the Wages Council industries. In some respects the previous tradition of avoiding the direct regulation of factory regimes has been strengthened. Yet there has been a reversal of tradition in so far as the state has either kept out of the three limited areas of intervention or has shifted the basis of intervention away from providing the conditions for collective bargaining to take place towards questioning the value of such bargaining.

The British state, like other states, has traditionally intervened in labour relations in ways which have helped to shift capitalism away from a laissez-faire model: supporting collective bargaining and mediating in disputes questions the operation of pure laws of supply and demand. Its interventions were limited by the character of labour relations and the economic context in which the state was operating. Developments since 1979 suggest an attempt to re-establish laissez-faire conditions. The implications will be pursued in the concluding section of the chapter.

Australia
The contrast with Australia is dramatic, for in that country the state has for many years been heavily involved in labour relations. About 90 per cent of employees are covered by industrial tribunals operating

at the national (Commonwealth) level or at the level of tl
states (K. Walker, 1970: 11). The tribunals can set b
together with conditions of work such as hours. Sta
arbitration performs many of the functions carried out b
bargaining in Britain and America. The arbitration system
fully shaped the rest of the industrial relations landscape: since it implies the existence of permanent workers' organizations, it has
stimulated union growth; and, as discussed in chapter 5, it has
affected the pattern of strikes, with frequent, short strikes being used
as demonstrations to tribunals of the seriousness of a case.

How did this system, the legislative basis of which is the Conciliation and Arbitration Act of 1904, come about? The position of the
state itself was important, for during the nineteenth century it had
played a significant role in economic development. Australia began as
a penal colony in which the state directed most aspects of the
economy. 'Penal colony beginnings had determined that the state
would be both centralized and positive' (Gollan, 1960: 85). In dealing
with railways, education and the distribution of land, governments
became major forces in the economy. The state was responsible for
half of all capital formation during the nineteenth century, and public
expenditure accounted for a large part of the gross national product:
38 per cent in 1911/12, as against 13 per cent in Britain in 1910 (Encel,
1970: 62–3). It was thus likely that the state should play a role in
labour questions, although precisely what role remained to be
established.

/ Direct wage regulation had been practised during the early nineteenth century, as an offshoot of the government's determination of
the conditions of labour of convicts, but such regulation was, by the
1850s, increasingly impractical (Plowman *et al.*, 1980: 97–8). During
the second half of the nineteenth century, unions and employers began
to develop ways of dealing with each other directly. In the coal industry, for example, there was a pattern which had strong similarities
with developments in industrial relations in Britain and America: in
periods of rising demand unions were established and gained some
concessions from employers, but periodic slumps led to wage cuts and
the collapse of union organization (Gollan, 1963). In general, according to Macarthy (1970a: 4), labour market conditions favoured such
independent and non-state-directed endeavours: a shortage of labour
made for high real wages, so that workers did not feel the need for
government protection, while employers tended to be suspicious of
government involvement/ It is possible that a 'voluntaristic' system
based on collective bargaining would have developed. But, for many
observers, events in the 1890s prevented this. A slump between 1890

and 1893 unleashed a powerful onslaught by employers on unions in many key industries such as shipping, coal, and sheep farming: there had been growing concern at union encroachment, and employers took the opportunity to fight back, making as the key issue the right to employ non-union labour and to pay non-union wages. Up to 50,000 workers were on strike for between two weeks and two months (Sutcliffe, 1966; Gollan, 1963: 78–88). The unions were defeated.

The unions had never been interested only in bargaining with employers. At the level of cities and states they had had considerable political involvement, and when they turned to political solutions at the national level at the end of the nineteenth century they used methods that were already well-established (Dabscheck and Niland, 1981: 64). To understand why they did so, and did so successfully, their position must be considered.

Several conditions promoted the early development of union organization and solidarity. One was the concentration of the population in a few urban centres and the homogeneity of the labour force: as early as 1880 half the population lived in towns of at least 1,000 inhabitants, and ethnic homogeneity was such that even as late as 1947 only 2 per cent of the population was born in non-British countries (K. Walker, 1970: 5, 8). The importance of an egalitarian mateship in Australian working-class culture has been widely stressed (Mayer, 1964: 442–3). Australian unionists were convinced that their standards were better than those in Europe, and attributed this to their own independent efforts (Gollan, 1960: 73). Workers' self-confidence and power was evidenced by the winning of the eight-hour day in most skilled trades during the 1850s (Gollan, 1960: 69–72), an achievement well in advance of developments in Britain or America. In view of the tradition of independent action, what explained unions' involvement in politics? According to Gollan (1960: 80–6), unionists felt that, in principle, politics lay outside their proper interests, but the logic of their activities, in seeking such things as limits to working hours and provision for the unemployed (both of which became established policies during the 1860s and 1870s), led them into political campaigns. In addition, the established role of the state meant that for unions the gap between collective bargaining and political action was smaller than it was in countries in which state regulation of the economy had to overcome established practice. That is, in a country such as Britain a move into politics involved a new step for unions, whereas in Australia the established role of the government made it natural to turn to it to secure the unions' aims. The role of the state thus had a direct effect on the eventual legal regulation of industrial relations (because the state was itself predisposed to control the terms and conditions of employment) and an indirect effect (because it encouraged unions to take an early interest in politics).

The defeats of the 1890s might have made unionists disenchanted with politics, for the employers' onslaught was actively supported by the state (I. Turner, 1978: 54). Yet, according to Rawson (1978: 46), 'since there was no strong native tradition of union suspicion of the law as such, this seemed to show only that the forces which had been used against the unions could equally be used in their favour'. It should not be inferred that unionists were naively optimistic about their ability to use state intervention to suit themselves. But the events of the 1890s seem to have generated less of a profound suspicion of the law than existed in Britain. The unions had enjoyed, and continued to enjoy even during the 1890s, some success in the individual states in building labour parties and in securing the passage of employment legislation. The state would not have been seen as a monolith, and its activities would, on the basis of experience at local level, have been felt to be adaptable to the needs of the unions.

As for the employers, it seems that they were, when compared with their American counterparts, weak and divided. Goodrich (1928: 202) noted that America has had a 'group of industrial and financial magnates far more powerful and equipped with a far more varied arsenal of weapons than the scattered squatters who formed the chief Australian aristocracy'. Divisions were apparent in the response to demands in the 1900s for the regulation of wages by the law. Macarthy (1970b) identifies two groups of employers. One, comprising mainly manufacturers, wanted tariff protection so that domestic industries could be promoted, while also being concerned about under-cutting from low-wage sweatshops. The other, composed chiefly of exporters, feared the increase in their costs and the possible retaliation from abroad that tariff barriers would bring. The protectionists were prepared to do a straight deal: wage regulation (which would also help them to deal with competition from low-wage producers) in return for tariffs. The absence of a powerful and united opposition to state intervention by employers thus assisted state regulation. In 1907 came the famous 'Harvester' case in which the president of the Court of Conciliation and Arbitration, Justice Higgins, laid down the minimum wage for labourers of seven shillings a day. This was not the first time such a standard had been used, but it was a watershed in bringing together some disparate rulings and in establishing that the Court would determine rates of pay and apply them throughout its area of jurisdiction: the level of wages was to be set according to standards of fairness and social need and not the vagaries of market forces (Macarthy, 1967).

A 'state manager' of the 1900s could thus have identified at least four influences. First, the unions, although weakened by the events of the 1890s, were not destroyed and were, partly as a result of these events, turning to political demands. Then there were the employers, who were, although industrially powerful, unable to develop a unified policy on state intervention. Third, the strikes had brought into focus the traditional role of the state in trying to articulate a 'public interest' and in preventing damaging industrial disputes. Direct intervention to place the relations of managements and unions on a more rational and orderly basis would have seemed not merely feasible but positively desirable. Finally, there was the long-standing tradition of state involvement in setting the terms and conditions of employment. This gave the state the resources and authority to act.

It was not, then, a matter of any of the parties having a developed strategy. As Macarthy (1967: 81) puts it in the case of the unions, 'labour's policies may be thought of more as a series of short-term expediencies evolved as experience taught, rather than a continuum of inter-related policies'. But, he goes on, in the process of responding to changing economic and political conditions 'the Australian labour movement inadvertently helped to carve out for itself, and for Australia, the most complete system of state regulated industrial conflict outside the present day socialist countries'. This neatly captures the dialectics of the process, with social actors making choices in particular structural circumstances and with their choices helping to shape subsequent developments, often in unintended directions. The unions' demands, traditions of state involvement, social norms about fairness, and the absence of a unified employers' view interacted in the particular climate of the 1900s to produce an outcome that may have been unintended but was hardly accidental.

Conclusions
These examples do not cover all the circumstances in which states can be called on to intervene in the capital-labour relation. But they illustrate some of the processes involved and some of the sources of variation therein. Australia shows how powerful state regulation can emerge where there is a tradition of intervention and where employers' and workers' demands are compatible with, or not strong enough to prevent, further involvement. Britain illustrates the problems facing a state trying to manage an increasingly crisis-prone economy which has a long-established tradition of voluntarism with its deep suspicion of the law. And America shows how even a non-interventionist state can be led to make substantial moves to regulate factory regimes, how the relative autonomy of the state can vary, and how a labour policy is

often the result of the assembly on an *ad hoc* basis of a range of expedients and not of a clear plan. In all three cases, it is clear that neither 'capital' nor 'labour' is a united bloc. The development of labour policy is not a matter of a homogeneous state reacting to the demands of capital and labour, but of state managers trying to handle the contradictory needs of accumulation and legitimation and having to respond to specific demands, which may conflict with other demands, stemming from particular groups within the ranks of capital and labour.

The idea that state intervention reflects a strategy to ensure the better functioning of the capitalist economy is thus too simple. The state has to manage contradictory pressures, and there is no guarantee that even such an explicit attempt to restore the conditions for accumulation as America's NIRA will be effective. This is not, however, to dismiss the notion of strategy. Although some uses of the concept have implied that states have clearly articulated policies that fit into an overall strategy of economic and social management, reaction against such uses has tended to suggest that there are never any overall policies and that events are no more than a sequence of accidents. A view between these extremes is that state managers may have available competing strategies and that they have to choose between them according to the conflicting demands with which they are faced. A strategy may well fail to work. And situations will vary according to the extent to which strategies can be formulated: in some cases reasonably coherent plans may exist, whereas in others short-term expedients may be all that can be put together. It is not a matter of strategy versus day-to-day management but of variations in the coherence of strategies and in the number of competing strategies from which state managers have to fashion a policy.

Conclusions

This chapter has argued that the state has a relative autonomy in the field of labour relations: it is neither independent of the forces of civil society nor a mere reflection of those forces. Any capitalist state can be called upon to perform tasks connected with accumulation, that is the need for a capitalist economy to continue to generate profits and to use these profits in subsequent circuits of capital, and with the legitimation of the system. The basic role of the state thus stems from the nature of the productive system. But if the state is to perform its functions adequately it cannot be tied directly to the 'interests' of capital. It must have some real independence from capitalists. There may, moreover, be differing priorities within different groups of capitalists, so that there need be no clear capitalist interest. Demands from other groups will also have to be managed. And the functions of accumulation and legitimation contain contradictions within themselves as well as being in contradiction with each other. The task of state managers is to manage these contradictory pressures and to fashion a policy with the tools to hand.[2]

The task can be performed in different ways. Burawoy has suggested that in the area of labour relations the state's activities can be assessed in terms of the regulation of factory regimes and support for the reproduction of labour power. It was suggested above that this framework needs developing in two respects: to explain why the state's interventions are conditioned by the economic base; and to consider in some detail examples of state intervention so that the character of different states' relative autonomy may be indicated. This chapter has tried to carry through these two points.

One conclusion arising from the second warrants emphasis. Australia, like Sweden, would score high in Burawoy's two dimensions. Yet patterns of labour relations in the two countries are patently very different; most obviously, and for reasons explored in the following chapter, Australia has been far the more strike-prone, particularly with respect to small, short stoppages. Countries falling into the same box of Burawoy's typology thus have different patterns of workplace industrial relations. As shown elsewhere (P. Edwards, 1983), a similar problem besets other typologies. How serious it is depends on one's view of the purpose of the typologies. Burawoy himself would seem to see his approach as doing more than classifying types of state intervention, for he places it in the context of differences in shopfloor relations and argues that state actions have been important in creating these differences. That is, the typology aims to categorize an overall pattern of industrial relations and not just the role of the state. It thus has problems with explaining differences between similarly located countries, and also with showing where other countries fit within it. Such an approach also has the difficulty of dealing with specific historical developments in different countries. Burawoy's account of how and why each of his four countries came to fall within each of his categories is very brief, and the dynamics of the situation are far from

2 Zeitlin (1985) has recently argued against any use of the idea of the relative autonomy of the state, suggesting that the state is either totally constrained or totally free to pursue its own objectives. This is to pose the issue in far too stark a way. The economy constrains the state without determining everything that it does. Zeitlin makes some useful points about the weaknesses of existing theories of state intervention, but he offers little by way of resolving these.

clear. To continue with the case of Sweden, more would need to be said on the policies of unions and employers and on how these policies interacted with the behaviour of state agents to create a particular shape of industrial relations. This is certainly possible, as the fore-going discussion has attempted to show in the case of America. Sisson (forthcoming) has explored the strategies of employers in different countries, generating a more detailed and subtle account than that offered by Burawoy.

If, however, the typology is seen as a way of looking at forms of state intervention, it retains some considerable value. States differ in the extent to which they regulate factory regimes, and it is important to consider why. Burawoy's framework indentifies two key dimen-sions of state involvement and thus helps in the analysis of the dif-ferent forms which this intervention can take. It does not work as a typology of workplace industrial relations, and to the extent that it reduces the complexity of history in a particular country to a box of a classificatory scheme it gives insufficient attention to process, but it provides some tools for understanding the relationship between the state and the labour process. This conclusion echoes that reached in chapters 1 and 2 about typologies of managerial strategy. Not only do ideal-type characterizations neglect the complexity and ambiguity of empirical cases, but they also tend to imply that the categories iden-tified are clear-cut and mutually exclusive. It was argued that managerial stategy is better seen as an assembly of many different elements than as a consistent package. State interventions should similarly be viewed less as the working through of a distinct type of activity than as developments which have logics of their own. A typology can be a useful tool of analysis but it cannot capture the dialectics of concrete practices.

One important substantive conclusion arises from this argument. As noted above, there have been tendencies in Britain away from traditional forms of state intervention. Burawoy's model would characterize this as a shift away from the category of low regulation of factory regimes and high provision of social security to that of being low on both dimensions. This second box is filled by Japan. Now, several commentators have discerned in trends at the level of the workplace a tendency for Japanese styles of labour relations to emerge. If state intervention is moving in similar directions, there is a neat symmetry. The problem, however, is that the British case remains very different from the Japanese. To see the two states as becoming similar has to contend with the fact that the British state has been aiming to re-establish a type of laissez-faire, whereas in Japan internal labour markets are of great importance, as are the links between productive industries and banks. Both of these features encourage a long-term approach such that, for example, banks and manufacturing firms take a strategic view of industrial development instead of being driven by the demands of short-term profit maximization. To the extent that the British state's stress on short-term economic viability reproduces behaviour characteristic of laisser-faire economies, in which long-term investment strategies are impossible, the gap between Britain and Japan is widening and not narrowing. The danger of characterizing the complexities of such developments within an ideal-typical scheme that identifies only two dimensions of state intervention are obvious.

State intervention is dialectically related to the capital-labour relation because the need for it stems from the character of the relation while it is itself capable of influencing the shape of factory regimes. The circularity implied in this statement (A affects B and B affects A) can be avoided in two ways. The first, deriving from the overall approach suggested in chapter 2, is to see different agents as interacting to produce specific outcomes. Just as a pattern of workplace relations should be seen as the product of the activities of managers and workers, in which outcomes emerge, often unintentionally, from the process of struggle, so states' activities can be viewed in terms of the inter-relationship between state managers and other parts of a social formation. The second is to consider events historically, asking why a particular structure arose and then charting its effects once it had been created: social structures are human products but once they exist they have effects independent of the wishes of those subject to them.

The methodological point made at the start of the analysis of cases of state intervention thus warrants emphasis. In considering the interactions between social actors within particular social structures, the account does not try to identify a list of 'factors' which distinguish between countries. Such factors have their effects only in the context of other influences, and they do not exist independently of each other. Instead, each country needs to be analysed in its own right, with the ways in which aspects of structure and action come together to produce specific outcomes. This is not to retreat into a methodological relativism in which each case is seen as unique and self-contained. The real contrast is not between accounts of each case and attempts to generalize across cases. It is between a method which identifies various independent variables and tries to analyse their impact across countries and one which develops tools of analysis at a general level of analysis and tries to apply them to concrete cases. Thus, the foregoing discussion has considered the general characteristics of capitalist states before examining the specific conditions which led some different states to behave in different ways. It is not a matter of saying that this or that factor will have a certain effect, but of considering how a set of factors operated in a particular situation. The tools of analysis that have been employed include, at decreasing levels of generality, the nature of the capital-labour relation, the roles of the capitalist state, the relative autonomy of the state, the variability of this relative autonomy as economic conditions vary, and the divisions that exist within state machineries and within the sides of capital and labour. These tools have been employed not to generate typologies of state intervention but to understand the logic of particular cases of intervention.

One point about this approach warrants emphasis. It is common to link state intervention to class struggle, and to see this struggle as a cause of state activity. It has been argued above that there are substantial problems in seeing struggle as a source of direct demands on the state, with labour, for example, making clear claims for state support. This approach pays little regard to divisions within the ranks of labour and capital. And it assumes that direct demands are, indeed, made. Such demands are far from being the rule. But the role of struggle should not be neglected. In all of the cases considered above, the struggles that were going on within the workplace affected state managers' perceptions of their own role: the strikes of the 1890s in Australia increased demands for an arbitration system that would permit less damaging resolutions of differences; industrial unrest during the American New Deal highlighted the problem of employers' autocracy and also that of the effects of disputes on 'the public'; and so on. State managers have responded to these issues by trying to use their power to mediate in disputes or to establish institutions that can prevent their occurrence. Thus, workplace struggles can often have an indirect effect on what the state does. This underlines one feature of the state's relative autonomy, for the consequences of patterns of struggle have to be interpreted by state managers before they act as inputs to the decision-making process.

In most capitalist economies the state plays a significant role in economic management, and this often includes intervening in relationships between managements and workers, either directly, as with labour laws, or indirectly, for example with incomes policies. A theory of work relations cannot, therefore, ignore the state. This chapter has tried to fill the gap in this area which exists within the labour process tradition. Yet state intervention is not a once-for-all thing. It continues to have effects. Indeed, a major part of the argument is the point that, because the state has a relative autonomy, it acts in ways which are not directly dependent on the demands of employers or unions and workers. It follows that state activities will help to shape the conduct of workplace industrial relations. The following chapter therefore considers trends in the three countries considered above and assesses the connections between the state's actions and those of employers and unions.

5

The Workplace,
Employers and the State

This chapter continues the discussion of the three countries, the United States, Britain and Australia, analysed in chapter 4. The main focus shifts from the state as such to the workplace. Contrasting trends in workplace relations during the period since 1940 are identified, and reasons for the contrasts are suggested. The activities of the state, and in particular the different forms of interaction between state regulation and the modes of regulation worked out by employers and unions and workers, comprise one set of explanatory factors. The contrast between Britain and America is the major focus, for in these two countries the tradition of handling the employment relationship at the point of production was particularly well-developed. The similarity was strengthened by the American state's support for collective bargaining in the 1930s and by the emergence of shopfloor bargaining during the late 1930s and, in particular, during the Second World War. Yet this did not lead to workplace bargaining of the British type. The reasons for this contrast can be found in the interaction of employers, the unions, and state agencies. State intervention was not the key feature, for its effects depended on the use made of it by employers and unions. Indeed, the shape of this intervention can be related to the form of workplace bargaining, and in particular the strategy of employers, in place before the state's involvement.

Australia provides some useful contrasts with the Anglo-American picture. In particular, its arbitration system has had a dramatic effect on the development of collective bargaining and the pattern of workplace conflict. It thus helps to illustrate the different connections that can exist between states and workplace relations.

The first two sections of this chapter outline the different patterns of workplace relations in the three countries and consider the reasons for the differences, paying particular attention to the policies of state agencies and employers. But is there a more fundamental explanation of these differences than one based on institutions and strategies that have operated since 1940? What explains why these structures and policies have come into existence? In the case of Australia the early involvement of the state was crucial in subsequent developments, and little more will be said about it. But the contrast between Britain and America raises some deeper issues. It will be argued in the third section of the chapter that the policies for managing the workplace adopted by employers have played a vital and somewhat neglected role and, moreover, that reasons can be adduced as to why British and American employers acted differently.

After this consideration of causes, the final section turns to some of the consequences of different patterns of job control. It suggests that the effects of the British pattern of shopfloor bargaining and custom and practice, as contrasted with the American one of formal contracts and bureaucratic grievance procedures, should not be seen in terms of the strength of workers and the weakness of employers. The American system has also constrained employers, and each system has produced results that may have been desired by none of its participants. In Britain, both sides were weak, and the fact that unions had a certain defensive power, based on their implantation at shopfloor level, should not be confused with an ability to re-structure labour relations or to break out of a cycle of disputes and disruptions. This argument illustrates one of the general themes of this study, namely that patterns of workplace relations have contradictory features and that a given pattern cannot be reduced to the 'zero sum' idea that one side is more powerful than the other; a set of relations can develop such that neither side is able to attain its long-term objectives.

Trends in Workplace Relations

In this section the main elements of the different paths of development of British and American shopfloor relations are outlined. The starting date of 1940, and not the more usual 1945, is taken because wartime experiences were important in shaping subsequent developments. The Australian situation is considered more briefly after this main contrast has been made. The focus, it must be stressed, is the workplace and forms of control practised within it. No pretence is made of dealing with wider questions of class consciousness or workers' perceptions of power and inequality in society at large. Analysis at the level of the workplace is pertinent to these questions, and it may be suggested that many of the discussions of, in particular, the reasons for American workers' distinctive class attitudes have been weakened by a lack of attention to experience within the workplace. This point will be considered briefly in the third section of the chapter, but to deal with class consciousness and its variations between countries would require a study of its own.

Contrasts in Workplace Behaviour

There has been some debate as to whether Britain and America have really been as different as might appear. Two publications in 1980 suggested that in the early 1940s there were substantial similarities but that there was subsequently a significant divergence: in Britain, autonomous shopfloor organizations flourished whereas in America such organizations were contained by formal agreements which prevented day-to-day bargaining about effort and reward. Brody (1980: 206), while recognizing that American work groups had some ability to alter through shopfloor struggle the formal structure of bargaining, argued that

> it was, however, an unequal struggle. The force of legitimacy lay on the side of the workplace rule of law. In England, where union contracts did not penetrate down to the factory floor, the shop stewards carved out a bargaining realm quite independent of the union structure.

Lichtenstein (1980: 348–9), analysing car workers in particular, similarly suggests that Britain developed a system based on the bargaining of production standards on the shopfloor while in America workgroup power was not legitimized or institutionalized in the same way.

Tolliday and Zeilin (1982) have questioned this contrast. They suggest that it exaggerates the strength and vitality of shopfloor organizations in Britain, which in fact emerged only during the late 1950s and the 1960s and which were, as subsequent events have shown, vulnerable to managerial counter-attack. And in America, they argue, shopfloor power was not snuffed out and there remained very substantial constraints on managerial freedom. Seniority rules and grievance procedures may have been acceptable during periods of growth, but they placed considerable limits on management's freedom to introduce more flexible systems of working in the face of growing competition. The authors go so far as to reverse the Brody-Lichtenstein view, arguing that 'for most of the postwar period unions were stronger and cut more deeply into managerial prerogatives in American than in British auto plants' (p. 33).

This way of looking at the matter is not, however, very helpful. It is true that powerful shop steward organizations in Britain are more a product of the 1960s than the 1940s and that American shopfloor organizations did not disappear overnight. But this is to amend only the timing of the process of divergence. It is also true that American managements have been constrained by the pattern of bargaining that emerged. But this is not at all the same as saying that American unions were stronger than their British counterparts. The constraints emerged from the system of industrial relations as a whole. The system was powerfully shaped by managerial policies. It will be argued below that American firms had a clearer view of what they wanted than did British ones and that they were able to institute a formalized system which limited the possibility of bargaining on the shopfloor. The system brought with it some unintended consequences such as inflexibility, but these results cannot be seen as the outcome of the strength of the unions.

Discussion in terms of the relative power of unions and workers also has difficulty in getting to grips with the facts, analysed below, that the number of strikes has risen in Britain and not in America, and that the length of strikes in the latter country has remained high. If American unions have been 'weak' in fighting few strikes, they have been 'strong' in prosecuting disputes with vigour. Shopfloor relations cannot be reduced to 'more or less' terms because they contain several elements: the frontier of control has many features, which can vary independently. The frontier refers, moreover, only to detailed control, and the outcomes in terms of general control be read off from it. The problem in examining consequences is to explore the contradictory results of workplace bargaining. Thus it is possible that American workers, while losing the right to challenge managerial actions on the shopfloor, have been compensated by the emergence of formalized workplace rules that are binding on management and that thus limit managerial discretion. Similarly, the retention of shopfloor bargaining in Britain may have preserved and extended aspects of detailed control while also locking workers and managers into a battle over day-to-day issues which has suited neither side in the longer term. Such things cannot be reduced to the one dimension of the relative bargaining power of the two sides.

It is true, as Tolliday and Zeitlin argue, that shop stewards in Britain have not always had the bargaining power to exert much control of the effort bargain. But there is an important distinction between the power to challenge management and the underlying principle on which workplace relations are based. In Britain this principle continued to be the settlement of issues through the direct confrontation

of workers, stewards, and management, and not through written contracts, grievance procedures, and arbitration arrangements.

In order to expand on these contrasts, it will be useful to review
some of the workplace studies that have been conducted on each side
of the Atlantic. Given that these studies are generally focused on
specific issues and that there are no systematic comparisons of similar
factories in the two countries, drawing inferences about differing
contexts and patterns of behaviour is necessarily risky. But some
points emerge fairly clearly. The engineering factories studied by
Edwards and Scullion (1982a) indicate the position in Britain. In two
plants, called the Large Metals and Small Metals factories, stewards
had developed a very powerful position on a wide range of issues and
were constantly dealing with foremen about production standards,
line speeds, man allocations, and overtime. In the other two engineering plants, the Components and the Electrical Factories, the frontier
of control was less advanced but there were full-time conveners and
the stewards had an established place in the factory. In particular,
problems were dealt with by foremen and stewards on the shopfloor
so that a grievance about, say, safety matters would be considered as it
arose. Although actual stoppages of work were rare, it was taken for
granted by all sides that they were a constant possibility and that a
steward who was dissatisfied with management's response to a com-
plaint could call for a stoppage or other sanctions. Clack (1967)
describes in detail how the use of 'downers' was built into the day-to-
day operation of a car factory. Batstone *et al.* (1977) analyse the
activities of shop stewards in a vehicle-assembly plant and show how
stewards operated largely independently of the national union;
there were close ties between workers and stewards, and stewards
played an important role in the running of the factory.

Now it is true that these may be extreme or atypical cases, but findings from less powerfully organized factories suggest that some of the
underlying principles were the same. Thus, Nichols and Beynon (1977)
discuss workers' sources of power where shopfloor organization was
weak. A little sabotage or absenteeism was practised, but workers had
few other means of influencing the effort bargain. They were not
entirely powerless, but they lacked the resources to challenge
managerial decisions. In all these cases the immediate effort bargain
assumes considerable significance: as demonstrated in detail in
chapter 6, in cases where shopfloor organizations are well developed,
workers have been able to influence the effort bargain and the factors
impinging on it, whereas in the absence of such organizations they
have had much less control.

The American pattern is very different. What comes out of descriptions of unionized factories is the importance of the collective bargaining contract, which is often a lengthy and detailed document, and the procedure for handling individual grievances. Herding (1972: 142–224) documents changes in four steel and four car factories over the post-war period. He argues that unions' substantive rights in terms of such things as seniority and production rules have generally increased, but contrasts this with a decline in their procedural influence on such matters as representation, procedures and arbitration, and strikes. That is, unions have lost the power to challenge managerial logics, and such power as unions have has been shifted from the level of the shopfloor and has been concentrated in the hands of union officials. The shop steward system has atrophied. Pfeffer (1979) produces similar arguments, based on his experiences working in a factory producing piston rings. He describes the great distance between union leaders and the shopfloor, the main interest of the leaders in administering the contract, and the leaders' lack of concern with shopfloor issues. And, as has been shown in previous chapters, Burawoy (1979) sees the rise of collective bargaining and grievance procedures as the consolidation of the internal state, wherein workers have the right to protest about work assignments or production standards, but this right depends on going through a bureaucratic procedure that removes the issue from the immediate work group.

Burawoy also stresses a further feature of the American system, namely the seniority rules that are widespread in unionized sectors and are also used outside them. These rules establish seniority as a criterion for the right to bid for desirable jobs and for protection against lay-offs; when the size of the labour force is cut, the most senior workers can 'bump' others out of their jobs, with the least senior suffering the lay-off. The consequence has been an emphasis on individual rights and the administration of the contract to ensure the protection of these rights, and not the prosecution of collective matters. The rules certainly constrain management, in that labour cannot be deployed as managers may want, but they also tend to limit a collective orientation among shopfloor workers.

Some examples further illustrate this point. D. Peach and Livernash (1974) studied grievance procedures in the steel industry. They report that in the plants which they studied foremen and stewards at shop level had little role in the handling of grievances, most matters being dealt with at a higher level; they consider this to be typical (p. 76). Gersuny (1973) reports a study of grievance handling and discipline in a Ford engine plant. He suggests (p. 67) that overt punishment for individual acts of disobedience was rare but that collective acts were dealt with severely. A case in point was a wildcat strike which ended with 20 workers, including four union stewards, being sacked after the International union had urged a return to work and a court injunction against the strike had been obtained.[1] Action at the level of the work group certainly occurs, but it tends to have a covert existence, being outside the agreed rules and subject to severe penalties. Zabala (1983) helps to develop this point, using observational and other material from a General Motors assembly plant in California. His main concern is to demonstrate the extent of what he calls subterranean bargaining, namely attempts to alter the effort bargain at the point of production. His work is therefore useful in refuting the naive view that American workplace relations are completely within management's power. He documents several instances in which sabotage was used as a bargaining lever, and he also produces evidence of the use of the slowdown as a tactic. One interesting datum about effort levels is that on some sub-assembly jobs it was possible to complete eight hours' work in five hours (p. 256), a situation not markedly different from that in well-organized British factories. There are, however, important differences. The contract exerted a powerful influence in Zabala's plant so that he reports (pp. 268–76), for example, a tightening of production standards by the company which was met with the filing of a grievance and, eventually, sabotage after the worker concerned became dissatisfied that nothing had been done about his grievance. It may reasonably be suggested that in a similar British factory a worker would have refused the new tasks and would have received his steward's support. Instead of having to file a grievance and, if he was sufficiently ingenious and willing to take the necessary risks, then engaging in sabotage a worker would have the means at his disposal to bargain directly with the foreman and to summon assistance from his steward.

These studies certainly do not suggest that shopfloor action has disappeared in America. Some, notably those by Herding and Zabala, stress its continuation but see it as something separate from the union organization in the plant. It would, indeed, be surprising had managerial power become total. As writers such as Brody and Lichtenstein stress, immediately before and during the Second World War a considerable degree of shopfloor organization was built up. Detailed historical work on the war period (Lichtenstein, 1982; Glaberman, 1980; Harris, 1982a; Jefferys, 1984) has shown that, the no-strike pledge at national level notwithstanding, at factory level

1 Many American unions are called internationals because they include Canadian members.

employers often had substantial problems of labour control. Tight labour markets increased workers' bargaining power; there was limited opportunity to bargain about wages because of the wartime controls on wage movements, so that shopfloor matters were the only possible focus of disputes; these matters in any event took on an increased importance in view of longer hours and the demands of military production; shopfloor organizations had emerged only recently and were keen to establish their authority and position as against management; and the influx of new workers increased problems of discipline. There was, in short, growing tension on the shopfloor which managements sometimes found it impossible to control. Although there is disagreement as to the extent and significance of shopfloor movements, the studies agree that they were substantial and that they challenged the myth that there was national unity of purpose in the war effort.

The factory floor in Britain during wartime has been less well served by historians, but Croucher (1982) has produced an important study of the engineering industry. The picture that he paints has interesting similarities with the American situation, with an image of national unity being belied by a continuing struggle over production standards. Although it would be dangerous to speculate too much about differences between the two countries, one contrast seems to have existed. In America, as Harris (1982a) in particular argues, employers were actively reconstructing their labour policies to meet the challenge from below. General Motors took the lead in establishing an industrial relations department and in re-asserting the right to manage. Other companies followed more slowly. In Britain, employers appear to have lacked this strategic sense. Croucher (pp. 202–3) documents the efforts of government ministers to improve managerial practice by providing training courses and encouraging the appointment of personnel managers. More generally, his account suggests that British managements did not have any developed policy for dealing with labour. They were certainly active in resisting shopfloor demands and in victimizing militant stewards. But this activity seems to have stemmed from a desire to retain traditional rights. While American employers were learning how to deal with unions, their British counterparts were operating on much the same principles that they had always followed.

The reconversion to peacetime conditions shifted the balance of power in the employers' favour. In both countries, redundancies were accompanied by a campaign against left-wing stewards, with employers who had been willing to seek the stewards' co-operation during the war turning against them in the 'red scare' atmosphere of the Cold War (Croucher, 1982: 356; Harris, 1982a: 203). Again, however, the difference seems to have been that American employers continued their policy of constraining the powers of autonomous shop steward organizations. Herding argues for a progressive development, but with a rapid upward surge during the recession of 1957–9, an interpretation consistent with contemporary analyses (Strauss, 1962). It also fits Jefferys's (1984) brilliant reconstruction of the history of labour relations at Chrysler's chief Detroit factory, Dodge Main. Chrysler differed sharply from General Motors in having a particularly well-developed shopfloor organization during the 1930s and in the lack of any articulated managerial policy of containment. Effective shopfloor bargaining continued into the 1950s, one index of which was the much higher rate of unauthorized strikes than occurred in the other car firms. By the late 1950s, however, the company's competitive position was worsening, and an attack was launched on the steward system, which was successful. Studies conducted during the 1950s also point to the survival of shopfloor bargaining. Perhaps the best known is that by Kuhn (1961), who studied plants in the tyre and electrical industries and argued that 'fractional bargaining', that is continuous shopfloor bargaining within the grievance process, played an important role in altering formal managerial rules and giving workers a degree of influence over the labour process. Seidman *et al.* (1958) studied six union locals and found that in the case of the Steel Workers there was a fairly active shopfloor tradition. The authors comment, however, that slowdowns had been widely used in the immediate post-war period but that there had been none since 1953, attributing this to the organization of an industrial relations department and the removal by the company of the right of supervisors to make their own decisions on grievances (p. 69). Similarly, Kuhn recognizes the limitations of fractional bargaining, given its covert nature. In short, shopfloor bargaining was coming under fairly systematic pressure.[2]

2 To underline this point, data on the rise of grievance procedures may be cited. Thomson and Murray (1976: 168–9) point out that in America grievance procedures were more or less universal by the early 1960s, as were arrangements for sending disputed issues to arbitration. In Britain, grievance procedures developed only during the 1970s (Institute of Personnel Management, 1979), and even then it is questionable whether the formalization of procedures involved a thorough-going attempt to contain shopfloor action: some writers see it as no more than an administrative tidying up. In America, arbitration has become particularly important, with grievances going through a clear procedure and with arbitrators following the rule that workers must obey commands and grieve any complaints, and not refuse a management order (Stessin, 1960: 294). Workers certainly gained some important rights, and the system was far from being one of simple incorporation. What it did was to shift the locus of disputes away from the shopfloor.

In Britain, managements were not idle. Around the time that their American counterparts were imposing a tough line, they, too, were taking on their shop stewards. Turner *et al.* (1967: 282–6) speak of a 'firm line' which was adopted by the Pressed Steel and Rootes firms, and throughout the 1950s there were cases of substantial disputes in other car firms such as Standard. But the approach seems to have been qualitatively different from that of the American firms. These had a clear policy of re-structuring industrial relations on the basis of formal contracts, the aim being to escape from the informal bargaining that had begun to emerge during the Second World War. The British firms attacked steward organizations when circumstances seemed to require or permit it, but they did not use their victories to build a system of workplace relations in which their own authority was buttressed by a bureaucratic rule of law. Short-term gains were not made part of longer-term policies of constraining shopfloor bargaining when the balance of power swung back in favour of the workers.

Tolliday and Zeitlin (1982: 11) note, in a remark which conflicts with their view that British employers were relatively powerful, that the British situation during the 1950s was not one in which 'management exercised effective control over the workplace'; foremen were given the discretion to make concessions to workers in order to secure a steady stream of output. Quite so. Although stewards were often quite weak, management was not able to establish effective control on its own terms. Shopfloor bargaining remained legitimate, whereas American managements were able to constrain it.

Strike Trends

Before considering the causes of these developments, one quantitative index of them, strike trends, may be examined. For all their well-known deficiencies, such as the omission of small and short strikes, official strike data can be used to chart broad tendencies in the number and length of industrial disputes. They demonstrate dramatically some of the key differences between Britain and America, while also serving to introduce the distinctive character of Australian shopfloor relations.

For each country, data have been assembled on strike trends for the period since records began; such a long-term perspective helps to put the recent period in context. It is also useful to separate, where possible the coal industry from other sectors: as is well known, in Britain during the 1950s and 1960s trends in coal differed sharply from those elsewhere and, given the dominant position of the industry in the strike statistics, its inclusion can give a misleading picture. Accordingly, Table 5.1 and 5.2 report data for all industries, and for coal and other

TABLE 5.1
Trends in Strike Indices, United States

	Frequency	Involvement	Loss Ratio	Strikes Lasting under 1 Week (%)
1897-1905	149	33.5	—	44.4[a]
1906-15	146	29.9	—	—
1916-18	153	53.6	—	40.9
1919-22	101	79.6	—	24.8
1923-30	34.0	13.9	—	28.9
1931-6	60.1	33.4	532	37.8
1937-41	106	41.7	533	38.0
1942-5	99.6	51.0	391	70.5
1946-9	90.1	67.5	1350	38.6
1950-9	84.6	43.8	682	44.8
1960-9	67.5	29.8	454	45.3
1970-9	75.7	33.0	568	38.6[b]

Note:
Frequency   = Number of strikes per million employees
Involvement = Number of workers involved per thousand employees
Loss Ratio   = Number of days lost per thousand employees
[a] 1881-94.
[b] 1970-8.
Sources: Third and Tenth *Annual Reports* of the U.S. Commissioner of Labor (Washington: U.S. G.P.O. 1888 and 1896); F. Peterson, *Strikes in the United States, 1880-1936* (Washington: U.S. G.P.O., 1938); annual articles on strikes and lockouts in *Monthly Labor Review*, 1916-58; *Analysis of Work Stoppages*, (Bureau of Labor Statistics, annual); J. I. Griffin, *Strikes: A study in Quantitative Economics* (Columbia University Press: New York, 1939). Employment data are based on non-agricultural employment, reported in G. S. Bain and R. Price, *Profiles of Union Growth* (Oxford: Blackwell, 1980), Table 3.1, and *Monthly Labor Review*.

industries separately for the United States; the following four tables report similar figures for Britain and Australia. The periodization adopted will generally be obvious.[3]

An outstanding feature of the data is the increase in the frequency of strikes in Britain and Australia during the post-war period. In Britain during the 1970s there were, on average and after allowing for changes in the size of the working population, three times as many strikes in the non-coal sector as there were during the period 1946-9. In Australia the figure was a remarkable eight times. In the United

3 For the period since the Second World War, decennial averages are given. Before then, the periods used are those of war, post-war adjustment, and so on. Some minor variations between countries also reflect the availability of data.

TABLE 5.2
Strike Trends, Coal and Other Industries, United States

	Coal			All Other Industries		
	Frequency	Involvement	Loss Ratio	Frequency	Involvement	Loss Ratio
1881-1905	352	262	—	114	22.9	—
1908-15	—	190	9530	—	25.7	—
1916-18	397	183	2770	145	49.7	—
1919-22	136	461	30400	99.6	67.5	—
1923-30	135	181	11070	31.4	9.7	—
1931-6	154	347	5540	58.1	26.5	422
1937-41	140	497	6580	105	33.8	428
1942-5	1040	827	8850	88.3	41.6	289
1946-9	1002	1720	25700	79.5	48.3	1070
1950-9	828	396	4600	80.0	41.6	658
1960-9	1160	447	2150	63.8	27.5	415
1970-8	4890	2010	17700	57.6	25.9	478

Sources: As Table 5.1 plus employment data for coal industry from *Historical Statistics of the United States, Colonial Times to 1957*, (Washington: U.S. G.P.O. 1960), and *Statistical Abstract of the United States* (Washington, annual). Total employment 1881-96 estimated from census data reported in S. Lebergott, *Manpower in Economic Growth* (McGraw Hill: New York, 1964) pp. 510-12. Strike data for coal industry 1908-26 reported in *Statistical Abstracts*, 1930 and 1936, based on U.S. Geological Survey records.

States, the index fell. These trends are even more notable when set in historical context. In Britain strike frequency rose slowly to the end of the First World War, before falling sharply during the 1920s and 1930s; the recovery during the 1940s was to fairly normal levels by historical standards, with the rise of the 1960s and 1970s being to unprecedented heights. There was a broadly similar story in Australia. In America the peak of the frequency index occurred during the First World War, and the steady decline from the 1950s left the number of strikes at a level that had not been seen since the rise of mass production unionism during the 1930s.

Britain and Australia are again similar in the rise in worker involvement and in the loss of working days during the post-war period. The increases in the two indices are, however, less dramatic than the rise in the number of strikes. The British loss ratio, outside coal, in the 1970s, for example, was similar to that during the upsurge of industrial conflict before the First World War, and well below the level recorded in the conflicts after that war. The United States is marked by relative constancy of the involvement and loss ratio indices.

TABLE 5.3
Trends in Strike Indices, United Kingdom

	Frequency	Involvement	Loss Ratio	Strikes Lasting under 1 Week (%)
1893-1909	38.4	15.1	431	—
1910-14	54.3	47.1	939	45.5
1915-18	42.9	37.6	234	52.8
1919-22	64.8	104	2520	39.0
1923-30[a]	27.1	38.3	1490	54.1
	(28.6)	(21.3)	(355)	
1931-9	37.8	18.9	150	68.8
1940-5	81.5	25.4	99.5	88.4
1946-9	87.5	24.8	103	—
1950-9	98.5	30.9	151	91.7
1960-9	106	58.7	154	85.5
1970-9	115	71.7	571	67.4

Note:
[a] Figures in brackets exclude 1926
Sources: British Labour Statistics: Historical Abstract, 1886-1968, (HMSO, 1971); annual article on 'Stoppages of Work due to Industrial Disputes', *Employment Gazette.* Employment data based on employees in employment, reported in G. S. Bain and R. Price, *Profiles of Union Growth* (Oxford: Blackwell, 1980) and in *Employment Gazette.*

TABLE 5.4
Strike Trends, Coal and Other Industries, United Kingdom

	Coal			All Other Industries		
	Frequency	Involvement	Loss Ratio	Frequency	Involvement	Loss Ratio
1893-1909	205	194	5620	31.0	3.9	200
1910-14	162	385	8830	47.3	25.1	428
1915-18	87.1	207	887	39.8	25.4	188
1919-22	146	746	20000	58.2	51.9	1110
1923-30[a]	122	211	16900	20.4	26.0	386
	(131)	(103)	(1070)	(21.2)	(15.4)	(304)
1931-9	274	201	1100	25.0	9.0	98.2
1940-5	897	319	1070	43.5	11.7	54.4
1946-9	1290	284	753	35.2	13.5	74.3
1950-9	1950	284	671	28.5	21.3	132
1960-9	1520	241	697	70.9	54.2	140
1970-9	661	354	5780	106	67.7	497

Note:
[a] Figures in brackets exclude 1926
Sources: As Table 5.3.

TABLE 5.5
Trends in Strike Indices, Australia

	Frequency	Involvement	Loss Ratio	Strikes Lasting under 1 Week (%)
1913-14	211	47.0	664	67.6
1915-18	293	88.1	1360	64.7
1919-22	388	111	2240	71.8
1923-30	232	80.5	1070	71.0
1931-9	148	46.8	307	78.0
1940-5	314	112	577	86.3
1946-9	406	133	700	90.7
1950-9	455	138	358	88.9
1960-9	367	153	236	90.6
1970-9	500	290	664	81.4

Sources: *Labour Statistics* (Canberra: Australian Bureau of Statistics, annual), *Official Yearbook of the Commonwealth of Australia* (Canberra, annual). Employment data based on estimates of non-agricultural wage and salary earners. Calculated from N. G. Butlin and J. A. Dowie, 'Estimates of Australian Work Force and Employment, 1861-1961' *Australian Economic History Review*, 9, pp. 138-55 (1969); *Labour Statistics, 1978*, p. 44; and Census data on numbers of employers and employees, reported by Butlin and Dowie and the *Official Yearbook*. Calculations based on interpolation between Census years, and rely on several estimates of the agricultural work force and the number of employers and unpaid helpers in the non-agricultural work force.

It is generally accepted that the loss ratio is the most suitable index for direct international comparisons, being less subject to differences in recording practice than the other measures. It will be seen that the United States continued to score highly on this index, with the other two countries coming close to its levels only recently, and for a few years in the past when industrial conflict was at its height. One reason for this high loss ratio is the great length of American strikes. As Table 5.1 shows, most American strikes have, apart from the years of the Second World War, lasted over a week. In Britain, there has been a growing tendency for strikes to become shorter, so that two-thirds were over within a week during the 1970s. Data on strike duration by industry are not generally available, but if the coal industry were to be excluded, reasonable estimates are that there was a dramatic rise in the proportion of short strikes in the non-coal sector during the 1960s and 1970s (P. Edwards, 1982). Strikes in Australia have been even shorter, with about 90 per cent being settled within a week throughout the post-1945 period.

TABLE 5.6
Strike Trends, Coal and Other Industries, Australia

| | Coal | | | All Other Industries | | |
	Frequency	Involvement	Loss Ratio	Frequency	Involvement	Loss Ratio
1913-14	5330	1520	17900	64.9	10.0	188
1915-18	7330	2390	25100	107	29.8	599
1919-22	8550	3410	20850	89.3	24.5	1170
1923-30	7510	2770	30700	45.6	13.4	269
1931-9	8410	2760	13480	25.8	7.4	87.3
1940-5	22170	6760	23050	62.2	30.9	244
1946-9	33430	7530	21980	56.5	43.5	359
1950-9	30340	5310	9460	144	70.2	211
1960-9	12670	2310	3260	246	114	178
1970-8	9360	2370	7550	429	236	496

Sources: As Table 5.5 plus employment data for coal industry calculated from D. W. Oxnam, 'The Incidence of Strikes in Australia', pp. 18-46 in J. E. Isaac and G. W. Ford (eds), *Australian Labour Relations: Readings* (Melbourne, 1966) and K. F. Walker, *Australian Industrial Relations Systems* (Cambridge, Mass, 1970) pp. 190 and 314. The data from the latter source refer to New South Wales only, and are used to allocate employment in mining and quarrying in Australia as a whole between coal and other mining. No data on coal strikes are available before 1930, but data exist for New South Wales, which accounts for the majority of the coal industry, and these data have been used to estimate the total number of coal strikes in Australia. Note that the N.S.W. data are more comprehensive than the Australian, in that the number of strikes in this one State's records sometimes exceed the total for Australia. The *ratio* of coal to other mining strikes in the N.S.W. data has thus been used to allocate the mining and quarrying total between the two sectors of the industry.

One important implication is that a unidimensional view of 'worker militancy' is inadequate. Although American workers have been striking less often than their forebears, when they do stop work they continue to do so for very long periods of time. Any view that managerial control has successfully been re-asserted has to be faced with this uncomfortable fact. The data are consistent with the argument that American managements have restructured workplace relations in such a way as to make frequent use of the strike weapon difficult. But it has remained a significant element in labour relations, with disputes being as long as they ever were.

In accounting for these differences, some of the proximate influences on the British post-war pattern may firstly be indicated. The rise in the power of shop stewards, the decentralization of bargaining, full employment, and inflation are all likely to have encouraged stoppages (Clegg, 1979: 277). As the argument that shop steward organization was not fully in place until the early 1960s suggests, it was not until the 1960s that the frequency index outside coal accelerated. The small, short unofficial sectional stoppage became a major focus for analysts and policy-makers during the 1960s. In Australia some of these forces were also at work. In addition to inflation, there were influences specific to the country. Bentley (1974: 39–42) suggests that the arbitration system was coming under strain: full employment gave workers the ability to demand wage increases, and inflation provide the incentive. The system was less able to cope than it had been during the 1950s.

In a longer-term perspective, Australian strikes reflect two forces. First, there is the arbitration system itself. As numerous commentators have pointed out, the system has always tended to encourage a brief stoppage to reinforce a point that is being made to a tribunal: such strikes serve as useful demonstrations that a case should be taken seriously. Second, however, the system has its weaknesses for, as is equally frequently noted, the existence of the tribunals has tended to discourage collective bargaining and the development of disputes procedures (Dabscheck and Niland, 1981: 70–1; J. Kuhn, 1955). There has been little point in accepting an employer's offer if something better could be obtained by holding out and seeing what a tribunal would award. The lack of close attention to grievance handling at shopfloor level means that a strike is a useful way of drawing attention to a grievance and of ensuring a quick tribunal hearing (Niland, 1976: 378). It is thus not surprising that stoppages have been so short, for they have been demonstrations and not battles in their own right. Their growing frequency in the post-war period can be attributed to the way in which new pressures have impacted on a system which has not been geared to the resolution of disputes at shop level before they become strikes.

The British and Australian cases exemplify two situations in which post-war economic conditions have interacted with traditions of shopfloor relations to produce a rise in the number of strikes. In Britain, the key element in these traditions was the principle of the settlement of disputes at the point of production, with the growth of shop steward organization encouraging existing tendencies in this direction. In Australia, it was not direct bargaining but the settling of disputes through the arbitration system which was important. But in both cases there was a lack of systematic attempts to reconstruct shopfloor relations through grievance procedures and the like. In America, by contrast, such attempts were widespread. The strike data are thus consistent with the picture of changing workplace relations presented above, the American employers being keen to develop their own internal arrangements for settling disputes.

Employers and the State in the Post-War Period

What explains these diverging trends? As already suggested, the role of American employers in acting to re-shape workplace relations has been crucial. One influential argument is that American labour law, and not the actions of employers, has been the decisive influence. The argument developed here is that this view exaggerates the autonomy of the law and neglects the congruence of the law with the systems of workplace regulation that employers were evolving: state law and private law interacted.

Role of the Law

Among those concentrating on the law, Klare (1978) has argued that the legal cases settled during the early years of the Wagner Act, that is the period 1937–41, although apparently pro-labour in establishing the duty of the employer to bargain, tended to restrict autonomous union activity. There developed a 'modern American legal consciousness that came to stand, whatever the intentions of its authors, as an ineluctable barrier to worker self-activity' (p. 270). Klare identifies three elements in this process: the restatement of the traditional legal policy of contractualism, that is the right of parties freely to make contracts and their duty to abide by them; the development of a doctrine of public rights; and the inhibition of unions' self-activity, by, for example, treating the union as separate from its members and as a body which is a trustee of the public interest and which therefore has a duty of acting responsibly in return for its legal privileges.

Stone (1981) analyses post-war developments in similar terms. She argues that labour law has been based on a doctrine of industrial pluralism, which holds that the parties to collective bargaining should determine their own arrangements, that the workplace under collective bargaining is a democracy because of the rights and duties enshrined in the collective agreement, that private arbitration is necessary to settle disputes within this democracy, and that labour's only rights are to bargain collectively and to submit disputes to arbitration. Stone charts the growth of the legal supposition that arbitration is the natural situation and that courts should not intervene in the substantive conclusions reached by arbitrators. She argues that the model of an equal democracy is not applicable to reality because there are numerous areas on which employers are not required to bargain, notably the introduction of new technology and investment decisions (p. 1548). In addition, the arbitration system is not neutral: 'only in the midst of "disorder" do workers have the leverage to press for their demands. Thus by intervening to preserve order, arbitrators are not only non-neutral, they are acting consistently on the side of management' (p. 1565). In short, the law has been active in creating a structure in which workers' rights are constrained and in which the right to use strikes and other weapons is limited by a general presumption that industrial peace should rule and that difficulties can go through the grievance procedure. Stone quotes at several points the views of Harry Shulman, who was the first arbitrator at Ford, which introduced the 'umpire system' for settling disputes in 1942. In 1943 Shulman wrote in a decision that an employee may refuse an order which involves a health hazard or doing something illegal

> but in the absence of such justifying factors, he may not refuse to obey merely because the order violates some rights of his under the contract. The remedy . . . lies in the grievance procedure . . . . To refuse obedience because of a claimed contract violation would be to substitute individual action for collective bargaining (quoted in Gersuny, 1973: 80).

In short, action at the point of production is illegitimate.

Tomlins (1980) presents perhaps the most ambitious argument on these lines. He argues that the Wagner Act created a publicly regulated system in which the role of trade unions was increasingly defined by the state. 'Eventually, the peaceful negotiation of contracts by certified agents on behalf of employees acting in association became almost the only manifestation of collective behavior, whether of workers or of unions, which the Act's administrators and the courts were prepared to accept as legitimate' (p. 274). The stabilization of labour relations on the basis of a negotiated contract became the cornerstone of the policy of the courts and the National Labor Relations Board. The Taft-Hartley Act of 1947 further developed the split between unions and the process of work itself, and the employer was 'established in complete control of work assignments' (p. 355).

These analyses are valuable in trying to relate the law to the conduct of work and in exploring the unintended consequences of legal decisions. As Klare, in particular, stresses, there was no legal conspiracy to contain shopfloor power, and instead there was a process whereby courts used legal reasoning in labour matters which had the effect of undermining the basis of shopfloor organization, namely the ability to respond collectively to immediate issues and to use collective resources to secure desired ends. As Harris (1982b) argues, however, there are difficulties. Klare tends to exaggerate the role of the courts, as against that of the NLRB, and to imply that the Wagner Act was more radical than it really was. And both Klare and Tomlins give too great a weight to judicial and administrative rulings and insufficient attention to the context of power of the legal apparatus. This latter point is crucial. These analyses of the law concentrate on judicial rulings, which are treated as self-contained and as independent of other influences. There is the obvious danger of treating what the courts said as evidence of what actually happened, as in Tomlins's view that total employer control was established by 1947. And why the courts said what they said is not considered in detail.

Employers and the Law

A more adequate analysis would look at the interaction of employers' policies and the behaviour of state agencies. There would have been little point in the courts' stressing the importance of arbitration and the rule of law if employers were not actively moving to make such pronouncements practical achievements within the workplace. The law did not independently shape the course of labour relations, but it reflected other developments. As Harris again argues, even during the New Deal period forces were building up against the Wagner Act. Employers had been very unhappy with it, and in Congress there was a growing political movement to rescind some of its clauses. This movement began as early as 1938, and continued through the war up to the passage of the Taft–Hartley Act. The NLRB was thus under considerable pressure and, its general pro-labour sentiments notwithstanding, it had to operate in a political climate in which apparently pro-labour decisions sparked off enormous protests and endangered the position of the Board itself. Between 1935 and 1947, 169 bills concerned with national labour policy were presented to Congress (Millis and Brown, 1950: 333), and these reflected growing concern about the labour problem and the supposed role of the Wagner Act in giving excessive powers to the unions. As argued in chapter 4, the passage of the Act reflected very special circumstances, and it is not surprising to find attempts to limit its operations growing as the economy moved out of the crisis of the recession and as 'normality' was re-established.

Many commentators have stressed that the Act was designed only to permit 'proper' collective bargaining to take place; its aims were in fact very limited. Employers came to recognize this, and were willing to operate within it, while attempting to ensure that unions' powers were not extended. They thus insisted on reserving managerial rights on issues concerned with the overall operation of the enterprise, and on defining areas on which bargaining would take place. In these areas, they aimed to set clear rules as to how bargaining should be carried out, in other words to ensure that labour relations were placed on an orderly and predictable footing. It is true that they were not always successful in this, but they were able to give a clear lead to the NLRB and the courts as to what would be acceptable.

It is important to be clear about the argument here. Some treatments, notably those associated with 'radical' critiques of what is seen as corporate liberalism (e.g. B. Bernstein, 1968; Hurd, 1976), suggest that there was a deliberate policy of incorporating labour and that capital's power was thereby strengthened. Such an interpretation is not consistent with capitalists' opposition to the Wagner Act. And neither does it fit the ensuing period. If capital's powers were simply reinforced, how is the continuance of shopfloor struggle to be explained, and why is it that employers have, since the late 1970s, begun to experiment with quality circles and other attempts to gain workers' compliance? The situation was, rather, one of capitalists responding to the rise of unionism and attempting to find ways of living with unions. The new post-war structure placed limits on some managerial powers as well as enhancing other. As Piore (1982) has argued, rules on seniority and the like may be acceptable to employers under full employment but may place serious constraints on what can be done under more difficult economic conditions. The relationship between capital and labour necessarily contains contradictory elements, as the two sides struggle for advantages while also depending on each other. A particular pattern of relations has to be assessed in its own terms and not reduced to such simple terms as 'incorporation' of unions. Employers had to concede benefits to workers, and not just in terms of wages and working conditions. Rights within the plant were granted which would have been unthinkable prior to the Wagner Act, for workers now had the right to protest managerial decisions on discipline, production standards, and other things. Management was certainly able to contain the exercise of these rights, but their significance should not be devalued.

Before taking the causal chain further back by investigating the origins of managerial policy, the position in the other two countries must be briefly considered. In Australia there is little hard evidence, for workplace relations have not been such an area of research interest as they have in the other two countries. This lack of interest reflects the nature of the Australian system, for with arbitration being so important neither unions nor employers have had any incentive to develop internal systems of regulation. The employer's authority thus remains considerable in dealing with day-to-day matters of discipline and the like. Kriegler (1980) provides an account of work in a shipyard owned by Australia's largest firm, Broken Hill Proprietary. Although highly coloured, the account points to the absence of developed shop steward organizations or even less formal means of developing collective challenges to management. Unions lacked the power to develop their own shopfloor job controls, while employers had no need to create complex internal states.

In Britain, it is widely argued, engineering firms took advantage of the 'soft' product market conditions of the 1950s by letting prices rise and by concentrating on producing as much as possible regardless of cost. Firms were willing to cede control to the shopfloor. Thus Friedman (1977: 208–10) points to the high level of profits that were enjoyed by car firms in the post-war period, suggesting that 'firms competed for raw materials and labour rather than car buyers'. They were willing to permit gang systems and other forms of shopfloor control to emerge. A similar picture comes from material collected by P. Edwards and Scullion (1982a) in their study of the Small Metals Factory: during the 1950s the plant was owned by an independent company, which was taken over by a larger firm in 1959, and managerial policy was based on the simple dictum of producing as much as possible, not worrying about price, and granting such controls to the shopfloor as were necessary for continuous production. There was a policy, or perhaps practice would be a better word, of drift, with the market looking healthy and with there being no perceived need to restructure labour relations.[4]

Other aspects of firms' behaviour are their marketing and investment policies. Williams *et al.* (1983) argue that the largest British car firms failed to identify markets and to develop appropriate products, and also that there was a high level of distributed profits and a low level of investment in new productive capacity. In the short term it was possible to increase production and to make substantial profits, but longer-term expansion was inhibited and the resurgence of competition from European firms left the British industry weak. The authors develop similar arguments about other parts of manufacturing industry.

The consequence for labour relations was an essentially short-term perspective. Managements did not consciously choose to cede shopfloor control or to make such a policy the basis for gaining workforce compliance. They permitted control to drift away and, when faced with crises of competitiveness, reacted to the needs of the immediate situation through declaring redundancies and attempting to attack practices which they had formerly tolerated. Such an approach is unlikely to engender a sense of confidence in management among shopfloor workers, who will, quite reasonably, criticize the

4 Further research on the plant, using company and shop-steward records, has developed this point (Scullion and Edwards, 1985). During the 1950s the plant was making good profits and appeared to be working on virtually a 'cost plus' pricing agreement with its main customer. Shopfloor relations posed few problems to managers, who permitted the stewards considerable conrol of effort levels. By the 1950s the stewards' controls were being perceived as serious constraints, but it was difficult for management to root them out.

inconsistency of managerial practice and will resent attacks on practices which managers had been all too willing to condone during periods of prosperity.

The American economy has also faced competitive pressures. In both countries, widespread plant closures in traditional manufacturing areas led to discussions of 'de-industrialization' (Blackaby, 1978; Bluestone and Harrison, 1982). The relative importance of workplace relations and other factors in the process is, of course, a hotly debated issue. Some comments are offered in the final section of the chapter, the present concern being more with the origins than the consequences of differing paths of development. But it should be stressed that it is not being argued that labour relations were important in Britain but not in America. In both cases, relations in the sphere of exchange have to be taken into account. And, in the workplace itself, patterns of control are multi-faceted and have correspondingly complex consequences. What has been suggested is that American employers were, in general, able to shape labour relations such that day-to-day effort bargaining was constrained by a framework of law. This law was the product of the employers' own efforts and of the development of case law by the courts and agencies such as the NLRB. Since private and public law appeared to fit so neatly, it might be argued that the latter was merely an arm of the former, that is that the relative autonomy of the state was very limited. Such a reading is not accurate. As noted above, many American employers resented the Wagner Act, and it is highly unlikely that they would have changed the basis of their factory regimes, from arbitrary authority to the rule of law, without the pressures of the state law and of developing workers' shopfloor organizations. Private and public laws reinforced each other.

A hypothesis that the state's activities were secondary to the needs of the capitalist economy can, however, be sustained with reference to the reasons for state intervention, as suggested in chapter 4. But even there it was contradictory pressures stemming from the operation of the economy, and not the needs of capital, which governed the state's interventions. A question that remains, however, concerns the reasons why, even by the 1930s, labour relations in Britain and America were so different.

The Origins of Diversity

Some Explanations Considered

From the middle of the nineteenth century, scholars have been puzzling over the question, why no socialism in the United States? Their efforts are usefully summarized by Lipset (1977). The present concern is with workplace relations and not directly with such large issues as class consciousness. Yet consideration of the workplace in fact throws light on the tangled debate on American exceptionalism. The debate has concentrated on the characteristics of the working class itself and not the context in which workers lived. Various characteristics have emerged, notably the ethnic diversity of the American working class and high rates of geographical and social mobility. But such a listing of factors does not identify which ones were crucial or how they came together. Thus, a paper such as that of M. Davis (1980), which sets out to explain 'why the U.S. working class is different', in fact provides a review of labour history that does not answer the question. Political conservatism has, moreover, been taken to be a self-evident category. Karabel (1979: 221) is unusual in identifying 'one of the great riddles of American history', as being 'why a working class so evidently capable of extraordinary militancy in its struggle at the point of production was apparently incapable of translating this tradition of economic militancy into a broader demand for fundamental political change'. Yet he provides little by way of answer to the riddle. What is required is a closer examination of 'economic militancy' than has been provided with in the existing debate.

Since it is generally accepted, and has been demonstrated above, that American workers have been at least as active as their British and Australian counterparts in prosecuting workplace struggles, there is no need to invoke such factors as traditions of egalitarianism to explain some supposed natural conservatism among American workers. Several possible explanations of international differences may thus be ruled out because they aim to explain a false contrast between the countries in question. Thus there is no need to suppose that American unions have had an inherent tendency either towards conservatism in general or towards a distrust of political involvement in particular. In their craft origins and their concern to control relations at the point of production, the early American unions had far more similarities with than differences from their British and Australian counterparts. In the steel industry, for example, unions in Britain and America were based on the skilled men, and reflected the concerns of these workers to control the supply of labour and to preserve their considerable control over the production process itself, with many of the details of work operations being left to the leader of each crew (Holt, 1977; Brody, 1960; Wilkinson, 1977).

If the inherent characteristics of workers and unions are unlikely to develop the explanation very far, perhaps the American environment was crucial. Comparisons with other countries have pointed to a range of contrasts. In an important early study Goodrich (1928) looked at America along with Britain and Australia. He noted three factors commonly used to explain differences between the last two in the extent of political involvement of unions: the concentration of 'democratic and rebellious elements' among emigrants to Australia; the bargaining power of labour in a sparsely populated country; and the less entrenched position of labour's opponents. Yet, as he pointed out, the first two factors hardly differentiate between Australia and America. Goodrich put most weight on agrarian developments: in America the land offered the chance for individual escape, whereas in Australia it was tied up in large holdings. In the latter country the land, far from being a drain on collective organization, encouraged it. As Mayer (1964) argues, both countries have had strong egalitarian traditions, but the American tradition has emphasized rugged individualism whereas in Australia mateship and solidarity were significant, even in the rural areas, where a landless and migratory proletariat faced the land-owning class.

American individualism is, of course, a well-worked theme. Goodrich's contrast is important but not decisive. It helps to show why the land did not undermine collectivist tendencies in Australia. But it does not explain the nature of American individualism, for the picture of individual striving sits awkwardly with the enormous solidarity that has characterized many industrial disputes throughout American history. The question is why American workers were pressed into an individual orientation.

Three more recent studies have pursued the question of class radicalism further. Lash (1984) has compared American and French workers, finding, not surprisingly, a higher degree of radicalism among the latter. His explanation lies in the class alliances that the working classes of the two countries have made. Such alliances may have played a role, but Lash's account, like that of Davis (1980) mentioned above, becomes a review of labour history in which the key causal influences are hard to disentangle. The reasons for the making of particular alliances with other classes are not really pinned down, and the role of groups such as employers, in shaping the context in which alliances were made, is not considered. Gallie's (1983) comparison of France and Britain is more helpful. Gallie argues that 'French workers are much more resentful about inequality in their society' (p. 91), and he sees one important reason as the power structure of the firm, with French employers adopting a highly authoritarian approach and being unwilling to grant unions any rights within the workplace. French workers were thus dissatisfied with their position in the workplace, and this fed through into resentment about inequality in society in general. What accounts for the authoritarianism of French employers? For Gallie (p. 161), 'the most convincing explanation lies in the relative power of the trade union movements': the British unions, being stronger in terms of membership and less divided on political lines, were the better equipped to contest managerial authority. French employers were able to sustain their autocracy because it was not subject to any permanent challenge. In explaining the Anglo-American contrast, however, it is necessary to go rather further in considering the role of the employers. In both countries employers were faced with direct challenges on the shopfloor, for example from craft unions at the end of the nineteenth century and again from semi-skilled workers during the Second World War.

Littler (1982) has identified some of the proximate influences at work, of which two are of particular importance here. First, 'huge, managerialist corporations' emerged in America whereas British firms retained 'familial and proprietorial' forms of organization until well into the inter-war period (p. 163). American firms thus had the power to transform the labour process. Littler discusses the demise of inside contracting, arguing that, although it occurred at about the same time in both countries, the reasons were different: in America, the pressure came from above as employers asserted their authority and tried to destroy all opposition, while in Britain pressure from the semi-skilled unions was more important. Second, American employers needed 'to reduce and keep down unit labour costs in the context of a high-wage economy' (p. 178). Littler attributes such things as the early rise of systematic management in America to this need to control unit labour costs.

These influences help to explain why American employers were able to establish, in the period between 1890 and 1910, their dominance of the factory. They are also pertinent in accounting for the response to unionsim since the 1930s. Employers had become accustomed to exercising unrestrained control in the workplace, and had developed the managerial techniques to enable them to do so. When faced with the challenge of unions they had the resources to respond by adapting their methods of control. They were thus able to bring unions within an already established system of factory governance. French employers were able to retain a traditional form of authoritarianism because they were not challenged at shopfloor level. British firms came to live with the challenge. American ones dealt with it by reconstructing their authority through new ways of organizing the labour process (such as systematic management) and by reshaping their factory regimes (with internal labour markets, welfare schemes, and so forth). But a problem remains. Although the size of American firms gave them the power to take on craft unions, this size must also have reduced the incentive to do so; given their oligopolistic position, they were in a position to control prices and thus to pass on to the consumer their high wage costs. And, although in retrospect their victory over the unions appears inevitable, at the time this was far from obvious; in fact, the destruction of craft unions was a lengthy and costly process. Why should employers have taken all the risks that such a policy entailed?

Employers and the Drive to Control

The answer lies in the need of American employers to establish their own authority. It is widely noted that they have been far more hostile to unions than have their European counterparts. Goodrich's comments, cited above (p. 175), are echoed by those of Tawney (1979: 9) and Clegg (1976: 22, 26), among others. The frequency and stridency with which the 'right to manage' was asserted have also been documented (Berthoff, 1964; Fine, 1956). But, apart from some references to the effects of general social values such as individualism, the reasons for this have not been systematically explored. Yet they must be considered if the fundamental origin of the American pattern of workplace relations is to be identified. Once a clear idea of employers' behaviour is obtained, several of the puzzles mentioned above can be resolved. In particular, why have strikes been so long and so bitterly fought, and why, therefore, have workplace relations had their dual character, with the intensity of struggles in strikes apparently contradicting employers' attempts to prevent overt conflict at the point of production? If it can be shown that employers had a distinctive and continuing interest in asserting their own control, it follows that they will have wanted to prevent challenges to their authority and also that they will have fought strikes intensely so as to prevent any weakening of this authority.

Some detailed studies within particular industries have pointed to the importance of employer activities. Thus, Holt (1977) argues that traditional explanations of the differing experiences of trade unions in the steel industry do not work. In America, a powerful craft union was attacked and destroyed during the final years of the nineteenth century. In Britain, unions retained a significant presence. One argument has stressed ethnic and skill distinctions in America as crucial factors weakening the workforce; but skill differences were probably more marked in Britain, which also had some significant ethnic divisions. Such divisions were, moreover, sometimes overcome in America, as in the crucial Homestead strike of 1892, in which the whole workforce displayed remarkable solidarity but in which the Carnegie

Corporation was still able to deliver a crippling blow to the union. For Holt (pp. 230–4), differences in employer behaviour were the most striking differences between the countries, with the British adopting a conciliatory approach and with the Americans using the opportunities presented by technical change to attack the position of skilled workers. Holt makes the interesting suggestion, to be pursued below, that the extent of the American employers' hostility to craft unionism may have reflected the novelty of the 'labour problem' in America and their need to establish their own authority.

Elbaum and Wilkinson (1979) have pursued this contrast. They argue that craft unions established a place within the early development of the iron industry in both countries. Firms faced highly competitive product markets and were willing to collude on wage levels so as to introduce some stability; the unions were useful in this process of stabilization. With the development of giant steel firms in America, however, craft unions ceased to hold any attractions for employers. In Britain, by contrast, a fragmented industrial structure, foreign competition, and a slow rate of technical change left employers weaker and less willing to take on the unions, which were able to consolidate their position in the new industry. This argument does not, however, establish why American employers were so hostile to unions. The differences from Britain in technology, industrial structure, and level of competition might just as well have encouraged American employers to be particularly tolerant of craft unions: with their size and technical sophistication they could afford to live with the unions. It remains to be explained why they used the opportunities that were presented to them, and why they were so vigorous in rooting out any organized challenge to their own authority within the workplace.

Before pursuing this point, it needs to be shown that steel was not a special case. Lazonick's (1981) comparison of the Lancashire and New England cotton spinning industries provides useful further evidence. In Britain, the spinners' unions were very powerful, and their members were among the best-paid manual workers in the country. An enduring system of collective bargaining was established, and workers had considerable influence over such things as piecework price lists and the detailed operation of the labour process. In New England unions were much weaker and the employer's authority within the workplace was correspondingly greater. Lazonick suggests two reasons for the contrast: the concentration of ownership in New England as contrasted with the fragmentation of the Lancashire industry; and the high rate of geographical mobility among the American spinners, whose bargaining power relied less on collective agreements than on the willingness to quit factories which were unsuitable. American workers were thus not powerless, but they were largely excluded from any joint determination of the conditions of work. On Lazonick's second point, there is plainly a problem of causality: individual mobility can reflect as well as cause a low level of collective organization, and the origins of the pattern of geographical mobility would require detailed investigation. The first point parallels the evidence from the steel industry, but does not directly establish why American employers used the opportunities that the structure of the industry made available.

These industry-level studies are, however, of great importance in establishing in detail the general impression that American employers have been particularly active in asserting their own control within the workplace. An attempt to consider why this should be so can begin from the firm basis that there is a genuine difference from British employers to be explained. This is not to suggest that the difference was equally marked in all industries. As was stressed above in discussing more recent developments, the explanatory focus is on the manufacturing sector, especially its mass-production part. In other industries American employers were not successful in rooting out craft unions. In printing and building in particular these unions flourished (Jackson, 1984). And in the coal industry, where there was, of course, no craft tradition, employers' practices do not seem to have differed very much from those of their British or Australian counterparts: collective bargaining emerged from time to time on a district, and eventually national, basis but tended to collapse in the face of product market pressures. Employers certainly engaged in struggles with unions that were often lengthy and violent, but so did their counterparts elsewhere. It may be that an argument consistent with the present one could be developed for coal, taking account, for example, of the very intense hostility to unions that has existed in areas such as West Virginia and which may be qualitatively different from the behaviour of employers in other countries. But the account here will exclude the industry.

It may be suggested that American employers faced two sorts of problem in a more extreme form than did their British counterparts: securing their position of authority within the factory, and establishing themselves as a class against other classes. On the latter, they faced opposition from farmers, the traditional middle classes, and other groups which were suspicious of capitalist monopolies, as well as from workers. In the workplace itself, several developments brought the question of the employer's authority to the fore. First, there was the rapid industrialization and urbanization of the country during the second half of the nineteenth century. Between 1860 and 1910 the population almost trebled, as against a less than doubling in Britain. The proportion of the population in urban areas (defined as those with 2500 or more inhabitants) rose from 20 per cent to 45 per cent of the total. More than 22 million immigrants entered the United States be:ween 1861 and 1910, as against a population in 1910 of 92 million. In that year, 22 per cent of the white male population had been born abroad. As Gutman (1977: 14–15) argues, in Britain the transition to industrial society was largely complete by 1850, whereas in America the whole of the period between 1815 and 1919 was marked by the movement of significant numbers of pre-industrial workers into industrial work.

Second, this massive series of changes occurred in a context in which there were few established lines of authority or understandings as to how to proceed. Rules in industry had to be worked out from scratch. Factory masters had to recruit, organize, and discipline workers with differing cultures, languages, and customs (Korman, 1967: 195–6). And employers could rarely rely on established habits and customs existing outside the workplace. As Joyce (1982) argues, in Britain local and national politics developed a set of understandings concerning civic rights and duties, so that, regardless of what went on inside the factories, employers could feel reasonably secure that wider questions of their rights of ownership would not be raised. The great controversy regarding the causes of the growth of political stability in mid-Victorian Britain notwithstanding, it seems to be common ground among scholars that stabilization took place and that the potential for 'radical' challenges was reduced. This does not, of course, mean that authority within the workplace went unchallenged. Quite the contrary. But challenges within the factory were limited to the frontier of control and did not raise larger issues about the bases of employers' rights. American employers lacked such a secure position. Aronowitz (1973: 183) thus argues that the success of American employers lay in their creation of a set of authority relations in which their own position was paramount.

When the problem facing employers is seen in this way, the extent of their hostility to craft unions can be understood. It might be argued that, faced with an influx of new workers and uncertain as to their own position, employers would have been disposed to rely heavily on craft workers. They might, for example, have strengthened the inside contracting systems that were widespread in several industries (Clawson, 1980: 71–122) with the aim of 'incorporating' the craft elite and simultaneously putting onto that elite the responsibility for industrial discipline. But they could not afford to do so. A reliance on traditional forms of authority would have interfered with attempts to modernize, and in particular to create very large plants and large companies using bureaucratic rules and procedures. More importantly, it would have contained the danger that the craft unions could have used the powers ceded to them to challenge the whole basis of managerial authority: instead of accepting delegated powers to control the details of the work process, they could have begun to question the wider organization of work and the capitalist's role within it. Now, it is known with the benefit of hindsight that such a challenge might not have developed far: craft unions had limited objectives, there were divisions between them as well as between the skilled and the unskilled, and so on. But it would not necessarily have looked like that to an employer who was insecure about his own authority and who was faced with an established and determined body of skilled workers who had considerable control over the work process.

The employers' insecurity was heightened by the second factor mentioned above, namely their need to establish themselves as a class. Numerous scholars have described the opposition faced by the early capitalists. Pollack (1962) has analysed the Populist movement of the late nineteenth century. This was primarily an agrarian movement which, although not opposed to industry in general, objected to the capitalist form of organization and saw farmers and workers as groups in a similar situation. Pollack argues that farmers often supported unions in their struggles with employers. Gutman (1963) similarly argues that, outside the large cities, pro-capitalist sentiments were slow to emerge, that workers in the smaller communities were often politically influential and were not as separated from the middle classes as they were in the cities, and that, therefore, there was often a good deal of community support for workers as against capitalists. In a case study of Paterson, New Jersey, Gutman (1977) develops the point: 'as a new class, the industrialists had not yet achieved high social status . . . Paterson is a good illustration of the frustrating search by the industrialist for status and unchallenged authority' (p. 237). This pattern was not limited to the eastern cities. Dubofsky (1966), in a study of hard-rock miners in the western states, argues that workers and the middle classes were not initially sharply divided and that there were important ties between various social groups; the arrival of large corporations, however, shattered this pattern, and the eventual victory of the corporations was achieved in the face of considerable opposition.

Employers faced a potential crisis of authority which they dealt with by adopting a policy of attacking alternative sources of authority within the workplace. There was nothing peculiar about this: they were not inherently different from other capitalists, but they faced problems that required specific solutions. They thus acted to develop the logic of capitalism in an extreme way. In Britain, capitalists had a degree of general control and were able to cede some detailed control to craft unions and to engage in a policy of compromise and accommodation. American employers were unable to follow this route, and needed to secure detailed control of work in order to establish their own authority and thus create general control.

Once this tendency was established, several features of the industrial relations pattern were decisively influenced. The period up to and including the First World War was one of a battle for control between employers and unions, with strikes being frequent and lengthy. During the 1920s the employers reaped the fruits of the conjuncture of their post-war victories with the success of their longer-term strategy of rooting unions out of the plants. By contrast, British employers certainly attacked the unions during the 1920s, but this was more a matter of tactics than of long-term strategy, and shopfloor organization was not destroyed. The New Deal was traumatic for American employers, but they found in their previous experience means of accommodating to it. Thus, several firms experimented with welfare plans and employee representation schemes during the early years of the century; one of the best-known examples was U.S. Steel where, after the destruction of the craft unions, the company turned to welfarism (Eggert: 1981: 41–54). These schemes were the basis, in the early New Deal, for company unions and other attempts to forestall organizing drives. Company unionism proved to be unworkable but it again increased companies' experience of dealing with their workers. It was not until 1937 that firms had to take the threat of unionization supported by the state seriously; they had had many years to prepare. In the case of Ford, union recognition did not come until 1941; this was 27 years after the five-dollar day had been introduced, and in this period the company had learned a great deal about the 'labour problem'.

Ford exemplifies the American case, for neither the five-dollar day nor union recognition was half-hearted: in both cases, the company rapidly developed a new policy and implemented it thoroughly. American employers displayed tactical flexibility based on a strategic firmness about the right to manage. British employers were often tactically tough, as when they sacked militant shop stewards, but strategically weak.

Conclusions

These remarks can be no more than tentative: they cannot prove that American employers' behaviour reflected particular problems of authority in the workplace. But they help to deal with some long-standing puzzles, notably why the employers were so hostile to unions and why struggles within the workplace were so important to the unions. It was not something inherent in American unionism which led it to eschew politics, but the nature of the difficulties that it faced in establishing itself at factory level.

In addition, the uniqueness of the American strike record, namely the continued very great length of American disputes, can be placed in historical context. Although now recognizing unions, employers are unwilling to concede more than they are forced to do: bargaining remains a trial of economic strength. At shopfloor level, employers have been able to restrain the challenge from below, which explains the relatively low number of strikes as compared with earlier periods, when unions were in formal terms far weaker but when strike activity was more common. But unions have not been destroyed: they have considerable financial resources, and the ritual of holding lengthy strikes at the end of contracts provides an escape valve for rank-and-file discontents while also putting pressure on the employer. On the employer's side, strikes are probably less immediately threatening than they were in the past, for they do not pose any direct challenge to authority. But to settle rapidly would be seen as a sign of weakness and would undermine attempts to keep unions at bay. The expectation that strikes will be trials of strength has become deeply rooted.

More generally, it has been possible to see how, and also to suggest some reasons why, the histories of workplace relations in Britain and America have been different. There has been a complex interaction between workers, unions, employers, and the state; each party had a degree of autonomy within constraints. For example, the pattern of labour relations established in America before the New Deal profoundly influenced the way in which the state intervened, for the direct settlement of disputes between workers and employers was taken for granted. At the same time, the state had some freedom to decide how to intervene, and it did not perform the role of the ideal capitalist. There was nothing approaching total agreement between the state and employers, as indicated most dramatically by the significant minority of employers who refused to accept NLRB instructions to bargain and who waged lengthy campaigns against the Board. But administrative and court rulings were broadly consistent with employers' needs to establish how bargaining could be carried out, what representative rights unions had, and so on. The practice of workplace relations was thus shaped by state activities, and cannot be understood outside them. But at the same time the constraints on the nature of state activities can be assessed.

Finally, the above discussion highlights the weaknesses of those typologies of managerial control, discussed in chapter 1, that posit distinct periods in methods of gaining compliance. Ever since they began to attack traditional forms of work organization in the late nineteenth century, American employers have used a variety of means of controlling their workers, including the organization of work itself and the factory regimes within which work tasks were carried out; US Steel and Ford are good examples. There have certainly been changes, most obviously in the replacement of arbitrary managerial power with the workplace rule of law. But in the large firms arbitrary power existed for the end of protecting the employer's right to manage, and it was buttressed with such things as welfare schemes, and the rule of law also had the defence of the right to manage as its fundamental rationale. In that sense, there is an important degree of continuity in firms' practices of labour control. Changes in these practices, moreover, have come about as much as a result of external pressures, such as the activities of the state and changes in the competitive environment, as they have through problems within systems of labour control themselves. This last point may be pursued by considering some of the consequences of patterns of shopfloor relations.

Conclusion: Some Consequences of Job Control

The foregoing discussion has described and analysed some international differences in patterns of workplace relations. It has thus tried to illustrate one of the arguments of the study as a whole, namely that these patterns develop logics of their own which shape the extent and character of overt industrial conflict. Most obviously, in the strongly organized parts of British industry, strikes and other sanctions are an ever-present possibility because effort bargaining is largely unrestrained by public or private laws. In the unionized sector in America strikes are not such a natural outgrowth of the day-to-day negotiation of order. In Australia they take yet a third form reflecting the absence of developed systems of shopfloor regulations. Strikes are, of course, far from being the whole story. Patterns of relations are complex and multi-faceted. A given practice can assist employers in some respects and constrain them in others. American seniority systems, for example, have helped to undermine collective orientations among the workforce while also creating a set of individual rights which have reduced the employer's freedom of action.

This perspective may be used to throw some light on the consequences of workplace relations for productivity. The debate on th⸱

question is complex, and no claim is made that decisive answers will be given. What is claimed is that a perspective can be developed which goes beyond some of the rather simplistic formulations currently on offer.

There are two extreme positions on the effects of shopfloor job controls. One, exemplifed by Kilpatrick and Lawson (1980), sees these controls as a major constraint on capitalists and, in the British case, as a key reason why the economy has performed less well than others. The opposite view denies any significant role to job controls, seeing complaints about trade union restrictions as attempts to find scapegoats for problems whose causes lie elsewhere and arguing that there is no evidence that British employers have lost control of the labour process (Williams *et al.*, 1983).

The inadequacy of the former view has been demonstrated by Hyman and Elger (1981): to celebrate job controls is to exaggerate their strength in the face of employer counter-attacks, to ignore their sectional, defensive, and ambiguous nature, and to imply that they have been widespread whereas they have in fact been limited to very specific parts of manufacturing industry. The latter view has more to commend it. It is true that criticisms of trade union power have been greatly inflated and that many other factors have to be taken into account. But completely to dismiss the labour process is unwise. This is particularly so in the case of Williams *et al.*, who in their conceptual analysis correctly view the labour process as one area which is likely to affect productivity, only to dismiss its role in their empirical discussion. Other authors (e.g. Aaronovitch *et al.*, 1981: 69) adopt a less extreme view, arguing that shopfloor controls have been a secondary influence, as compared with such things as the structure of capital, in the slow growth of the British economy. Yet the problem remains of explaining the interaction between workplace relations and other influences. Although these relations are conceptually distinct from activities in the sphere of exchange, the two aspects are empirically connected. It is not as though British firms had problems with marketing and investment policies while also facing completely separate constraints on the shopfloor. Approaches to both areas stemmed from common sources.

Consider for example the discussion by Williams *et al.* (mentioned above, p. 203) of the policies of British car firms during the 1950s. Factors such as low investment and a low level of profit per vehicle are identified as sources of weakness. It is also argued that the firms had not lost effective control of the labour process, although little hard evidence on this is produced. Yet the latter argument fits oddly with the evidence surveyed above that it was during the 1950s that shop steward organizations were emerging and with subsequent evidence on fragmented bargaining structures and unofficial strikes. It is reasonable to suggest that the firms took an essentially short-term approach to labour relations as to other matters. The structural problems that Williams *et al.* identify were not immediately apparent at the time, but their consequences were serious as competitive conditions changed. In the same way, it may be suggested, a weakness in labour relations arrangements did not bring any immediate problems but left firms unable to cope subsequently, when external pressures were greater and when steward organizations had become more firmly established.

The argument needs to be taken further, for there is a danger of implying that there is a path of perfect capitalist development from which countries such as Britain have strayed: if only employers had been more long-sighted, everyone would have prospered. This view neglects the costs that a strategic re-structuring of labour relations would have involved. It also implies that such re-structuring was feasible. Although, with hindsight, weaknesses can be identified, these were not necessarily apparent. It would, for example, have seemed thoroughly perverse for British engineering firms to have attacked piecework and its associated methods of bargaining as early as the 1950s. Finally, a model of perfect development ignores the benefits that ceding control to shopfloor workers could bring. Firms were aware of these benefits. Thus, Hyman and Elger (1981: 135) cite the belief of BL management that piecework was an important incentive to workers; in its evidence to the Donovan Commission the firm claimed that its 'Cowley assembly line was between 30 and 50 per cent more productive in terms of manning than were comparable lines at Ford'.

It is thus questionable whether British employers or unions had the incentive and opportunity to act in ways that were significantly different from the courses that were in fact taken. It is, thus, not a matter of identifying failures but of examining why structures that worked well in one period seemed to bring problems later. Now, in talking of 'problems' it may seem that a managerialist perspective is being taken: as critics of industrial relations reformism (e.g. Goldthorpe, 1977) point out, what employers see as problems may be desirable from the workers' point of view in so far as wages are increased or effort levels are made more tolerable. Yet, as Maitland (1983) argues, on the basis of contrasts between a British and a German tyre factory, British shopfloor relations are characterized by a disorder which neither stewards nor managers actively want. Stewards do not deliberately seek sectionalized wage bargaining or a constant round of strikes. But in the bargaining context in which they find themselves they have little alternative to using the tools that are available. Neither they nor managers have traditionally been able to escape a battle over day-to-day issues, even though both sides may have a vision of breaking through to a high-wage, high-productivity productive system.

These remarks suggest that the problem of 'restrictive practices' in British industry should be recast into that of why workplace relations have had particular consequences; these results may, moreover, have been intended by no one. It may thus be possible to reconcile two views that are often expressed: that restrictive practices have been limited to only a very small part of industry, and that the productivity problem is widespread. The former is correct to point out that the shopfloor organization necessary to sustain 'restrictions' is far from universal; it is also true that such organization can bring benefits as well as costs to management. But factories with powerful organizations can be seen not as exceptions to a general rule but as particularly developed examples of a wider phenomenon. This phenomenon is not 'trade union power' but the practice of dealing with labour relations at the point of production itself, and of doing so without a long-term strategic policy. This practice has not been separate from other parts of firms' activities but has been closely connected with them; a short-term approach was also evident in marketing and investment decisions, and shopfloor relations have permitted such an approach to continue. British trade unions have, in a very important sense, been too weak and not too strong, for they have not forced firms out of their narrow horizons to reconstruct labour relations. And such a reconstruction might also have encouraged them to plan a different approach in the sphere of exchange. In short, shopfloor resistance has been a small part of the productivity problem, but labour relations arrangements have been a significant part of a larger managerial approach, and this has been important in a failure to overcome constraints both inside and outside the workplace.

The American system has involved problems of its own. Thus, it is widely argued that the system of collective bargaining was not only put under pressure as economic growth slowed, but was also a prime cause of the downturn in productivity growth that has been a major concern for analysts. Piore (1982) argues that seniority rules and the like have created institutional rigidities that make change difficult. Bluestone and Harrison (1982: 16–17, 138–9) develop a similar point. And Gordon *et al.* (1982: 219) argue that by the 1970s the 'truce' between capital and organized labour was breaking down. They see 'this erosion' as 'a principal source of the well-known slowdown in productivity growth in the U.S. economy'. There are two aspects of this argument that its proponents have not always kept distinct. One is the claim that there has been rising conflict in the workplace which has made management's control of the labour process less certain: workers' resistance has restrained the growth of productivity. The other is the more limited suggestion that the rigidities of the system have become increasingly evident without there necessarily being any rise in overt conflict. The second, but not the first, will be endorsed here.

The difficulty with the first part of the argument is that it has to impose an unrealistic picture on trends of shopfloor action. Proponents of the thesis of growing shopfloor discontent use data on such things as the number of strikes over working conditions and the number that were not authorized by a union (wildcats) to measure the extent of the 'revolt' on the shopfloor. The problem of declining productivity began to become apparent during the 1970s. Yet the evidence from the official statistics, on which writers such as Gordon *et al.* rely, shows that most indicators of the revolt were pointing to a decline during the period (Nolan and Edwards, 1984: 211–13). Surveys of job satisfaction show some decline between 1973 and 1977, but no change between 1969 and 1973 (Staines, 1979): there is certainly no evidence of a massive rise in worker discontent. The more detailed workplace-level study by Jefferys (1984) points to the same conclusion. The plant studied by Jefferys, Dodge Main, had been in the forefront of shop-steward activity during the 1930s and 1940s, and significant organization had been retained until the 1950s. By the 1970s, however, organized resistance to management had all but disappeared. There is, in short, little evidence of an erosion of the 'truce' between capital and labour brought about by rising levels of shopfloor action.[5]

Where there had been an erosion, it has been in management's willingness to live with the consequences of the system of institutionalized bargaining. The flight of firms from collective bargaining and a crisis for organized labour are widely discussed trends (e.g. Juris and Roomkin, 1980). This is where de-industrialization comes in. There is a curious contradiction in Bluestone and Harrison's (1982) analysis of the process for, while they argue that collective bargaining was constraining

5 Gordon (1981) has tried to produce a direct test of the argument that weakening control of the factory has been an important influence on the productivity slowdown. He develops an econometric model in which measures of labour control are shown to perform better than such measures of external shocks as energy prices. The effectiveness of labour control is measured by the ratio of non-production hours to production hours, a rise being seen as a reflection of management's need to increase supervision and thus of a weakening of control. Since, however, non-production workers include clerical and administrative personnel, the measure can be seen as an index of the complexity of firms. It may reflect rigidity but it is a very indirect and imperfect indicator of labour control.

,erial freedom, they also provide an account of labour history
, stresses the weakness of workers and their inability to resist
,igerial changes in work rules (p. 136). The answer lies in the
au..iors' recognition that management's accommodation with
organized labour was coming under increasing pressure as economic
growth slowed. The system of institutionalized bargaining, which was
probably more the creation of management than the outcome of
unions' demands, had always involved rigidities. These became increasingly apparent not just because of a general slowdown in
economic growth but also because of rising competition. American
firms increasingly saw Japan as a major threat and compared their
own systems of management unfavourably with what they took to be
the Japanese model. They have set about reforming their arrangements. Katz (1984), for example, notes the transformation that has
been made in the collective bargaining system of the car industry.
Work standards have been altered at plant level as local unions have
been persuaded to change working practices. There have been
attempts to involve workers more fully, as in the quality of working
life programme at General Motors and the 'after Japan' scheme at
Ford. Common to these has been the wish to replace the old pattern,
based on precisely defined duties and obligations, with one in which
workers have a sense of commitment to the enterprise and act flexibly
instead of clinging to rigid job descriptions.

Similar tendencies have been observable in Britain, where flexibility
and involvement have been widely seen as new principles for organizing work (*Financial Times* 21 August 1985; Thomas, 1985). This is not
the place to comment in detail on the extent to which work relations
have been re-structured or on whether such re-structuring reflects a
specific and short-term response to the post-1979 recession or a more
long-lasting development in workplace relations. Instead, three points
arising out of the foregoing discussion will be considered.

First, there is the general issue of the connection between patterns
of workplace relations and 'efficiency'. Does shopfloor power constrain management? Several otherwise opposed approaches would say
'yes': conservative critics of restrictive practices and radical analysis
of the struggle for control may agree that shopfloor power is a means
of restraining management. The argument contains several errors. It
assumes that 'efficiency' is unproblematic and that, in the absence of
shopfloor resistance, management would know what it was and have
the means of running the highly complex organization that is the
modern firm in such a way as to achieve it. The argument also tends to
treat 'resistance' as something separate from 'control'. And, of
course, it does not link relations inside the workplace to the economic

and political environment in which firms operate. It has been argued above that firms, as much as workers, can create practices that are subsequently seen as 'restricting'. And the co-operative aspects of workers' behaviour have been stressed throughout. This is not to suggest that workplace relations can never seriously impede the pursuit of firms' goals, although it certainly is to raise large questions about the easy equation of these goals and efficiency. It is to argue that their role has to be seen in the context of firms' overall situations and that matters that are satisfactory at one point can come under attack at another.

This may seem to be obvious, but it is to give a rather different interpretation from that offered by those who see attacks on shopfloor controls as attempts to find scapegoats for failures elsewhere. The error is to suppose that, just because management has tolerated practices in an easy competitive environment, it is irrational for it to attack them in harsher times. There is also the danger of confusing causes and cures. It is true that patterns of control are unlikely to have been prime causes of economic decline, in either Britain or America. Witness the concentration of extensive effort bargaining in small parts of the economy, and the other influences operating even in firms where it was present. But, if firms are to respond to competitive pressures, they may find it necessary to try to re-structure their workplace relations. This is no more than the most recent manifestation of the problem of labour in the capitalist firm, namely that workers have no guarantee that, regardless of how much commitment they give, they will not be required to give even more or to accept the sack if their employer can no longer make adequate profits. The analytical conclusion is that patterns of control in the workplace are connected with other parts of firms' operations. Labour relations arrangements do not exert a distinct and separate effect on productivity, for a firm's approach to them is likely to be part of a wider approach to the managerial task. Their consequences have to be assessed accordingly.

This leads to the second point, namely the question of whether British labour relations have put greater constraints on management than have their American counterparts. There is plainly no straightforward answer to this question, for a given pattern produces several different effects. Although the British shop-steward system has given workers the ability to challenge managerial decisions immediately, it has, precisely because of its informal status and its tendency to make the unit of action the work group or factory and not the whole company, been prone to counter-attack. With the benefit of hindsight from the mid-1980s, interpretations of the rise of steward

.s are increasingly stressing the fragile and temporary
which it rested. And in America, although collective
. power was reduced, the system of formal rights could not
ɔe destroyed by management. The economic context has also
different; periodic economic crises, and in particular the recession since 1979, have put particularly strong pressures on British
labour relations, pressures that have, arguably, been weaker in
America. It still appears, however, that the British system has permitted employers rather less freedom of action than has the American.
This has not been because of greater resistance getting in the way of
management but of a tradition of bargaining in which management
has wanted and needed to assert the right to manage less forcefully.
Management has not had the same determination to shape labour relations to its own ends, and traditions of settling issues as and when they
arise have encouraged compromise and the growth of implicitly
acknowledged limitations to what management will do. The American
system has encouraged a greater degree of strategic thinking by
management. Whether or not the move to flexibility and involvement
marks a shift in this long-established contrast remains to be seen,
although it may perhaps be suggested that British firms are more likely
than American ones to face difficulties in establishing a new form of
co-operation. This is not to suggest that they will necessarily find it difficult to attack the old methods of regulation. Evidence from the
private and public sectors points to the removal of demarcation lines,
the introduction of new working practices, and so on. But this is only
half the story. The other half goes beyond the removal of existing
practices to embrace the development of new ones that work in the
long-term and not just as an immediate response to crises. British
workers may have accepted many new things, but long-term commitment and the replacement of informal bargaining with involvement in
the aims of the firm will require a massive change of attitudes and
assumptions. And it is not just a matter of workers' assumptions.
Managements will have to think of ways to generate co-operation. The
problem of harnessing workers' creative capacities does not go away,
and it remains to be seen how far managements can develop the means
to do so.

Finally, how are these new modes of management to be conceptualized? Burawoy (1985: 149–52) develops the concept of hegemonic
despotism to capture the process. Increasing competition has forced
firms to alter their hegemonic regimes, in which concessions were
granted to workers in return for their co-operation, into a more
despotic form wherein workers have to accept effort intensification in
order to keep their jobs. This new despotism differs from the

despotism of competitive capitalism because it is no longer based on arbitrary managerial authority and the threat of the sack. Instead, it is fear of plant closure that binds workers collectively to their firms.

This approach certainly grasps something of recent developments, even if the precise basis of the new despotism is not portrayed very clearly. It is also true that trends towards flexibility have been noted in several countries. But it is not clear what is really new, for capital relocation has always been a threat, even if the threat is somewhat greater now in view of the increased mobility of capital. Neither may it help to see relations inside the factory as despotic. In many ways, they stress consent even more than hegemonic regimes did, for ideas of involvement and commitment, sometimes but not necessarily expressed in such things as quality circles and briefing groups, require workers to adopt the ends of the firm and to strive actively to achieve them. The rewards, for those fortunate to retain jobs in such rationalized corporations, can also be considerable. As Burawoy notes, moreover, this pattern exists for a small declining minority of the workforce, with many more workers being pushed into casual and temporary jobs. It is doubtful whether any one concept can grasp these different tendencies, and it is perhaps too early to try to do so. It may be that there will be a convergence between British and American arrangements. If so, this will not be the first time that similar developments have occurred, the rise of shopfloor bargaining during the Second World War being a case in point. But historically these similarities have masked some deeper differences, in which the role of the employer in managing the workplace has been a key feature.

This chapter has looked at broad patterns of workplace relations and considered some of their causes and consequences. One major consequence is the different ways in which workers behave, with overt effort bargaining and the strikes associated with it being more common in Britain than America. This contrast is, however, very broad. It remains to consider in detail the range of workplace behaviour and the differing circumstances permitting one form rather than another to emerge. This is the task of the following chapter.

6

Conflict and Control
in the Workplace

Previous chapters have examined conflict at the levels of a mode of production as a whole and of different nation states. This chapter adopts a more detailed focus, that of the individual workplace. It is in many ways the most important empirical chapter of the study, for it deals with concrete behaviour and considers in detail the simultaneous production of accommodation and struggle. It attempts, moreover, to take account of differences between workplaces. In any workplace there is a continuing negotiation of the effort bargain. But the form that this negotiation takes differs markedly, with important consequences for the type of overt 'conflict', be it strikes or sabotage, that occurs.

Industrial sociology has always had a tradition of examining what happens inside the effort bargain, with names such as Roy and Lupton being prominent. It has never, however, been a very strong tradition as compared, for example, with that of assessing orientations to work and class consciousness. It has not, moreover, been integrated into the consideration of conflict. In an orthodox, indeed old-fashioned, textbook such as that by Hirszowicz (1981) work group behaviour is considered in terms of the development of group identities and social solidarity; 'industrial conflict' is seen as a quite separate concern. Watson (1980) has provided a more adequate approach in which studies of life on the shopfloor are related to a model of conflict and control. Yet the space which can be devoted to the issue within a general account of industrial sociology is limited. This has two results, which are characteristic of sociological treatments more generally. Some activities, in particular the 'individual' ones of sabotage and absenteeism, receive only passing mention. And behaviour tends to be seen in universalistic terms: bargaining about effort levels, committing sabotage, or 'restricting effort' are presented as ways of responding to the frustrations and pressures of work which are equally open to all workers. Although it is important to present these things as rational and understandable, they are not equally available to all workers. The question of why some occur only among some groups is not addressed.

The re-orientation introduced by the labour process perspective might be expected to have altered this picture. Terms such as conflict and control are now widely used, and the history of work relations has been given attention. But there have been few attempts to look in detail at workplace behaviour and to integrate a treatment of this behaviour within a theoretical perspective. There have been even fewer efforts to take account of 'individual' forms of activity. Thus, in texts describing this new industrial sociology (Hill, 1981; Salaman, 1981) little or no attention is given to the details of workplace behaviour or to the classic studies that dealt with it. This chapter attempts to deal with this substantial deficiency.

A set of workplace studies will be used to assess the pattern of behaviour in different contexts.[1] One approach would be to take each phenomenon in turn and to look at variations in its occurrence. This has, however, two great drawbacks: it treats an activity such as 'sabotage' as a self-evident entity, instead of asking how and why specific activities come to have this label attached to them; and it fragments behaviour into separate 'forms of conflict', whereas the occurrence of one form and not another in a particular workplace depends on the overall organization of work. It is necessary to have some way of categorizing different forms of work organization so that the consequences for forms of behaviour can be systematically considered. The first section of the chapter thus outlines a method of classification before applying it to a range of workplaces. The following two sections draw out the results, in terms of 'collective' and 'individual' action respectively. Once the links between patterns of behaviour and forms of work organization have been considered, two questions arise: how far are these forms influenced by factors from outside the workplace, that is how much relative autonomy do labour processes have; and, more generally, why do workplaces differ in their patterns of control? The first question will be considered with special reference to the position of women and the links between extra-workplace roles and behaviour at work. In assessing the second, a variety of possible causal influences will be considered.

1 The emphasis is heavily on Britain. It is useful to restrict analysis to one country, in order that national differences do not complicate an already complex picture. Britain is the obvious choice because of the number of workplace studies that have been conducted.

Patterns of Workplace Relations

Heuristic Classification

It is obvious that workforces differ in the extent to which they challenge management at the point of production. Or, to put the point in a way which does not imply that it is the workers' own characteristics which are the key source of variation, work organizations differ in the way in which social relations at the point of production are created. Three dimensions can be identified as ways of locating these variations. They are most conveniently described in terms of workers' approaches and organization, but these things should be taken as reflections of wider forces to be discussed below. The dimensions are: the extent to which workers have a militant or acquiescent orientation to the employer; the degree to which an individual or collective orientation exists; and the extent to which a collective orientation has been translated into a collective organization. 'Militant' does not mean politically left-wing, but refers to the extent to which workers perceive themselves as having interests which are opposed to or are inconsistent with the interests of management, and act accordingly. 'Orientation' in this context means, not a set of attitudes or beliefs, but an approach which influences behaviour within the workplace. And a position on any of the dimensions is to be assessed not by means of attitude surveys but by investigation of how work is organized and what activities the workers engage in. The terms refer to the characteristics of groups of workers and not to individual beliefs. A group of workers would, for example, be counted as militant to the extent that it challenged managerial demands on manning levels or piecework prices even though its members may, when interviewed, accept the right of management to manage, agree that the firm is like a football team, and report good working relationships with their supervisors. In short, it is what people do that is important.

This classification refers only to what has been termed earlier detailed control, that is the shape of the frontier of control at the point of production itself. It does not deal with general control. It is not, therefore, to be interpreted as a simple more *versus* less, or better *versus* worse, model of control. Consider, for example, a group of workers who were deemed to be individualistic and to lack any oppositional orientation. They would not necessarily be assessed to be worse off with respect to their working lives than more militant groups. This comes out most clearly in relation to employees of firms practising job enlargement, using autonomous working groups, and offering relatively high wages and good working conditions. Workers here would have some detailed control over such things as job assignments between members of a work group, and they might be considered to be 'better off' than workers with a highly developed collective organization but worse working conditions. The aim of the classification is to assist in describing such different arrangements so that their implications for patterns of conflict can be worked out. Having done this, it is then possible to consider wider questions of the reasons for the existence of a given pattern and its consequences.

If each of the three dimensions is dichotomized, eight categories emerge, as shown in the top panel of Table 6.1. Several combinations are, however, impossible. It is not possible to have an organizational means of controlling the effort bargain without a collective orientation, for an organization implies collectivity; this disposes of cells 2 and 6. Cell 4 is similarly empty because collectivity and organization require militancy in the sense defined above. A counter-example might be a trade union or staff association which represents workers who are non-militant. The present classification, however, is concerned with

TABLE 6.1

Classification of Characteristics of Workplace Relations

a. *Matrix of Notionally Possible Combinations*

		Collective			
		No		Yes	
		ORGANIZATIONAL		ORGANIZATIONAL	
		No	Yes	No	Yes
	No	1(G)	2(X)	3(?)	4(X)
MILITANT					
	Yes	5(G)	6(X)	7(G)	8(G)

Note:
G indicates a combination in the Guttman-type scaling below;
X is an impossible combination;
? indicates an uncertain case discussed in the text.

b. *Guttman-type Scaling*

	Militant	Collective	Organizational
Cell 1	No	No	No
Cell 5	Yes	No	No
Cell 7	Yes	Yes	No
Cell 8	Yes	Yes	Yes

action within the workplace. If workers have not developed a sense of opposed interests as against management, then an organization representing them will not be able to develop organized challenges to managerial control. Cell 4 is thus of little practical relevance. Cell 3 might seem to represent a conceivable combination of a non-militant work force which lacks organizational means of influencing the effort bargain but which has a collective orientation. An example might be the case of autonomous work groups, where the work groups are significant collectivities but where there is no militant opposition to management. But, as explained above, the typology does not aim to classify every possible form of workplace relations but analyses only the extent of explicit challenges to managerial authority. This sort of case would fit into cell 1 because of the absence of any collective orientation in the sense of a set of interests which are seen as being opposed to those of management.

This leaves four possible combinations, which can be arranged as shown in the lower panel of Table 6.1. They take the form of a Guttman scale; that is, a case which passes a 'difficult' item will also pass all the 'easier' ones. For example, someone who can do complicated mathematics will also be capable of conventional algebra and arithmetic, someone who cannot do the complicated work but who can do the algebra will also be capable of the arithmetic, and so on. In the present case, the development of an organizational approach depends on the existence of militancy and collectivity, a non-organizational but collective orientation also requires militancy, and so on.

Examples of each of the four cases will be given below. Several workplace studies will be used in outlining the examples, and these will also be referred to in more detail in the discussion of patterns of conflict and the reasons for the existence of one set of relations and not another. Other studies will be considered that bear on one particular topic such as sabotage. The main 'panel' has been chosen with two considerations in mind. First, the published case study contains sufficient information for a picture of the frontier of control to be developed. This is not always possible, for a study may have a particular concern such as the fixing of piecework prices which means that all the aspects of the relevant frontier of control are not described. Second, it must be possible to assess the implications of a pattern of control for workplace behaviour and at least some of the causal influences at work. Both considerations lead to heavy use of the writer's previous work (Edwards and Scullion, 1982a). The study in question was based on a comparative analysis of seven British factories and tried to develop a comprehensive picture of patterns of conflict and their relationship to the frontier of control. The present discussion is an extension of some of its arguments, and it is natural to draw on it. In addition, personal familiarity with the research material makes it possible to make more soundly based inferences and generalizations than are possible if one's only source of information is a published report.

Examples of the Four Patterns

The first case (cell 1) covers a wide range of situations in which militancy is absent. These situations are probably far more common than the heavy analytical focus in the past on strikes, shop-steward organizations, and open struggles to control the labour process would suggest. In many parts of industry workers either lack union organization or have an organization which is insufficiently powerful to challenge managerial authority. Some detailed studies have, however, begun to emerge.

Armstrong *et al.* (1981) studied three factories producing respectively plastics, electrical mouldings, and footwear. Each employed between 300 and 800 workers. There was very little tradition of collective opposition to management, and managerial definitions of the situation were dominant. Workers accepted, for example, the centrality of profitability and the right of management to manage. If managers argued that it was necessary to cut piecework prices in order to remain competitive, workers accepted this argument and they did not develop any of the controls of the piecework system that have been widely noted in other studies of piecework factories. They did not, for example, establish output quotas or engage in bargaining over the pricing of new jobs. Some informal rules and practices developed, but managers had the power to challenge these whenever they chose. They could, indeed, turn them to their own advantage. As the authors point out (p. 171), 'custom and practice' tends to be seen as a set of arrangements that workers have an interest in defending. Yet here managers could use custom and practice to meet their own ends. For example, managers in one factory successfully argued against the claim that fork lift truck drivers must be properly qualified, citing in support the custom that trucks had been driven by unqualified personnel.

Some very similar findings emerge from two of the factories studied by Edwards and Scullion, which the authors called the Hosiery and Underwear Factories. As their pseudonyms indicate, they were both in the clothing industry; the former was a 200-strong department of a firm employing 650 workers in all, while the latter had 350 employees. Both were managed by the members of the families that owned them. The managerial principles employed were straightforward: the industry was highly competitive, and the only way to stay in business was to maintain price levels, meet delivery dates, and establish a high level of quality and reliability. The last factor was very important, particularly in the Underwear Factory where the main customer was a large retail chain which put considerable weight on quality. The consequences for the management of the labour process were that very strict discipline was enforced on the shopfloor, with break times being strictly enforced and with supervisors firmly discouraging workers from moving around or talking to each other. There was virtually no sense of collectivity among the workers, as was revealed dramatically in workers' secrecy about how much they earned. Even limited attempts to challenge management on effort levels and piecework prices require some degree of collective orientation, but this was largely absent. There were thus no controls over the piecework system, and a detailed investigation of workers' output and earnings revealed that workers operated entirely as individuals with no sense of an output norm.

One significant feature of these factories was the different ways in which men and women were controlled. The foregoing description applies to the women, who carried out all the main operations of sewing up, inspecting, and packing the garments. There were a few male labourers, but most of the men worked in the 'knitting rooms', tending banks of automatic machines which knitted the basic fabric. The men were subject to far less strict supervision than were the women: they had considerable freedom to move about, and were able to indulge in illicit smoking breaks with the toleration of management. They did not, however, have anything that could be described as a militant approach to management: there were complaints about particular issues such as the low level of shift bonus but there was a sense that such problems were inevitable and that there was nothing that could be done about them. At the time of the study of one of the factories, for example, management was in the process of introducing new machinery and asking for redundancies. There was no serious questioning by the workers of the amount of redundancy compensation on offer or of who was to work on the new machines.

This contrast between men and women shows that 'direct control' can contain significant internal variations. It is not to be equated with a total absence of freedom on the part of workers. Neither should it be thought that protest is impossible, for in these two factories and in those studied by Armstrong *et al.* there were cases in which workers protested about alterations in work arrangements, and there were also customs, such as an understanding that 'good' and 'bad' jobs would be distributed 'fairly', which served workers' interests. What is distinctive is an absence of resources among workers to make their demands effective as against the demands of management: managers may tolerate a few ways of giving workers a little freedom, but the limits are tightly controlled.

Very different examples of non-militant workforces come from large firms characterized by highly sophisticated personnel policies. A well-known example is IBM, whose employment policies have been described by one of the company's senior managers (L. Peach, 1983). In brief, employee relations are not carried out through a trade union and, instead, the firm tries to secure the commitment of its workers as individuals through a policy of no redundancies, basing pay on personal merit within job bands, having a well-developed grievance procedure, and regularly monitoring worker attitudes. Other examples come from unionized firms. In the 'Process Factory' studied by Edwards and Scullion man-made fibres were produced under a continuous shift system. The firm sought the loyalty of its workers by guaranteeing the annual wage, providing generous sick pay and other benefits, and organizing production around work teams which were given considerable amounts of discrection over how tasks were allocated between team members. At 'ChemCo' (Nichols and Beynon, 1977) workers were similarly individualized, in particular through a collective agreement which removed the opportunity to bargain from the shopfloor.

There are, then, two distinct cases within the non-militant pattern, which may be called direct control and sophisticated managerialism. The difference should not be seen as one of coercion in the former and hegemony in the latter: direct control involves significant elements of consent, as when workers accept the right of management to manage or value the personal privileges that they may be granted. Control is direct because it is vested in the person of the manager, with little by way of formal procedures, and because managerial techniques are primitive. A sophisticated approach involves a much more conscious personnel policy and is more bureaucratic, with workers having clear rights and with there often being a deliberate policy of being in the forefront in terms of wages and fringe benefits. Compliance is sought in very different ways, but the two patterns have the similarity of discouraging workers from developing a militant perspective.

The second pattern identified in Table 6.1, that of a militant but non-collective approach, has been somewhat neglected in general considerations of work relations. It has generally been assumed that militancy and collectivity necessarily go together. Yet two detailed case studies in the industrial sociology literature point to very different circumstances in which militancy and individualism go together. The first (Cunnison, 1966) coined the term militant individualism to characterize the behaviour of workers in the 'Dee' waterproof garment factory who were studied using participant observation methods for six months in 1956. There was 'an individual struggle between worker and manager over the fixing of the weekly wage, and over matters affecting it, such as piecerate prices and the allocation of work' (p. 89). In one of Dee's workshops 52 women and 28 men worked alongside each other on the 'making-through' system which was characteristic of much of the industry at the time. The system involved a pair of workers in carrying out all the operations required to produce a garment. Each worker bargained individually with the manager over the allocation of work and various allowances and extras that might be added to the basic piecework price of a given task. In addition to this bargaining, workers asserted their independence in a number of ways, notably through their right to plan their work as they saw fit, to talk and move around the shop, and generally to decide when they made their efforts. On working hours, for example, the manager made no attempt to enforce formal factory rules on times of starting and leaving work, but approached workers individually, using as a rationalization not the rules but the efforts put in by other workers. Although there was an occupational community in the sense that workers were closely identified with the trade and were tied together by patterns of residence, kinship ties, and common ethnic and religious affiliations (pp. 64–73), they were also divided by skill and occupation. Their shared background was not strong enough to encourage a collective approach within the workplace.

The second study demonstrating individualism based on a shared occupational culture is that of Sykes (1969a, 1969b), who carried out a project in 1953 on the work attitudes of navvies on Scottish construction sites. Sykes stresses the importance of 'jacking', that is the sudden and unannounced leaving of a site, in the navvies' culture. Navvies boasted of the frequency and suddenness of their moves, and those who did not jack were treated with contempt; jacking was a way of asserting the worker's independence of the employer. In addition, the navvies valued independence of each other: no permanent social groups were formed, and independence and self-reliance were seen as manly and a source of esteem. Yet the men were certainly not hostile to each other. On the contrary, they were amiable and helped each other out at work. They saw themselves as independent workers who were willing to help out a workmate but who did not wish to be tied into more permanent relations of dependence.

In considering the implications of his material, Sykes argues that the characteristics of an industry will tend to create certain orientations among its workers, which will in turn encourage a common response: 'the means whereby this response is practised will become an *interest* for the workers and will be *valued* by them'. Where, as in the case of the navvies, 'the means is individualistic the interest will be a *like interest*; if it is collective then it will be a *common interest*' (1969b: 167, emphasis in original). He therefore draws a contrast between groups such as navvies and clerks, who have an individualistic approach and have developed only like interests, and a group such as printers, who have strong common interests. The distinction is important, but it is plainly inadequate on its own. At first sight, clerks and navvies have more differences than similarities: the one is the archetypal middle-class employee and the other is the tough, self-reliant manual worker. In the classification proposed here, the difficulty is overcome by placing clerks (or at least clerks as they appear in Sykes's account) in the non-militant category. Navvies differ from them because they have developed like interests in that they have a militant approach to the employer, whereas clerks do not. The case of workers with like interests should be seen as a distinct situation, different from the non-militant case and from the case of collective orientations.

The four-fold categorization used here also distinguishes within the 'collective' category. Not all workers with a collective orientation have the developed sense of organization and the tight-knit control of the work situation which is commonly attributed to printers. It will be convenient to begin with this most developed, or organizational, category before dealing with the more heterogeneous non-organizational one. The chief characteristic of the organizational group is a substantial set of controls over the effort bargaining which rest on a shopfloor organization which embraces all the relevant workers. The shopfloor organization plays a central part in the organization of the labour process. It has become a commonplace that in the printing industry (or, more precisely, in certain parts of it, especially the Fleet Street newspaper print rooms) management has little or no discretion over the hiring of workers or who shall do what jobs. The union organization exercises a tight control over all aspects of work. And this control is exerted not only against management. It also operates to discipline workers, such that those stepping outside the rules are subject to punishment.

Examples outside the special case of printing can be drawn from the Edwards and Scullion study. In two plants, the Large Metals Factory and the Small Metals Factory, owned by a large engineering firm, shop-steward organizations had developed a substantial degree of control over the effort bargain. In addition to a pre-entry closed shop, there were important controls over the deployment of labour within the factories. The allocation of workers to jobs depended on the stewards' agreement; that is, the matter was not just negotiated, but the stewards had an effective veto over assignments of which they did not approve. Stewards totally controlled the allocation of overtime: they drew up the rotas, and supervisors played no part in the process. In both factories the stewards boasted that 'we run the factory', and the role of first-line supervision was correspondingly limited. In both, moreover, the controls operated across all grades of workers: they were not limited to skilled craftsmen but also covered semi-skilled assemblers and machine operators and unskilled labourers.

This situation is probably unusual. Possibly more typical is the position in another engineering company in which two plants, the Electrical Factory and the Components Factory, were studied. Here, skilled workers such as toolmakers, electricians, and fitters had developed powerful steward organizations, and in some respects their controls were stronger than those exercised in the Large and Small Metals Factories. In the Components Factory toolroom, for example, a worker was not permitted to shift from one type of machine, for example a lathe, to another machine such as a turning machine. And overtime controls had been extended to a point at which, if management wanted any overtime at all, it had to be offered to the whole shop for a twelve-week period. By contrast, production workers in the two factories, although having steward organizations that were quite well developed in formal terms, had relatively few controls: there were none on overtime, and very few on manning levels.

Three points about the organizational pattern warrant emphasis. First, its strong controls do not imply a powerful sense of solidarity among workers. Indeed, it is often associated with intense hostilities between different groups of workers, for example between compositors and machine-minders in printing and between different skilled trades in the engineering industry. Second, the controls are imposed on members of the work group as well as on management: shopfloor discipline can be enforced very strictly, and this discipline is important in establishing a sense of organization in which, in many respects, the organization itself plays a larger role than does management in determining what members can and cannot do. Third, to underline the point made above, the organizational pattern is a type of detailed control. It should not be assumed to be more in workers' interests than other patterns: it certainly gives workers powers that are absent elsewhere, but it can go along with general levels of wages and working conditions that are worse than those enjoyed by workers employed by sophisticated managerialist firms.

The final pattern, of a collective but non-organizational orientation, has rather imprecise boundaries with the individualistic and the organizational patterns. The main difference from the former is that effort bargains cease to be worked out by managers and individual workers and take on a collective character. The difference from the organiz- ational pattern lies in the lack of a developed struggle over the frontier of control, with workers' organizations being looser and less dis- ciplined than they are in the organizational pattern and with disputes with management concentrating on the specifics of the effort bargain and not the frontier of control which governs the bargain. Examples include some of the classic industrial sociology studies of piecework. Roy (1952, 1953, 1954) studied an American steel fabrication plant during 1944 and 1945. He discovered some powerful collective con- trols of earnings, with work groups establishing clear norms and warning people not to go above the norms. Similarly, Lupton (1963) analysed the range of 'fiddles' used by workers in a British engineering factory to control their level of earnings, together with the consider- able toleration of the practices on the part of management. In both cases, workers were actively engaged in effort bargaining, and the establishment of group norms differentiated them from the pattern of militant individualism. But they had not developed a more organized challenge to managerial power on such issues as manning levels, the allocation of overtime, or the right to apply disciplinary sanctions. The collective orientation patterns is not limited to pieceworkers. Ditton (1979a) reports a study of bakery workers designed to discover whether workers paid by time control the level and timing of their own efforts. His answer is that they do, with a range of methods, notably the manipulation of machine cycle times and arrangements allowing workers to clock each other out at the end of the shift. Ditton's description appears to place these workers within this pattern: they operated as a group, but their effort controls were often informal, being limited to exploiting managerial leniency and not developing into organized pressures to shift the frontier of control in workers' favour on a more permanent basis.

These four patterns (or five if the two sorts of non-militant orien- tation are taken into account) are simplifications and idealizations. Some cases to be discussed below fall between two of the patterns, and there are significant variations within each pattern. In view of the strictures against ideal types of managerial strategy made in previous chapters, the patterns are not offered as typifications of complete modes of control. They avoid some of the problems identified with ideal types, for they do not treat management as the key actor or view labour relations in terms of control *versus* resistance. They are, instead, pictures of the different ways in which struggles for control can develop. They do not suggest that the links between conflict and co-operation can be deduced from a strategy of managerial control. They simply aim to identify some contrasts in the ways in which the dialectical relationship between conflict and co-operation is managed in different workplaces. In short, they have a very specific function, namely to point to differing positions of the frontier of (detailed) control, and to examine the consequences for patterns of overt conflict.

The Collective Control of Effort

In this and the following section, the literature of shopfloor industrial relations is used to analyse the patterns of concrete behaviour associated with each of the types of workplace relations identified above. This use is selective, in that no attempt is made to summarize all the studies that exist. It is also a constrained use, for not every study contains information on all the issues of interest. As noted above, the systematic analysis of 'individual' forms of behaviour is rare. But several studies contain snippets of information that can be used, in the light of other research, to develop plausible arguments about the place of the behaviour in question in the workplace under scrutiny.

This section begins by considering patterns of effort bargaining. These patterns can then be related to the frontier of control more generally. No attempt will be made to survey the voluminous writings on the collective use of sanctions such as working to rule or going on strike. The interest is in continuing patterns of behaviour and not in, say, the reasons why some industries are more strike-prone than others. But some important conclusions emerge about how collective sanctions should be viewed, and these are presented by outlining a perspective on strikes.

Effort Bargaining

The concern here is not with why effort bargaining takes a developed form in some workplaces and not in others; this will be considered later. It is with the prior question of how systems of effort bargaining work: how are the uncertainties of the labour contract (in terms of how much effort is expended, under what conditions, at what times, and for what reward) managed in different sorts of workplace?

Among non-militant workforces effort bargaining is absent or tightly constrained. Armstrong *et al.* (1981: 68) note that in their factories quality standards were accepted as being entirely a managerial responsibility, so that workers accepted managerial alterations of cycle times on grounds of quality without question. The researchers also stress (p. 143) workers' extreme privacy about their earnings. Similar features were noted by Edwards and Scullion in their Hosiery and Underwear Factories. In addition, the piecework system itself remained under managerial control. When new jobs were brought in, workers accepted the standards for them that managers set. Most notably, in many piecework factories it is taken for granted that, when jobs are timed so that piecework prices can be established, the 'average' speed of the 'average' worker will be the baseline. A price should enable such a worker to attain the accepted level of bonus under normal levels of effort. In addition, workers take it for granted that they will try to get a loose time by working slowly when under study. In these two factories, however, management had successfully established the practice that the 'best' and not the average worker should be studied. Workers also said that there was no point in restricting effort when under study, for this would simply cut their own earnings. Such an attitude reflected the workers' extreme individualism, for the aim was to maximize individual earnings and not to negotiate a good price on behalf of the group. A further feature of the system was the very low basic wage paid when workers were not on piecework, for example when a machine had broken down. In the Electrical and Components Factories, by contrast, such waiting time was paid at 85 per cent of average earnings. Finally, the established rules on quality were that anyone doing faulty work had to rectify it 'in her own time', that is without extra payment. This meant that any incentive to workers to increase earnings by cutting corners was kept tightly in check, for any-one attempting to work an angle would find her work being returned to her and, if she persisted, there would rapidly be disciplinary warnings for bad work.

The important point about all these features is the way in which they came together to form a co-ordinated system. They were not independent items, but were part of a set of arrangements which closed off various possibilities for exerting control of effort levels such as working angles, trying to fiddle time studies so as to obtain loose times, and seeking payment for waiting time. There were some counterbalancing customs, in particular the practice that workers would have 'good' and 'bad' jobs allocated to them in turn. This prac-tice was not, however, a formal rule. And it did not cost management very much, for it kept workers happy without significantly affecting output. The practice, moreover, related only to the allocation of jobs within a specific department; in one shop, for example, where garments were prepared and packed there were three basic sizes of garment, and batches of each size were distributed in turn. The practice did not extend to movements of workers between entirely different jobs. As noted above, managerial discretion here was absolute. Armstrong *et al.* (1981: 61) similarly describe a case in which workers were required to move to new work; when they queried this, they were told that they could do the work, quit, or go home until their normal work was available.

As emphasized earlier, managerial domination even in these situations is not total. Workers can question requests, and they have some resources at their disposal. Those with skills that are valued can exploit their strategic position to some degree. Thus, in a case observed by Edwards and Scullion, a group of long-serving and skilled employees was moved to new work which they feared would lead to a cut in earnings. They were able to delay the transfer and persuade management to guarantee their old earnings for a longer period than management originally proposed. They had to move, and their resistance was based more on the worries of each worker as an individual than on a collective refusal to do the new work; hence, managers were able to persuade them to move one at a time. But there was some possibility of resistance. More generally, there is a wide range of ways in which day-to-day matters are negotiated between workers and supervisors, and workers can grumble and generally make life difficult for their superiors.

This suggests that there is no rigid dividing line between the non-militant and militant individualism patterns. The latter is an extension and development of some of the possibilities of the former. In particular, workers have a degree of bargaining awareness and make use of their tactical opportunities. Thus, Cunnison (1966: 103) describes how workers initiated increases in piecework prices when product demand was buoyant. Her account reveals the pattern of mutual dependence between workers and managers that developed. Managers had to go to some lengths to try to keep workers satisfied, in particular by ensuring a steady supply of work. Given the rapid and unforeseeable fluctuations in the market, managers had the difficult task of keeping a steady flow of work while meeting urgent orders. They thus depended on workers to deliver output. In addition, they relied on the workers' exercise of skills. In the case of the 'Dee' factory analysed by Cunnison, skills were particularly important, for in the making-through system there was only a rudimentary division of labour between makers and machinists, with each worker performing all the making or machining tasks on each garment. There was little by way of task fragmentation or the separation of conception and execution. The importance of this lies not just in the demonstration that workers have skills that they must be willing to give up if the production process is to continue. In addition, it shows how notions of skill can assist management. It is commonly argued that skilled workers are more powerful than the unskilled because they are less replaceable. This may be true as a general proposition, but the degree to which workers can make use of their skills as bargaining resources will depend on the pattern of control as a whole. Cunnison's workers were certainly highly skilled in the difficult operations that they had to carry out, but the absence of any collective norms on output and the general acceptance of managerial authority limited their bargaining powers. As Cunnison stresses (p. 96), managers generally had the whip hand on matters of prices and the allocation of work, and individual bargaining was constrained by this overall balance of power. The workers were unable to move beyond their individual bargaining to develop notions of the autonomous craft worker which might have posed a broader challenge.

The position under the 'sophisticated non-militant' pattern is very different from these sorts of arrangements. Piecework, even where it is tightly under management control, makes explicit the relationship between effort and rewards. Sophisticated systems avoid these matters by using time methods of payment, often accompanied by broader guarantees on total earnings. There may also be such things as profit-sharing schemes and bonuses related to total company sales. Workers' efforts are secured not through the immediate carrot of piecework but through inducing a broader willingness to work. Effort bargaining at the point of production is effectively organized out of the employment relationship: job gradings and bonus systems operate at the level of the company and there is little left to bargain about. It is, of course, true that workers can try to restrict their efforts, but the system is so organized as to make this unlikely. Most workers have been imbued with the company's way of doing things, for one of the characteristics of the system is to encourage long service. Any protest is likely to involve a minority of workers and to be difficult to sustain. Given that the firms in question generally try to provide generous wages and conditions, there is probably not a great deal to bargain about, and potential issues are far less central than, say, a proposed rate cut in a piecework factory. In short, effort bargaining is highly constrained.

By contrast, piecework where workers have developed a collective organization, as in the cases described by Roy and Lupton, is an extreme case of continuous effort bargaining. There is little to add to the description already given concerning the bargaining itself. But one important question concerns the motivations of the parties. On the workers' side, the analytical focus has traditionally been why workers do something as apparently irrational as to restrict their output and thus their earnings. This focus stems from the celebrated Hawthorne studies (Roethlisberger and Dickson, 1939), which found a fixed ceiling on output in the 'bank wiring room' and which explained it as the result not of rational economic calculation but of 'social' factors, in particular the function of the ceiling in promoting a sense of solidarity among the workers. The errors of this view have been widely documented. Sykes (1965) has argued that many of the arguments which Roethlisberger and Dickson advanced against an 'economic' explanation were spurious; for example, they claimed that the workers did not understand the operation of the pay system and thus could not be manipulating it in their own interests, whereas Sykes argues that there was no need for a detailed understanding and that a rough-and-ready appreciation of its main point was sufficient. Franke and Kaul (1978) have recently re-examined the Hawthorne data and have concluded that the best predictors of output variations (across all the experiments and not just the bank wiring room) were the effects of the recession (many of the studies were carried out during the early 1930s) and the re-assertion of managerial discipline, with intra-group solidarity being less important.

More generally, one of Lupton's main achievements was to question the whole approach in terms of 'restriction':

> To support a judgement that a group of workers was restricting output, one would have to have a neutral measure of a proper day's work . . . I have therefore discussed the 'fiddle' not as part of a policy of restriction of output but as a form of social adjustment to a given job environment (1963: 182).

It is possible to make even more of this point than Lupton himself does, for his empirical work at Jay's demonstrated that the 'fiddle' involved means to speed production as well as to limit it. The whole point of working angles is to do work in less time than work study standards suggest. Workers are thus using their detailed knowledge of the job and their experience of what exactly can be done with specific tools to increase output. In effect, they are saving management from itself by replacing formal and unrealistic work study standards with skills on the job.

Lupton also significantly advanced the understanding of managerial behaviour, for the earlier focus on workers' motivations had left management entirely out of the picture. His focus on fiddles and not restriction provides an important part of the explanation of managerial toleration of the activity: to the extent that workers are deploying their skills in the pursuit of production they are acting in line with managerial interests. He also explains why those aspects of the fiddle, such as exploiting loose times and being booked on two jobs at once, which did not assist production were not attacked by managers. It was realized that too tight an application of the formal rules would lead to resentment on the shopfloor and possibly to more systematic effort restrictions and also to increased absenteeism and labour turnover. Tolerating a certain amount of rule-breaking was necessary to get production out and, for Lupton, it was relatively cheap because permitting the fiddle bought worker satisfaction at a low cost. Some attempt at fiddling was, in the circumstances, inevitable and it was better to live with it, controlling only cases of gross 'abuse', than to try to stamp it out.

Such an argument is, however, specific to a given payment system and a given frontier of control and should not be used to explain capitalist control of the labour process in general. It plainly does not work, at least without substantial modification, in non-piecework situations. Neither does it apply to cases where workers have insufficient power even to play these 'games', as Burawoy (1979) calls them, or to situations in which they have gone beyond operating within specific wage-effort bargains to affecting wider aspects of the frontier of control. A particularly clear example of the latter point is provided by the organizational pattern within the Small Metals Factory. At the time of the research this plant was on measured day work, but it had for many years operated under piecework. A key feature of the control that the stewards had developed was an earnings ceiling that was applied across the factory. This had two main effects. It took effort bargaining away from the individual work group and enforced union discipline on the whole factory. And it was a useful weapon against management, for if the firm wanted to increase output the stewards could refuse to raise the ceiling if they felt that there was insufficient work in the factory to justify an increase. This and other associated controls went far beyond playing games in the sense of gaining the satisfaction of 'making out' while also accepting the rules of the game. Stewards had taken issues such as manning levels and the pace of work away from the individual effort bargain and made them part of a wider struggle to establish and defend a frontier of control in their own favour.

Effort bargaining under the organizational pattern thus has a much wider significance than it does under the collective orientation pattern. As noted above, these two patterns are not rigidly separated. A case which falls between them, and thus illustrates the differences, is that of Ford's Halewood plant as described by Beynon (1973). The case is also useful in illustrating the controls of effort that can emerge where there is no piecework but where workers have developed a collective approach to the matter.

As is well known, Ford has had a reputation, even within the conflict-prone car industry, for an aggressive style of labour relations based on management's right to manage and the refusal to tolerate any form of 'mutuality'. When forced to recognize unions, the company aimed to keep bargaining at the level of national union officials and to prevent shop stewards from establishing a position on the shopfloor. The establishment of the new factory on Merseyside, away from traditional centres of the industry, gave the firm an opportunity to re-assert its aims. It was not, however, successful. Beynon (1973: 68) identifies three factors that were important in the establishment of a shop-steward organization: traditions of militancy on Merseyside, the fact that nearly all workers were members of the Transport and General Workers' Union, and the daily experience of life in a Ford factory. In the early period of the plant the pressure of work was unremitting, and there grew up an intense antipathy between managers and stewards in which neither side was willing to show any concern for the other: there was a straightforward battle for control (pp. 75, 105). By 1968, however, the shop stewards' committee was in a position to establish a degree of consistency in the job control exercised by each of its stewards on their section. 'Its ability to secure this consistency derived from the actual controls over job regulation that had been built up unevenly throughout the plant' (p. 142). These controls included such things as line speeds, the allocation of overtime, and work allocation. On some sections there were informal rotas for time off with, for example, a team of eight workers taking it in turns to have Friday afternoon off (p. 148).

Some of these controls, as will be seen below, are characteristic of the organizational pattern. Controlling such things as line speeds and the allocation of work within a team plainly goes beyond conflicts over individual effort bargaining as described by writers such as Lupton. Yet there are degrees of organizational control, and the Halewood case contrasts with the cases of the Large and Small Metals Factories, in two main respects. First, as Beynon stresses, controls at Halewood developed patchily, and such things as rotas for overtime were far from universal. This seems to have reflected the limited extent to which stewards could establish their controls. In the two Metals factories many controls were deeply entrenched and were taken for granted by all sides. At Ford they appear to have been less universal, more covert, and more subject to managerial attack. This obviously reflects Ford management's policy on retaining the right to manage, as contrasted with the attitude of the various managements that had owned the Metals Factories, which can be summarized as one of having no overall policy on labour relations and of seeking accommodation with the shop stewards on whatever terms seemed sensible at the time. Second, Beynon (p. 149) stresses the vulnerability of controls at Halewood to fluctuations in the market, having previously documented how declining market demand stimulated managerial attempts to tighten up shopfloor control. Similar forces were at work in the Metals Factories (Edwards and Scullion, 1982a: 195–9). Yet there were at least some means of insulation from the market, as with the earnings ceiling described above, which enabled stewards in the Small Metals Factory to prevent market fluctuations from affecting their members immediately.

The example of Ford helps to point up some of the variations within a given pattern of relations. The aim here has not been to suggest that every workplace can be fitted into one of four types. It has, on the contrary, been to develop some analytical tools with which some concrete situations can be examined. Patterns of effort bargaining can be related to the frontier of control, and it can be shown how different social relations develop within the production process.

Parameters of the Effort Bargain

The discussion now needs to be broadened to consider influences on individual effort bargains. Of particular importance is an issue that has received very little systematic attention in the literature, namely the mobility of workers between jobs. This is not the narrow question of allocation of particular tasks, for example whether on a particular day a car factory press operator is to produce bonnet panels or boot lids. It is the larger question of how mobility between completely different sets of operations is handled. This is important because a management facing few constraints has considerable freedom to treat workers as interchangeable and to prevent any collective orientation from developing. Workers will correspondingly lack any means to control relations among themselves.

As already indicated, the non-militant pattern under direct control is associated with very few shopfloor controls over the mobility of labour: managers can move workers as the perceived needs of production dictate. There may be some notions of property rights in specific jobs (Armstrong et al., 1981: 117–18) but these are weak and are always open to managerial challenge. From Cunnison's study, it appears that militant individualism is associated with a great stress on job property rights, with workers feeling that they had a right to their own jobs. Even here, however, such feelings were undercut by the workers' all-pervasive individualism. Cunnison (1966: 246–9) demonstrates how divisions necessarily emerged as workers fought on an individual basis for the work available and accused the manager of favouritism in his allocations.

Even under a collective approach, workers rarely have many well-established controls of the supply and allocation of labour. In practice, management is unlikely to make the sorts of demand which seem to be common under non-militant arrangements, where workers are asked to move from one job at short notice and with no rights of return to their 'own' jobs after the transfer. Even in the fairly weak form of collective orientation that existed in the Electrical Factory, there was a custom and practice rule that anyone moved had a right of return to her old job. Elsewhere, managers do not seem to have asked for moves between different sections of factories, but movements within sections, for example from one machine to another, lie largely within managerial prerogative. Given that some sort of bargaining relationship exists, this prerogative is unlikely to be enforced as a totally unilateral right. A manager will try to persuade a worker to move, will choose the 'reasonable' workers and not the 'troublemakers', and will explain the reasons behind the request. But the matter will largely be one of individual negotiation between a supervisor and a worker, and workers have few formal rights to refuse to move.

In the organizational pattern, by contrast, management is far more tightly constrained. In the Large Metals and Small Metals Factories there were several aspects of these constraints. Most basic were numerous demarcation lines, across which it was always impossible to move workers (with one important exception, noted below). Now, demarcations in craft areas have been common throughout British industry such that the duties of an electrician, a pipe-fitter and a machine-tool fitter are distinct. In these two factories there were, in addition, similar distinctions between grades of production worker. In the assembly shops of the Large Metals Factory, for example, there were two distinct trades claiming skilled status and two further semi-skilled trades. Some of these divisions were reinforced by the pattern of union organization, with different unions organizing different trades, but some occurred between workers in the same union. The exception to the impermeability of demarcations occurred in the Small Metals Factory where, because of a number of peculiarities of the plant, the strict imposition of demarcations would rapidly lead to manpower shortages in particular areas and thus to lay-offs, and the stewards permitted mobility from skilled jobs to less skilled ones. This policy was assisted by the fact that all the production jobs were organized by one union. Such mobility was, however, strictly voluntary and could be refused at any time.

In addition to demarcations between trades, within each trade stewards played an important role in assigning workers to jobs. This 'labour loading' was carried out by negotiations between foremen and stewards, and was often highly detailed; stewards might, for example, argue that a particular worker should not work on a section because of his health problems. This points up the contrast between such arrangements and those characterized by managerial discretion. The latter is illustrated at perhaps its extreme by Linhart's (1981) description of his work as an operative in a Citroen factory near Paris. He was moved from job to job as and when management demanded and had no rights to protest. He describes graphically his lack of freedom, his subjugation to managerial directives, and the lack of any sense of belonging to a stable social group. The important thing about controls in the two British factories is not that they were used continually to frustrate management. They certainly meant that labour loading could be a time-consuming task. But these delays were not the aim of the stewards; they were the consequence of the frontier of control that had developed. Stewards did not want to hold up production, but neither did they wish to give up their rights to determine man assignments through negotiation, for these rights were important to their members and also to their own power as against management. The first important result of the controls is thus their unintended consequence of interfering with production. Their second was that they gave stewards considerable power to make intentional stoppages: when stewards resented a managerial initiative they could refuse their 'normal' co-operation in negotiating the allocation of tasks, thus making life very difficult for foremen.

In the organizational pattern, then, and to a lesser extent in cases such as Halewood, potential overt conflicts in the effort bargain become institutionalized within the frontier of control. By 'institutionalized' in this context is meant not that formal institutions channel and contain overt disputes, but that the possibility of day-to-day struggle over every aspect of the labour process have come to be expressed in a set of understandings and assumptions about the social organization of work. It is accepted, for example, that foremen cannot ask anyone to move jobs without the steward's agreement. Such an arrangement can suit managers: it means that potential arguments between workers and foremen are dealt with by established rules, and it removes from managers the responsibility for taking some decisions. If, however, managers gained the right to allocate workers to tasks, they might well be faced with resentment among workers who felt that their long-established rights were being challenged. But institutionalization cannot be perfect, for the rules themselves are open to challenge. It does not remove the contradictory relationship between capital and labour, but is a reflection and expression of it. Whether or not the many possible sources of friction within the effort bargain develop into open conflicts will depend on the position of the frontier of control.

A Perspective on Strikes

Before leaving the question of collective forms of control of the labour process, a brief comment on strikes is required. Strikes are among the most studied of British industrial relations phenomena, and an account of patterns of conflict should be able to say something about them. At the same time, however, a neat picture is unlikely since, even in highly strike-prone plants, stoppages of work are far from being daily occurrences and since the causation of strikes is highly complex, with many idiosyncratic elements. All that can be put forward is a view of the significance of strikes under different patterns of control, and not a causal explanation of strike activity.

In non-militant circumstances strikes are obviously very unusual. Where they occur, they are likely to be almost entirely divorced from day-to-day relationships on the shopfloor. A good example is described by Pollert (1981: ch. 10) in a study of female tobacco workers which will be examined in more detail below. Pollert demonstrates a lack of control of the work process on the part of the workers. A one-day strike was called by the union and, although this encouraged feelings of freedom from the routines of the factory, it had little bearing on these routines and was something apart from workers' daily experiences. A similar point can be made about strikes that emerge within the factory instead of being organized outside it. Edwards and Scullion (1982a: 229) report a strike which occurred in one of their clothing plants some years before their research. It had been a spontaneous walk-out over a rumour, which was in fact unfounded, that piece rates were to be cut. It was written off by management as the result of a misunderstanding, and there was a good deal of truth in this view, for it was, apparently, more of a protest than an attempt to exert bargaining pressure, and it had no lasting consequences.

At the other extreme are strikes in the organized pattern which represent an extension of the normal round of bargaining. Workers and stewards here have a wide variety of sanctions available to them, and in some circumstances they will strike. As Batstone *et al.* (1978: 218) put it at the end of their detailed study of strikes in a large, well-organized, and highly strike-prone vehicle-assembly plant, strikes in this sort of factory are just a development of other methods of controlling the effort bargain. Strikes are taken for granted as an

ever present possibility and, apart from those which raise great issues of principle, no one is likely to be unduly exercised about them. They are not exactly predictable, but they have an understood place in such factories.

With the exception of Halewood, the other plants used in the previous discussion seem to have had too few strikes for anything systematic to be said about them. Strikes certainly do not loom large in the classic studies of piecework bargaining. Halewood, by contrast, has had a history of a large number of strikes. Examples which have been described in detail include an unofficial dispute analysed by Beynon (1968) and the case used by Hyman (1972: 11–16) to illustrate an 'unexceptional dispute'; many others have attracted press attention. What emerges from these cases is the high-profile approach adopted by management and the way in which the factory was a perpetual battlefield. In contrast to the well-institutionalized organizational pattern, where strikes emerge as part of a process of bargaining within broadly accepted parameters, strikes at Halewood seem to have reflected struggles in which there were few established rules of the game. As Beynon (1968: 337) puts it, 'the conflict was between bureaucratic rational efficiency and the rationality of worker experience – a fundamental conflict of values'. It is possible that incidents that provoked strikes at Ford would, under a more fully developed organizational pattern, result in a quiet compromise between foreman and steward: the foreman would want to discipline a worker, the steward would point to the consequences which might arise if he did so, the foreman, fearful of his reputation with higher management if he were seen to be pursuing a minor incident that could cost the company far more in lost time than the immediate point at issue could justify, would back down, and the steward would suggest to the worker that he watch his step for a while.[2]

An incident in the Large Metals Factory illustrates the point (Edwards and Scullion, 1982a: 139). A foreman discovered that, out of a team of four welders who were supposed to be doing overtime, only two were present. The issue was, in principle, one that could lead to very severe penalties for the workers: if justly accused, they would

2 A further example of the Ford approach is the now-famous 'Kelly' case of 1983 in which a worker was sacked for allegedly damaging a bracket. A large strike ensued. This is exactly the sort of incident that under a less directive managerial approach would probably be settled informally at shopfloor level. The case is described in the *Financial Times* of 10, 11, and 23 March, 8 April, and 28 May 1983. There is, of course, no certainty that the approach is limited to Ford. Thus, Willman (1984) in analysing industrial relations at British Leyland draws parallels between it and events at BL's Longbridge plant: as managers there tried to re-assert their control, strikes over working arrangements and the right to manage emerged.

be guilty of seeking earnings to which they were not entitled, and there would also be questions about conspiracy with others to enable them to be clocked in when they were in fact absent. That there was not a managerial attempt at instant dismissal itself indicates the extent to which control of discipline had been surrendered by management. The practice of leaving early had, as noted below, become widely established. All that the foreman attempted to do, therefore, was to stop the pay of the two alleged absentees. The rest of the welders immediately banned overtime, and the dispute was resolved when the union convener promised that, in future, stewards would formally submit to management a list of names of those doing overtime. This result reflected the institutionalization of stewards' power over the effort bargain: in this case their controls of overtime, the weakness of managerial authority over discipline, and the ability of the workers involved to impose sanctions at will. In non-organizational patterns a similar issue might well provoke a strike or, where workers' collective orientation was less developed, simply result in the sacking of the workers involved.

Individual Action

The case just discussed points to the connections between collective controls and supposedly individual issues: discipline is formally a matter of the employer's application of sanctions against individuals who break the rules, but collective controls prevented managers from dealing with the welders in this way. The degree to which 'individual' responses are shaped by collective controls varies according to their position on the frontier of control, as the following discussion tries to demonstrate. Four types of behaviour, sabotage, pilfering, absenteeism, and labour turnover will be considered.

Sabotage
There is more to these labels, and particularly the first two, than meets the eye. What is sabotage? An apparently specific definition is the deliberate destruction of the product or the machinery used to produce it. But how do we know what is deliberate? A good example is described by W. Walker (1969: 221–2). In a press shop, some jobs were timed for 'single-stroke' operations, that is for the operator to activate the press for each pressing. But long experience had taught operators that on some of the jobs the presses could be run continuously, which increased earnings but carried the risk of damaging the raw material or even breaking the tool. In such cases, damage

should be seen not as deliberate destruction but as the by-product of effort bargaining. Geoff Brown (1977: xi) has developed a broader definition, seeing sabotage as any direct action at the point of production which clogs 'the machinery of capitalism'. But this would cover almost any form of bargaining, and is too imprecise. The approach adopted here is to see sabotage not as a self-evident category but as a label that may be applied to some actions and that itself requires explanation. It refers to destruction and also to the production of goods below acceptable levels of quality. Quality standards, like effort levels, are necessarily contestable, and definitions of what is acceptable or unacceptable cannot be divorced from the bargaining context in which they take place.

The meaning of sabotage will vary according to the pattern of work organization, as Taylor and Walton (1971) set out to demonstrate with their classification of it into three types: individual and collective attempts to reduce tension and frustration; efforts to facilitate or ease the work process; and attempts to exert control. These categories plainly overlap to a significant degree. Easing the work process, for example, is also likely to moderate frustration. The authors' main example of this second type, or utilitarian sabotage as they call it, is the study by Bensman and Gerver (1963) of an American aircraft factory. These investigators discovered that workers used an illicit tool known as the 'tap' with which to force into position the bolts holding the wings to the fuselage. Although possession of a tap could lead to instant dismissal, workers used it widely because to fix the bolts 'properly' required an excessively lengthy and difficult task. Hence frustration was also eased. It is notable, in addition, that foremen not only acknowledged the use of the tap but even instructed workers in its use. This illustrates a major point about sabotage: it grows out of shopfloor arrangements and is taken for granted by participants, and to see it simply as a deviant or criminal act is not helpful.

Taylor and Walton (p. 243) note that existing accounts of sabotage tended to be 'too abstract' and too far 'removed from the actual industrial setting in which the critical behaviour occurs'. They suggest some ways of moving away from abstraction to locate sabotage in context. For example, sabotage expressing frustration will occur where workers are powerless and individualized; utilitarian forms will be observed in environments where workers have to take on the machine to push up earnings; and attempts to assert control will be associated with a history of militancy in situations in which official protest, for example through strikes, is difficult (p. 242). It is possible, using the present classification of patterns of control, considerably to extend this picture.

First, where workers are powerless and individualized, that is in non-militant settings, sabotage is likely to be rare. As noted above, in the clothing factories studied by Edwards and Scullion, management had a wide range of techniques which made it difficult for workers to lower quality standards. There may on occasions be outbursts of destruction, and it may be that such outbursts can be related in a general way to the pressures that workers are under. But they will not be a day-to-day occurrence and will not be an integral part of the organization of work like the tap in the aircraft factory.

On utilitarian sabotage, Taylor and Walton are correct that it will occur where workers are under pressure to increase their earnings, typically under piecework. But this is not the whole story. As just suggested, tight managerial control can prevent such sabotage in a range of piecework factories. A degree of militancy is necessary before it can emerge. There are some suggestions in Cunnison's study (1966: 117–18) that militant individualism can be associated with some alterations of quality standards to ease the work process: she cites the practice of 'dabbing' adhesive onto the waterproof material instead of fixing it properly, a practice that managers tried to eliminate from time to time but which had become fairly firmly established. She also notes, however, the contempt in which workers producing poor-quality work, who were known in the shop as 'murderers' of the job, were held. This illustrates a general point, namely that workers have conflicting interests about sabotage: they want to do the job as quickly as possible, but they need to ensure that 'reasonable' standards are maintained so that the firm does not lose orders. In firms in the clothing industry, where customers can rapidly switch suppliers, this need is very apparent.

With a collective orientation two possibilities regarding utilitarian sabotage can be discerned. The first is that covered by the cases described by Lupton, Walker, Roy, and others. Here, workers will look for 'angles', and foremen will tolerate those which do not go beyond some implicitly set standard of reasonableness. The managerial interest here is clear: foremen can meet their production targets. And, to the extent that they can get away with goods of uncertain quality, more senior managers also benefit from the practice. Tolerating 'sabotage' is just part of a broader toleration of piecework fiddles. Whether or not a fiddle reaches the stage of sabotage is likely to depend on specific features of the product and the technology. In the plants studied by Lupton and Roy, for example, the label seems to have been applied rarely. In Edwards and Scullion's Components Factory most departments similarly had few cases. But in one shop producing plastic mouldings a problem arose: workers wanted to make machine cycle times as short as possible in order to increase earnings, but in doing so they ran the risk of turning out scrap. Production foremen tolerated the practice by experienced workers, although not by newcomers, because, as they explained, it increased output and kept the workers happy. The problem was as much an intermanagerial one, with the quality department bemoaning poor quality and the failure of production supervision to deal with it, as a workermanager one. The case described by Walker (see above, p. 248) is another illustration of the point.

The second possibility arises where, as at Halewood, management asserts the right to manage and workers oppose them in a collective and militant manner. Here, sabotage is unlikely to emerge out of making out strategies; instead, from the incidents reported by Beynon, it appears to have been an expression of frustration with the monotony of work. One case, for example, involved workers in removing the 'style line' on car bodies so that they would emerge from the paint shop with bare patches. Such activities are plainly not part of making out strategies. Neither do they involve attempts to push up earnings or the activities of workers who are 'powerless' in the sense intended by Taylor and Walton. The workers were, after all, strongly unionized and, on any continuum of degrees of 'power' as against management, would be more powerful than a great number of other groups. The sabotage reflects, rather, the growth of considerable collective orientations among workers in a context in which outlets for the use of collective power are restricted by the pattern of negotiations between management and workers: there was some power, but it could not be directed to, say, fiddling piecework systems, and resentment thus grew up.

Within the organizational pattern, then, it seems that sabotage is rare, for the simple reasons that workers have many other ways of putting pressure on management and also have established an effort bargain which reduces many of the strains of factory work. In the Large and the Small Metals Factories, manning levels were such as to give workers considerable leisure on the job. Although the work tasks themselves were as tedious as those of other workers, the important thing was that workers were not tied to them for eight hours a day. They were able to do a series of tasks and then enjoy a break, and tedium was not a serious problem. The general absence of sabotage in these plants is particularly notable in view of the fact, noted above, that the workers felt extremely disgruntled about their decline in the earnings league. This together with nature of the work itself, meant that there were plenty of forces encouraging sabotage, but these were outweighed by collective effort controls which rendered resort to sabotage unnecessary.

It is possible, then, to begin to explain sabotage as the product of two sorts of influence: the general character of the social relations of production and specific features such as the precise nature of the technology. A similar perspective can be applied to pilfering.

Pilfering and Fiddling

Systematic pilferage can be a significant way of affecting the wage-effort bargain. The shop assistant who over charges and the dockers who divert goods to their own uses are familiar figures. As with sabotage, however, the label 'pilfering' can be misleading if it implies that the activity in question is separate from other work-related behaviour or that it is seen by everyone involved as stealing. As one of the main students of occupational theft, Gerald Mars (1983), notes, people in Britain use the term 'fiddling' to describe the diversion of the firm's property to their own uses (the parallel terms in America are skimming and gypping). Now, fiddling is also the term used by Lupton's workers to characterize their ways of bending the piecework system. This is not surprising, for whether or not a fiddle involves the theft of goods (as with the dockers) or the payment for work not done (as when the same output is booked twice) or the manipulation of time (when workers go home when they are still clocked in) represents simply the surface form taken by various means of altering the effort bargain. Yet it remains important to know why the form of theft occurs in some settings and not others. And the relevant fiddles need to be kept distinct from the generality of means used to bargain about effort. The term fiddling will be used below, but with reference only to activities that result in theft.

Mars categorizes occupations into four types according to how prone they are to fiddling. He calls the types hawks, vultures, donkeys, and wolves. These categories arise from a classification according to 'grid' and 'group'. 'Grid' is the extent to which broad social norms are imposed on individuals. 'Group' is the degree of collectivity among work groups. Hawks are weak on both dimensions, their main trait being individual entrepreneurial activity. They tend to be in occupations such as the self-employed professions and independent businesses where fiddles can be directed against the customer by over-charging. Hawks are largely autonomous, and act creatively on their own. Vultures are strong on group and weak on grid; that is, they have a high degree of solidarity and are relatively immune to social norms. Examples are sales representatives and roundsmen of all kinds. Workers here are members of a group for some purpose but act in-dividualistically for others. Collectivity is provided by a shared employment situation, but, within this shared context, vultures operate as individuals to take advantage of the opportunities for fiddling that present themselves. Donkeys have low group and high grid, being isolated and subordinated. They can be extremely powerless but there are also circumstances in which they can be powerful if they reject the constraints imposed on them. The prime example is the supermarket check-out operator, who performs a tightly constrained set of tasks but who can find ways round the system. Finally, there are the wolves, who are high on both dimensions. They act collectively and, unlike the vultures, see an injury to one as an injury to all. Good examples are dustmen and dockers, who have strong collective norms over what can be fiddled and the allocation of the rewards.

Mars's work, together with the detailed studies on which it draws,[3] is very valuable in analysing the organization of fiddles and revealing not only the motivation of those involved in them but also the reasons why managers tolerate them: opportunities to fiddle allow basic wages to be kept low, and also give workers some job satisfaction. There are, however, some difficulties.

One problem relates to the control of fiddling. In many occupations fiddles are endemic, but there are occasional attempts by management to prevent them. For example, someone committing a blatant fiddle may be sacked. Ditton (1979b) has developed a general theory of 'contrology' to analyse the cycles of discipline that seem to characterize fiddle-prone occupations. As he points out, managerial offensives seem to have little rationale since they stamp out fiddles only temporarily. Yet, as argued elsewhere (P. Edwards and Scullion, 1982b), it is incorrect to suggest that controllers are necessarily as all-powerful as Ditton implies. With donkeys and vultures, who are on their own, managers may be able to crack down at will. But where a more wolf-like orientation has developed attempts at discipline may be met with organized opposition. The argument was developed in connection with an incident in the Large Metals Factory in which managers tried to prevent the widespread practice of leaving before the end of the shift and in which strenuous opposition, from shopfloor workers and stewards alike, forced them to give way. In cases where a collective but non-organizational orientation exists, management may face less powerful resistance but may still find it difficult to penalize 'offenders' without collective opposition. In short, the position of the frontier of control affects the ability of management to attack fiddles and hence the degree to which they shift from being covert activities and become relatively respectable forms of bargaining.

3 Studies include those of dockers (Mars, 1974) hotel workers (Mars, 1973), bread roundsmen (Ditton, 1977) and bakery workers (Ditton, 1979b).

Organization is also important in affecting whether a job is a donkey or a wolf job. According to Mars (1983: 70) 'jobs on long and noisy mass-production belts are good examples of donkey jobs', and he quotes Beynon on what it is like being tied to the track for eight hours a day. But his statement should be amended to read: assembly-line jobs are donkey jobs to the extent that workers lack collective means to control their efforts. Assembly-line workers in the Large Metals Factory were more like wolves than donkeys, because they had a collective organization that overcame the fragmentation and isola-tion that can characterize assembly lines. 'Identical' jobs would fall into different parts of Mars's classification according to the extent of the shopfloor controls surrounding them. The phrase 'to the extent that' is also important. Mars presents his four types as distinct, but there are plainly several intermediate cases. Thus he discusses Klein's (1964) study of piecework fiddles under the rubric of donkey jobs, even though these fiddles represented a considerable degree of collec-tive orientation and were thus not the activity of isolated and powerless individuals but were an expression of work group power. The typology proposed here deals with this by distinguishing between cases where militancy is absent and those where some degree of collec-tive awareness exists: the latter involve cases falling between the 'donkey' and the 'wolf' ideal types.

It is also important to bear in mind the distinction between jobs and the fiddles that characterize them. Thus, as Mars notes, some donkey jobs are very tightly controlled and presumably cannot produce fid-dles. An example is the absence of effort controls in the factories studied by Armstrong *et al.* Other donkey jobs, however, can create fiddles, with supermarket cashiers being Mars's main example. The difference seems to represent the degree to which tasks can be tightly constrained by management. A cashier dealing with many customers and handling money has more opportunities to fiddle than does a factory worker who is limited to fiddling time or bending quality standards or work study timings. And, as stressed above, these factory fiddles can be tightly constrained by managements practising direct control.

Finally, fiddles are far from being the whole story of a work group's relations with management. In cases with a high level of collective organization controls over effort can emerge from the shady world of fiddles to become relatively respectable rules. The toolmakers' rule on overtime in the Components Factory, for example (see above, p. 234), was a 'fiddle' in so far as it brought benefits to workers from work that was not required by management. Yet it was very different from, say, someone fiddling time by being booked for overtime and then leaving the plant. Rules can make fiddles legitimate, and thus, under the organized pattern, workers do not need to be wolves but can act as respectable individuals with an established right to take their leisure in the factory.

There are, then, some difficulties with Mars's classification. Jobs do not fall neatly into the four boxes, and, more importantly, there is a question as to whether the dimension of 'grid' really differentiates between jobs. Vultures and wolves supposedly differ because the former have a weak grid, that is have weak external constraints on them, while the latter are subject to tight external constraints. But is there really a sharp distinction between bread roundsmen (vultures) and dockers (wolves) in the extent to which managerial authority and the technical requirements of work impose constraints on them? In both cases, the nature of the job necessarily gives workers a considerable amount of discretion in the carrying out of their tasks, and bureaucratic factory-like rules have been difficult to apply. The 'grid' dimension fails to differentiate between them. Mars implies as much when he labels vultures and wolves as, respectively, weak and strong work groups.

This approach in terms of work group organization seems to avoid some of the problems of the group-grid classification. If hawk fiddles are left on one side, because they do not stem from relations of domination and subordination in employment but instead reflect the exploitation of uncertainty in market transactions by autonomous people, the types of fiddle can be linked to the present classification of workplace relations. Non-militant workforces either produce no fiddles, in cases where the technical division of labour permits management to exercise tight control of the recording of output, or engage in donkey fiddles, in situations where there is necessarily uncertainty, typically where money changes hands. Vulture fiddles represent the individualistic pursuit of goals based on socially constructed understandings; there are some loosely-articulated shared understandings about appropriate behaviour but there is no strong sense of belonging to a work group, and no powerful pressures to conformity to group norms. There are degrees to which workers are 'vultures'. Under militant individualism, there is an extremely individualistic outlook. As work forces move more towards the collective orientation pattern, social norms develop more force. With a very strong collective orientation vultures become wolves. Finally, the organizational pattern can obviate the need to engage in fiddles: workers establish certain practices openly, and have the power to resist managerial efforts to alter them. A similar perspective applies to the apparently even more individual and spontaneous activities of absenteeism and labour turnover.

Absenteeism and Turnover

Since going absent and quitting are more clearly individual acts than is following the culture of fiddling in a particular occupation, and since they reflect many personal contingencies that are unrelated to the effort bargain, they pose a large challenge to an account in terms of control. The problem is exacerbated by the fact that most of the voluminous literature on them relates to the characteristics of individuals, with hardly any attention being given to the social meanings of the behaviour or to its place within a pattern of employer-employee relations (P. Edwards and Scullion, 1984).

The study by Edwards and Scullion (1982a) had as one of its major aims the consideration of 'individual' behaviour through a framework which is usually deployed only to look at relations at the point of production. It argued that, in the two clothing factories, absence and turnover among the women production operators was a direct reflection of the tight system of control to which they were subjected. Several pieces of evidence were deployed in support of this argument. First, rates of absence and turnover were much higher than those for men in the same factories, and they were also higher than those of women in the other plants studied. These rates could not be written off, then, either to an 'industry effect' or to a 'sex effect' (even leaving to one side the question of what such an effect might signify). Second, observation suggested that women were subject to far more strict control than were men. Going absent or quitting seemed a likely response to the system of control, particularly because other possible means of asserting some influence within the workplace, such as a little sabotage or fiddling, were not available. Third, workers themselves reported that they had taken days off when they had been able to get into work, and they did so in much larger numbers than workers in the other factories that were studied. They were, moreover, quite clear about the need to go absent once in a while to escape the pressures of work. They did not, for example, invoke their domestic commitments as reasons for going absent. And they also expressed strong dissatisfaction with discipline on the shopfloor, which they experienced as harsh and arbitrary.

There were thus strong grounds for seeing absenteeism as a manifestation of conflict. At the same time, however, it had limited implications for shopfloor relations. Although being clear on the need to go absent, workers did not make any direct connections between it and the control system. They did not view going absent as a way of 'getting back' at management. And there were no collective norms governing the behaviour. It was a reflection of social relations at work but was not directly controlled by social standards of behaviour. Its effects on the shopfloor were also limited. It imposed few direct costs on managers, for there were no company-financed sick pay benefits, and, as noted above, managers were free to move workers to cover for absentees. As an important 'escape valve' it helped workers to accommodate to the system. These facts were reflected in managerial accounts of the behaviour, which stressed the domestic duties of married women, problems of getting to work from outlying areas, and similar extra-plant factors.

Similar points apply to labour turnover. Turnover was very high, especially among workers with very short periods of service. Workers apparently tried the job for a while, and moved on if they did not like it. This movement was often to a very similar factory, and seems to have reflected a general desire for change and not a total escape from factory work. One plant might be marginally better than another, for example if it was nearer home or offered more steady work. A further important reason for mobility directly reflected managerial control: it seems to have been quite common for a worker who had received a couple of warnings for bad work to decide to try her luck elsewhere. Thus movement helped to reinforce managerial control to the extent that the discontented left 'voluntarily'. In addition to this volatile population, however, was a group of employees with longer periods of service. They were skilled male machine operators, and some of the older women, who typically did the more complex sewing operations. Management needed these workers and, as noted above, was willing to make some concessions to them. They thus gained a degree of satisfaction from their favourable position.

This sort of pattern probably applies to much of the 'direct' control type of non-militant pattern. And it has some important similarities with militant individualism. As noted above 'jacking' was a central feature of navvies' relations with their employers. And Cunnison (1966: 69–71) describes the habit of mobility in the waterproof garment industry, with workers moving between jobs freely and thus sharing common experiences of the trade. She also describes the long-serving minority of the employees, and notes how managers depended on them and would suffer if they left; as a 'quid pro quo' managers tried to protect them when work was scarce (Lupton and Cunnison, 1964: 114). An important feature of those various clothing plants (in different parts of the country and producing for very different markets) is thus a tradition of the 'trade' that was shared by workers and managers. Movement assisted management since there was a pool of experienced labour available: the costs of turnover were thus minimized. For workers some form of limited escape was possible from a factory suffering shortage of work, or with a particularly harsh style of management, or where a worker had developed a bad reputation.

Although apparently quite common, this picture is not universal. Lupton (1963: 45–8, 87–90), in his discussion of the 'Wye' waterproof garment factory, which was located in the same area as the 'Dee' plant studied by Cunnison and which shared many of the characteristics of the industry, suggests that absenteeism was more of a problem for management than it was in the plants considered above. He suggests, in line with an argument based on the nature of control, that going absent was related to work-based pressures; for example, workers given new jobs where they could not 'make their money' tended to go absent. The behaviour created problems for management because it disrupted a tightly knit productive system. Management's ability to replace absentees (and also, it may be inferred, leavers) was limited by a lack of what Lupton calls 'trained female, semi-skilled labour' (p. 87). The reason was the unique nature of the plant's productive system, that is its use of a fragmented flow-line system in place of the traditional making-through technology. The plant could not draw on a pool of labour in the same way that Dee could. The significance of absenteeism will thus vary according to its impact on management. Even at Wye, however, its impact must have been moderated by the overall power of management within the factory, and in particular the ability to move workers at will. Lupton does not, for example, document any attempts by management to limit absence.

As for 'sophisticated' non-militant cases, the pattern is very different. In the Process Factory, and also, it would appear, at 'ChemCo', absenteeism and turnover ran at very low levels and long spells of service were the norm. In highly complex technological environments managers wanted stable and reliable workers, and considerable emphasis was placed on training. Yet compliance could not be taken for granted. Thus the Process Factory had a clear policy for monitoring absence, such that anyone developing a 'pattern' of absence on desirable shifts was first approached by his foreman for what one worker called a 'hand on the shoulder' chat. Should performance fail to improve, further chats would take place, with the emphasis being on helping the worker to correct his behaviour and not on punishment. The sack always remained as a final option, used rarely but always present. Because of the creation of a committed workforce, this system could operate to prevent matters getting out of control. It affected only a small minority of employees and the majority apparently endorsed the need to deal with those unwilling or unable to tolerate shift work. Turnover, although low, reflected shift work's pressure, for a significant number of workers left either through early retirement or for health reasons. It was not a large or immediate problem, but it can be related to the technical conditions of work and the demands that they placed on the workers. It was a muted reflection of the demands of shift work and the long-term inconsistency between these demands and the needs of workers who, after several years of it, felt that enough was enough. Again, managers dealt with the problem sympathetically, using 'early retirement' and not the sack. But they were, as they themselves stressed, able to do no more than moderate the effects of the shift system, whose demands were paramount. 'Sophisticated' managements deal with such issues by organizing out of their labour relations any overt, collective conflict.

A sharp contrast is provided by the organizational pattern. In the Small and the Large Metals Factories absence and quit rates had traditionally been low, but this reflected not a sophisticated managerial policy for gaining compliance but the position of the frontier of control and the nature of the wage-effort bargain. The availability of considerable spells of leisure within the factory reduced the need for days of absence. This situation had also limited labour turnover, but the factories' slide down the earnings league had stimulated a rapid rise in quitting, especially among skilled workers. This quitting was seen by workers and managers alike as a major problem and as a reflection of workers' increasing discontent. It also has a broader implication: despite their considerable controls at shopfloor level and despite their pride in their organization, workers were unable to exert much influence over the 'wage' aspect of the effort bargain, and leaving was seen as the only way of improving one's position. Many workers remained in the hope that redundancies would be declared, so that they could take some redundancy money instead of leaving voluntarily. Here is a prime example of the limits of shopfloor controls.

These controls remained influential, however, within the plants themselves. In particular, they exerted a powerful effect on absenteeism. In addition to providing leisure in work, they permitted workers in the Large Metals Factory to leave the plant without being recorded as absent. Typically, a gang of workers would so organize its activities that its members could take turns at leaving the plant for half a day or so. As noted above, foremen had few means of dealing with this, although they were plainly aware of its widespread occurrence. Thus shopfloor controls meant that the meaning of recorded absence was entirely different from its meaning in many other plants, where absence records provide some kind of indication of the frequency with which workers absent themselves. In this factory, going absent was tightly bound up with collective effort controls and could hardly be seen as an 'individual' act. It was, instead, a direct reflection of workers' collectivity.

The typicality of such an arrangement is hard to assess. Practices in this factory have important similarities with those that have been observed among dockers, for whom the 'welting' system whereby half a gang works and the other half rests has been an established practice, and some printers. These are, however, unusual situations in which a team of workers controls its own efforts and management has given up any practical efforts to determine when and how work shall be done. The practice is not universal among workers under an organizational pattern, as is shown by its absence in the Small Metals Factory even though workers here had, if anything, a more developed sense of collectivity than those in the Large Metals Factory. This difference seems to have reflected several influences. In the Large Factory, there were distinct gangs, usually with about a dozen workers each, each with a gang leader chosen by the workers themselves. As a working group, a gang was largely independent of foremen and also of other gangs, and it was natural for it to develop its own private arrangements. The absence of gangs in the Small Factory constrained the development of such arrangements.

These examples illustrate some of the ways in which rates of absence and turnover, and also the social meanings of the behaviour, are connected to patterns of control of the labour process. It should not, however, be inferred that there is always a simple and direct connection. Nothing has been said above about the collective orientation pattern. Accounts such as those of Lupton, Roy, and Burawoy give little or no attention to absence or quitting, and it seems that these behaviours had little resonance on the shopfloor. The argument advanced by Edwards and Scullion in connection with the Electrical and Components Factories was that these plants fell between the extremes of the organized pattern and the 'direct' non-militant pattern. That is, absence and turnover rates were lower than in the Hosiery and Underwear Factories and higher than in the two Metals factories. And, since the position of the frontier of control could also be seen as falling between the extremes a plausible argument could be developed. But it was no more than a reasonable 'ex post' conjecture. It was suggested that in situations of this type the effects of personal contingencies are likely to be particularly noticeable, with the direct role of the pattern of control being less obvious than it is elsewhere. Plainly, however, further work would have to be done to develop this argument and to explore the links between personal contingencies, experience within the workplace, and external factors such as the availability of jobs elsewhere.

The lack of a strong tradition of sociological research on absenteeism and quitting makes it hard to be more precise. But the findings reported above, together with attempts to provide new conceptual frameworks (e.g. Johns and Nicholson, 1982), point to the fruitfulness of trying to relate patterns of behaviour to the social organization of work. In particular, research that relates the behaviour to individuals' job satisfaction or other personal characteristics has limits that are increasingly being recognized. The significance of going absent, in terms of how far it reflects a state of conflict, of what meanings it has for those who engage in it or try to control it, and of its impact on the system of control of the labour process, can be understood only by relating the behaviour to the pattern of control in which it takes place.

Conclusion: Alternative Forms of Conflict
The foregoing discussion has suggested that forms of workplace behaviour do not come in discrete chunks labelled sabotage, effort restriction, or whatever. Instead, their occurrence and nature depend on the social relations of work. There is, however, the danger of treating behaviour as an undifferentiated mass, with pilfering or absenteeism being seen as equally likely responses and with the specific characteristics of each type of behaviour being neglected. The analysis has thus tried to consider concrete sets of actions without, however, treating them as self-contained.

It thus becomes possible to deal decisively with the debate about alternative forms of conflict. That is, are 'individual' and 'collective' forms alternatives, or do they tend to occur together? There have been numerous empirical investigations of this question using, for example, correlations between absence and strike rates. Such investigations are necessarily limited by their assumption that these rates of behaviour are, indeed, indexing individual and collective forms of behaviour. That is, it has to be assumed that absence and quitting are measures of individual activity that can be contrasted with collective behaviour. Yet this assumption is often questionable, for patterns of individual action are powerfully shaped by collective controls of effort. It may happen to be the case that absence and strike rates tend to be inversely related. But such correlations do not explain why the two forms of behaviour might be alternatives. An approach in terms of the pattern of control can do so by considering why absenteeism is used in some circumstances and not others. It can also deal with cases such as the Process Factory where rates of both types of action are low. These represent anomalies for an argument that there are alternative forms of conflict, and have to be explained in terms of the system of control and its ability to organize overt expressions of discontent out of the factory. In short, to look at correlations of rates of behaviour is to consider only surface phenomena and to miss the underlying mechanisms which explain why the phonemena take place and what ties them together.

A similar point emerges with reference to such possible influences on workers' behaviour as their job satisfaction. It has repeatedly been found that there is no clear connection between these attitudinal measures and an activity such as going absent. The solution to this dilemma, which has puzzled analysts for many years, is to consider the circumstances in which job satisfaction is likely to have an effect. Under direct control, many workers will feel the need for time off, so that job satisfaction will play little role. Similarly, an organizational pattern gives workers freedom to take leisure, and it is again unlikely that variations in job satisfaction will affect behaviour. In other circumstances, where the control system exerts less powerful influences, forces such as job satisfaction may be permitted to play a role. Instead of worrying about the inconclusive results that arise from looking at the direct connection between attitudes and behaviour, it is possible to indicate the conditions under which different sorts of connections between the two will exist.

One other point warrants emphasis. In line with most writing on workplace relations, the foregoing discussion has concentrated on the central features of each set of arrangements. But there is always a possibility of 'deviance'. That is, an individual worker may behave differently from the norm. The 'rate-buster' is an established figure in the literature. To deal with individual idiosyncracies would require a different approach. In the case of absenteeism, for example, Nicholson (1977) provides a model of absence based on the contingencies of individuals' situations and on the forces encouraging or discouraging going absent. A full account of fiddling would also need to explain why only some individuals exploit the opportunities that are available. What the present account suggests, however, is that individual variations will reflect the social organization of work, a point developed elsewhere in connection with Nicholson's studies (Edwards and Scullion, 1984: 556–7). In particular, individuals will be less free to make their own choices where there is a strong collective organization than in cases where workers are individuated. Most obviously, printers and workers in the Small Metals Factory are not free to exceed collective effort standards.

Once the importance of the frontier of control has been established, there remains the question of why it takes a given shape. That is, what explains the dramatic differences in social relations which have been analysed above? This question is addressed in the rest of this chapter.

Women in the Workplace

Numerous explanatory variables have been put forward to account for differences in patterns of workplace organization at one point in time and for changes over time. These include payment systems, technology and the nature of product markets. One factor which requires special attention, however, is the sex composition of the workforce. There has been a recent, and welcome, growth in interest in the position of women at work. But this has not necessarily been associated with theoretical clarity: some writers have argued that no theory of the labour process can be complete unless it specifically takes account of gender relations, but this is to confuse levels of analysis. It is important, however, to consider whether at the concrete level gender relations are important and, if so, in what way.

To follow Richard Brown's (1976) classification, traditional industrial sociology has treated women in two ways. The first is to see them as a source of problems: for employers, for themselves or for their husbands. The second way, to treat employees as 'unisex', is arguably an analytical advance: instead of seeing women as the cause of their own problems, the motivations of female employers are related to the characteristics of their jobs, and the fact of their being women is not seen as particularly important. The advance is to refuse to write off, say, an observed high rate of absence among women as a self-evident 'sex effect'. The remaining problem is that specific gender-related issues are neglected. The problem has been the focus of the new wave of studies of women which attempt to demonstrate that there are particular problems faced by women because they are women and that gender relations on the shopfloor are important.

Lupton (1963) was quite clear that a 'unisex' approach was adequate for his purposes. He cited evidence that women at 'Jay's' followed the men's practices of output restriction and that, at 'Wye' when it had been dominated by men, output controls had been absent: industrial, and not personal, characteristics were dominant. Cunnison (1966), although questioning aspects of Lupton's model in some important ways that will be considered below, similarly treated shopfloor behaviour as a reflection of a worker's occupational position. The shop that she studied employed 52 men and 28 women, but her account of their behaviour generally stresses matters of skill and occupation, and not gender-specific influences. Edwards and Scullion (1982a) similarly explained differences in behaviour in terms of patterns of control and not supposed 'sex effects'.

In discussing this last study Purcell (1983: 107) argues that its attempt to avoid a sexist account of absence rates leads to a neglect of features of workers' lives outside the factory as possible influences on behaviour within it; specifically, domestic responsibilities could affect women's absence behaviour. Yet this is to miss the point. The study did not aim to discount such points but to show that control within the factory is also significant, not only in explaining the amount of absenteeism but also, and crucially, in considering the significance of the behaviour in the context of social relations within the workplace. Thus it pointed to substantial differences between women in the clothing factories and women in the Electrical Factory, differences which did not seem to reflect any obvious differences in domestic duties. And it showed that the former group of women themselves saw going absent in terms of a need to escape. No doubt other factors are important, but these do not necessarily need to be built into studies exploring differences in the internal characteristics of different factories. This is not to endorse a 'unisex' view of workers. Men and women enter workplaces with different backgrounds and expectations, they have different obligations outside work, and their treatment in the workplace (for example, the ways in which their skills are evaluated in job gradings) differs markedly. The interrelationship of these factors is crucial in understanding the specific nature of women's work experience, but it does not follow that it needs to be addressed by every study that includes women workers.

It has been the focus of several valuable studies of women workers (Pollert, 1981; Cavendish, 1982; Westwood, 1984). The aim here is not to review them in detail but to consider the light they throw on the central question of the rest of this chapter, namely why differences in patterns of control exist and how influences internal and external to the workplace interact. The light is less clear than might be expected. There are several reasons for this. First, the starting point of the studies is the traditional neglect of women workers and the need to assess what semi-skilled factory jobs for women are actually like. The result is thus more of an ethnographic analysis of the nature of experience than a developed theoretical account of how work and non-work influences interact. Second, the method is one of single-factory case studies, which does not lend itself to the consideration of how different influences operate in different circumstances. Third, the ethnographic approach means that the structures that affect experience and also some of the consequences in terms of concrete behaviour are not put in the centre of the picture. On the former, methods of allocating work, the nature of managerial control, and the nature of effort bargaining come into the picture somewhat indirectly.

On the latter, information on rates of behaviour such as quitting is presented sketchily or not at all. Finally, the concern of relating work and non-work lives notwithstanding, the studies tend to concentrate heavily on activity within the workplace, with non-work demands entering indirectly. (These points should not be taken as criticisms. The studies emerged from a neglect of women, and had to start somewhere. There are also likely to have been difficulties in obtaining the resources to carry out more ambitious projects, given the hostility or suspicion that the research may have aroused in conventional circles. But it remains true that the studies do not directly provide answers to the questions being considered here).

Some points emerge, however. An important one concerns the prevalence of methods of direct control. A common argument is that these methods survive only in small firms in competitive industries, such as footwear and clothing. Yet Westwood's plant was owned by a very large firm in the clothing industry. Pollert's factory was owned by Imperial Tobacco, a large multi-national in an oligopolistic industry, and Cavendish's anonymous plant was also part of a large corporation which appears to have been in an oligopolistic sector. Similarly, Herzog (1980) describes her experience of work in factories owned by several large German firms such as AEG, where the pressures caused by working under a piecework system that was under tight managerial control seem to have been at least as great as those reported from plants in competitive industries. The general lesson is, of course, that firms which 'ought' to practise hegemonic or bureaucratic methods do not always do so. As Lawson (1981) for example points out, there is no necessity for firms in primary product markets, that is where competition is limited, to employ such methods. If they can institute such secondary labour market practices as paying low wages and exercising strict discipline they are likely to try to do so. This leads to the specific lesson, namely that one of the major conditions which permits firms this opportunity is the presence of a supply of female labour. A complex array of forces in society in general and in the employment relationship in particular means that 'women's work' is equated with the least desirable jobs. Not least of these is the fact that women 'want' these jobs as a result of the socialization to which they have been subject. In the particular context of factory jobs, such wants have to be seen in the context of alternatives: as several of the studies mentioned above show, factory work may be monotonous and frustrating but the wages are still higher than in other jobs for working class women such as cleaning or working in a shop. In short, women do not just happen to fill the least desirable jobs. Such jobs cannot exist outside the availability of a work force to fill them. That is jobs are not specified according to product market and technological conditions, with women and other disadvantaged groups filling those at the bottom of the pile. Many firms could structure their jobs within hegemonic modes of control but they are able to avoid doing so because they can secure an adequate labour supply using other means. The structure of the jobs and the nature of the labour force interact.

It does not follow, of course, that all undesirable jobs are held by women or that all women have such jobs. On the latter point, Toynbee (1971) has described work in a factory owned by the Lucas car components firm. This firm has for many years employed large numbers of women on its assembly lines, and it has practised a paternalistic policy. Thus Toynbee documents the relaxed atmosphere on the shopfloor and the absence of strict supervision. To explain this case would require attention to the detailed history of the firm and its product and labour market circumstances. But it illustrates the point that policies of labour control are not determined by these circumstances. An apparent opportunity to employ direct control methods may not be grasped, and firms in similar positions choose to manage their labour relations in different ways. Thus women can be subject to differing sorts of control, and it is likely that these differences will affect their experience of work over and above any influences stemming from domestic circumstances.

Studies of women in the workplace are very useful in explaining how relations inside the factory help to produce and reproduce notions of women's subordinate position. They show, for example, how working in an environment in which their work is accorded little status leads women to accept their subordinate position and to agree that, because they are only working for 'pin money', they should be the first to go redundant. Pollert and Westwood point to the ideology of marriage as a means of escape from drudgery. The image of escape leads young workers to tolerate their lot, even though, as older married women had come to recognize, the escape was only apparent, because many of them had returned to the same jobs, but with the added burden of domestic duties. The result was a stolid and resigned acceptance. The general implication to be drawn is that relations in the workplace are not just affected by extra-workplace factors. They also react back on roles in the home. They help to produce wider forms of domination and subordination. As Westwood in particular argues, girls learn to be women through their experiences at work. For those concerned that workplace studies neglect influences from outside, it must be said, first, that these influences do not have determinate effects but have to be interpreted within particular relations of production and, second, that forces run in the opposite direction. These forces, moreover, are not just the general ones of the ways in which a mode of production puts demands on such things as the educational system. They also operate at the concrete level of lived experience.

What do the studies of women have to say about the effects of work and non-work situations on concrete behaviour? Pollert (1981: 118) makes an interesting point about absenteeism. It was 'one response to the strain' of work but, whereas for men absenteeism represents a real if temporary escape from the demands of work, for 'working-class women there is no relief, no escape. A break from wage work merely brings them face to face with a pile of work at home'. This characterization helps in identifying the specific nature of women's work. But to build an account of absenteeism from it would require going much further to investigate patterns of attendance at work, the closeness with which management monitored absences and the strictness with which rules were enforced, the detailed links between work and non-work roles (for example, how domestic duties were allocated), and differences between different types of worker. On the last point, Pollert's argument does not obviously apply to young women with few domestic responsibilities. For such women, going absent may have more to do with the pressures of work and the desire for leisure than the double burden of paid and domestic labour.

On turnover, Pollert (1981: 34) produces data on the length-of-service characteristics of workers in her factory, showing that 46 per cent of the women had been employed for less than two years. Although not in itself demonstrating the pattern of turnover, the statistic is interestingly similar to that for women in the Hosiery and Underwear Factories, where the average was 42 per cent (calculated from Edwards and Scullion, 1982a: 64). Thus women in very different firms display similar high rates of turnover. Pollert (p. 104) goes on to consider the forces underlying this pattern. Women were encouraged to accept the idea that, for them, work is temporary and less important than marriage. Young women therefore move around from one dull job to another: they are expected to treat work as an interlude between school and marriage, and react accordingly. Pollert admits that young male workers also have high rates of turnover but argues that there is an important difference: when they come to settle down some young men can enter proper jobs and their early pattern of mobility does not militate against the establishment of some sort of a career, whereas for women there is no such possibility. It can be concluded that women's propensity to quit work can be considered as the result of three influences: the fact that women tend to work in jobs which are likely to encourage a high degree of instability, namely those where managerial control is intense and where there are few attempts to tie workers to individual firms (sectors such as clothing, but also catering, where turnover is very high); the operation of an 'age effect' which affects men and women equally; and domestic and broader social influences which create expectations that women will leave work when they marry, that they will move jobs if their husbands' careers so demand, and so on.

One important point about this turnover, and about women's position in the labour process more generally, relates to the skilled or unskilled nature of female employees. As soon as the notion of skill is addressed, however, it loses much of its apparent clarity: it is difficult or impossible to disentangle 'genuine' accomplishments and socially constructed claims to status. Thus female employees are often classified as being unskilled, but the abilities which women deploy in the work process are often considerable. The studies mentioned above cite the intricate tasks which women are called on to perform and the tacit recognition of their skills by supervisors who remark that men could not do the work. The ambiguity of conceptions of women's work is neatly captured in Lupton's reference, quoted above, to 'trained female semi-skilled labour': employers want capable and experienced women workers, but treat this labour as a distinct category from semi-skilled labour in general and deny it the same claims to have a degree of skill which justifies appropriate rewards. It appears, therefore, that 'low skill' is not a clear correlate of women's employment in the way in which being employed in small firms in highly competitive industries is a characteristic of much female employment. It is true that women's skills are recognized and rewarded to a lower extent than those of men, but this is a reflection of the way in which female labour is devalued in general and not an objective characteristic of the work that women do, which often calls for a high degree of dexterity and application.

The discussion has moved a long way from the idea that there is a self-evident 'sex effect' in workplace behaviour or that this behaviour is unrelated to external influences. It has been argued that, although there are substantial gaps in our knowledge of how work and non-work influences interact, the case of women in the workplace shows that work relations have a 'relative autonomy': patterns of control of women are not uniform; extrawork statuses have to be interpreted within the context of the workplace; the workplace is itself important in producing and reproducing broader patterns of domination and subordination; and the distinctive effects of systems of control on behaviour have been demonstrated. This argument needs to be taken further by assessing other possible influences on the modes of control whose internal dynamics have been examined above.

Causal Influences

Several points need to be made about how these causes should be viewed. First, they are not independent of what happens in the labour process. External influences do not have determinate effects but have to be interpreted in action. As has already been stressed, an influence such as technology can have differing effects depending on the social relations of production: an assembly line can produce intense feelings of alienation and discontent, but, if it is subject to controls associated with the organized pattern, it can lose several of these consequences. In addition, internal and external factors cannot be rigidly separated. Consider an influence such as high labour turnover which may be seen to be characteristic of whole industries. Treating this as 'external', it might be argued that rapid turnover is an important reason for the absence of collective controls in a particular factory. On the other hand, as indicated at length above, turnover is also a product of factors that might be treated as internal to the labour process such as the organization of work and managerial policy as to whether a permanent or a dispensable work force is desired. Second, causal influences are not independent of each other. As Lupton and Cunnison (1964: 124) argue, features such as the competitive structure of an industry, the level of technology and the size of plants are systematically related, coming together in clusters. It thus makes little sense to inquire about the effects of technology as such, for particular technologies will be found within particular constellations of other variables, and the 'effects' of one variable cannot be separated from those of other influences.

To see how these points work in practice, consider Lupton's (1963) explanation of why piecework fiddles existed at Jay but were absent at Wye. Lupton identifies several contrasts between the engineering and waterproof garment industries which may account for the contrast. Engineering has a relatively stable market situation, with little price competition between a small number of firms. Demand in the garment industry fluctuates sharply, price competition is intense, and entry to the trade is very easy. Trade union structure also differs, with the unions in engineering encouraging shopfloor bargaining while the waterproof garment workers' union discourages it to the extent of having a rule banning any negotiation of piece prices at shop level. Labour costs account for a higher proportion of total costs in garment than in engineering. And there are differences in the location of the industries (whether they are localized or widespread) and in the type of product (whether it is for the consumer or capital goods markets). As Cunnison (1966: xxiv) argues, this listing of factors is not entirely satisfactory, for they cover several very different aspects of social structure. Neither is it very clear how important some of the influences are: localization, for example, is a descriptive characteristic of each of the industries considered, but what is its explanatory role? Is it not equally arguable that a high degree of localization, as in the garment industry, encourages shared knowledge of the trade and thus leads to collective challenges to management? Neither are all the external factors really 'external' to the labour process. The character and policy of the unions, for example, is not an independent and inherent aspect of the unions in the two industries but obviously reflects the type of industry in which they were operating. The waterproof garment workers' union's hostility to shop bargaining, for example, can obviously be seen as part of a policy of preventing fragmentation and price cutting within a highly competitive industry: the union depended above all on establishing an agreed set of prices and enforcing them on all employers.

As Emmett and Morgan (1982) note, Lupton's argument also lacks conviction because it does not explain why workers at Wye did not attempt to act together to influence piece rates and because other plants with similar external circumstances have been characterized by such attempts. A decisive answer cannot be given, but it is possible to point to some of the possible influences at work. The nature of the product market in engineering meant that managers at Jay's did not have to worry too much about price competition, and they could afford to tolerate a few piecework fiddles. Firms in the garment industry lacked such leeway. Yet 'internal' factors must also have been important in the patterns of relations that emerged. At Jay's, shopfloor workers were able to use the opportunities presented to them. A plausible story is that workers began to challenge managers, for example on allowed times for breakdowns of machinery, and found that shop managers, concerned with delivery dates and under no direct pressure from above on labour costs, were willing to compromise. Hence a tradition of bargaining emerged. At Wye, by contrast, similar attempts would have been met with resistance from managers. As Armstrong *et al.* (1981) demonstrate, in their poorly-organized plants shopfloor workers had some 'resistance principles', but were unable to make these effective because of the forceful reaction that any attempts provoked from management; hence managerial legitimacy was reinforced. In short, shopfloor struggles interact with 'external' conditions to create particular outcomes.

Before considering these external conditions in more detail, it will be convenient to consider why the two garment firms, Wye and Dee, differed despite the fact that they shared similar product market circumstances, were organized by the same trade union, and were located in the same part of the country so that they shared similar traditions of the trade. This is an issue to which Cunnison gives little attention, despite her more general criticisms of Lupton's approach. It is reasonable to suggest that technology was the key influence. Or, more precisely, it was not technology in the sense of particular hardware (moving assembly lines versus static work stations, or automated versus mechanical processes) that was important but the technical organization of the work process. At Dee, the traditional making-through system involved little fragmentation of tasks and left workers with considerable discretion over the making of the garments. At Wye, a more 'modern' and more deskilled system had been established, and Lupton describes the separation of conception from execution and the division of work into a series of minute operations. As noted above, Lupton comments on two consequences: absenteeism was disruptive because it interfered with the flow of work, and labour supply was problematic because the plant's productive system placed it outside the labour market based on making-through. In addition, it can be suggested that the fragmentation of tasks prevented the emergence of militant individualism because workers could no longer see themselves as independent skilled workers but instead depended on management to be told what tasks to perform. A very good example is the freedom of workers at Dee to come and go as they pleased: they saw themselves as independent workers, whereas employees at Wye were tightly constrained by the time clock. Workers' bargaining power at Wye was also weakened in fairly obvious ways.

This is not to suggest that technology has determinate effects. It is to argue that, when other factors are relatively constant, it can exert an identifiable influence on workplace behavior (see C. Davis *et al.*, 1973). Neither should it be thought that technology is a fixed and asocial influence. In this particular case, it would be interesting to enquire what led Wye management to break with the traditional practices of the industry. Lupton (1963: 13–16) does not directly consider this question, but cites some important influences: the size of the firm; and a general wish to be 'progressive', both in modernizing labour relations through the use of joint consultation and the provision of welfare benefits and in improving the technical organization of work 'in accordance with modern principles of work flow and motion economy'. Given the absence of a labour problem in the industry, it is doubtful whether a desire to control labour was a major cause of the firm's decisions. It is more plausible to suggest that the firm wanted to 'modernize', and that de-skilling was a consequence of this general policy. This view is, of course, consistent with a standard criticism of the view that technical change has the control of labour as one of its central aims: the evidence that firms have deliberately sought 'labour control' is thin, and there is the danger of seeing firms as conspiratorial and omniscient. It is preferable to see labour control as emerging from a set of decisions and as often being unintended. The comparison of Wye and Dee also shows that technical re-organization brought with it a new set of problems, notably regarding absenteeism and the supply of labour. Its consequences can therefore be two-sided.

A further illustration of the importance of the technical organization of work is provided by the contrast between the Process Factory and the 'ChemCo' plant. The similarities in terms of the shift system and the sophistication of the managerial approach are considerable. Yet the latter factory appears to have had more discontent on the shopfloor and a greater sense of antipathy towards management. In the absence of detailed comparative research such a judgement must obviously be provisional, but Nichols and Beynon's accounts of workers' experience of work, reflecting boredom and monotony and yet also tension and worry, stand in something of a contrast with the picture of the Process Factory. Work at ChemCo was of two sorts: handling bags of fertilizer, and sitting in control rooms monitoring the chemical process. On the former, the authors describe the pressures of the unremitting routine of filling and stacking bags: the automatic machine dispensing the fertilizer was a relentless taskmaster. On the latter, they stress the isolation of the control rooms, together with the boredom of watching dials and the sense of responsibility if something went wrong. In the Process Factory, there were two main operations: setting up and minding the machines that produced the basic material; and loading this material onto a second set of machines that spun it onto bobbins, which were then removed and packed. Each of these tasks was carried out by teams. Moreover, once the machines were running they required only a little monitoring, so that teams could decide when they would work. In their periods of leisure they would retire to rest rooms set around the walls of each shop. In this environment, work teams tended to develop a considerable identity of their own, and the rest rooms were havens in which workers could talk, away from the machines and also away from managers. There was none of the continous work pressure of bagging fertilizer, and also none of the isolation of the control rooms. Such work conditions served to take the edge off potential discontents and to make work bearable because a particular set of tasks had a clear end in view. At ChemCo, by contrast, attempts to enlarge and enrich jobs meant little, and workers remained closely tied to the machine.

It is now possible to return to the influence of the product market. Many studies have pointed to its importance. In addition to those mentioned above, William Brown (1973: 168-9) concludes from his study of piecework bargaining in engineering factories that the product market and the technology are 'significant factors' in determining the amount of control that management has over the payment system. It is, however, necessary to distinguish between different aspects of the product market and the nature of competition. It is, for example, possible to explain an absence of shopfloor controls by reference to the instability of market demand and an intense level of competition. Yet a feature such as instability could also be used to explain the emergence of shopfloor organization. A good example is the car industry during the 1930s, which was characterized by very sharp seasonal fluctuations; accounts of unionization stress that, although these fluctuations made permanent organization difficult, they were a major source of grievance and were influential in workers' efforts to organize (e.g. Fine, 1969). Similarly, H. Turner *et al.* (1967) see the insecurity and uncertainty that continued to characterize the industry during the 1950s and 1960s as major causes of workers' discontents and thus of strikes and other forms of organized protest. It is, then, unsatisfactory simply to cite 'instability' as an explanation of a low level of collective organization.

What is crucial is the overall context of the industry. Instability in a sector such as the car industry or engineering is different in its effects from instability in the clothing or the footwear industry. In the latter, instability occurs in the context of a larger number of firms, intense price competition, relative ease of entry, and a rapid alteration in the types of goods produced. In the former, the smaller number of firms and the difficulty of entry make the firms themselves more secure. In addition, the demand cycle tends to affect the whole industry: whereas clothing firms will be affected differently by seasonal and cyclical changes in demand for their particular products, and will thus be very exposed to shifts in fashion and will have to retain the flexibility to adapt rapidly, car firms are more likely to be affected in broadly similar ways. There is thus less pressure on them to keep a very tight control of labour costs. And, once some sort of collective awareness has developed among the workers, instability is likely to produce resentment and attempts to control its effects. A major function of the fiddle at Jay's was thus to minimize earnings fluctuations, while in the Small Metals Factory a major concern of the steward organization was to limit the effects of fluctuations in market demand: the recruitment of new workers and the operation of night shifts were resisted if it was felt that there was insufficient work to justify an increase in the plant's capacity.

In addition to the structure of an industry, which has been quite widely discussed, the role of changes in product mix requires emphasis. What emerges from descriptions of competitive sectors is the speed with which styles and whole ranges of products alter as market demand shifts. An engineering factory, by contrast, is likely to turn out much the same goods from one year to the next. A firm in the competitive sector needs to be able to react very quickly to demands from customers, or it will find the business going to a competitor. It cannot, therefore, afford any institutional constraints on its ability to change product lines rapidly or, even more important, to introduce new lines. It cannot, for example, tolerate a long period of negotiation about the prices of new jobs, but needs to have them running as quickly as possible. Such a management is therefore likely to insist on retaining a high degree of control over the details of work operations.

Some further causal influences arise in connection with Millward's (1972) study of female workers in an electronics plant who had very little control of the effort bargain; in the terms used here, they would probably fall into the non-militant category. The factory had several characteristics in common with Jay's, in particular the nature of market competition. Lupton had placed considerable weight on this factor as an explanation of the difference between Jay and Wye. But plainly other forces must have been at work to prevent the emergence of collective controls in an environment conducive to them. Millward identifies four: the presence of women workers; the minute sub-division of jobs; the weakness of unions at shopfloor level; and a low degree of work group stability. He suggests that the first three were not important. An argument for a sex effect, for example, could not deal with the presence, in another factory that he observed, of considerable collective effort controls among women workers. This is certainly pertinent, and work group stability is plainly important if any sense of collectivity is to emerge. But it is surely preferable to treat it as one among a set of conditions, each of which is a necessary precondition for a collective orientation, and not as a sufficient explanation in its own right. 'Stability' is not an exogenous condition, but is affected by the way in which the labour process is organized and is likely to be related to other influences such as gender relations. As indicated above, high rates of labour turnover tend to be associated with women workers because of the types of jobs that they do and because of social expectations about attachment to work (for example, that they will move jobs if their husbands go to work in different parts of the country).

The upshot is that no factor or set of factors can be isolated as the key causes of differences in patterns of workplace relations. Effects work together, such that there are clusters of characteristics whose separate components cannot be pulled apart. This is not to say that causal analysis is impossible. The foregoing discussion has shown how particular contrasts can be explained. But a given factor, such as the technical division of labour, which can explain one set of differences does not have determinate effects. Its impact has to be assessed in the context of the operation of other forces. It is, moreover, unhelpful to try to identify 'external' and 'internal' forces, for the two often interact. Thus something that is certainly external to a specific workplace, such as the policy of the trade union that covers it, is not really external to the relations governing the mode of control that operates, for the union's policy will have been shaped by the nature of the industry and by the forms of struggle characteristic of it. When Millward, for example, cites the weakness of unions at shopfloor level as a possible explanation of the absence of collective controls, he is really pointing to something that is itself intimately related to this absence.

A further important consideration has run through this study as a whole. This is the proposition than specific struggles for control develop logics of their own. Managers, stewards, and workers struggle within a context shaped by the product market and the technology. But, first, they are not entirely passive in the face of these forces. In the short term the forces are more or less fixed, but in the longer term they are not, as is most obvious with managerial decisions to introduce one form of technology and not another. Second, even within the same context, actors can create different outcomes. The various forces discussed above establish constraints and facilitate certain actions. But they do not determine how people will operate within these constraints and possibilities. Thus a determined shop steward organization can build up means of challenging management that a less committed body fails to do. Once it has begun to do so, it may start to alter some of the 'external' conditions of its activity; for example, labour turnover may fall and work group cohesiveness may rise, thereby creating conditions for the further development of a collective orientation.

A good example is the firm that owned the Electrical and the Components Factories. A third plant had a reputation of being very militant, the Electrical Factory was reputed to be quiescent, and the Components Factory fell somewhere in the middle. Since all the plants were in the same area, differing local traditions of militancy do not seem to be the explanation. Technological conditions were also broadly similar. And the two plants other than the Electrical Factory were dominated by men, so that a sex effect cannot be the answer. The exploitation of the possibilities provided by an identical piecework system by a group of committed stewards seems to be the key factor.

To identify such an influence certainly raises further questions about why such a group arose and why management tolerated its controls. But these are in principle answerable through detailed comparative investigation. And it is not suggested that this was the only influence. The acknowledgement by the company of the skilled status of production workers in the Components Factory, for example, may have encouraged a sense of pride and helped to develop the use of 'skill' as a bargaining resource; this was not possible in the Electrical Factory. The explanatory task is to show how different factors interacted to produce a given outcome.

In examining the logics of individual struggles for control it is important to remember the ways in which particular ways of doing things come to be taken for granted. A great strength of Armstrong *et al.*'s study is its demonstration of the ways in which managerial legitimations were accepted on the shopfloor. They might be questioned for a while but workers lacked the resources to develop alternative arguments. In citing the importance of individual traditions, one is not falling back on 'history' as a catch-all category to explain everything. It is being argued, instead, that traditions have a certain autonomy and their ability to influence constraints and opportunities is in principle demonstrable. Workers at Jay's did not develop their fiddles overnight. These must have grown up over a considerable period, with workers trying one fiddle and continuing with it and refining it if they found that it worked. There are, it is true, few studies that describe in detail the evolution of patterns of control at the level of the individual workplace: the general approach has been to examine the workings of a system at one point in time, and there are likely to be severe problems in securing the evidence necessary for a thorough reconstruction of past events. Yet some of the work cited in the previous chapter indicates what is possible. There is a growing body of work that looks at the history of workplace relations. Of particular interest here is the study by Jefferys (1984), which reconstructs the shape of shopfloor struggles in one plant, Dodge Main in Detroit, over a fifty-year period. This considers how 'external' events impacted on the frontier of control, but also how the tradition of bargaining developed a life of its own.

There is not need here to pursue in detail the question of how historical reconstruction should proceed. The aim has simply been to establish the point that traditions of shopfloor relations have, and must have, an independent role in mediating the effects of structural conditions such as the state of the product market. One feature of these traditions warrants attention, however. This is the way in which a collective orientation can develop into an organizational pattern of relations.

The reasons why work relations fall into one of the non-organizational categories can be found in a range of factors such as the nature of the product market, the technical division of labour, managerial policy, and the characteristics of the workforce. But why does a specifically organizational form emerge? Relatively autonomous traditions of bargaining help to provide the answer. As argued in Chapter 5, an organizational pattern tended to develop in some industries in Britain, but not in the same sectors in America, because managerial policy was not based on a developed attempt to establish a rule of law. Shopfloor bargaining were able to use the space that this created to build an organizational challenge. One reason that has been advanced for their ability to do so is the craft tradition of British unions. Zeitlin (1980) in particular has suggested that the peculiarity of British shopfloor relations lies in the extension of craft practices to semi-skilled workers. As pointed out elsewhere (Scullion and Edwards, 1985), this formulation takes for granted what a craft tradition actually is. The idea that craft practices were diffused to non-craft workers, moreover, lacks an explanation of how diffusion took place. In a plant such as the Small Metals Factory, where there was a strong and clear craft tradition, the process is obvious. But such a plant is notable because it is very unusual in this respect. In the vehicle-assembly plant studied by Batstone *et al.* (1977), for example, small craft societies played a very limited role. And why, in a case such as the Components Factory, where craft groups such as toolmakers had developed powerful controls, was there no diffusion from craft to non-craft groups? The explanation does not lie in craft controls as such; these can in some ways be seen as a reflection and not a cause of the frontier of control, for they were able to flourish because of the wider character of bargaining. They were a special case of a more general phenomenon, namely continuous effort bargaining and the shifting of the frontier of control in workers' favour.

It may not be possible to indicate the sufficient conditions for the emergence of this phenomenon. Why, for example, did workers at Jay's or in the Components Factory not build on their existing collective strength to develop an organizational challenge to management? But some necessary conditions can be identified. First, there is the existence of the general principle that labour relations will be handled at the point of production. This is not the sole influence, for in many ways it operated as much in Armstrong *et al.*'s factories as in the Small Metals Factory. But without it, as the American case suggests, shopfloor bargaining is constrained. Second, product market and technological conditions must encourage management to tolerate shopfloor bargaining. Third, workers must be able to generate and sustain a powerful sense of collectivity that embraces more than just the immediate work group and that goes beyond the terms of the immediate effort bargain. Factors lying behind this tradition include the existence of a core of long-serving employees and a sense of identity among this group. But also important is the deployment of this sense against management, and here the argument must return to specific shopfloor traditions and the role of leadership in building an organizational challenge to management.

In short, to understand how different patterns of workplace relations have arisen it is not sufficient to list a set of internal and external factors. Influences inside and outside workplaces interact, and they operate not as forces independent of each other but as parts of clusters of characteristics. And structural characteristics have to be interpreted by actors in concrete situations. Workplace struggles cannot be reduced to the working through of the effects of background conditions. These conditions establish constraints and provide opportunities, but the constraints can be altered and the opportunities have to be grasped. Struggles necessarily have a relative autonomy in the double sense that there are logics which are specific to the labour process and that these logics are developed through the interaction of workers and managers over the terms of the effort bargain.

Conclusion: Interdependence and Relative Autonomy

This chapter has tried to analyse a range of workplaces, to describe the frontier of control in them, to consider the association between the position of the frontier and behaviour on the shopfloor, and to identify some of the causal factors influencing the position of the frontier. The third of these aims, namely the systematic examination of a range of collective and individual activity and the connection of this activity with the social organization of work, is perhaps the most important: the linking of concrete behaviour to broader patterns of social relationships has rarely been carried out in a detailed way. For any overall assessment of conflict, however, such an analysis is essential if the relationships between apparently different types of behaviour are to be grasped and if the analysis is to explore the connections between behaviour and broader notions of conflict between workers and management. Workplace behaviour does not come in pre-packaged forms such as absenteeism and pilfering but is the product of the wider social relations governing work; this chapter has tried to demonstrate this point empirically.

The chapter has stressed the multiplicity of ways in which workers' compliance is generated. In the case of the non-militant workforces subject to direct control in the clothing factories studied by Edwards and Scullion, several forces tied workers to the firms. For the women, there were wages that were relatively high compared to what was available elsewhere; close supervision and the careful checking of quality controlled the effort bargain; managers were 'fair' in the allocation of work; for some groups of longer-serving workers the overt application of discipline was rare, and there were benefits such as being able to alter working hours to suit family commitments; workers lacked any means of comparison with effort levels elsewhere because they lacked experience in other industries; managers promoted the image of the family firm and the overriding need to maintain competitiveness; and the union organization was distant from the shopfloor and unwilling to take up, let alone actively seek out, problems concerning piecework prices. Other factors could be added to the list. For the men, high wages were probably less important, but this was balanced by the sense of commitment to the firm that had grown up. This commitment was certainly not a total loyalty to all that management stood for, but was based on a curiously double-edged view of the firm in which cynicism about managers was mingled with appreciation of the personal ties that had developed; there was also uncertainty about what an alternative might have looked like. The 'ideological' aspects of workers' compliance were more evident than they were in the case of the women, as was evidenced by differing attitudes about absenteeism. Under the system of sophisticated control practised at 'ChemCo' the main elements in the pattern were: high wages and generous fringe benefits; the bureaucratic system of job gradings and other rules; the individualization of the workforce; and the constant demands that the technology placed on the workers. 'Technical' and 'bureaucratic' control operated together, but it was not just the technology or the rules that were important but the way in which management created an acceptance of them.

Similar points could be developed about the other factories examined above, but the main implication is clear. It is possible to assess the ways in which different parts of a firm's operations generate compliance. Two points in particular stand out. First, firms' modes of control contain many elements which cannot be reduced to one type or style; these modes are not created consciously but emerge out of concrete situations. Second, workers have some part in creating patterns of control: they are not passive recipients of managerial actions. Various modes of adaptation have been described above. Even where discipline is imposed strictly, understandings can emerge about, for example, how often one can go absent, and these means of escape are very important in generating acceptance of the system. Acceptance and adaptation are part of the same phenomenon. Thus it is not the case that workers would simply not work if managerial control mechanisms were somehow removed. Workers have general expectations about the duty to work which are derived from experiences in home and school as well as work. What systems of control do is to define and specify the general duty according to the needs of the particular employer. Workers have varying abilities to alter managerial rules. According to the interaction between such struggle at the point of production and demands derived from the process of exchange, for example pressures stemming from rising international competition, a particular pattern of control develops.

Patterns of work relations thus have a 'relative autonomy' from outside forces. This issue of relative autonomy has been a significant part of the labour process debate. It overlaps with the traditional concern of industrial sociology to unravel the relative importance of 'internal' and 'external' factors in the explanation of attitudes and behaviour. As noted in chapter 1 (see p. 47), Burawoy's (1979) argument for a very high degree of autonomy of the labour process is not satisfactory, but criticisms of it are also inadequate to the extent that they fail to develop a theoretical means of grasping the links between internal and external forces. A useful analogy is provided by Emmett and Morgan (1982) in their consideration of the work of Lupton, Cunnison, and other members of the Manchester ethnographical school. They liken the wall of a factory to a 'semi-permeable membrane'; the factory is not immune to external forces, and its own arrangements filter and transform them. They take the example of Jewishness from Cunnison's study. As in other parts of the garment industry, there was a long tradition of the employment of Jews, and Cunnison demonstrated that the division between Jews and other workers was important in the formation of social groups and in many other aspects of work. Yet, Emmett and Morgan argue, it would be incorrect to criticize the study for failing to study the Jewish community as a whole. The fact of being Jewish took on a particular significance in the factory. In another factory it might play a different role, or have no significance at all. A factory study needs to consider how external conditions are transformed in the workplace, and need not concern itself with every aspect of the external social lives of the workforce.

Now it might be argued that religion is a poor example and that the effects of gender, say, are far more pervasive. But the same general argument applies: the status of being a man or a woman takes on a particular significance in particular workplaces. It is not simply an external effect with automatic consequences, but its role is mediated by the structures and traditions of the workplace. As noted above, the experience of women at work varies according to the type of control system in operation. Here, then, is one sense of the relative autonomy of the workplace. Another is the way in which patterns of workplace relations evolve as a result of the process of struggle. External and internal structural conditions do not in themselves determine outcomes, for these depend on actors' behaviour. Once the analytical principle that the labour contract cannot be specified in advance is accepted, it must also be accepted that this indeterminacy means that struggles have lives of their own. Personal abilities, the unintended consequences of action, and luck are all involved. A third feature of relative autonomy is the interaction between 'internal' and 'external' factors. What is apparently external may well be influenced by patterns of control, the character of trade unionism in an industry being a good example. These aspects of relative autonomy at an empirical level can be understood within the analytical point that the process of production is a distinct sphere of social life, with demands and logics of its own stemming from the need to transform labour power into labour. The idea of relative autonomy can thus be developed and refined to explain why work relations can be analysed in their own right.

This chapter concludes the analysis of capitalism begun in chapter 3. The theory outlined in chapter 2 claimed, however, to refer to work relations under other modes of production. The following chapter takes up the task of applying it outside the familiar terrain of capitalism.

7

Conflict under Non-capitalist Modes of Production

Orthodox studies of trends in indices of industrial conflict have concentrated on the capitalist world, a focus which has been reproduced in most of the labour process debate. This chapter tries to go some way towards correcting the balance, not by providing a detailed account of the patterns of work relations in non-capitalist societies (which would be an impossibly large task, even if suitable studies were available from all the main countries and historical periods) but by indicating in broad terms how some of the themes pursued in previous chapters can be applied outside capitalism. The principal theme is the indeterminacy of the labour contract, the ability of subordinate groups to affect the terms of their exploitation, and the simultaneous accommodation to and alteration of the system of domination that occurs within relations of production. Each mode of production creates distinct ways of dealing with these things. As indicated in chapter 2, each has a structured antagonism which makes it possible to say that 'conflict is inevitable'. But the organization of this conflict differs markedly. The common statement that conflict is not limited to capitalism is correct when taken literally, but incorrect if it is taken to imply that the principles on which conflict in the workplace is based are invariant.

There are, or have been, numerous non-capitalist forms of work organization. The following discussion will concentrate on three, feudalism, slavery, and state socialism, because each stands as a reasonably pure case whose principles of organization contrast with those of capitalism. There are, of course, significant internal variations in each. Some of these will be mentioned where relevant. For example, slave systems have differed in the intensity of slave-owners' control of the slaves, and the nature of and reasons for these differences are pertinent to the general argument that the power of subordinates to amend the effort bargain varies within a mode of production. Each mode of production also contains elements of change and development which will not be considered in detail. No pretence is made of offering a comprehensive picture of variations over time and space. The aim is merely to illustrate some general arguments and to draw out the contrasts with capitalism.

This may provide some justification for the very heavy reliance on the work of others, particularly Hilton in the case of feudalism and Genovese for slavery. The aim is not to offer new substantive interpretations of the social formations in question, but to present the key implications of this work for a materialist account of conflict. As both authors note, the social relations of work have been given very little attention within the respective historiographical traditions. Their work represents a major corrective, and warrants inclusion within general debates about the labour process.

Feudalism

'Industrial conflict' under feudalism has often been equated with mass movements such as the famous Peasants' Revolt in England in 1381. Hilton (1977) has provided an account of it which goes beyond the specifics of the case to locate it within a general interpretation of peasants' action. This rests in turn on a characterization of feudalism as an exploitative mode of production. Thus, Hilton quotes (p. 11) the significant remark of Marc Bloch that peasant movements were as 'natural to the seigneurial regime as strikes were to large-scale capitalism'. And he does not limit the implications to the obvious one that peasant movements and strikes punctuate developments. They are not incidental but are extreme examples of a more general phenomenon, namely overt conflicts arising from protests about or attempts to alter the existing balance of effort and reward. Such conflicts are themselves reflections of continuing struggles around this balance, and these struggles need not involve anything as dramatic as a rebellion or a strike.

Hilton thus considers early developments in the twelfth and thirteenth centuries (pp. 74–89). A typical demand was for a charter freeing the peasants from various feudal obligations to the lord. The fight for a charter was less spectacular than a revolt, but it was arguably more significant, for a charter secured permanent gains while a revolt might achieve nothing. In the terms used here, a charter institutionalized some aspects of conflict over rights and obligations in a way similar to that in which workplace rules under capitalism limit the terrain of effort bargaining. Hilton relates the demand for charters to the growth of production for the market, which made the wealthy peasants ambitious and eager to reduce their feudal obligations. The movement was most advanced in those countries, namely France and Italy, where the development of the market had proceeded furthest. In England, by contrast, development had been less rapid, and the nearest approach to a 'charter of enfranchisement was the legal definition of fixed custom' (p. 89), although even here the lords tended to be more successful than the peasants when disputes came to litigation.

This point about custom is of some general significance, and, as will be seen, it applies also to a slave mode of production. Just as in capitalism the transformation of labour-power into labour is a complex process whose parameters can never be fully fixed, so in feudalism the relations of lord and peasant were governed by a web of rules, some legal, some written, and others unwritten. The precise timing and nature of labour services, the character of the many other exactions which could be made, rights to the use of forests and common land, and many other matters could never be fully specified. Custom grew up as a way of handling elements of uncertainty, and it was a victory for the peasantry to have customary practices recognized in formal statements of rights and obligations, for here was one way in which the terms of exploitation could be varied. If it is true that the peasant movement is the equivalent of the strike, then it is not too farfetched to draw an analogy between the peasant's concern with customary rights and the ability of a shop steward to have a local factory custom on, say, the payment to be made when no work is available given managerial recognition as a rule and not merely a habit without legitimate status. It follows, moreover, that just as the active pursuit of 'custom and practice' is not universal in capitalist factories but depends on organization and the development of legitimatory rhetorics which challenge managerial arguments, so peasants were not always and everywhere pursuing the legal enforcement of custom.

The fact that they sometimes did so can be related to specific developments such as the growth of wealth and independence among a section of the peasantry. It can also be linked to the nature of the mode of production, for central to this was not the sale of labour power but the specification of obligations of labour service on the part of the peasants. Peasants were not free, but depended on their lords for the right to use the land that they farmed on their own account, and they had to provide labour services (or equivalent rents) in return for this right and the lord's protection. Bargaining thus took the form not of negotiating levels of effort within the labour process but of trying to alter the extent of the obligations that peasants owed to their lords.

What accounts for the occurrence of revolts at one time and not another? As Hilton argues (p. 114), it is insufficient to prove that lords and peasants had opposing interests, for the two sides co-existed for centuries without engaging in open conflict. Something more than inevitable antagonism 'must therefore have precipitated movements which often seemed to participants on both sides a break in the "natural order" of things'. Peasants' movements reflected a series of influences, and their character changed as the feudal mode of production developed and came to reveal differing pressures on lords and peasants. As Hilton puts it, in an important statement of the position, 'peasants, even more than their lords, tended to cling to custom even when, without knowing it, they were constantly seeking to mould custom to suit their own interests'. It is this dual nature of custom, as something constant and yet changing, as reflecting existing forms of accommodation and yet also suffering the possibility of change, which must be grasped. Peasants respected custom not because they were backward-looking or introspective or otherwise lacking in allegedly modern values, but because it was the means by which their antagonism to their lords was simultaneously expressed and altered.

Hilton goes on to note an apparent paradox about the English rising of 1381: it occurred not when the peasants were worst off but when the distribution of income was moving in their favour (pp. 154–7). The paradox disappears when the trend is placed in context: the government had been increasing its tax demands across the whole country, and lords and government officials were together trying to re-establish their dominance in the face of the economic disruption, and in particular the tightening of the labour market, which followed the Black Death. The resulting tensions formed the basis of discontent among the peasantry. Two conclusions are warranted. First, the peasants did not cling blindly and ritualistically to custom; they used it, and in the period after the Black Death were able to mould it as the shortage of labour enabled them to amend the terms of the obligations. Second, the correlation between relative prosperity and the occurrence of the rising was not a product of the peasants' situation in and of itself. It reflected the efforts of the lords to regain their position of dominance.

Again, a parallel suggests itself. It is frequently noted that rebellions and strikes tend to occur not when conditions are worst but during upturns in economic activity. This may reflect a lack of confidence and organization in the depths of a depression, followed by a recovery once conditions start to improve. The other side of the story is less often told. A period of tight labour markets may force dominant groups to grant concessions that they subsequently try to claw back. The sources of overt conflict lie as much in these groups' attempts to protect their dominant position as in subordinates' efforts to exploit their bargaining power. The situation also involves more than the settlement of particular disputes according to the relative size of the parties' power resources. A successful challenge by subordinate groups to the conditions of their exploitation involves more than an alteration in the balance of power; it can also begin to undermine the basis of a system of domination. Once peasants challenged long-established arrangements, how much further might they go? Would they begin to question the lord's right to demand labour services? A lords' offensive or an employer' offensive is required lest the system drift dangerously out of their control.

This is not to suggest that feudal lords articulated such thoughts consciously. No doubt they were genuinely shocked at the erosion of the natural order of things, just as capitalist employers may be shocked to find workers challenging their authority. But they were acting in response to the contradictions within the social formation, notably the ability of the peasants to amend the terms of exploitation. Their reaction challenged the peasants' new expectations and the new forms which custom was taking, and thus laid the basis for the rising of 1381.

Now it may be argued that the Black Death was the most important factor, and that, because its occurrence was exogenous to the feudal mode of production as such, the rising cannot be seen as a reflection of contradications inherent in feudalism. Instead, it would be seen as the product of a set of particular circumstances. This argument deserves to be taken seriously. It is inadequate to point to the fact of rebellions in different modes of production as though their mere presence provides analytical justification for the view that conflict is inherent in each mode. For the purposes of the argument it may be accepted that the Black Death was, indeed, exogenous and that it had a crucial effect on the supply of labour and hence on the relative power resources of lords and peasants. Yet the mere presence of such an exogenous influence is hardly sufficient to explain the occurrence of rebellions. The suggestion that it is sufficient takes us back to the view, criticized in chapter 1, that we can understand conflict by positing the existence of antagonistic groups and charting the balance of power between them. What is needed in addition is an explanation of the material basis of antagonism. In the particular case of feudalism the basis of exploitation in extra-economic institutions helps to explain at least two things about peasant rebellions. First, of course, it establishes the character of antagonism and the bases of conflict between lords and peasants. Second, it helps us to understand something of the particular shape of the rebellions themselves. Why, for example, did the rebels display concern about the law and lawyers, apparently wishing to establish a new basis for the law? And why was freedom from serfdom and villeinage at the centre of the demands of the rebels in 1381? The answer lies in the peasants' experience of exploitation, for they were challenging existing obligations which lay at the heart of the feudal system, namely the obligations to provide surplus labour-time to the lord. The problem of the character of the rebels' demands cannot properly be grasped without an understanding of what lay beneath them. In short, although there were particular reasons for the size and significance of the rising of 1381, its more general characteristics can be related to the antagonisms of the feudal mode of production.

The rising was, of course, defeated. As Hilton suggests (p. 232), this defeat had important long-term consequences in that it helped to strengthen the hand of the lords, which in turn meant that a patriarchal form of organization became established in English agriculture even after the end of feudalism. How far such domination can be traced directly to the consequences of 1381 is, of course, a moot point. But the general point, namely that the outcome of struggles over the terms of exploitation has real and lasting consequences, is of some significance. It is not simply that large victories or defeats have long-term consequences for the power positions of the two sides, although that, of course, is true. The more general point is that the shape of the relationship between peasant and lord, or worker and capitalist, has a powerful influence on subsequent developments. Relationships which define the terms of exploitation do not simply reflect the balance of power resources. They are an important resource in their own right, for they mediate the influence of external factors such as changes in the demand for and supply of labour. And the way in which they have been shaped by past struggles will determine how this mediation is carried out. There is no automatic correlation between resources and outcomes, either over time or between different places. The tightening of the labour market after the Black Death, for example, did not necessarily mean that peasants would begin to press for changes in the terms of their feudal obligations. Also required was a tradition within which such changes were felt to be legitimate, to some degree at least, and which was capable of sustaining particular struggles. Struggles at the point of production have a certain autonomy, with their shape helping to determine future developments.

Moreover, as the example of feudalism shows clearly, these struggles should not be interpreted as straightforward bargaining games.

They expressed several different elements of the relationship between dominant and subordinate groups: economic struggles over the division of rewards; political and legal disputes over the rules governing the extraction of the surplus; and ideological battles reflecting the legitimacy of custom and competing definitions of customary rights. These elements were fused together, a point which will be pursued, with reference to other modes of production as well, in the concluding section of this chapter.

The feudal mode of production rested on an insecure base, since the extraction of a surplus was obvious and visible. The importance of political and ideological forces can therefore readily be understood. An apparent contrast is provided by slavery. Unlike feudal lords, slaveholders did not have to rely on extra-economic means to secure a surplus: they took the whole of the product, providing for the slaves only the means of subsistence. Unlike capitalists, however, they were not faced with a class of free wage-labourers who could leave their employment without legal penalty. Their problems of securing a surplus might thus appear to have been largely solved. As will be seen, however, they too faced the potentially problematic task of securing the compliance of their subordinates.

Slavery

The interest in slavery is not in the legal institution as it has appeared in various parts of the world or in the practice of enslaving enemies defeated in battle. It is in slavery as a means of putting workers to work and with the distinctive patterns of domination and subordination that result. Slavery is thus being viewed as a mode of production in the sense that it is a way of deploying labour-power to produce goods and services. This is not to suggest that it is a self-contained system. In the cases discussed below, goods were produced on slave plantations to be sold on markets dominated by capitalist principles: the goods were produced for their exchange value and not for the direct consumption of the masters, as was the case in a feudal economy. A fully functioning capitalist system has a close connection between the spheres of production and exchange. The principles governing the labour process are tied to those for the operation of the economy as a whole. The slave labour process was in some ways parasitic on a capitalist market. It raises, none the less, some specific problems with labour control. The owners' domination of their slaves was not as total as might appear, and there were important differences between slave systems. The case of the American South indicates most clearly the conditions under which slaves can develop a limited counter-control to the control of the owners. Contrasts with other slave systems may then be considered.

The American South

Fogel and Engerman (1974a) have used a wide range of econometric evidence to challenge the standard picture of slavery in the South. This traditional view, namely that slavery was inefficient and economically moribund, that slave-owners had none of the capitalist's interest in profit maximization, and that slaves were lazy and unproductive, is challenged on all counts. It is argued that slave farms were substantially more efficient than Northern agriculture, that the rate of return to slaveholders was better than that in many capitalist enterprises, that slaveholders had a close appreciation of profit and loss, and that slaves were more efficient than free workers. The last point is crucial, for Fogel and Engerman (1974a: 231) do not draw back from the full implications of their analysis: early writers accepted the myth of the slaves' incompetence and laziness, and this has been only partially corrected by writers such as Stampp (1964), who sees in problems of labour discipline not laziness but 'day to day resistance' by the slaves against their conditions of work. For Fogel and Engerman the debate between the critics of an apologists for the slave system has been based on the false premise that there was a low level of labour productivity and a high degree of cruelty and repression of the slaves. Once the leap is made to recognize the superiority of slave labour it is no longer necessary, in their view, for writers such as Stampp to defend the slaves' actions by describing them as forms of resistance to unjust oppression: the ordinary slave was a diligent and efficient worker.

Starobin's (1970: 148–58) research suggests that the economic benefits of slavery were not limited to agriculture: the detailed evidence indicates that in manufacturing enterprises the efficiency of slaves was not less than that of free workers. Any tendency to low productivity was balanced by the ability to enforce strict discipline and to use female and child labour freely; and free workers were prone to quitting and being intractable.

Much of the argument about the economic viability of the slave system, and about other features such as the importance of an autonomous or semi-autonomous black culture, provides a very proper corrective to earlier writings. But Fogel and Engerman's account of labour efficiency is curious. They go on (pp. 234–40) to discuss the economies of scale in Southern agriculture, arguing that it was only on the slave plantations that these economies could be realized. The reason given for this is not, however, the inherent efficiency of slave labour but the fact that the kind of work required, namely highly regulated labour in gangs under direct supervision, would have required a high wage to persuade free workers to accept it. Slaves, by contrast, could be made to tolerate the system because the masters could use force, for this was the only way to operate the gang labour system without a high financial premium. The stress on force fits uneasily with the earlier argument that slaves were willing and diligent workers. This is more than a minor inconsistency, for it reflects an important confusion in the concept of efficiency. The standard measure of labour productivity is output per worker or per hour, and it is quite proper to argue that slavery was, on this measure, more efficient than other forms of agriculture. But what is left out is the intensity of labour, that is how 'efficiently' the master can extract labour power from the worker. As Fogel and Engerman stress, slave plantations were efficient in the first sense precisely because there were means of extracting effort, which they summarize as 'force', which were not available to employers of free labour. Or, more precisely, such means were more costly to employ with free labour although, as many indictments of the factory system show, force was certainly not absent.

In their additional comments on this, Fogel and Engerman (1974b: 155–7) rightly argue that it is wrong to see force and financial inducements as incompatible, for all societies rest on a combination of both. And they show how a curve can be drawn to represent the amounts of force and financial rewards that can be used to produce one 'unit' of labour. Under slavery force was relatively cheap, and hence masters used a combination of a relatively large amount of force and a relatively low level of other inducements. The mistake, however, is to compare directly slave systems, which have one trade-off between force and inducements, with systems of free labour where the trade-off was very different, for the 'efficiency' of the former was based on the use of force whose costs do not directly enter the calculation of productivity. Fogel and Engerman estimate that slaves gained 20 per cent of the increase in production attributable to large-scale operations. Such estimates obviously rest on several assumptions, but they show very clearly the confusions that can arise if different notions of efficiency are not kept distinct. The economies of scale certainly increased production per worker, but the fact that 80 per cent of these economies went to the masters reflects the high rate of exploitation that they entailed.

It is also important to distinguish between the threat of force and its exercise. As the authors rightly stress it is a mistake to assume that slave plantations were characterized by large numbers of overseers who kept the slaves in a condition of fear. Direct repression was often not needed, and the success of the system rested on masters' ability to generate the compliance of the slaves. Yet to understand the operation of the system requires attention to its internal workings. What, in other words, were the characteristics of the system which led to the establishment of a particular trade-off between force and rewards? When this question has been tackled it will be possible to come to a more complete view of resistance than Stampp's inversion of the traditional view or Fogel and Engerman's virtual denial of the presence of resistance.

The complex question of the relationship between resistance and accommodation to the system has been pursued in great depth by Genovese (1976). He insists 'upon the centrality of class relations' in slavery and stresses the contradictions of the system: although slave masters had a paternalist concern for their slaves, this paternalism 'grew out of the necessity to discipline and morally justify a system of exploitation. It did encourage kindness and affection, but it simultaneously encouraged cruelty and hatred' (p. 4). It is this grasp of the ambiguities and contradictions of the system which marks Genovese's treatment. He does not argue simply that the slaveholders were either fair or unfair, but places slaveholders' behaviour in the context of the paternalist system as a whole. He does not deny the cruelty of the system but he rejects any simply moral condemnation of it. He stresses that Southern paternalism was one means, and certainly not the only one, as his comparisons with slavery elsewhere in the New World suggest, for mediating irreconcilable class interests. 'It mediated, however unfairly and even cruelly, between masters and slaves, and it disguised, however imperfectly, the appropriation of one man's labor power by another' (Genovese, 1976: 6). Masters and slaves had antagonistic interests, and paternalism was one distinct means of mediating this antagonism in such a way that life for both sides could continue. Open hostility was far from common, but at the same time the contradictions of the system meant that there was certainly not total harmony.

Hence Genovese discusses at length the slaveholders' position. Although the law created the fiction that the slave was the master's property, to be treated as the owner saw fit, in practice masters were forced to recognize the slaves' humanity, for otherwise the system would have been unworkable. Similarly, white overseers were not given absolute authority to do as they liked, and masters did not always take the word of overseers against the slaves. As Genovese (p. 16) puts it, the masters recognized that the slaves could exercise some free will and 'had an interest, however psychologically antagonistic, in the smooth running of the plantation which fed black and white alike'. Masters had to temper the legal fiction of absolute authority with the recognition that any master who wanted production at a high level relied on winning the co-operation of the slaves. Hence a variety of customs grew up to control such things as the amount of land which slaves could have to grow their own crops, the hours of work that would normally be required, and the operation of discipline. Masters who infringed customary understandings knew that they risked considerable trouble.

The parallel here with analyses of the effort bargain within capitalist firms should come as no surprise. The point is simply that labour processes rest on gaining consent, and that neither a detailed contract of employment nor 'absolute' employer authority can guarantee that work will be performed in the desired manner. The surprise is that many treatments of slavery fail properly to grasp this, with the debate turning on whether the masters were cruel or the slaves were lazy instead of placing cruelty and laziness within the context of an exploitative relationship. Genovese's approach enables him to put the matter in a completely different light, because he has an understanding of the contradictions of the system which meant that masters and slaves had interests in common although this was in the wider context of an antagonistic relationship.

Genovese's treatment of slaves' resistance illustrates this point. He notes (p. 587) that scholars such as Aptheker (1963) have tried to overturn the myth of the contented slave by stressing slave revolts and organized resistance. But, he goes on, the evidence for a revolutionary tradition in the South is far from strong and, more importantly, concentration on slave revolts 'drew attention away from the slaves' deeper cultural and social resistance and from the organic relationships inherent in the slaveholders' hegemony'. Genovese stresses the intimate relationship between accommodation and resistance under paternalism, an approach which is again excluded by simple distinctions between contentment and rebelliousness. He discusses, for example, the practice of feigning illness to avoid work (p. 620): this plainly reduced the labour power available to the master, but Genovese argues that it was a form of resistance only in so far as it helped to reduce the general pace of work and that, because only a few slaves could successfully play this game, the remainder often suffered and hence had little sympathy for shirkers. More generally, various means of limiting the pace of work were, for Genovese, important attempts to wrest some control from the master which were also, however, reflections of a partial acceptance of the system in that they were far from being direct challenges to the slave system as such. Yet they were in many ways more important than more spectacular activities such as running away or murdering the overseer because they produced clear gains in slaves' everyday living and working conditions and because they encouraged a collective community spirit in place of spontaneous and unconnected individual acts of defiance.

Finally, as his concluding comments (p. 568) make clear, Genovese, despite his heavy reliance on the concepts of paternalism and hegemony, does not treat the masters' domination as simply a cultural product. He stresses two points about hegemony, first that it was based on deep class antagonisms and second that 'command of the culture could not readily have been established without command of the gun'. The first point is not developed further, but it is a crucial rejoinder to those who use notions of exploitation without basing them in a materialist analysis. Genovese is clear that to speak of hegemony makes sense only if this domination is seen in class terms: slave masters exercised hegemony not because they were devious or because their market power happened to be greater than that of slaves but because they were in a class relationship in which they had to create the basis of slaves' willingness to work under, and hence sustain, the system of exploitation.

The second point is more debatable. As stated it implies that cultural or ideological control rested directly on control of the means of force without there being any reciprocal linkages. Yet as Genovese himself notes (p. 25), treatments of the law as simply superstructural obscure the degree of autonomy which the law can create for itself. Perhaps the most useful reading of these passages is that different levels of analysis are being employed. In the analysis of specific historical circumstances the law should be seen as a factor having a degree of autonomy from other features of society. To treat it as the direct result of the slaveowners' control of the means of violence would be to retreat to a very narrow instrumentalist view of the state as a simple reflection of the needs of the dominant group. Under slavery, as under other economic systems, the law had a degree of autonomy, and the slaves had some limited rights. Yet, at a more abstract level of analysis, the law can be seen as a reflection of a deeper class relationship: it took the form that it did because of the pattern of domination. Thus Genovese charts the tortuous reasoning of legal authorities: were the slaves no more than the owners' property, in which case they had no responsibilities or rights, or were they people to whom normal standards of reasonable behaviour could be applied? Using different levels of analysis removes the confusion as to whether the law is merely superstructural or has some autonomy, and means that the law's links to the nature of the economy need not be reduced to 'command of the gun'.

Genovese's account makes clear the ways in which different modes of control were brought together. Although the stress is on hegemony, this concept, as used by Genovese, should not be taken to refer only to ideological means through which acceptance of the system was generated among the slaves. The analysis explores the way in which the system cohered. Everyday life on the plantations became so taken for granted that it was hard to break out of the rhythms that it created. Modes of bargaining reflected accommodation to the principles of the system in the same way in which, as Burawoy argues, playing games in capitalist factories induces consent to the rules of these games. Outside the individual plantation stood the political and legal power of the owners, for the structure of the polity and the law rested on the requirements of a slave-based economy. Slaves were the owner's property and had no independent political or legal existence. Behind this power lay the ultimate sanction of force.

For Genovese (1976: 303), the 'actual work rhythm of the slaves' was hammered out 'as a compromise between themselves and their masters. The masters held the upper hand, but the slaves set limits as best they could'. This perspective integrates a treatment of 'resistance' into a consideration of the operation of the system of domination. It thus goes beyond traditional Marxist attempts to construe permanent resistance out of the occasional rebellions that occurred, and also points up the one-sidedness of Fogel and Engelman's focus on the 'diligence' of the slave. Slaves were neither latent rebels nor happy and diligent workers but were workers placed under a repressive system of control who developed some means of moderating the system and of making their lives tolerable.

Other Slave Systems

The pattern of mutual accommodation that developed in the American South rested on several specific features of the economy. In contrast to the Caribbean sugar plantations, the Southern plantations were small, and the whites formed a large part of the population. As early as 1680 the native-born comprised a majority of American slaves whereas the proportion of imported slaves remained high in the Caribbean (Fogel and Engerman, 1974a: 22–3). And there were important technical differences between the production of cotton and sugar: the former required more skill and was less easily supervised. The massive plantations of the Caribbean, run by a small group of whites and employing slaves who were unaccustomed to the system to perform highly routinized tasks, resembled 'factories in the field' (Genovese, 1976: 286). Their highly repressive system of control contrasted sharply with Southern paternalism.

Genovese (1979) has developed this contrast between slave systems. He sees a key difference as lying in the need for Southern slaveholders to improve the material conditions of slave life. If they did not do so, they would be unable to ensure an adequate supply of labour power. The system grew most rapidly after the closure of the slave trade, and the owners were thus forced to rely exclusively on internal sources of slaves. The relative size of the white population was presumably also important, in that fears of revolts were reduced, such that the owners felt that they could afford a paternalistic approach. The result, for Genovese, was that Southern slaves became so accommodated within the system that rebellion was increasingly pointless: the chances of success were slim, and the benefits of the existing system were sufficient to reduce the attractiveness of risking open revolt. Elsewhere, repression meant that the existing arrangements offered few benefits to the slaves. The smallness of the white community gave revolts a reasonable chance of success. And in the South the countryside was settled and cultivated, which made it difficult for rebels to find areas in which to hide and group together. In the Caribbean, however, the terrain made it possible to establish substantial rebel camps. Thus, the need to engage in open revolts, and the probability of success, were both greater than they were in the South.

Genovese's (1979: 52–81) work here provides an important insight into one aspect of slaves' resistance to which he had earlier given little attention, namely running away. At first sight, a slave system which gives masters absolute rights over their property leaves slaves few opportunities apart from escape. Yet matters are more complex than this. First, as noted above, the essence of Genovese's account of Southern slavery is to point to several aspects of the labour contract which were open to influence by the slaves. Quitting was far from being the only option. Second, the costs of running away were larger than they were in other slave societies. During the eighteenth century, Florida in particular provided a haven for runaways, but antagonism between blacks and the Indian tribes made the development of distinctive ex-slave communities difficult. By the nineteenth century the growing white majority, the presence of armed whites in the countryside, and the inhospitability of the land as the frontier shifted westwards further reduced the chances of communities of runaways. Elsewhere, such communities were certainly small, and they tended to be limited to guerilla activities. But some of them existed for many years, and their very presence was a reminder that slaves could escape and rebel.

The implication seems to be that running away and staging open revolts, although apparently at the opposite poles of 'individual' and 'collective' forms of resistance, in fact depended on similar conditions. Whereas under capitalism, individual escape through labour turnover tends to reduce a work force's ability to engage in collective protest, under slavery it appears that different connections existed. Where slaveholders' control was based on paternalism and accommodation neither activity offered much hope, whereas more repressive regimes made bargaining within the labour process impossible and rendered escape and revolt important possibilities.

Conclusions: Viability of Slavery

As Genovese concludes, Southern slavery tended to be like peasant agriculture whereas that in the Caribbean was more like a factory. By this is meant not that Caribbean slavery resembled modern forms of economic organization but that there was no paternalist system of legitimation and accommodation: relations between exploiters and exploited were naked and brutal.

A 'factory in the field' differs from a capitalist factory because of the absence of a free labour market and because of the overt and simple nature of the exploitation. The analogy does, however, raise the question of how slave and free labour compared. G. Cohen (1978: 191–2) argues that accumulation requires increasingly sophisticated productive forces and that slavery is incompatible with this. The costs of supervising slave labour and the fact that slavery is unlikely to encourage the skilful and willing application of the slaves' creative capacities render the system inappropriate to the long-run development of the productive forces. In the short term, however, slave labour may be as efficient as free labour (Starobin, 1970: 154). A study of textile mills argues that the slaves were 'an efficient and self-confident work force that was not brutalized by industrial bondage, but rather found sufficient social space to fend off the total domination of their masters' (Miller, 1981: 490). Free workers were often as subject to harsh supervision and dangerous working conditions as were slaves. In addition, along with the benefits of freedom came the costs of uncertain employment and of being treated as no more than a wage labourer: whereas the slaveholder had an interest in the long-term health of his slaves, the capitalist need take no concern with such things as long as he could hire workers when he wanted them. Against this, however, must be set the special nature of Southern slavery. Slavery could produce paternalism but did not necessarily do so. In the conditions of the South slavery and 'freedom' may not have differed much, but this should not be made a general rule.

It is impossible to establish whether slavery had a long-term future because it was destroyed. Temperley (1977) provides an indication why. He rejects the common argument that the system was coming into growing conflict with the rising capitalist economic order, pointing out that conflicts were more apparent than real. Yet he also rejects an explanation in terms of the moral arguments of the abolitionists. There was an indirect link between slavery and capitalism: the ideology of political economy equated freedom with prosperity, and took it for granted that the latter was impossible without the former. Interpretations of slavery were based on assumptions about what a slave economy ought to look like (unwilling workers, repression, and an absence of innovation) and not how it, in fact, worked. The ideology also neglected the repression and lack of freedom characteristic of early capitalism. In short, slavery may have come up against its incompatibility with accumulation, but there is little evidence that existing slave systems fell apart because of their internal contradictions.

State Socialism

Analysis of the societies of Eastern Europe is complicated by the number of competing interpretations available. There is the official view that social relations are non-antagonistic because the basis of antagonism under capitalism, the private ownership of the means of production, has been abolished. Society is seen as involving the harmonious co-operation of two classes, the workers and the peasants, and one stratum, the intelligentsia. In particular, there can be no grounds for industrial conflict as it is known under capitalism, since the workers collectively own the means of production and since it is impossible to engage in conflict against oneself. Any manifestations of discontent are written off as the actions of deviants or troublemakers. Few Western commentators would accept such an argument. Indeed, as will be seen below, the Soviet authorities in practice recognize that a certain amount of discontent will be present, and there is a degree of toleration of it, even though that toleration can receive no official sanction.

Once the official view is rejected, a range of interpretations of state socialist societies, and of the place of industrial conflict within them, is available. One argument shares with the official view the claim to be Marxist while otherwise being completely opposed to it. This is the thesis of 'state capitalism', namely that these societies have in fact reproduced all the inequalities of capitalism and that the dominant group within them has in fact become a ruling class which exploits the working class (Cliff, 1974). A contrasting view, associated with the name of Trotsky (for an exposition and discussion of whose views, see Deutscher, 1963: 298–324), sees Soviet society as a degenerate workers' state. Capitalism has not been re-invented, but instead the state bureaucracy has choked any genuine democracy and has become the enemy of the working class. Several other interpretative schemes (usefully reviewed by Lane, 1978: 171–98) are available. They do not require detailed comment here. They tend to be rather general statements about the nature of society as a whole, and the evidence which they call up in their own support is not always as decisive as their proponents seem to think. Consider, for example, the recent collection of articles on the Soviet worker edited by Schapiro and Godson (1981). This takes what may be called the totalitarian perspective, namely the view that Soviet workers are repressed by an all-powerful bureaucracy and that everything in Soviet society is worse from the point of view of the workers than is the case under capitalism. The result of the Soviet system is found to be 'a collection of sullen, disillusioned, unproductive workers who have little say in economic decisions and who have no outlet for their grievances' (Seeger, 1981: 105). Trade unions, for example, often fail to defend workers' interests: any dismissal of a worker is supposed to have the agreement of the enterprise's union committee, but 'in practice this agreement is either not sought by management or is treated as a mere formality' (Godson, 1981: 116). Such arguments appear to contradict their own evidence of absenteeism and low effort levels, which surely are outlets for grievances. More importantly, the deployment of evidence is used not to try to develop an analysis of the social formation but to buttress some view of it. It is true that Soviet workers go absent, steal, and get drunk, but this does not in itself prove that they are totally powerless tools of the bureaucracy. It is true that private property has been abolished, but this demonstrates only that the societies are different from capitalism, not that exploitation has ended. It is also true that there is considerable inequality, but this does not show that capitalism has been re-invented. What is needed is an approach which can take due account of these facts.

Lane (1982) has made a valuable contribution in charting the extent of social inequality in Eastern Europe and in trying to explain it in terms of the societies as they are and not on the basis of facile generalizations about the inevitability of inequality. Thus he argues that, by abolishing private property, they have ceased to be capitalist, for the direct inheritance of wealth has been ended. They are not, however, socialist because, as he frequently points out, the level of productive forces remains undeveloped, which means that problems of scarcity and distribution loom large. Hence, he concludes, they are transitional. But in transit to what? Is it implicit in this approach that, when the productive forces have developed far enough, socialism will become possible? Yet how are we to know when the moment has arrived? Or, to reverse the argument, is it necessarily impossible for 'socialism' to emerge in, say, China because the country is technologically backward? Such difficulties reflect Lane's method of analysis. Despite some very pertinent observations about the Soviet productive system and the tensions within it (e.g. Lane, 1978: 197–315; Lane and O'Dell, 1978), empirical discussion is not connected to a view of state socialism as a distinct mode of production. Its contrast with capitalism is seen in terms of the abolition of private property, and the main interest is in the outcome of the system, in terms of income inequality and other aspects of the distribution of life chances. The operation of the productive system and the generation of social relations within this system is not made a central focus; such a focus is essential if the nature of industrial conflict is to be understood.

The Mode of Production

As noted in chapter 2, it is common for Marxists such as Roemer (1982), as well as for non-Marxists such as Lane, to see the abolition of private property as the key break between capitalism and state socialism. But this is not decisive. It is incorrect to see the ownership or non-ownership of property as central to the basis of exploitation in capitalism, since workers can own property and still be exploited. It is the effective control of productive resources that is important. State socialism differs from capitalism because the principles governing the economy are different. Garnsey (1982: 18, 29) argues that, although the occupational structure resembles that of the West, the reasons for the growth of the structure are not the same as those operating under capitalism: governmental decisions and not market forces were the reason for such things as the shift of workers out of agriculture. She goes on to identify four ways in which capital accumulation differs from that under capitalism: it is carried out by central planning authorities and not the market; planners, not managers, choose the technology to be employed; profit is not the aim; and market competition is not involved.

The system has contradictions, but they are different from those characteristic of capitalism. Ticktin (1973) sees one major contradiction as lying in relations between the central administration and local officials. The economy is not so much planned from the centre, in the sense of there being internally consistent sets of targets that can be put into practice locally, as administered. Planners cannot decide prices and quantities for every product, and instead they administer the economy by setting targets for each enterprise. The enterprises will try to meet their targets without regard for the consequences elsewhere in the economy and without regard to the overall rationality of their endeavours. An output target, for example, will encourage the production of low-quality goods that may not meet any real need. The result, according to Ticktin, is an enormous wastefulness in the use of productive resources. Enterprises have an interest in hoarding labour and materials to make the attainment of output targets as easy as possible, and there is no means of attacking this hoarding, which is widely seen as a central feature of the Soviet economy. Some interesting, if dated, information emerged from interviews carried out with 26 emigres in 1950 (Berliner, 1952: 353–6). Practices used to attain targets included inflated estimates of raw materials needed; the simulation of plan achievement by reducing quality and producing an assortment of goods that was easiest to manufacture; and producing only those goods that were included in the formal aims of the plan, for example, making machines but no spare parts.

In addition to what might be called these structural contradictions of an administered economy, there are various dynamic contradictions. Nuti (1979) has developed a model in which the interaction of capital accumulation, economic decentralization, and political liberalization produces a cycle of development. There is an inherent tendency to over-investment. Unlike capitalism, in which constraints on profitability lead to a lack of investment and to crises of unemployment, state socialism is dominated by the long-run aims of the planners to develop the system: investment and growth are highly valued. A cycle emerges in which rigid central planning and problems with integrating enterprises lead to dislocations and declining economic performance. Economic decentralization is seen as the answer, but the bias towards accumulation still exists and is worsened by problems of inflation, which were previously suppressed. The production of consumer goods is not greatly increased, and groups adversely affected by decentralization such as the old-style enterprise managers complain. Decentralisation is abandoned, and centralized control is re-established.

The state's planners are thus actively involved in managing the economy in a far more direct way than occurs within capitalism. As Lane (1978: 300) puts it, 'it is the state bureaucrats who have the power and organisation to run the economy, the industrial manager is a subordinate'. Yet the managers are not totally powerless, for they decide how centrally determined targets are to be achieved. The contradiction between their position and the demands of the central plan provides a major dynamic for the operation of the system.

This perspective can be taken further by considering Arnot's (1981) case study of a productivity experiment. Arnot begins by arguing that the conflict between central administrators and enterprise managers, although important, is not the basic contradiction of the system. Administrators and managers are members of the ruling group, and disputes between them are secondary to the fundamental contradiction, namely that between those who produce the surplus and those who dispose of it (pp. 38–40). The present argument shares this view. As indicated above (p. 63), state socialism can be considered to be exploitative because the immediate producers own neither the means of production with which they work nor all of their labour-power. There is therefore a structured antagonism between them and all those involved in the organization of the production process. As argued in detail below, forms of industrial conflict can be seen to be integral to the mode of production and not mere anachronisms arising from a feudal past or the result of capitalistic modes of thought among a few 'deviants'. But this fundamental antagonism is shaped by the other conflicts that are endemic in state socialism. Thus the ways in which workers use their ability to influence how their labour-power is deployed reflect the opportunities open to them. The systemic tendency for enterprise managers to be wasteful, for example, gives workers useful bargaining leverage in that managers may be willing to tolerate a high level of manning because it provides them with a cushion in meeting their targets. Just as, in capitalism, workers' general ability to act within the labour process is shaped by the managerial control system, the competitive environment, and other things, so, in state socialism, this same general ability is affected by other features of the economic system.

This point emerges from the details of Arnot's case study of the Shchekino Experiment, which was basically a productivity deal introduced in a chemicals works in 1967. The aim was to reduce manning levels and to distribute the benefits among the remaining workers, and the experiment was hailed as a success. This must be seen in context, however, for, as Arnot (p. 46) notes, even after the experiment manning levels were very high: a new Western-built facility designed to be operated by 178 workers required 806 Soviet operatives (a good example of the size of the tendency to hoard labour). There were also problems with the experiment itself, notably in persuading workers that they were redundant when they had been brought up to believe that such a thing was impossible under Soviet planning. Moreover, profit is not the means to allocate scarce resources and thus there were no benefits in terms of profitability and 'performance' that accrued to the enterprise itself; there were, and are, thus powerful barriers against the generalization of the experiment to the economy as a whole. A further condition for the extension of the experiment is, as Arnot (pp. 53–5) stresses, the reintroduction of unemployment. This might have the benefit of increasing industrial discipline but would have the crucial drawback of undermining the legitimacy of the system. In capitalism the logic of the market is so established that firms can explain the need for redundancy in terms of market forces: such things are inevitable if undesirable. State socialism lacks any similar means of legitimation, for the use of unemployment would plainly be a political decision and would contradict many of the claimed benefits of the system.

Apart from illustrating how the cycle of decentralization and centralization identified by Nuti works, this case points to some broad problems facing central planners and plant managers. Workers are exploited but they are told that private property and exploitation have been abolished. How then are they persuaded to work? Burawoy (1985: ch. 4) has made a notable attempt to answer this question.

Social Relations of Production
Burawoy uses the well-known description of piecework in a Hungarian tractor factory by Haraszti (1977) as his starting point. The major feature of the factory was a coercive regime involving strict supervision, the forcing of workers to neglect safety standards in the pursuit of production, the cutting of piecework prices, and the absence of any real rights for the shopfloor workers. Workers tolerated this system for a variety of reasons. Once they were playing the game of trying to make out they were sucked into it and accepted its logic. They had to work hard because basic wages were so low as not to support even a subsistence level of earnings: workers had to work or starve. The workforce was divided, the auxiliary workers sharing many interests with management; and with promotion to an auxiliary grade such as that of tool-setter being an important aspiration for shopfloor workers, production workers were forced into competition with each other. In short, piecework was used by a dominant management in ways having important similarities to the 'market despotism' of competitive capitalism: powerful managements were able to force workers to work hard, for if they did not do so they would lose their livelihoods. The difference is that state socialism cannot rely on loss of the job as a means to remove a worker's source of income: instead jobs are guaranteed, but wages are kept very low. Crucial to the process is the state itself. Under market despotism, the market itself provides the necessary discipline, whereas under state socialism there develops a bureaucratic despotism involving extra-economic forms of coercion. 'Distinctive to the politics of bureaucratic despotism is the harnessing of the party and trade union structures to the managerial function' (Burawoy, 1985: 181). For example, party officials support

the dictatorship of management, and trade unions do not provide a means to express grievances.

The connections between political apparatuses and management require some further comment, for, as noted above, the usual interpretation of state socialism is that the party is dominant and that managers are subordinate. Burawoy takes a perhaps exaggeratedly shopfloor perspective on the issue. It is true that, to the shopfloor worker worried about piecework prices, the party or trade union official may simply appear to back up the power of management. But to what is this power directed? — to the achievement of production goals that themselves depend on the politically determined central plan. Managerial power and authority has no independent role in the way in which, in capitalism, managers represent the demands of the system as a whole for profit and accumulation. Party and trade union bureaucracies may be used to support managerial authority at shopfloor level, but at a higher level this authority must necessarily depend on the political structure, for it is the structure which determines the dynamics of state socialism.

There is, then, a complex array of economic, political, and ideological factors which generate a set of social relations of production, which in turn shape workers' expectations and behaviour. Workers are presented with an overwhelming reality of domination, and they have to cope with the situation as best they can. Burawoy goes on to suggest, however, that the position in the tractor factory may not be characteristic of state socialism as a whole. (This appears to be a development of his earlier comparison of piecework machine shops in the West and the East (Burawoy, 1980), in which he treated Haraszti's account as being broadly characteristic of a whole structure of bureaucratic despotism).[1] He argues that the extreme form of

1 In the course of this discussion Burawoy (1985: 183) makes a significant alteration to his overall perspective, when he compares bureaucratic despotism with capitalist market despotism. He had formerly argued that the latter arose under conditions of competitive markets, and was criticized for neglecting cases such as building where competition has been associated with craft control. He now accepts that, in sectors 'such as construction, we find craft workers retaining control of production despite the existence of a competitive market structure'. But it is not clear how he can integrate this aside into his overall framework: if competition in the market and despotism in the factory do not necessarily go together, how is the development of the capitalist labour process to be explained? The present argument, developed below, is that workplace control reflects a complex of elements so that, within parameters established by the nature of the mode of production and by the characteristic of the social formation, individual industries vary in their modes of control. In the case of building, the size of employing organizations, the craft nature of the work process, and the peculiar nature of the product (with a high degree of competition but also with contracts for specific pieces of work that gave firms short-run monopolies) interacted to sustain craft controls. These often helped

managerial domination observed by Haraszti reflected an unusual financial squeeze. This was caused by attempts to increase enterprises' performance and accountability associated with Hungarian efforts to decentralize decision-making and to strengthen the market. As will be seen below, there is evidence that in several state socialist countries, including Hungary, workers have been able to exert some influence over the labour process and to develop informal bargaining. The nature of the administered economy necessarily makes this possible.

The problem with Burawoy's account, however, is what conclusions should be drawn about the concept of bureaucratic despotism from the considerable modifications that have to be made to it if the breadth of experience under state socialism is to be understood. Is despotism still the underlying principle of social relations in the workplace, or is it merely an extreme case? If the latter; then what other concepts have to be deployed? As indicated in chapter 2, the approach adopted here is to abandon the attempt, which characterizes numerous writers apart from Burawoy, to extract the essential principles of the social relations of production associated with particular modes of production. Each mode certainly has characteristics peculiar to itself which place distinct pressures on relations within the workplace. But there are contradictions between the two aspects of relations between dominant and subordinate groups, namely the elements of co-operation and conflict. How these aspects are brought together depends on a range of contingent factors. In the case of state socialism the concept of bureaucratic despotism does not advance the analysis of work relations. These can just as readily be assessed in terms of the pressures that are characteristic of the mode of production and the forms of adjustment that people make to these pressures. Despite these difficulties, Burawoy's analysis is valuable for its careful assessment of the characteristics of different patterns of control and of the connections between the component parts of each pattern. For present purposes, however, it is more important to turn to actual behaviour. That is, having outlined the key points of the mode of production and the social relations of the labour process, the most concrete level of analysis, namely forms of behaviour and their significance as indices of 'conflict', must be addressed.

Forms of Workplace Behaviour

It is now well known that industrial conflict has not been eradicated from state socialism. Most attention has been devoted to the strikes

employers to regulate the industry (Price, 1980; Jackson, 1984). It is not a matter of 'competition' producing despotism but of the precise nature of this competition and its interaction with other aspects of work organization.

and mass protests that have broken out from time to time (described by, for example, Belotsevkovsky, 1978). Yet, just as conflicts at work under slavery have to be understood in terms of day-to-day behaviour and not the rare outbreaks of mass protest, so forms of bargaining within the labour process under state socialism warrant particular attention. This is often recognized, but lack of information obviously makes detailed analysis difficult. Holubenko (1975: 8), for example, notes in a much-cited article that the general pattern of protest is individualized and is expressed in forms that officialdom labels as 'social problems' or 'deviance': absenteeism, labour turnover, and alcoholism. Yet the bulk of his article is taken up with describing strikes and not with assessing the role of 'deviant behaviour'. Other writers (e.g. Connor, 1979: 318) stress that the style of the industrial organization is tolerant of absenteeism and slacking. 'Despotism' is in practice greatly modified.

As already noted, there is a day-to-day toleration of these formally unacceptable practices because managers have to ensure that the production process continues. Turnover as such is not frowned upon, because it can be for good reasons. There is, however, considerable concern about the rate of job-switching; numerous studies have appeared about turnover (their main points are summarized by Teckenberg, 1978; Pravda, 1979: 334–8), although they tend to focus on proximate influences, leaving implicit the question of how far turnover can be seen as some sort of index of discontent. Teckenberg (p. 194) produces figures suggesting that average turnover rates in the Soviet Union are higher than those in the West. Yet such direct comparisons may be dangerous. Given the permanently tight labour markets of a state socialist system, it is not surprising that workers readily change jobs. Since, moreover, basic welfare provisions depend on the state, and not on service with a particular employer as do such benefits in the West as redundancy payments (irrelevant in the Soviet Union in any event) and pension rights, the constraints on moving are also weak. Some conclusions can, however, be reached. First, the possibility of changing jobs without too many questions being asked represents an important safety-valve, although it would be unwise to equate high turnover directly with a state of conflict. Second, frequent quitting is possible only because enterprise managements tolerate it by, for example, taking on workers who have not gone through the proper procedures in leaving their previous jobs. This implies that turnover can involve accommodation with the system in so far as workers are willing to exchange one job for another. It need not involve any specific challenge to the system, being an individual response to a given set of opportunities. Third, however, it may put some pressure on managements to moderate the terms of exploitation so as to retain labour and ensure the fulfilment of production targets.

Various forms of rule-violation in the workplace, especially absenteeism and alcoholism, are more disliked by the authorities since they have no balancing aspects; they are, however, tolerated and some workers are able to defy disciplinary codes in the knowledge that they are important to the enterprise and that they will not be dismissed (Pravda, 1979: 339–41). In the absence of detailed investigations of the social meanings of absence and of its effects in different types of enterprise, it is difficult to go beyond this general point to consider, for example, how far workers consciously view going absent as an escape from an intolerable authority in the workplace or under what conditions managements are willing to bend or ignore the rules. It is certainly possible to conclude that the behaviour is too systematic and widespread for official explanations, in terms of the lack of socialist virtues of absentees and their generally 'deviant' characteristics, to be sustained. Yet, as with turnover, and in common with the position in the West, going absent contains elements of accommodation to the system, albeit an accommodation which is at variance with the official ideology. It is a way in which individual workers can gain some satisfaction, not only by escaping work but also by enjoying the act of beating the system for its own sake. Managements tolerate it because they need workers' co-operation, and the behaviour cannot therefore be interpreted directly as a form of 'industrial conflict' that is as an action in which workers and managers have directly opposing interests. It plainly says something about the average Soviet worker's commitment to the productive system as a whole. But even then it should not be interpreted as an action which is necessarily anti-authority. In their day-to-day lives workers know that they have to attain a production target but they also know that this target is often set arbitrarily. In adopting a pragmatic approach, wherein absenteeism at one time is balanced by another characteristic feature of the Soviet system, namely 'storming' to attain targets in the days at the end of each production period, they are able to gain some control over the timing of the expenditure of their own labour power. There may not be any wider or continuing consequences.

What of the other side of workers' workplace behaviour, namely their rights as employees? Just as arbitrary management power in the West is moderated by legal rights and collective bargaining agreements, so the Soviet worker is not simply subject to managerial whims. As already indicated, a major difference from capitalism is the general absence of unemployment and the inability of management to declare workers redundant. In addition, there are constraints on managerial freedom to dismiss workers for breaches of working rules. Workers cannot be sacked without the agreement of the enterprise union committee, and even if this agreement is given individuals have the right of appeal to the courts. The courts have routinely re-instated workers in cases where, regardless of the merits of the case or the endorsement of managerial actions by the union, the union's agreement has not been sought prior to a dismissal. The re-instatement remedy is used in about half of all cases coming to the courts (Ruble, 1979: 60–3). Facile comparisons with the West again have to be avoided, and there remains the question of how far, in practice, workers' rights are defended by trade union committees. But it should not be concluded that, just because unions share the managerial aim of attaining targets, they necessarily fail in their representative duties. Western unions, after all, can be production-conscious while being able and willing to protect individuals from what they see as management victimization or a managerial failure to follow proper procedures.

Again, the absence of detailed studies makes it impossible to reach a proper assessment. It is certainly possible to question the simple view that workers are powerless, and hence to accept the general conclusion of Sabel and Stark (1982: 461) that workers are not powerless and that the situation of effort bargaining is similar to that in capitalism during a prolonged spell of full employment. Thus, in a rare case-study at factory level, Hethy and Mako (1974) demonstrate that work group behaviour in a Hungarian factory making railway carriages has obvious similarities with behaviour observed under capitalism. They discovered, for example, the phenomenon of quota restriction which is familiar from the work of Roy (1952): when 'bad' jobs on which it was difficult to attain satisfactory levels of piecework earnings were introduced, there was a collective withdrawal of effort, and workers were willing to increase their efforts only when 'good' jobs were introduced which made the expenditure of effort worthwhile.

Yet there is the danger, in challenging the picture of the repressed and powerless worker, of implying that the situation is totally open and that workers have as much bargaining power as their Western counterparts. The point of trying to identify distinct features of a state-socialist productive system is to try to identify specific parameters that shape the labour process. Bargaining power cannot take the same significance that it has under capitalism because workers are not free wage-labourers: collective and individual withdrawals of work are in practice possible but they involve behaviour which generally remains formally illicit and they cannot be legitimized by reference to the official ideology. As Hyman and Brough (1975: 21, emphasis in original) note, 'capitalist ethics might appear to invite the worker to apply *in his own interests* the principle of buying in the cheapest and selling in the dearest market, to seek the maximum earnings for the minimum effort'. There is no similar invitation under state socialism.

The consequences of struggles at the point of production are thus likely to be more diffuse and uncertain than they are under capitalism. It is, of course, true that the contrast should not be made too sharply. Capitalism does not, in general, involve a clash between overtly class-conscious groupings of capital and labour. Instead, a series of day-to-day struggles takes place which may come to influence subsequent relationships without either side having the outcome which in fact emerges as a deliberate aim. Yet a wider class-consciousness remains a possibility, and there is nothing in the organizing principles of capitalism to prevent class-based organizations from emerging. Under state socialism there are constraints on such developments which are not just quantitatively greater but which are qualitatively different. Capitalism is based on the explicit recognition of the separation between capital and labour, whereas state socialism is supposed to overcome this separation by expropriating the class of capitalists. Any developed class-based action necessarily challenges this supposition. It is thus not surprising to find that the authorities' reaction to large collective protests tends to be swift and relentless. Yet activities at the point of production reflect the duality of relations: workers' attempts to alter the wage-effort bargain are limited by the potential challenge that they can offer to the legitimations of the system as a whole, but at the same time the authorities have to tolerate some such attempts if the system is to continue to function.

There are, of course, significant variations between state socialist countries, for example in the extent to which market-like mechanisms are used to try to obviate the problems of central planning. Specialists have assessed the causes and consequences of these differences in terms of the overall operation of the economy. But there appears to be little systematic information on differing patterns of workplace relations. The patchy information above certainly suggests that conditions in Hungary may have been different from those in the Soviet Union, with market mechanisms in the former country leading to two contrasting outcomes: intense despotism and a degree of collective piecework bargaining. Which of the two arose in a given factory must have depended on the nature of market pressures and the sense of solidarity of individual work groups. In the Soviet Union, it may be argued, market-like mechanisms were absent, and labour hoarding and its associated practices of slacking, absenteeism, and labour turnover were more in evidence. But the hard evidence to support this contrast or to extend it to other countries is lacking.

Feasible Socialism?

To conclude this section, and also in a sense the discussion of exploitative modes of production as a whole, it will be useful to consider briefly the possibility of overcoming the conflicts within state socialism. Socialism's promise is to transcend the class divisions of feudalism and capitalism. But is a non-exploitative mode of production conceivable?

Nove (1983) has addressed this issue in his consideration of what he calls feasible socialism, which he defines (p. 11) as that which is attainable within one lifetime, that is without wishing away the problem by assuming material abundance or a massive change in human attitudes and behaviour. Much of Nove's work is in fact less a blueprint for feasible socialism than a detailed analysis of the problems of existing state socialist systems and a refutation of attempts to minimize the size of these problems. He focuses particularly on issues of pricing and allocation, arguing that there have been, and remain, huge problems with operating an administered economy. Even in the case of Yugoslavia, where statist centralization has been replaced by self-managed enterprises, there are difficulties (pp. 135–7). Within each enterprise there is a tendency for the surplus to be distributed so as to maximize incomes, with accumulation for the future being neglected. And even if this problem were overcome there would remain the difficulty of integrating enterprises into the economy. If a genuine capitalist market is rejected, and if central planning is seen as too directive and is also abandoned, there is no way of co-ordinating production and investment decisions. Inflation and unemployment are ever-present possibilities because each enterprise considers only its own position, and externalities are neglected.

Although Nove refuses to shy away from these problems, there is one area where he fails to follow through his rigorous approach. This is the production process. He writes (p. 212, emphasis in original) 'there would be no exploitation' under his model of feasible socialism 'except in so far as a *working* owner-manager may be thought to be deriving additional income from his few employees'. There would be few employers, and these would be working proprietors and not capitalists living on the work of others, so that the problem of exploitation would be very small. This seems to take a very narrow view of exploitation as something that occurs on a face-to-face basis. But Nove is assuming that there would not be material abundance, and it follows that a complex division of labour would be required. A group of workers would exist whose tasks were defined by others. There would, presumably, be a high degree of detailed control of work tasks, but there would have to be co-ordination and direction. This would, in turn, mean that workers were subjected to general control in the sense that the broad aims of the production process and the principles of co-ordination were established elsewhere. It might be the case that some of these principles were open to democratic discussion, but in a highly complex production system authoritative decisions would still have to be made. It is, in short, unlikely that the production process could become one of the smooth transformation of inputs into outputs.

This is not to suggest that struggles to control the labor process would necessarily resemble those in currently existing societies. The aim of this chapter has, indeed, been to point to the different shape of struggles in different modes of production. Neither is it being argued that an attempt to introduce feasible socialism is necessarily naively utopian. It may be that workers would find the forms of control that it produced preferable to those practised elsewhere. But it should not be supposed that the general problem of extracting effort from producers that characterizes any mode of production other than the simplest would disappear.

A similar point applies to Wright's (1985: 115) model of the succession from one mode of production to another. He argues that there are four forms of 'exploitation-generating asset inequality'. The first relates to labour-power: in some modes of production, producers do not own their own labour-power, feudalism and slavery being cases in point. The second covers the means of production: in these two cases and in capitalism, effective control of the physical means of production lies with the exploiting class. The final two assets are less familiar. First, 'the way the process of production is organized is a productive resource' distinct from other resources (p. 79). Under capitalism the power to co-ordinate production within a complex division of labour lies largely with managers, but because of the anarchy of the market there is no effective co-ordination across firms. These organizational assets become much more significant under state socialism because of the central planning process. The final set of assets is skill: the ability of one group, either through genuine ability or the use of credentials to limit entry to its activities, to secure for itself the fruits of the labour of another group. For Wright, there is a tendency for modes of production to succeed one another. In feudalism all four forms of exploitation are present. Capitalism removes that based on the ownership of the labour-power of other people. State socialism eliminates private control of the means of production. True socialism ends the control of organizational assets by a ruling class. Finally, communism destroys exploitation based on the differential distribution of skills.

This analysis of state socialism is broadly consistent with that advanced above, although the terms are different: there is exploitation because of a division between workers and those who plan the production process. But there are some specific problems. One concerns the treatment of skills as a source of exploitation. As Wright admits (p. 106), his view that exploitation is rooted in the monopolization of productive assets is very similar to Parkin's (1979) decidedly non-Marxist account of class structure as the result of practices of social closure. But, underlying detailed questions about Wright's approach, there is the central issue of the organization of the production process. Wright is clear that, as the level of 'social productivity' increases, the probability of accomplishing a transition from one mode of production also increases. Along with writers such as Lane, he would see state socialist societies as being in transition to a higher form of socialism in which exploitation based on the control of organizational assets is eliminated. But, regardless of the level of social productivity, issues concerning the co-ordination of production would still arise. It may be that, in conditions of abundance, a complex division of labour would be unnecessary. But there could be no magic mechanism for deciding who worked at what jobs, how the surplus was to be invested, how prices were to be fixed, and so on. Problems would still arise about the social relations of production.

This is not to suggest that the problems would be identical with those of current societies or that new modes of production cannot supersede existing ones. It is, however, more difficult to assess Wright's view of the future than the view of Nove since the latter is clear that feasible socialism must be achievable within a lifetime: existing problems of scarcity and co-ordination might be altered but would not have disappeared. There is no point in speculating at length about the precise shape of possible future societies. The aim has simply been to underline the point that the production process in existing societies has inherent structured antagonisms between the organizers of production and those who do the work. A future society may alter the nature of these antagonisms but it is not clear how they could be eliminated.

This links with the point, made in chapter 2, that Marxism must presume some necessary trajectory of history. Wright's presentation is honest and lucid. Thus he does not rely on some vague idea of progress but insists that the level of development of the productive forces is the key motor of change. It is not the only factor, but as development proceeds it is more and more likely that a transition from one mode of production to another will occur. Yet it is plain that state socialism did not emerge out of the most developed forms of capitalism. Neither is it clear why the form of exploitation practised under it is more 'advanced' than that existing under capitalism. Private owership of the means of production may have ended, but other elements of the system make the domination of the exploiting group in some ways more total than it is under capitalism. The political apparatuses of the employing organization and the state are fused, so that workers cannot use power in the national political arena to by-pass or challenge controls imposed on them at the level of the firm, whereas there is more freedom in this respect under capitalism. Ideological control is also considerable. Now it is true that this is not total: just as a capitalist worker can use the ideology of the free market to justify trying to increase wages, so the worker under state socialism can sustain a claim for more say in decisions through reference to the fact that ownership is supposed to lie with the workers. But, given the domination of public opinion by the authorities, the extent to which this is possible is limited. In particular, forms of counter-control on the shopfloor can be dismissed as deviant, whereas workers under capitalism have more legitimatory arguments to sustain such behaviour.

It is thus not clear that a transition from more to less exploitative modes of production can be identified. It can be accepted that existing modes of production need not be the end point of history. But it must also be accepted that the control of the production process is likely to remain an issue for any mode of production in the forseeable future. There may be new types of exploitation, and new patterns of behaviour going along with them. Conflict at work will continue to be a significant feature of societies for a long time to come. But more than that cannot be said.

Conclusion: Modes of Control and Compliance

This chapter has had two main aims: to demonstrate the ways in which conflict, and in particular bargaining about the balance of effort and reward, is expressed in non-capitalist modes of production; and to relate these ways to the nature of the mode of production. The latter is the more difficult, for it could be argued that concrete experience is often similar (the similarities between Haraszti's factory and capitalist firms in competitive industries being a case in point) and that modes of conceptualizing this experience are also similar (for example, Genovese's analysis of the ways in which slaves negotiated an order for themselves and thus came to accept the principles of the system has strong parallels with Burawoy's model of workers playing games under capitalism). It is not surprising that there are similarities. The need to extract work from workers is common to all exploitative modes of production, as is the existence of uncertainty within the labour contract. Forms of behaviour also have similarities. The defence of customary rights in feudalism has parallels with custom and practice in a capitalist factory. But the underlying causes and consequences of behaviour are different. Thus the difference between Haraszti's factory and a similar Western one lies in the links in the former between the enterprise's method of control and global politics. These links had important consequences, for example the use of legitimations about the non-conflictful nature of social relations under socialism to induce workers to work hard. Similarly, feudal custom and capitalist custom and practice differ because the nature of the system is different: feudalism has no wage contract, exploitation involves extra-economic coercion, there is no free movement of serfs, and so on. It has also been shown that specific forms of behaviour take on different roles in different modes of production. In capitalism labour turnover is legitimate; under state socialism it has a more shadowy existence, while it is totally illegitimate in slavery. In this last case, moreover, the individual act of running away and the collective one of rebellion are likely to have stemmed from similar causes, whereas under capitalism a quite different logic operates.

In considering the links between behaviour and the nature of a mode of production, reference has been made to various ideological legitimations that may be employed. It will be useful to draw this discussion together. Feudal serfs accepted much of the ideology of a community of interest and mutual obligations. This is not to say that they totally internalized everything about the system. But it is to suggest that in their daily practice they took for granted, and also used, various features of the system. Thus the defence of custom or the attempt to have rights and duties specified in charters reflected means of operating within existing social relations. Similarly, as Genovese stresses, slaves developed views of what was a proper level of effort and disliked shirkers. This was part of an acceptance of the idea of rights and duties within a slave economy. Ideological elements are also important in the cohesion of state socialist systems. Thus the idea that workers cannot really want to strike because they own the means of production and would be striking against themselves is an important way of rendering collective industrial action illegitimate. Such ideological elements should not be seen as deliberate manipulations by ruling groups or as sets of ideas that are simply imposed on the subordinates. They are among a range of ways in which people make sense of the world and are not necessarily created by ruling groups with the aim of incorporating subordinates. In particular, like other parts of society, they have internal contradictions such that, for example, feudal serfs could use aspects of the ideology of feudalism to question, if not the fact of their subordination, at least the ways in which that subordination was expressed in concrete obligations.[2] Ideologies are not just means of persuading people to accept their lot. They are ways of thinking which reflect the contradictory nature of a mode of production as a whole. Thus in carrying out their duties workers develop ways of making sense of the world, they come to take certain things for granted while questioning others, and they operate with logics that are derived from the ideology of the system as a whole.

This is not the place to try to develop a detailed statement about the nature of ideology. The aim of this chapter, and of the study as a whole, has been to examine how work relations are structured under different conditions. The stress on ideology serves more as a way of drawing together some implications than as a focus in its own right. One key point running through the study has been that the problem of gaining compliance is general to all modes of production. Thus competitive capitalism does not rely solely on the coercion of the market to secure compliance. Management has to work actively to sustain the appropriate ideology of the need for hard work, and intense control of the effort bargain often goes along with paternalist traditions. Feudalism did not 'force' serfs to work on the lord's land but developed an ideology of reciprocity to explain why serfs owed obligations to the lord. And this ideology, it is crucial to note, was not just a sham. At the level of day-to-day life there was reciprocity: work and loyalty, in return for the lord's protection. The reciprocity was not based on the exchange of equivalents, for the lord was living on the surplus produced by the serfs. But an ideology based on ideas of reciprocity and customary understandings helped the system to cohere: it simultaneously expressed the contradictions of the system and provided the means of creating sufficient acceptance of its underlying principles to permit the labour process to continue to operate. Even slavery can involve powerful ideological elements, as Genovese's analysis of the South in terms of paternalism and

---

2 Abercrombie *et al.* (1980) have argued powerfully against what they call the 'dominant ideology thesis': the idea that the ruling class creates a coherent set of beliefs with the aim of incorporating the subordinate class into the system by inculcating the pertinent beliefs. Yet this is a very strong definition of ideology, and the authors' argument is not pertinent to other approaches (see Rootes, 1981). The approach outlined here owes much to Burawoy (1979: 17–18), although it must be admitted that the present argument, and possibly that of Burawoy too, does not constitute a developed statement about the character of ideology.

hegemony shows. Reliance on force alone seems to be limited to specific types of slave economies.[3]

The concept of hegemony thus has a broad application. Each of the modes of production considered above had a set of economic, political, and ideological structures that cohered to form a social order. Subordinate groups could influence these structures. Indeed, a further major theme of this study has been that 'resistance' is not just a response to an existing structure of domination but can also alter the nature of that structure. Subordinates also learn to live with the system and come to take for granted some of its assumptions.

If this is so, how is change to be explained? It has been argued in earlier chapters that typologies of modes of control under capitalism do not work very well. In particular, several models of development have been proposed, either with consent replacing force or with bureaucratic systems supplanting technical control and direct control. If these are rejected for their neglect of consent under competitive conditions and for their inability to grasp the duality of the capital-labour relation, then there arises the question of what should replace them. The answer suggested here is that a more modest, but at the same time more complex, view of development is needed.

Any mode of production can be subject to change as relations between constituent elements change. Capitalism is often seen as a particularly dynamic mode, because of the drive to accumulate. But studies of feudalism also point to changing relations between the towns and the country and the alteration of the bond between serf and lord (for example the commutation of labour services to rent). Change can be analysed at any of the three levels: the mode of production, the social formation, or the individual company or establishment. The degree of variability within a more concrete level will depend on factors at a higher level of generality. For example, state socialism as a mode of production puts fairly strong constraints on variations between individual countries, but plainly some variations are possible. Within each country the demands of central planning tend to govern the ways in which individual enterprises operate: either they are all subordinate to the central authority or they are all given quasi-market

---

3 A familiar theme from academic and literary studies of prison camps and similar organizations warrants mention. The person who rebels against oppression and brutality is often the focus. But among most subordinates there develop means of accommodation to the system in which loopholes are exploited and a structure of informal rules emerges. The subordinates impose an order on each other. The rebel stands apart, and may be admired from afar but is also disliked for upsetting existing arrangements and creating the danger that the authorities will punish everyone. Working within the system, and therefore engaging in practices that sustain the ideology of the system, is likely to be the preferred option for many people.

signals. The ability of enterprises to develop their own systems of control is limited. Under capitalism there may be more variation because the mode of production permits more variety at the level of the social formation. The latter level can constrain enterprises fairly tightly, most obviously where there is strong state intervention in factory regimes, or leave them free to develop their own solutions to the problem of compliance.

Paths of development at each level of analysis can be charted. Thus, changing technology and the growth of firms have dramatically altered the shape of capitalism over the past two centuries. The workplace, together with the forms of control practised within it, has changed as a consequence. But this change should be seen not as the unfolding of different self-contained types of control but as a complex and uncertain process. Economic, political, and ideological elements altered in different ways and at different speeds. Any account of such developments needs to be more modest than one based around models of control because it concentrates on the details of concrete developments and tries to understand their consequences instead of applying broad typologies to events that fit such typologies uneasily. Similarly, at the level of the social formation, different trends in different countries can be assessed. As argued in chapters 4 and 5, developments in the United States during the twentieth century, for example, should not be seen as a shift from technical to bureaucratic forms of control, not least because each 'form' can be discerned within the same pattern of relations. Instead, a complex of factors including the intervention of the state, the shape of trade unionism, and employers' own views of their labour problem led to a shift away from autocratic forms of management to more constitutional methods based on collective bargaining. The consequences for workplace behaviour can then be addressed. Finally, as indicated in chapter 6, it is possible to analyse patterns of relations at the level of the individual workplace. What emerges is that, even within one social formation at one time, there are wide variations in the types of control applied by managements and that workers have differing abilities to influence the frontier of control. These variations reflect such things as the precise nature of a firm's product market circumstances (for which the degree of competition is often an inadequate proxy) and the technical division of labour. But also crucial is the tradition of struggle within which these things are incorporated.

One result of giving attention to the impact of contingent influences and to the complex nature of modes of control is that the idea of clear-cut stages of control is lost. This is, however, a price that has to be paid if the analysis of concrete activities is to be advanced. The approach adopted here does not, however, simply reject broad interpretations in favour of concentrating on empirical detail. It suggests a way of analysing that detail through a hierarchy of concepts such as the mode of production, the relative autonomy of the labour process, the relative autonomy of the state, the frontier of control, and the effort bargain. With such concepts it is possible to make sense of reality without reducing it to a manifestation of an ideal type. Thus it is possible to ask how systems of control cohere, and to consider the interplay of economic, political and ideological elements which make up a given system. At the same time, space that subordinates have to affect the nature of the effort bargain can be analysed.

A similar perspective can be applied to changes from one mode of production to another. The point has already been made in differentiating between a materialist and Marxist model (above, p. 96), that a materialist approach does not espouse an evolutionary view of history: for a Marxist there must be a direction to history, whereas materialism not only has no need for such claims but also opposes them. Capitalism did not necessarily emerge from feudalism. As Holton (1985) argues in his assessment of this issue, feudalism may have had internal contradictions, but these are more useful in explaining the decline of serfdom than in accounting for the rise of capitalism. Capitalism emerged long after the decay of feudalism, and then only in some Western European countries. For Holton, the reasons lie in the extent to which a centralized nation-state was established and in the structure of land-holding. Change depended on a range of contingent factors and not on pressures stemming from the forces of production. Similarly, as noted above, it has been argued that capitalism's attack on slavery did not depend primarily on any incompatiblity between slavery and developing capitalist forces of production.

Modes of production differ in the nature of exploitation within them and in the patterns of work relations that emerge. The 'base' does not determine the shape of these relations, and neither does it impose a direction on the course of history. In looking at behaviour that goes under the rubric of industrial conflict or worker resistance, the task is to explore the complex ways in which compliance and conflict are produced and to relate them to the structure of the situation without reducing action to structure or seeing actions as free-floating. This study has tried to put this programme into effect.

Conclusion

This study has developed a theoretical approach to workplace relations and illustrated the applicability of the approach through discussion of a wide range of empirical examples. It has attempted not only to discuss issues such as conflict and control in the workplace in broad terms, but also to consider in some detail specific forms of behaviour and to discuss how the social organization of work gives them their shape and significance. To analyse behaviour in terms of conflict or resistance is unsatisfactory because it makes unwarranted assumptions about the characteristics and aims of the behaviour, in particular that a given activity involves either conflict or co-operation, and not a mixture of both. It does not help to analyse workplace relations as the outcome of capitalists' (or other dominant groups') attempts to control the labour process and workers' attempts at resistance. Capitalists do not necessarily seek control of every aspect of work relations, workers' behaviour involves adaptation as well as resistance, and the control *versus* resistance model has a curiously ahistorical flavour, with the interactions and development of employers' and workers' behaviour being given little role. Instead, workplace relations need to be seen as involving continuing struggles which develop logics of their own and in which the unintended consequences of actions are important. Shop stewards' controls of manning levels, for example, need not involve any clear resistance to capitalist domination, for they may in some respects ease the managerial task and they may be seen as traditional and sensible ways of getting work done and not as parts of an incessant conflict between workers and employers. Such controls can be seen as reflecting a particular pattern of struggle, defined as the actions which employers and workers take to influence the effort bargain. And they can have various consequences, such as the institutionalization of conflict, in the sense that potential overt conflicts about how many workers are required to do a particular job are treated through a set of rules and understandings. Workplace struggles thus develop in their own ways, and it is necessary to assess how they work and how aspects of conflict and co-operation are constituted through concrete practices, instead of assuming that conflict is a self-evident and self-contained phenomenon.

There is no point in labouring such arguments further. But two issues deserve some brief attention. The first is the theoretical one of the role ascribed to struggle at the point of production in the development of modes of production. The second is what practical message a personnel manager or shop steward might derive from a materialist approach.

On the former, there is a danger of treating struggle as the deliberate attempts that managements make to control the labour process and that workers make to resist this control. Actions are then reduced to the working out of a structural logic, and the aspects of historical development and of the processes of definition and negotiation that take place within the labour process are played down. And the structural logic is itself reduced to one in which capitalists are permanently trying to overcome workers' resistance. A dialectical process is rendered as a uni-dimensional and uni-linear one.

Struggle has been defined here as the behaviour of workers and managers that influence the terms of work relations. The extent of struggle is variable, and struggle can go along with behaviour that reflects an acceptance, by either side, of the current situation. Workers' struggles are not the sole, or even necessarily the most important, reasons for capitalists' attempts to rationalize the production process, for problems of realizing surplus value can be equally important and, within the workplace itself, there can be obstacles to the creation of surplus value which stem not from workers' actions but from the organization of the process as a whole.

The present approach has tried to avoid an extreme position in which class struggle is ignored or elevated to privileged status. Struggles at the point of production can have effects on capitalists' ability to direct production and on the process of accumulation, as the discussions in chapters 5 and 6 have suggested. Such struggles should not, however, be seen as ubiquitous or as separate from other aspects of capitalist development. Shopfloor controls and restrictive practices often depend on managerial behaviour for their growth and consolidation, and their effects on profitability and accumulation have to be seen in the context of many other aspects of the operation of the enterprise. As has been stressed throughout, moreover, such controls are unlikely to be seen by those operating them as being deliberate forms of struggle or resistance. Neither should struggle at the point of production be reduced, as it often is in practice, to workers' activities: it necessarily involves managers. Particular struggles develop logics of their own, and they reflect complex patterns of accommodation between the two sides. They are not the outcome of resistance on the part of workers to capitalist plans which, were it not for this resistance, would operate smoothly.

In developing empirical analyses that take account of these points, it has been necessary to develop rather complicated characterizations of modes of control and the nature of workplace behaviour. In avoiding the view that 'class struggle' is the motor of historical change and in eschewing stereotypes of modes of control and patterns of 'production politics' there is obviously the danger of providing few easy models. The foregoing account is less easily absorbed than one stressing a shift from despotism to hegemony or a move from simple to bureaucratic control. But, in view of the widespread scepticism about such accounts, it is important to try to move beyond them. The foregoing discussion has not attempted yet another textbook introduction to or simplification of complex issues. If one lesson, namely that workplace relations are complex and multi-faceted, has been absorbed then the study will have had some value. More importantly, a theoretical approach to the understanding of this complexity has been indicated and empirical illustrations have been developed. The world is complex, and a genuinely dialectical approach cannot, of necessity, reduce this complexity to a few slogans about control or class struggle. What it can do is provide the tools for thinking about and understanding linkages and mutual interactions.

This leads to the second issue, namely the study's practical consequences. Consider the following construction of what a thoughtful manager might say when confronted with writings taking a radical or Marxist perspective; a trade unionist's concerns would be rather different, but the principles involved are the same. The manager might be willing to grant that trying to understand the complex processes involved in work relations is a valid exercise and to concede that he should not expect immediate practical policy lessons to emerge. But he might be worried about the implication that everything in the workplace involves power and struggle, with any managerial attempt to improve working conditions or to reform payment systems being seen as no more than a ploy to undermine or incorporate workers' organizations. He might also question whether conflict really is inevitable, suggesting perhaps that good working conditions and wages can go together with high productivity and pointing to firms which appear to have overcome the confrontational approach to industrial relations. He could admit that in some very general sense there is still exploitation because workers have to be persuaded to work to goals that are set by others and because in any successful complex organization workers cannot have the right to challenge every decision. But he would point out that such exploitation is necessary to generate a high level of productivity, on which depends the immediate level of wages that can be paid to workers and also the future of employment, for it is only by being profitable that a firm can generate the funds for future investment. He might, finally, argue that in many cases the need for order, discipline and rules is not merely a cloak for the exercise of power. Disciplinary rules, for example, are necessary to ensure that the few workers who transgress against reasonable standards of behaviour, standards moreover that are shared by workers and managers alike, should be brought into line. There need be no policy of punishment for its own sake, and instead desired standards of performance can be achieved through identifying unacceptable conduct and helping the worker involved to correct his or her behaviour.

Whether or not such a reaction is justified, it must be conceded that the use of terms such as exploitation, conflict, and struggle may lead some managers to question the scientific objectivity of many studies of work organization, especially when these studies describe themselves as being radical. The basis of the present answer is that a materialist approach attempts to identify some of the principles underlying work organization and not to imply that actual workplace relations are straight battles for power. Several points warrant emphasis. First, the attention that has been given to non-capitalist modes of production, together with the attempt to define clearly what is meant by capitalism, should dispose of any view that conflict is being seen as peculiar to capitalism or that the term capitalism is little more than a term of abuse. Second, the role of co-operation in the organization of work has been continually underlined. Employers can seek the compliance of their workers in a number of ways, some of which not only rely on workers' creative capacities but also aim to develop these capacities. There is no presumption that workers and employers are continually in conflict, or that all managerially led reforms are, ultimately, attempts to mislead workers from their true destinies. Third, the consideration of exploitation is a theoretical and not an evaluative one. It is not assumed that workers have an over arching interest in overthrowing capitalist domination, and indeed such an assumption has been strenuously attacked. It is claimed that capitalism is exploitative in that surplus value is generated under the constraints of the accumulation process. But this exploitation establishes only the broad nature of the relationships between the abstractions of capital and labour. It does not follow that workers will have an interest in overcoming exploitation since the fact of being exploited cannot be separated from other aspects of the mode of production such as the generation of a certain level of income. The hypothetical manager can happily adopt the theory of exploitation, while also arguing that exploitation is unavoidable and that capitalist exploitation is preferable from the workers' point of view to other modes of exploitation.

This is not to suggest that a materialist approach is simply a sophisticated form of managerialism. A managerial social science is one that takes as its starting point problems as they are perceived by managers and seeks solutions which will be of specific use to managers; it will tend to neglect the interests of other groups in the firm and to pretend that solutions can be found that suit everyone. A materialist approach plainly avoids such problems by, for example, insisting that the effort bargain has to be continually negotiated and that firms are not unitary organizations but are instead based on power relations between groups with differing needs and demands. To argue that a sophisticated manager can accept some of the analysis of a materialist programme is not to suggest that the programme directly serves his interests.

This point leads to the final, and most difficult area, namely what practical lessons can be inferred. It should not be expected that direct prescriptions can emerge from a broadly based attempt to understand and analyse workplace relations. One implication, whose value should not be underestimated, is that the discussion has aimed to improve the understanding of behaviour that goes under the heading of conflict. Managerial decision-makers should have a more sophisticated view of such things as the restriction of effort and sabotage if they have considered carefully the analyses of these phenomena that are discussed in chapter 6. At a more practical level, they should also have an understanding of the circumstances which tend to give rise to particular forms of behaviour, so that they may, for example, come to the view that an amount of pilfering is inevitable in some types of firm and that to attempt to control the behaviour may create more problems than it solves. Another example is the controlling of piecework fiddles, for studies suggest that these assist as well as interfere with production and that attempts at regulation may be unsuccessful and even counter-productive, not least because shop managers cannot meet their production targets without the shopfloor co-operation that the fiddles encourage.

A realistic and critical view of the ways in which organizations work can, moreover, generate analyses that are more helpful than those deriving from a managerialist perspective. As argued at length elsewhere in the case of absenteeism (Edwards and Scullion, 1984), a managerialist approach tends to see absenteeism as the consequence of individual failings on the part of workers, with its connections with the social relations of work not being pursued. The understanding of the causes of the behaviour that results is unduly narrow, and the policy prescriptions that emerge may neglect the fact that for firms in some situations absenteeism is beneficial, to the extent that it reduces discontent in the workplace. In addition, the behaviour may be unavoidable if it is the consequence of a particular organization of work that managers cannot afford to alter. That is, when the behaviour is viewed in the context of the organization as a whole, the nature of the absence problem and the remedies available are seen in a realistic light. A related example is that of discipline, mentioned above in connection with the hypothetical manager's view of 'radical' approaches to industrial relations. Are not discipline and order in the context of public and clear rules better than disorder and confusion, and does not management have a duty as well as a right to develop appropriate rules and procedures? The point may have some relevance in criticizing an ultra-left argument to the effect that disciplinary rules are merely clever means of diverting workers from their true ends. But it does not damage careful attempts to relate discipline to the broader pattern of control of the work process. Such attempts note the assumptions underlying the view that management must create order. These include the idea that rules will necessarily be in the interests of all groups within an organization; the view that rules can cover every eventuality with their application to particular cases being routine and straightforward; and the belief that statements contained in rulebooks cover what actually goes on at shopfloor level. Analyses would then go on to point out that managements often do not live up to their ideals, with disciplinary rules being forgotten when it is convenient to do so. Although the rules do not simply confuse and mislead workers, neither are they objective statements of organizational rationality as some managerialist texts suggest. The argument has been pursued in detail elsewhere (Edwards and Dickens, forthcoming). For present purposes, the key point is that a critical appraisal of matters such as absenteeism and discipline can look at the organizational politics involved and assess possible courses of action in the light of such realities. The results may not be comfortable for managers if, for example, they suggest that managerial aims are unrealistic or that managers do not apply rules in the disinterested way that they claim to. The approach will neither condemn management out of hand nor take such a closely managerialist perspective that the real issues are ignored.

An approach claiming to be materialist is plainly not the only one capable of addressing matters of workplace relations in a disinterested way and of providing an informed basis for policy-making. There is a long tradition of research that does so. But the concepts and arguments of the present study range further than assessments of particular problems and situations. It is important to demonstrate that they do not prevent attention to matters of immediate concern and that they do not take a naively 'radical' view of the nature of conflict in industry. Most importantly, a materialist analysis can be accepted in principle by people committed to the capitalist system. In practice it may be unlikely that managers will accept critiques of their disciplinary arrangements, since it would require giving up the myths and convenient beliefs that any social group constructs around itself. It is the task of social science inquiry to hold up these myths and beliefs to critical scrutiny, but in doing so it does not imply that they are wrong. It tries to understand what they are and why they exist, and not to make evaluative judgements about them.

Two final points directed to analysts and not practitioners follow from the foregoing. First, the objectivity of social science has been affirmed. It may prove possible at some time to defend this affirmation in detail. But running through the whole of this study is the view that, although conflict involves relations of power and although the notion of a structured antagonism between employers and workers has been placed at the heart of the theory of conflict, concepts such as conflict and struggle can be developed which are genuinely objective. Analysis and prescription can, and indeed must, be kept separate. The identification of a structured antagonism between capital and labour does not imply that the antagonism can be simply removed or that attempts at such removal would necessarily be in workers' interests. Second, therefore, the materialist approach lies squarely within the non-Marxist tradition of social research. It claims to provide this tradition with an integrated theory of conflict which has hitherto been absent. Whether or not it does so is for others to judge.

References

Aaronovitch, Sam and Ron Smith, with Jean Gardiner and Roger Moore. 1981. *The Political Economy of British Capitalism: A Marxist Analysis*. London: McGraw-Hill.

Abercrombie, Nicholas and John Urry. 1983. *Capital, Labour and the Middle Classes*. London: Allen and Unwin.

—, Stephen Hill and Bryan S. Turner. 1980. *The Dominant Ideology Thesis*. London: Allen and Unwin.

Anderson, Perry. 1974. *Lineages of the Absolutist State*. London: New Left Books.

— 1980. *Arguments Within English Marxism*. London: Verso.

Aptheker, Herbert. 1963. *American Negro Slave Revolts*. New York: International Publishers. (Orig. publ. 1943).

Armstrong, Peter. 1983. 'Class Relationships at the Point of Production: a Case Study'. *Sociology*, Vol. 17, August, 339–58.

Armstrong, P. J., J. F. B. Goodman and J. D. Hyman. 1981. *Ideology and Shop Floor Industrial Relations*. London: Croom Helm.

Arnot, Bob. 1981. 'Soviet Labour Productivity and the Failure of the Shchekino Experiment'. *Critique*, no. 15, 31–56.

Aronowitz, Stanley. 1973. *False Promises: The Shaping of American Working-Class Consciousness*. New York: McGraw-Hill.

Auerbach, Jerold S. 1966. *Labor and Liberty: The LaFollette Committee and the New Deal*. Indianapolis: Bobbs-Merrill.

Bakke, E. Wight, Clark Kerr and Charles W. Anrod (eds). 1960. *Unions, Management and the Public*. 2nd edn. New York: Harcourt, Brace and Co.

Baldamus, W. 1961. *Efficiency and Effort*. London: Tavistock.

— 1969. 'Alienation, Anomie and Industrial Accidents: An Essay on the Use of Sociological Time Series'. University of Birmingham Faculty of Commerce and Social Science, Discussion Paper E12.

Barker, Diana Leonard and Sheila Allen (eds). 1976. *Dependence and Exploitation in Work and Marriage*. London: Longman.

Batstone, Eric. 1984. *Working Order: Workplace Industrial Relations over Two Decades.* Oxford: Blackwell.

— Ian Boraston and Stephen Frenkel. 1977. *Shop Stewards in Action: The Organization of Workplace Conflict and Accommodation.* Oxford: Blackwell.

—, Ian Boraston and Stephen Frenkel. 1978. *The Social Organization of Strikes.* Oxford: Blackwell.

—, Anthony Ferner and Michael Terry. 1984. *Consent and Efficiency: Labour Relations and Management Strategy in the State Enterprise.* Oxford: Blackwell.

Beechey, Veronica. 1978. 'Women and Production: a Critical Analysis of Some Sociological Theories of Women's Work'. In Kuhn and Wolpe, 1978, 155–97.

Belotsevkovsky, Vadim. 1978. 'Workers' Struggles in the USSR in the Early Sixties'. *Critique,* nos. 10–11, 37–50.

Bensman, Joseph and Israel Gerver. 1963. 'Crime and Punishment in the Factory: The Function of Deviancy in Maintaining the Social System'. *American Sociological Review,* Vol. 28, August, 588–98.

Bentley, Philip. 1974. 'Recent Strike Behaviour in Australia: Causes and Responses'. *Australian Bulletin of Labour.* Vol. 1 No. 1, September, 27–56.

Benton, Ted. 1981. ' "Objective" Interests and the Sociology of Power'. *Sociology,* Vol. 15, May, 161–84.

Berliner, Joseph S. 1952. 'The Informal Organization of the Soviet Firm'. *Quarterly Journal of Economics,* Vol. 66, August, 342–65.

Bernstein, Barton J. 1968. 'The New Deal: the Conservative Achievements of Liberal Reform'. *Towards a New Past: Dissenting Essays in American History.* Ed. Barton J. Bernstein. New York: Pantheon, 263–88.

Bernstein, Irving. 1950. *The New Deal Collective Bargaining Policy.* Berkeley: University of California Press.

— 1970. *Turbulent Years.* Boston: Houghton Mifflin.

Berthoff, Rowland. 1964. 'The "Freedom to Control" in American Business History'. *A Festschrift for Frederick B. Artz,* ed. David H. Pinkney and Theodore Ropp. Durham, N.C.: Duke University Press, 158–80.

Beynon, Huw. 1968. 'A Wildcat Strike'. *New Society.* 5 September, 336–7.

— 1973. *Working for Ford.* Harmondsworth: Penguin.

Bezucha, Robert J. 1979. 'The "Preindustrial" Worker Movement: The *Canuts* of Lyon'. *Conflict and Stability in Europe.* Ed. Clive Emsley. London: Croom Helm, 37–64.

Bing, Alexander M. 1921. *War-Time Strikes and Their Adjustment.* New York: E. P. Dutton.

Blackaby, Frank. (ed). 1978. *De-Industrialisation.* London: Heinemann.

Blau, Peter M. 1963. *The Dynamics of Bureaucracy: A Study of Inter-personal Relations in Two Government Agencies.* Rev. edn. Chicago: University of Chicago Press.

Block, Fred. 1980. 'Beyond Relative Autonomy: State Managers as Historical Subjects'. *Socialist Register,* 227–42.

Bluestone, Barry and Bennett Harrison. 1982. *The Deindustrialization of*

America: Plant Closings, Community Abandonment, and the Dismantling of Basic Industry. New York: Basic.

Bowles, Samuel and Herbert Gintis. 1976. *Schooling in Capitalist America: Educational Reform and the Contradictions of Economic Life.* London: Routledge and Kegan Paul.

— and Herbert Gintis. 1981. 'Education as a Site of Contradictions in the Reproduction of the Capital-Labor Relationship: Second Thoughts on the "Correspondence Principle".' *Economic and Industrial Democracy*, Vol. 2, May, 223–42.

Bradshaw, Alan. 1976. 'Critical Note: a Critique of Steven Lukes' "Power: A Radical View"'. *Sociology*, Vol. 10, January, 121–7.

Braverman, Harry. 1974. *Labor and Monopoly Capital: The Degradation of Work in the Twentieth Century.* New York: Monthly Review Press.

Brenner, Robert. 1977. 'The Origins of Capitalist Development: a Critique of Neo-Smithian Marxism'. *New Left Review*, no. 104, 25–92.

Brody, David. 1960. *Steelworkers in America: The Non-Union Era.* Cambridge, Mass.: Harvard University Press.

— 1980. *Workers in Industrial America: Essays on the 20th Century Struggle.* New York: Oxford University Press.

Brown, Geoff. 1977. *Sabotage: A Study in Industrial Conflict.* Nottingham: Spokesman.

Brown, Richard. 1976. 'Women as Employees: Some Comments on Research in Industrial Sociology'. In Barker and Allen, 1976, 21–46.

Brown, William. 1973. *Piecework Bargaining.* London: Heinemann.

Budish, J. M. and George Soule. 1920. *The New Unionism in the Clothing Industry.* New York: Harcourt, Brace and Howe.

Burawoy, Michael. 1978. 'Toward a Marxist Theory of the Labor Process: Braverman and Beyond'. *Politics and Society*, Vol. 8, nos. 3–4, 247–312.

— 1979. *Manufacturing Consent: Changes in the Labor Process under Monopoly Capitalism.* Chicago: University of Chicago Press.

— 1980. 'The Politics of Production and the Production of Politics: a Comparative Analysis of Piecework Machine Shops in the United States and Hungary'. *Political Power and Social Theory*, Vol. 1, 261–99.

— 1981. 'Terrains of Contest: Factory and State Under Capitalism and Socialism'. *Socialist Review*, no. 58, 83–124.

— 1985. *The Politics of Production.* London: Verso.

Cameron, David R. 1984. 'Social Democracy, Corporatism, Labour Quiescence, and the Representation of Economic Interest in Advanced Capitalist Society'. *Order and Conflict in Contemporary Capitalism.* Ed. John H. Goldthorpe. Oxford: Clarendon, 143–78.

Campbell, Alan B. 1979. *The Lanarkshire Miners: a Social History of Their Trade Unions, 1775–1974.* [Sic: 1874]. Edinburgh: Donald.

Cavendish, Ruth. 1982. *Women on the Line.* London: Routledge and Kegan Paul.

Child, John (ed.). 1973. *Man and Organization.* London: Allen and Unwin.

Clack, Garfield. 1967. *Industrial Relations in a British Car Factory.* Cambridge: Cambridge University Press.

Clarke, Tom and Laurie Clements (eds). 1977. *Trade Unions under Capitalism*. London: Fontana-Collins.

Clawson, Dan. 1980. *Bureaucracy and the Labour Process: the Transformation of U.S. Industry, 1860–1920*. New York: Monthly Review Press.

— and Richard Fantasia. 1983. 'Review Essay. Beyond Burawoy: the Dialectics of Conflict and Consent on the Shop Floor'. *Theory and Society*, Vol. 12, no. 3, 671–80.

Clegg, H. A. 1975. 'Pluralism in Industrial Relations'. *British Journal of Industrial Relations*, Vol. 13, November, 309–16.

— 1976. *Trade Unionism under Collective Bargaining: a Theory Based on Comparisons of Six Countries*. Oxford: Blackwell.

— 1979. *The Changing System of Industrial Relations in Great Britain*. Oxford: Blackwell.

Cliff, Tony. 1974. *State Capitalism in Russia*. London: Pluto. (Originally written 1948, first published 1955.)

Cohen, G. A. 1978. *Karl Marx's Theory of History: a Defence*. Oxford: Clarendon Press.

Cohen, Robin. 1980. 'Resistance and Hidden Forms of Consciousness among African Workers'. *Review of African Political Economy*, no. 19, September–December, 8–22.

Commons, John R., David J. Saposs, H. L. Sumner, E. B. Mittelman, H. E. Hoagland, J. B. Andrews and Selig Perlman. 1918. *History of Labour in the United States, 1*. New York: Macmillan.

Connor, Walter D. 1979. 'Workers, Politics and Class Consciousness'. In Kahan and Ruble, 1979, 313–32.

Crenson, Matthew A. 1971. *The Un-Politics of Air Pollution: A Study of Non-Decisionmaking in the Cities*. Baltimore: Johns Hopkins University Press.

Cressey, Peter and John MacInnes. 1980. 'Voting for Ford: Industrial Democracy and the Control of Labour'. *Capital and Class*, no. 11, 5–33.

Crew, David F. 1979. *Town in the Ruhr: a Social History of Bochum, 1860–1914*. New York: Columbia University Press.

Cronin, James E. and Jonathan Schneer (eds). 1982. *Social Conflict and Political Order in Modern Britain*. London: Croom Helm.

Crossick, Geoffrey. 1978. *An Artisan Elite in Victorian Society: Kentish London, 1840–1880*. London: Croom Helm.

Crouch, Colin. 1979. 'The State, Capital and Liberal Democracy'. *State and Economy in Contemporary Capitalism*. Ed. Colin Crouch. London: Croom Helm, 13–54.

— 1982. *Trade Unions: the Logic of Collective Action*. London: Fontana.

Croucher, Richard. 1982. *Engineers at War*. London: Merlin.

Cunnison, Sheila. 1966. *Wages and Work Allocation: a Study of Social Relations in a Garment Workshop*. London: Tavistock.

Dabscheck, Braham and John Niland. 1981. *Industrial Relations in Australia*. Sydney: Allen and Unwin.

Dahrendorf, Ralf. 1959. *Class and Class Conflict in Industrial Society*. London: Routledge and Kegan Paul.

Davis, Celia, Sandra Dawson and Arthur Francis. 1973. 'Technology and other Variables: Some Current Approaches in Organization Theory'. In Warner, 1973, 149–63.

Davis, Mike. 1980. 'Why the U.S. Working Class is Different'. *New Left Review*. no. 123, September, 3–44.

Deutscher, Isaac. 1963. *The Prophet Outcast. Trotsky: 1929–1940*. Oxford: Oxford University Press.

Ditton: Jason. 1977. *Part-Time Crime: an Ethnography of Fiddling and Pilferage*. London: Macmillan.

— 1979a. 'Baking Time'. *Sociological Review*, Vol. 27, February, 157–67.

— 1979b. *Controlology: Beyond the New Criminology*. London: Macmillan.

Dobb, Maurice. 1963. *Studies in the Development of Capitalism*. London: Routledge and Kegan Paul. Revised edition.

Dobson, C. R. 1980. *Masters and Journeymen: a Prehistory of Industrial Relations, 1717–1800*. London: Croom Helm.

Donovan Commission. 1968. Report of the Royal Commission on Trade Unions and Employers' Associations. London: HMSO.

Douglas, Paul. H. 1919. 'Plant Administration of Labor'. *Journal of Political Economy*, Vol. 27, July, 544–60.

Dubofsky, Melvyn. 1966. 'The Origins of Western Working Class Radicalism, 1890–1905'. *Labor History*, Vol. 7, Spring, 131–54.

— and Warren Van Tine. 1977. *John L. Lewis: a Biography*. New York: Quadrangle.

Dunbabin, J. P. D. 1974. *Rural Discontent in Nineteenth-Century Britain*. London: Faber and Faber.

Dunlop, John T. (ed.) 1961. *Potentials of the American Economy: Selected Essays of Sumner H. Slichter*. Cambridge, Mass: Harvard University Press.

Durcan, J. W., W. E. J. McCarthy and G. P. Redman. 1983. *Strikes in Post-War Britain*. London: Allen and Unwin.

Edwards, P. K. 1979. 'The "Social" Determination of Strike Activity: an Explication and Critique'. *Journal of Industrial Relations*, Vol. 21, June, 198–216.

— 1982. 'Britain's Changing Strike Problem?' *Industrial Relations Journal*, Vol. 13 no. 2, Summer, 5–20.

— 1983. 'The Political Economy of Industrial Conflict: Britain and the United States'. *Economic and Industrial Democracy*, Vol. 4, November, 461–500.

— and Linda Dickens. Forthcoming. 'Discipline'. *Personnel Management in Britain*. Ed. Keith Sisson. Oxford: Blackwell.

— and Hugh Scullion. 1982a. *The Social Organization of Industrial Conflict: Control and Resistance in the Workplace*. Oxford: Blackwell.

— and Hugh Scullion. 1982b. 'Deviancy Theory and Industrial Praxis: a Study of Discipline and Social Control in an Industrial Setting'. *Sociology*, Vol. 16, August, 322–40.

— and Hugh Scullion 1984. 'Absenteeism and the Control of Work'. *Sociological Review*, Vol. 32, August, 547–72.

Edwards, Richard. 1979. *Contested Terrain: the Transformation of the Workplace in the Twentieth Century*. London: Heinemann.

330   *References*

Eggert, Gerald G. 1967. *Railroad Labor Disputes: the Beginnings of Federal Strike Policy*. Ann Arbor: Michigan University Press.

— 1981. *Steelmasters and Labor Reform, 1886–1923*. Pittsburg: University of Pittsburg Press.

Elbaum, Bernard and Frank Wilkinson. 1979. 'Industrial Relations and Uneven Development: a Comparative Study of the American and British Steel Industries'. *Cambridge Journal of Economics*, Vol. 3, September, 275–303.

Emmett, Isabel and D. H. J. Morgan. 1982. 'Max Gluckman and the Manchester Shopfloor Ethnographies'. *Custom and Conflict in British Society*. Ed. Ronald Frankenberg. Manchester: Manchester University Press, 140–65.

Encel, S. 1970. *Equality and Authority: a Study of Class, Status and Power in Australia*. London: Tavistock.

Ferner, Anthony. 1985. 'Political Constraints and Management Strategies: the Case of Working Practices in British Rail'. *British Journal of Industrial Relations,* Vol. 22, March, 47–70.

— and Michael Terry. 1985. ' "The Crunch Had Come": a Case Study of Changing Industrial Relations in the Post Office'. Warwick Papers in Industrial Relations, no. 1, November. Coventry: Industrial Relations Research Unit, University of Warwick.

Fidler, John. 1981. *The British Business Elite: Its Attitudes to Class, Status and Power*. London: Routledge and Kegan Paul.

Fine, Sidney. 1956. *Laissez-faire and the General-Welfare State: a Study of Conflict in American Thought, 1865–1901*. Ann Arbor: University of Michigan Press.

— 1963. *The Automobile under the Blue Eagle*. Ann Arbor: University of Michigan Press.

— 1969. *Sit-Down: the General Motors Strike of 1936–7*. Ann Arbor: University of Michigan Press.

Fisher, Chris. 1981. *Custom, Work and Market Capitalism: the Forest of Dean Colliers, 1788–1888*. London: Croom Helm.

Flanders, Allan D. 1974. 'The Tradition of Voluntarism'. *British Journal of Industrial Relations*, Vol. 12, November, 352–70.

Fogel, Robert William and Stanley L. Engerman. 1974a. *Time on the Cross: the Economics of American Negro Slavery*. Boston: Little, Brown and Co.

— and Stanley L. Engerman. 1974b. *Time on the Cross: Evidence and Methods, A Supplement*. Boston: Little, Brown and Co.

Foster, John. 1974. *Class Struggle and the Industrial Revolution: Early Industrial Capitalism in Three English Towns*. London: Methuen.

Fox, Alan. 1966. *Industrial Sociology and Industrial Relations*. Research Paper 3 Royal Commission on Trade Unions and Employers' Associations. London: HMSO.

— 1973. 'Industrial Relations: a Social Critique of Pluralist Ideology'. In Child, 1973, 185–233.

— 1974. *Beyond Contract: Work, Power and Trust Relations*. London: Faber and Faber.

— 1979. 'A Note on Industrial Relations Pluralism'. *Sociology*, Vol. 13, January, 105–9.

— 1983. 'British Management and Industrial Relations: the Social Origins of a System'. *Perspectives on Management: A Multidisciplinary Analysis.* Ed. Michael J. Earl. Oxford: Oxford University Press, 6–39.

Franke, Richard Herbert and James D. Kaul. 1978. 'The Hawthorne Experiments: First Statistical Interpretation'. *American Sociological Review,* Vol. 43, October, 623–43.

Friedman, Andrew L. 1977. *Industry and Labour: Class Struggle at Work and Monopoly Capitalism.* London: Macmillan.

Gallie, Duncan. 1983. *Social Inequality and Class Radicalism in France and Britain.* Cambridge: Cambridge University Press.

Gardiner, Jean. 1976. 'Political Economy of Domestic Labour in Capitalist Society.'. In Barker and Allen, 1976, 109–20.

Garnsey, Elizabeth. 1982. 'Capital Accumulation and the Division of Labour in the Soviet Union'. *Cambridge Journal of Economics,* Vol. 6, March, 15–31.

Garside, W. R. and H. F. Gospel. 1982. 'Employers and Managers: their Organizational Structure and Changing Industrial Strategies'. *A History of British Industrial Relations, 1875–1914.* Ed. Chris Wrigley. Brighton: Harvester, 99–115.

Gartman, David. 1983. 'Review Essay. Structuralist Marxism and the Labor Process: Where Have the Dialectics Gone?' *Theory and Society,* Vol. 12, no. 3, 659–69.

Geary, Dick. 1981. *European Labour Protest, 1848–1939.* New York: St Martin's Press.

Geller, Jules. 1979. 'Forms of Capitalist Control over the Labor Process, I'. *Monthly Review,* Vol. 31 no. 7, December, 39–46.

Genovese, Eugene D. 1976. *Roll, Jordan, Roll: the World the Slaves Made.* New York: Vintage.

— 1979. *From Rebellion to Revolution: Afro-American Slave Revolts in the Making of the Modern World.* Baton Rouge: Louisiana State University Press.

Gersuny, Carl. 1973. *Punishment and Redress in the Modern Factory.* Lexington, Mass.: Lexington Books.

Giddens, Anthony. 1981. *A Contemporary Critique of Historical Materialism.* London: Macmillan.

— and David Held (eds). 1982. *Classes, Power and Conflict.* London: Macmillan.

Glaberman, Martin. 1980. *Wartime Strikes: the Struggle against the No-Strike Pledge in the UAW during World War II.* Detroit: Bewick.

Glen, Robert. 1984. *Urban Workers in the Early Industrial Revolution.* London: Croom Helm.

Godson, Joseph. 1981. 'The Role of the Trade Unions'. In Schapiro and Godson, 1981, 106–29.

Goldthorpe, John H. 1977. 'Industrial Relations in Great Britain: a Critique of Reformism'. In Clarke and Clements, 1977, 184–224.

— David Lockwood, Frank Bechhofer and Jennifer Platt. 1968. *The Affluent Worker: Industrial Attitudes and Behaviour.* Cambridge: Cambridge University Press.

Gollan, Robin. 1960. *Radical and Working Class Politics: a Study of Eastern Australia, 1850–1910.* Melbourne: Melbourne University Press.

— 1963. *The Coalminers of New South Wales: a History of the Union, 1860–1960.* Melbourne: Melbourne University Press.

Goodrich, Carter L. 1928. 'The Australian and American Labour Movements'. *Economic Record*, Vol. 4, November, 193–208.

Gordon, David M. 1981. 'Capital-Labor Conflict and the Productivity Slowdown'. *American Economic Review Papers and Proceedings*, Vol. 71, May, 30–5.

— Richard Edwards and Michael Reich. 1982. *Segmented Work, Divided Workers: the Historical Transformation of Labor in the United States.* Cambridge: Cambridge University Press.

Gospel, Howard F. 1983. 'Managerial Strategies and Industrial Relations: an Introduction'. In Gospel and Littler, 1983, 1–24.

Gospel, Howard F. and Craig R. Littler (eds). 1983. *Managerial Strategies and Industrial Relations.* London: Heinemann.

Gray, Robert [Q]. 1981. *The Aristocracy of Labour in Nineteenth-Century Britain, c.1850–1900.* London: Macmillan.

Groves, Reg. 1981. *Sharpen the Sickle. The History of the Farm Workers' Union.* (First published 1949). London: Merlin.

Gutman, Herbert G. 1963. 'The Worker's Search for Power: Labor in the Gilded Age'. *The Gilded Age: A Reappraisal.* Ed. H. Wayne Morgan. New York: Syracuse University Press, 38–68.

— 1977. *Work, Culture and Society in Industrializing America.* New York: Vintage.

Haraszti, Miklos. 1977. *A Worker in a Worker's State. Piece-Rates in Hungary.* Trans. Michael Wright. Harmondsworth: Penguin.

Harris, Howell John. 1982a. *The Right to Manage: Industrial Relations Policies of American Business in the 1940s.* Madison: University of Wisconsin Press.

— 1982b. 'Responsible Unionism and the Road to Taft-Hartley: the Development of Federal Labor Relations Policy, c.1932–47'. Paper presented to Colloquium on Shopfloor Bargaining and the State, Cambridge. (Revised version published in Tolliday and Zeitlin, 1985, 148–91).

Hartman, Heidi I. 1979. 'The Unhappy Marriage of Marxism and Feminism: Towards a More Progressive Union'. *Capital and Class*, no. 8, 1–33.

Herding, Richard. 1972. *Job Control and Union Structure.* Rotterdam: Rotterdam University Press.

Herzog, Marianne. 1980. *From Hand to Mouth: Women and Piecework.* Trans. Stanley Mitchell. Harmondsworth: Penguin.

Hethy, Lajos and Csaba Mako. 1974. 'Work Performance, Interests, Powers and Environment: the Case of Cyclical Slowdowns in a Hungarian Factory'. *European Economic Review*, Vol. 5, 141–57.

Hill, Stephen. 1974. 'Norms, Groups and Power: the Sociology of Workplace Industrial Relations.' *British Journal of Industrial Relations*, Vol. 12, July, 213–35.

— 1981. *Competition and the Control of Work: the New Industrial Sociology*. London: Heinemann.

Hilton, Rodney. 1977. *Bond Men Made Free: Medieval Peasant Movements and the English Rising of 1381*. London: Methuen.

— (ed.). 1978. *The Transition from Feudalism to Capitalism*. London: Verso.

Himmelstrand, Ulf, Goran Ahrne, Leif Lundberg and Lars Lundberg. 1981. *Beyond Welfare Capitalism*. London: Heinemann.

Hindess, Barry. 1982. 'Power, Interests and the Outcomes of Struggles'. *Sociology*, Vol. 16, November, 498–511.

Hinton, James. 1976. 'Reply [to Monds, 1976]'. *New Left Review*, no. 97, May–June, 100–4.

Hirszowicz, Maria. 1981. *Industrial Sociology: an Introduction*. Oxford: Martin Robertson.

Hobsbawm, E. J. 1964. *Labouring Men: Studies in the History of Labour* London: Weidenfeld and Nicolson.

— and George Rudé. 1969. *Captain Swing*. London: Lawrence and Wishart.

Holbrook–Jones, Mike. 1982. *Supremacy and Subordination of Labour: the Hierarchy of Work in the Early Labour Movement*. London: Heinemann.

Holt, James. 1977. 'Trade Unionism in the British and U.S. Steel Industries, 1888–1912: a Comparative Study'. *Labor History*, Vol. 18, Winter, 5–35.

Holton, R. J. 1985. *The Transition from Feudalism to Capitalism*. London: Macmillan.

Holubenko, M. 1975. 'The Soviet Working Class: Dissent and Opposition'. *Critique*, no. 4, Spring, 5–26.

Humphries, Jane. 1981. 'Protective Legislation, the Capitalist State and Working Class Men: the Case of the 1842 Mines Regulation Act'. *Feminist Review*, no. 7, Spring, 1–33.

Hurd, Rick. 1976. 'New Deal Labor Policy and the Containment of Radical Union Activity'. *Review of Radical Political Economics*, Vol. 8, no. 3, Fall, 32–43.

Huthmacher, J. Joseph. 1971. *Senator Robert F. Wagner and the Rise of Urban Liberalism*. New York: Atheneum.

Hyman, Richard. 1972. *Strikes*. London: Fontana-Collins.

— 1978. 'Pluralism, Procedural Consensus and Collective Bargaining'. *British Journal of Industrial Relations*, Vol. 16, March, 16–40.

— and Ian Brough. 1975. *Social Values and Industrial Relations: a Study of Fairness and Equality*. Oxford: Blackwell.

— and Tony Elger. 1981. 'Job Controls, the Employers' Offensive and Alternative Strategies'. *Capital and Class*, no. 15, Autumn, 115–49.

Ingham, Geoffrey, 1982. 'Divisions within the Dominant Class and British "Exceptionalism"'. *Social Class and the Division of Labour*. Ed. Anthony Giddens and Gavin Mackenzie. Cambridge: Cambridge University Press, 209–27.

Institute of Personnel Management. 1979. *Disciplinary Procedures and Practice*. IPM Information Report 28. London: IPM.

Jackson, Robert Max. 1984. *The Formation of Craft Labor Markets*. Orlando: Academic Press.

Jefferys, Stephen David. 1984. 'Management and Managed: a Study of the Development of Shop Floor Industrial Relations at Chrysler Corporation's Dodge Main, Detroit Factory, 1930–1980'. PhD thesis, University of Warwick.

Jessop, Bob. 1980. 'The Transformation of the State in Post-War Britain'. *The State in Western Europe*. Ed. Richard Scase. London: Croom Helm, 23–93.

— 1982. *The Capitalist State: Marxist Theories and Methods*. Oxford: Martin Robertson.

Johns, Gary and Nigel Nicholson. 1982. 'The Meanings of Absence: New Strategies for Theory and Research'. *Research in Organizational Behavior*, Vol. 4. Ed. B. M. Staw and L. L. Cummings. Greenwich, Conn. JAI Press, 127–72.

Johnson, James P. 1979. *The Politics of Soft Coal: the Bituminous Industry from World War I through the New Deal*. Urbana: University of Illinois Press.

Johnson, Terence J. 1972. *Professions and Power*. London: Macmillan.

Joyce, Patrick. 1982. *Work, Society and Politics: the Culture of the Factory in Late Victorian England*. London: Methuen.

— 1983. Review [of Price, 1980]. *Social History*, Vol. 8, May, pp. 239–41.

— 1984. 'Labour, Capital and Compromise: a Response to Richard Price'. *Social History*, Vol. 9, January, 67–76.

Juris, Hervey A. and Myron Roomkin (eds). 1980. *The Shrinking Perimeter: Unionism and Labor Relations in the Manufacturing Sector*. Lexington Mass.: Lexington Books.

Kahan, Arcadius and Blair A. Ruble (eds). 1979. *Industrial Labour in the USSR*. New York: Pergamon.

Karabel, Jerome. 1979. 'The Failure of American Socialism Reconsidered'. *Socialist Register*, 204–27.

Katz, Harry C. 1984. 'The U.S. Automobile Collective Bargaining System in Transition'. *British Journal of Industrial Relations*, Vol. 22, July, 205–17.

Kelly, John E. 1982. *Scientific Management, Job Redesign and Work Performance*. London: Academic Press.

Kerr, Clark. 1954. 'Industrial Conflict and Its Mediation'. *American Journal of Sociology*, Vol. 60, November, 230–45.

— John T. Dunlop, Frederick Harbison and C. A. Myers. 1973. *Industrialism and Industrial Man*. Second British edition. Harmondsworth: Penguin.

Kilpatrick, Andrew and Tony Lawson. 1980. 'On the Nature of Industrial Decline in the U.K.'. *Cambridge Journal of Economics*, Vol. 4, March, 85–102.

Klare, Karl E. 1978. 'Judicial Deradicalization of the Wagner Act and the Origins of Modern Legal Consciousness'. *Minnesota Law Review*, Vol. 62, 265–339.

Klein, Lisl. 1964. '*Multiproducts Ltd*': a Case Study on the Social Effects of Rationalized Production*. London: HMSO.

Kolko, Gabriel. 1965. *Railroads and Regulation, 1877–1916*. Princeton: Princeton University Press.

— 1967. *The Triumph of Conservatism: a Reinterpretation of American History, 1900–1916.* Chicago: Quadrangle (first published 1963).

Korman, Adolf Gerd. 1967. *Industrialization, Immigrants and Americanizers: the View from Milwaukee, 1866–1921.* Madison: State Historical Society of Wisconsin.

Korpi, Walter and Michael Shalev. 1979. 'Strikes, Industrial Relations and Class Conflict in Capitalist Society'. *British Journal of Sociology*, Vol. 30, June, 164–87.

Kriedte, Peter, Hans Medick and Jurgen Schlumbohm. 1981. *Industrialization before Industrialization: Rural Industry in the Genesis of Capitalism.* Cambridge: Cambridge University Press. Trans. Beate Schempp (first German edition 1977).

Kriegler, Roy J. 1980. *Working for the Company: Work and Control in the Whyalla Shipyard.* Melbourne: Oxford University Press.

Kuhn, Annette and AnnMarie Wolpe (eds). 1978. *Feminism and Materialism: Women and Modes of Production.* London: Routledge and Kegan Paul.

Kuhn, James W. 1955. 'Grievance Machinery and Strikes in Australia'. *Industrial and Labor Relations Review*, Vol. 8, January, 169–76.

— 1961. *Bargaining in Grievance Settlement: the Power of Industrial Work Groups.* New York: Columbia University Press.

Lane, David. 1978. *Politics and Society in the USSR.* London: Martin Robertson. Revised Edition.

— 1982. *The End of Social Inequality? Class, Status and Power under State Socialism.* London: Allen and Unwin.

— and Felicity O'Dell. 1978. *The Soviet Industrial Worker: Social Class, Education and Control.* Oxford: Martin Robertson.

Lange, Peter, George Ross and Maurizio Vannicelli. 1982. *Unions, Change and Crisis: French and Italian Union Strategy and the Political Economy, 1945–1980.* London: Allen and Unwin.

Lash, Scott. 1984. *The Militant Worker: Class and Radicalism in France and America.* London: Heinemann.

— and John Urry. 1984. 'The New Marxism of Collective Action: a Critical Analysis'. *Sociology*, Vol. 18, February, 33–50.

Lawson, Tony. 1981. 'Paternalism and Labour Market Segmentation Theory'. *The Dynamics of Labour Market Segmentation.* Ed. Frank Wilkinson. London: Academic Press, 47–66.

Lazonick, William H. 1978. 'The Subjection of Labour to Capital: the Rise of the Capitalist System'. *Review of Radical Political Economics*, Vol. 10 no. 1, Spring, 1–31.

— 1979. 'Industrial Relations and Technical Change: the Case of the Self-Acting Mule'. *Cambridge Journal of Economics*, Vol. 3, September, 231–62.

— 1981. 'Production Relations, Labor Productivity and Choice of Technique: British and U.S. Cotton Spinning'. *Journal of Economic History*, Vol. 41, September, 491–516.

— 1983. 'Technological Change and the Control of Work: the Development of Capital–Labour Relations in U.S. Manufacturing Industry'. In Gospel and Littler, 1983, 111–36.

Leiserson, W. M. 1922. 'Constitutional Government in American Industries'. *American Economic Review Papers and Proceedings*, Vol. 12, Supplement, March, 56–79.

Leuchtenburg, William E. 1963. *Franklin D. Roosevelt and the New Deal, 1932–40.* New York: Harper and Row.

Lewis, Roy and Bob Simpson. 1981. *Striking a Balance? Employment Law after the 1980 Act.* Oxford: Martin Robertson.

Levine, Louis, 1924. *The Women's Garment Workers: a History of the International Ladies' Garment Workers' Union.* New York: B. W. Huebsch.

Licht, Walter. 1983. *Working for the Railroad: the Organization of Work in the Nineteenth Century.* Princeton: Princeton University Press.

Lichtenstein, Nelson. 1980. 'Auto Worker Militancy and the Structure of Factory Life, 1937–1955'. *Journal of American History.* Vol. 67, September, 335–53.

— 1982. *Labor's War at Home: The CIO in World War II.* Cambridge: Cambridge University Press.

Linhart, Robert. 1981. *The Assembly Line.* Trans. Margaret Crosland. London: John Calder (original French edition 1978).

Lipset, Seymour Martin. 1977. 'Why no Socialism in the United States?' *Sources of Contemporary Radicalism.* Ed. Seweryn Bialer. Boulder: Westview, 31–149.

Littler, Craig R. 1982. *The Development of the Labour Process in Capitalist Societies.* London: Heinemann.

— and Graeme Salaman. 1982. 'Bravermania and Beyond: Recent Theories of the Labour Process'. *Sociology*, Vol. 16, May, 251–69.

Lockwood, David. 1964. 'Social Integration and System Integration'. *Explorations in Social Change.* Ed. G. K. Zollschan and F. Hirsch. London: Routledge and Kegan Paul, 244–57.

— 1981. 'The Weakest Link in the Chain? Some Comments on the Marxist Theory of Action'. *Research in the Sociology of Work*, Vol. 1, 435–81.

Lukes, Steven. 1974. *Power: a Radical View.* London: Macmillan.

Lupton, Tom. 1963. *On the Shop Floor: Two Studies of Workshop Organization and Output.* Oxford: Pergamon.

— and Sheila Cunnison. 1964. 'Workshop Behaviour'. *Closed Systems and Open Minds.* Ed. Max Gluckman. Chicago: Aldine, 103–28.

Macarthy, P. G. 1967. 'Labor and the Living Wage, 1890–1910'. *Australian Journal of Politics and History*, Vol. 13, May, 67–89.

— 1970a. 'The Living Wage in Australia: the Role of Government'. *Labour History*, no. 18, May, 3–18.

— 1970b. 'Employers, the Tariff and Legal Wage Regulation in Australia: 1890–1910'. *Journal of Industrial Relations*, Vol. 12, no. 2, 182–93.

Maitland, Ian. 1983. *The Causes of Industrial Disorder: a Comparison of a British and a German Factory.* London: Routledge and Kegan Paul.

Mann, Michael. 1970. 'The Social Cohesion of Liberal Democracy'. *American Sociological Review*, Vol. 35, June, 423–39.

— 1973. *Consciousness and Action among the Western Working Class.* London: Macmillan.

Mars, Gerald. 1973. 'Chance, Punters and the Fiddle: Institutionalized Pilferage in a Hotel Dining Room'. In Warner, 1973. 200–10.

— 1974. 'Dock Pilferage'. *Deviance and Social Control.* Ed. Paul Rock and Mary McIntosh. London: Tavistock, 209–28.

— 1983. *Cheats at Work: an Anthropology of Workplace Crime.* London: Counterpoint.

Marshall, Gordon. 1982. *In Search of the Spirit of Capitalism: an Essay on Max Weber's Protestant Ethic Thesis.* London: Hutchinson.

Martin, Roderick. 1977. *The Sociology of Power.* London: Routledge and Kegan Paul.

Martin, Ross M. 1983. 'Pluralism and the New Corporatism'. *Political Studies*, Vol. 32, March, 86–102.

Marvel, Howard P. 1977. 'Factory Regulation: a Reinterpretation of Early English Experience'. *Journal of Law and Economics*, Vol. 20, October, 379–402.

Mayer, Kurt B. 1964. 'Social Stratification in Two Equalitarian Societies: Australia and the United States'. *Social Research*, Vol. 32, Winter, 435–65.

Meyer, Stephen. 1981. *The Five-Dollar Day: Labor Management and Social Control in the Ford Motor Company, 1908–1921.* Albany: State University of New York Press.

Miller, Randall M. 1981. 'The Fabric of Control: Slavery in Antebellum Southern Textile Mills'. *Business History Review*, Vol. 55, Winter, 471–90.

Millis, Harry A. and Emily Clark Brown. 1950. *From the Wagner Act to Taft-Hartley: a Study of National Labor Policy and Labor Relations.* Chicago: University of Chicago Press.

Millward, Neil. 1972. 'Piecework Earnings and Workers' Controls'. *Human Relations*, Vol. 25, September, 351–76.

Monds, Jean. 1976. 'Workers' Control and the Historians: a New Economism'. *New Left Review*, no. 97, May–June, 81–100.

Montgomery, David. 1979. *Workers' Control in America.* Cambridge: Cambridge University Press.

Morris, Morris David. 1965. *The Emergence of an Industrial Labor Force in India: a Study of the Bombay Cotton Mills, 1854–1947.* Berkeley: University of California Press.

Mulder, Ronald A. 1979. *The Insurgent Progressives in the United States Senate and the New Deal, 1933–1939.* New York: Garland.

Musson, A. E. 1976. 'Class Struggle and the Labour Aristocracy, 1830–60'. *Social History*, Vol. 1, October, 335–56.

Nichols, Theo. 1975. 'The Sociology of Accidents and the Social Production of Industrial Injury'. *People and Work.* Ed. Geoff Esland, Graeme Salaman and Mary-Ann Speakman. Edinburgh: Homes McDougall, 217–29.

— and Peter Armstrong. 1976. *Workers Divided: a Study in Shopfloor Politics.* London: Fontana-Collins.

— and Huw Beynon. 1977. *Living With Capitalism.* London: Routledge and Kegan Paul.

Nicholson, Nigel. 1977. 'Absence Behaviour and Attendance Motivation: a Conceptual Synthesis'. *Journal of Management Studies*, Vol. 14, October, 231–52.

Niland, John. 1976. 'The Case for More Collective Bargaining in Australia'. *Journal of Industrial Relations*, Vol. 18, no. 4, 365–90.

Niven, M. M. 1967. *Personnel Management 1913–63: the Growth of Personnel Management and the Development of the Institute.* London: Institute of Personnel Management.

Nolan, Peter. 1983. 'The Firm and Labour Market Behaviour'. *Industrial Relations in Britain.* Ed. George Sayers Bain. Oxford: Blackwell, 291–310.

— and P. K. Edwards. 1984. 'Homogenise, Divide and Rule: an Essay on *Segmented Work, Divided Workers*'. *Cambridge Journal of Economics*, Vol. 8, June, 197–215.

Nove, Alec. 1983. *The Economics of Feasible Socialism.* London: Allen and Unwin.

Nuti, Domenico Mario. 1979. 'Th Contradictions of Socialist Economics: a Marxist Analysis'. *Socialist Register*, 228–73.

O'Connor, James. 1973. *The Fiscal Crisis of the State.* New York: St. Martin's Press.

Offe, Claus. 1975. 'The Theory of the Capitalist State and the Problem of Policy Formation'. *Stress and Contradiction in Modern Capitalism.* Ed. Leon L. Lindberg, Robert Alford, Colin Crouch and Claus Offe. Lexington: Lexington Books, 125–44.

— and Volker Ronge. 1982. 'Theses on the Theory of the State'. In Giddens and Held, 249–56. (Originally published 1975).

Panitch, Leo. 1976. *Social Democracy and Industrial Militancy: the Labour Party, the Trade Unions, and Incomes Policy, 1945–74.* Cambridge: Cambridge University Press.

Parkin, Frank. 1979. *Marxism and Class Theory: a Bourgeois Critique.* London: Tavistock.

Peach, David A. and E. Robert Livernash. 1974. *Grievance Initiation and Resolution: a Study in Basic Steel.* Boston: Harvard University Graduate School of Business Administration.

Peach, L. H. 1983. 'Employee Relations in IBM'. *Employee Relations*, Vol. 5, no. 3, 17–20.

Pfeffer, Richard M. 1979. *Working for Capitalism.* New York: Columbia Univeristy Press.

Piore, Michael J. 1982. 'American Labor and the Industrial Crisis'. *Challenge*, Vol. 25, no. 1, March, 3–11.

Plowman, D., S. Deery and C. Fisher. 1980. *Australian Industrial Relations.* Sydney: McGraw-Hill.

Pollack, Norman. 1962. *The Populist Response to Industrial America: Midwestern Populist Thought.* Cambridge, Mass: Harvard University Press.

Pollard, Sidney. 1965. *The Genesis of Modern Management: a Study of the Industrial Revolution in Great Britain.* London: Arnold.

Pollert, Anna. 1981. *Girls, Wives, Factory Lives.* London: Macmillan.

Poole, Michael, Roger Mansfield, Paul Blyton and Paul Frost. 1981, *Managers in Focus: the British Manager in the Early 1980s.* Aldershot: Gower.

Pravda, Alex. 1979. 'Spontaneous Workers' Activities in the Soviet Union'. In Kahan and Ruble, 1979, 333–66.

Price, Richard. 1980. *Masters, Unions and Men: Work Control in Building and the Rise of Labour, 1830–1914.* Cambridge: Cambridge University Press.

— 1982. 'Rethinking Labour History: the Importance of Work'. In Cronin and Schneer, 1982, 179–214.

— 1983. 'The Labour Process and Labour History'. *Social History,* Vol. 8, January, 57–75.

Prude, Jonathan. 1983. 'The Social System of Early New England Textile Mills: a Case Study, 1812–40'. *Working-Class America.* Ed. Michael H. Frisch and Daniel J. Walkowitz. Urbana: University of Illinois Press, 1–36.

Przeworski, Adam. 1977. 'Proletariat into Class: the Process of Class Formation from Karl Kautsky's *The Class Struggle* to Recent Controversies'. *Politics and Society,* Vol. 7, no. 4, 343–402.

Purcell, John. 1983. Review [of Edwards and Scullion, 1982a]. *Industrial Relations Journal,* Vol. 14, Autumn, 106–7.

Rawson, D. W. 1978. *Unions and Unionists in Australia.* Sydney: Allen and Unwin.

Reid, Douglas A. 1976. 'The Decline of Saint Monday, 1766–1876'. *Past and Present,* no. 71, May, 76–101.

Rex, John. 1961. *Key Problems of Sociological Theory.* London: Routledge and Kegan Paul.

Richardson, Reed C. 1963. *The Locomotive Engineer, 1863–1963: a Century of Railway Labor Relations and Work Rules.* Ann Arbor: Graduate School of Business Administration, University of Michigan.

Roberts, Robert. 1973. *The Classic Slum: Salford Life in the First Quarter of the Century.* Harmondsworth: Penguin.

Roemer, John E. 1982. *A General Theory of Exploitation and Class.* Cambridge, Mass.: Harvard University Press.

Roethlisberger, W. J. and William J. Dickson. 1939. *Management and the Worker: an Account of the Research Program Conducted by the Western Electric Company. Hawthorne Works, Chicago.* Cambridge, Mass.: Harvard University Press.

Rootes, C. A. 1981. 'The Dominant Ideology Thesis and Its Critics'. *Sociology,* Vol. 15, August, 436–44.

Ross, Philip. 1965. *The Government as a Source of Union Power: the Role of Public Policy in Collective Bargaining.* Providence: Brown University Press.

Rowthorn, Bob. 1980. *Capitalism, Conflict and Inflation: Essays in Political Economy.* London: Lawrence and Wishart.

Roy, Donald. 1952. 'Quota Restriction and Goldbricking in a Machine Shop'. *American Journal of Sociology,* Vol. 57, March, 427–42.

— 1953. 'Work Satisfaction and Social Reward in Quota Achievement: an

Analysis of Piecework Incentive'. *American Sociological Review*, Vol. 18, October, 507–14.

— 1954. 'Efficiency and "The Fix": Informal Intergroup Relations in a Piecework Machine Shop'. *American Journal of Sociology*, Vol. 60, November, 255–66.

Ruble, Blair A. 1979. 'Factory Unions and Workers' Rights'. In Kahan and Ruble, 1979, 59–84.

Rudé, George. 1981. *The Crowd in History, 1730–1848*. Revised edition (first edition 1964). London: Lawrence and Wishart.

Rule, John. 1981. *The Experience of Labour in Eighteenth-Century England*. London: Croom Helm.

— 1984. 'Artisan Attitudes: Skilled Labour and Proletarianization in Europe and New England'. Paper presented to the Fourth British–Dutch Social History Conference, Newcastle-upon-Tyne, April.

Russell, Bertrand. 1975. *Power: A New Social Analysis*. London: Unwin. (Originally published 1938).

Sabel, Charles F. and David Stark. 1982. 'Planning, Politics and Shopfloor Power: Hidden Forms of Bargaining in Soviet-Imposed State-Socialist Societies'. *Politics and Society*, Vol. 11, no. 4, 439–75.

Salaman, Graeme. 1981. *Class and the Corporation*. London: Fontana.

Schapiro, Leonard and Joseph Godson (eds). 1981. *The Soviet Worker: Illusions and Realities*. London Macmillan.

Schlesinger, Arthur M. 1960. *The Coming of the New Deal*, Vol. 2 of *The Age of Roosevelt*. London: Heinemann.

Schofer, Lawrence. 1975. *The Formation of a Modern Labor Force: Upper Silesia, 1865–1914*. Berkeley: University of California Press.

Scullion, Hugh and P. K. Edwards. 1985. 'Craft Unionism, Job Controls and Management Strategy: a Case Study'. Unpublished manuscript, Industrial Relations Research Unit, University of Warwick.

Seeger, Murray. 1981. 'Eye-Witness to Failure'. In Schapiro and Godson, 1981, 76–105.

Seidman, Joel, Jack London, Bernard Karsh and Daisy L. Tagliacozzo. 1958. *The Worker Views His Union*. Chicago: University of Chicago Press.

Sewell, William H. 1974. 'The Working-class of Marseille under the Second Republic: Social Structure and Political Behavior'. In Stearns and Walkowitz, 1974, 75–116.

— 1980. *Work and Revolution in France: the Language of Labor from the Old Regime to 1848*. Cambridge: Cambridge University Press.

Shorter, Edward and Charles Tilly. 1974. *Strikes in France, 1830–1968*. Cambridge, Cambridge University Press.

Sisson, Keith. Forthcoming. *The Management of Collective Bargaining: an International Comparison*. Oxford: Blackwell.

Skocpol, Theda. 1980. 'Political Response to Capitalist Crisis: Neo-Marxist Theories of the State and the New Deal'. *Politics and Society*, Vol. 10, no. 2, 155–201.

Skowronek, Stephen. 1981. 'National Railroad Regulation and the Problem of State-Building: Interests and Institutions in late Nineteenth-Century America'. *Politics and Society*, Vol. 10, no. 3, 225–50.

— 1982. *Building a New American State: the Expansion of National Administrative Capacities, 1877–1920.* Cambridge: Cambridge University Press.

Slichter, Sumner H. 1919. *The Trunover of Factory Labor.* New York: D. Appleton.

Staines, Graham L. 1979. 'Is Worker Dissatisfaction Rising?' *Challenge*, Vol. 22 no. 2, May, 38–45.

Stampp, Kenneth M. 1964. *The Peculiar Institution: Negro Slavery in the American South.* London: Eyre and Spottiswoode.

Stark, David. 1980. 'Class Struggle and the Transformation of the Labor Process: A Relational Approach'. *Theory and Society*, Vol. 9, January, 89–130.

Starobin, Robert S. 1970. *Industrial Slavery in the Old South.* New York: Oxford University Press.

Stearns, Peter N. 1974. 'Measuring the Evolution of Strike Movements'. *International Review of Social History.* Vol. 19, no. 1, 1–27.

— and Daniel J. Walkowitz (eds). 1974. *Workers in the Industrial Revolution.* New Brunswick: Transaction.

Stedman Jones, Gareth. 1975. 'Class Struggle and the Industrial Revolution'. *New Left Review*, no. 90, March–April, 35–69.

— 1984. *Outcast London.* (first edition 1971). Harmondsworth: Penguin.

Stessin, Lawrence. 1960. *Employee Discipline.* Washington: BNA.

Stevenson, John. 1979. *Popular Disturbances in England, 1700–1870.* London: Longman.

Stone, Katherine van Wezel. 1981. 'The Post-War Paradigm in American Labor Law'. *Yale Law Journal*, Vol. 90, June, 1509–80.

Stover, John F. 1961. *American Railroads.* Chicago: University of Chicago Press. (fourth impression 1967).

Strauss, George. 1962. 'The Shifting Power Balance in the Plant'. *Industrial Relations*, Vol. 1, May, 65–96.

Streek, Wolfgang. 1984. *Industrial Relations in West Germany: a Case Study of the Car Industry.* London: Heinemann.

Strinati, Dominic. 1982. *Capitalism, The State and Industrial Relations.* London: Croom Helm.

Sutcliffe, J. T. 1966. 'The Strikes of the 1890s'. *Australian Labour Relations: Readings.* Ed. J. E. Isaac and G. W. Ford. Melbourne: Sun Books, 99–113 (extract from a history of Australian trade unions, first published 1921).

Sykes, A. J. M. 1965. 'Economic Interest and the Hawthorne Researches: a Comment'. *Human Relations*, Vol. 18, August, 253–64.

— 1969a. 'Navvies: their Work Attitudes'. *Sociology*, Vol. 3 no. 1, 21–35.

— 1969b. 'Navvies: their Social Relations'. *Sociology*, Vol. 3, no. 2, 157–72.

Tawney, R. H. 1979. 'The American Labour Movement'. *The American Labour Movement and Other Essays.* Ed. J. M. Winter. Brighton: Harvester (essay originally published 1942).

Taylor, Laurie and Paul Walton. 1971. 'Industrial Sabotage: Motives and Meanings'. *Images of Deviance.* Ed. Stanley Cohen. Harmondsworth: Penguin, 219–45.

Teckenberg, Wolfgang. 1978. 'Labour Turnover and Job Satisfaction: Indicators of Industrial Conflict in the USSR?' *Soviet Studies*, Vol. 30, April, 193–211.

Temperley, Howard. 1977. 'Capitalism, Slavery and Ideology'. *Past and Present*, no. 75, May, 94–118.

Thernstrom, Stephan. 1964. *Poverty and Progress: Social Mobility in a Nineteenth-Century City*. Cambridge, Mass.: Harvard University Press.

— 1973. *The Other Bostonians: Poverty and Progress in the American Metropolis, 1880–1970*. Cambridge, Mass: Harvard University Press.

— 1974. 'Working-class Social Mobility in Industrial America'. In Stearns and Walkowitz, 1974, 278–96.

Tholfsen, Trygve R. 1976. *Working Class Radicalism in Mid-Victorian England*. London: Croom Helm.

Thomas, David. 1985. 'New Ways of Working'. *New Society*, 30 August, 300–2.

Thompson, E. P. 1967. 'Time, Work-Discipline, and Industrial Capitalism'. *Past and Present*, no. 38, December, 56–97.

— 1968. *The Making of the English Working Class* (first published 1963). Harmondsworth: Penguin.

— 1971. 'The Moral Economy of the English Crowd in the Eighteenth Century'. *Past and Present*, no. 50, February, 76–136.

— 1978. 'Eighteenth-century English Society: Class Struggle Without Classes?' *Social History*, Vol. 5, May, 183–221.

Thompson, Paul. 1983. *The Nature of Work: an Introduction to Debates on the Labour Process*. London: Macmillan.

Thomson, A. W. J. and V. V. Murray. 1976. *Grievance Procedures*. Farnborough: Saxon House.

Ticktin, H. H. 1973. 'Towards a Political Ecomony of the USSR'. *Critique*, no. 1, 20–41.

Tilly, Charles. 1982. 'Britain Creates the Social Movement'. In Cronin and Schneer, 1982, 21–51.

Tolliday, Steven and Jonathan Zeitlin. 1982. 'Shop Floor Bargaining, Contract Unionism, and Job Control: an Anglo-American Comparison'. Paper presented to the American Historical Association Convention, Washington, D. C., December.

— and Johnathan Zeitlin (eds). 1985. *Shop Floor Bargaining and the State: Historical and Comparative Perspective*. Cambridge, Cambridge University Press.

Tomlins, Christopher L. 1980. 'The State and the Unions: Federal Labor Relations Policy and the Organized Labor Movement in America, 1935–55'. PhD Thesis, Johns Hopkins University, Baltimore.

Toynbee, Polly. 1971. *A Working Life*. London: Hodder and Stoughton.

Turner, H. A., Garfield Clack and Geoffrey Roberts. 1967. *Labour Relations in the Motor Industry: a Study of Industrial Unrest and an International Comparison*. London: Allen and Unwin.

Turner, Ian. 1978. *In Union is Strength: a History of Trade Unions in Australia, 1788–1978*. Second edition. Melbourne: Nelson.

U. S. Strike Commission. 1895. *Report on the Chicago Strike of June–July 1894*. Washington, D. C.: Government Printing Office.

Vernon, H. M. 1940. *The Health and Efficiency of Munition Workers*. London: Oxford University Press.

Walker, Kenneth F. 1970. *Australian Industrial Relations Systems*. Cambridge, Mass: Harvard University Press.

Walker, W. M. 1969. 'Selection and Socialisation in a Small Workshop'. *Social Stratification and Industrial Relations*. Ed. John Goldthorpe and Michael Mann. Proceedings of an SSRC Conference, Cambridge, mimeo.

Warner, Malcolm (ed.). 1973. *The Sociology of the Workplace: an Interdisciplinary Approach*. London: Allen and Unwin.

Watson, Tony J. 1980. *Sociology, Work and Industry*. London: Routledge and Kegan Paul.

Webb, Sidney and Beatrice Webb. 1920. *The History of Trade Unionism, 1666–1920*. London: Longman.

Weinstein, James. 1968. *The Corporate Ideal in the Liberal State: 1900–1918*. Boston: Beacon Press.

West, Jackie. 1980. 'A Political Economy of the Family in Capitalism: Women, Reproduction and Wage Labour'. *Capital and Labour: A Marxist Primer*. Ed. Theo Nichols. London: Fontana, 174–89.

Westwood, Sallie. 1983. *All Day Every Day: Factory and Family in the Making of Women's Lives*. London: Pluto.

Wilkinson, Frank. 1977. 'Collective Bargaining in the Steel Industry in the 1920s'. *Essays in Labour History, 1918–1939*. Ed. Asa Briggs and John Saville. London: Croom Helm, 102–32.

Williams, Alfred. 1915. *Life in a Railway Factory*. London: Duckworth.

Williams, Karel, John Williams and Dennis Thomas. 1983. *Why Are the British Bad at Manufacturing?* London: Routledge and Kegan Paul.

Williamson, Oliver E. 1981. 'The Economics of Organization: the Transaction Cost Approach'. *American Journal of Sociology*, Vol. 87, November, 548–77.

Willman, Paul. 1984. 'The Reform of Collective Bargaining and Strike Activity in BL Cars, 1976–1982'. *Industrial Relations Journal*, Vol. 15, Summer, 6–17.

Winkler, J. T. 1974. 'The Ghost at the Bargaining Table: Directors and Industrial Relations'. *British Journal of Industrial Relations*, Vol. 12, July, 191–212.

Wolf, H. D. 1927. *The Railroad Labor Board*. Chicago: University of Chicago Press.

Wood, Stephen (ed). 1982. *The Degradation of Work? Skill, Deskilling and the Labour Process*. London: Hutchinson.

— and Ruth Elliott. 1977. 'A Critical Evaluation of Fox's Radicalisation of Industrial Relations Theory'. *Sociology*, Vol. 11, January, 105–25.

—and John Kelly. 1982. 'Taylorism, Responsible Autonomy and Management Strategy'. In Wood, 1982, 74–89.

Wright, Erik Olin. 1978. *Class, Crisis and the State*. London: New Left Books.

— 1983. 'Giddens's Critique of Marxism'. *New Left Review*, no. 138, March–April, 11–35.

— 1985. *Classes*. London: Verso.

Wrong, Dennis H. 1979. *Power: Its Forms, Bases and Uses*. Oxford: Blackwell.

Zabala, Craig Anthony. 1983. 'Collective Bargaining at UAW Local 645, General Motors Assembly Division, Van Nuys, California, 1976–1982'. PhD thesis, University of California, Los Angeles.

Zeitlin, Johnathon 1983. 'Trade Unions and Job Control: a Critique of "Rank and Filism"'. *Bulletin* of the Society for the Study of Labour History, no. 46, Spring, 6–7.

— 1985. 'Shopfloor Bargaining and the State: a Contradictory Relationship'. In Tolliday and Zeitlin, 1985, 1–45.

Index

Index compiled by Jacqueline McDermott